Cambridge Studies in Social and Emotional Development

The Development of Romantic Relationships in Adolescence

Although innumerable songs, poems, plays, and movies have been written about adolescent romantic relationships, no scientific book has been written on that topic. Numerous volumes exist on adult romantic relationships and on adolescent sexuality, but this is the first volume to examine adolescent romantic relationships. A group of eminent investigators met to discuss the topic and were charged with the task of writing about their conceptualization of these relationships and of romantic experiences in adolescence. The volume covers the full range of aspects of romantic relationships, and examines general processes and individual differences within the general context of adolescent development. Each chapter contains numerous provocative ideas that are designed to stimulate research on the topic.

Wyndol Furman is Professor of Psychology and Director of Clinical Training in the Department of Psychology, University of Denver.

B. Bradford Brown is Professor of Human Development in the Department of Educational Psychology at the University of Wisconsin, Madison.

Candice Feiring is Professor of Psychiatry at UMDNJ–New Jersey Medical School, Newark, New Jersey.

Cambridge Studies in Social and Emotional Development

General Editors: Carolyn Shantz, *Wayne State University*
Martin L. Hoffman, *New York University*

Advisory Board: Robert N. Emde, Willard W. Hartup,
Robert A. Hinde, Lois W. Hoffman, Carroll E. Izard,
Nicholas Blurton Jones, Jerome Kagan, Franz J. Monks,
Paul Mussen, Ross D. Parke, and Michael Rutter

The Development of Romantic Relationships in Adolescence

Edited by

WYNDOL FURMAN
University of Denver

B. BRADFORD BROWN
University of Wisconsin, Madison

CANDICE FEIRING
UMDNJ–New Jersey Medical School

CAMBRIDGE
UNIVERSITY PRESS

PUBLISHED BY THE PRESS SYNDICATE OF THE UNIVERSITY OF CAMBRIDGE
The Pitt Building, Trumpington Street, Cambridge, United Kingdom

CAMBRIDGE UNIVERSITY PRESS
The Edinburgh Building, Cambridge CB2 2RU, UK   www.cup.cam.ac.uk
40 West 20th Street, New York, NY 10011-4211, USA www.cup.org
10 Stamford Road, Oakleigh, Melbourne 3166, Australia
Ruiz de Alarcón 13, 28014 Madrid, Spain

First published 1999

Printed in the United States of America

Typeface Times Roman 10.25/13 pt.   *System* QuarkXPress™   [HT]

A catalog record for this book is available from the British Library.

Library of Congress Cataloging-in-Publication Data

The development of romantic relationships in adolescence / edited by
Wyndol Furman, B. Bradford Brown, Candice Feiring.
p.   cm. – (Cambridge studies in social and emotional
development)
Includes indexes.
ISBN 0-521-59156-2 (hardcover)
1. Love in adolescence. I. Furman, Wyndol. II. Brown, B.
Bradford (Benson Bradford), 1949–   . III. Feiring, Candice.
IV. Series.
BF724.3.L68D48   1999
155.5′ 18 – dc21   98-32339
                                                              CIP

ISBN 0 521 59156 2 hardback

Contents

Contributors

Brad Benson
Family and Human Development
Utah State University
Logan, UT

Cheryl Bonica
Department of Psychology
Columbia University
New York, NY

Pia R. Britto
Adolescent Study Program
Teachers College
Columbia University
New York, NY

Jeanne Brooks-Gunn
Adolescent Study Program
Teachers College
Columbia University
New York, NY

B. Bradford Brown
Department of Psychology
University of Wisconsin, Madison
Madison, WI

Gerald L. Clore
Department of Psychology
University of Illinois,
    Urbana/Champaign
Urbana, IL

Deborah L. Coates
Department of Psychology
City University of New York
New York, NY, and NYS Institute
    for Basic Research

W. Andrew Collins
Institute of Child Development
University of Minnesota
Minneapolis, MN

Jennifer Connolly
Department of Psychology
York University
North York, Ontario, Canada

Lisa M. Diamond
Department of Human Development
Cornell University
Ithaca, NY

Geraldine Downey
Department of Psychology
Columbia University
New York, NY

Eric M. Dubé
Department of Human Development
Cornell University
Ithaca, NY

Candice Feiring
Department of Psychiatry
UMDNJ–New Jersey Medical
    School
Newark, NJ

Wyndol Furman
Department of Psychology
University of Denver
Denver, CO

Adele Goldberg
Department of Psychology
York University
North York, Ontario, Canada

Julia A. Graber
Teachers College
Columbia University
New York, NY

Lauri A. Jenson-Campbell
Department of Psychology
Florida Atlantic University
Fort Lauderdale, FL

Reed W. Larson
Human Development and Family
    Ecology
University of Illinois,
    Urbana/Champaign
Urbana, IL

Brett Laursen
Department of Psychology
Florida Atlantic University
Fort Lauderdale, FL

Brent C. Miller
Family and Human Development
Utah State University
Logan, UT

Claudia Rincón
Department of Psychology
Columbia University
New York, NY

Marjory Roberts Gray
Department of Psychology
Temple University
Philadelphia, PA

Ritch C. Savin-Williams
Department of Human
    Development
Cornell University
Ithaca, NY

Valerie A. Simon
Department of Psychology
University of Denver
Denver, CO

L. Alan Sroufe
Institute of Child Development
University of Minnesota
Minneapolis, MN

Laurence Steinberg
Department of Psychology
Temple University
Philadelphia, PA

Gretchen A. Wood
Human Development and Family
    Ecology
University of Illinois,
    Urbana/Champaign
Urbana, IL

Foreword

Once the exclusive domain of poets, novelists, artists, and musicians, romance has been claimed as a legitimate subject by social scientists. Since the beginning of the modern era in sociology, anthropology, psychology, and psychiatry, an immense and diverse literature has accumulated on romantic relationships. A vast number of works now catalog the varieties of romantic attachments that characterize human beings, the role of romantic relationships in reproduction and their functions in evolution, cultural variations, their cognitive and emotional bases, and ethical and legal issues involving them.

The vast majority of these inquiries into romantic activity concern relationships among adults – mostly adults in their 20s and 30s. Far fewer studies deal with romantic relationships in middle and old age; a relatively small number focus on these relationships in adolescence; and romantic relationships between children have been completely ignored, although, some years ago, Elaine Hatfield developed a questionnaire instrument that she called the Juvenile Love Scale. Even when adolescents are studied, attention is usually focused on dating relationships (which may or may not be romantic, depending on the definition) or sexual activity (which may or may not occur in the context of romantic relationships). Consequently, one can argue that a developmental psychology of romantic relationships scarcely exists.

The current volume shows that this situation is changing, and changing rapidly. First, empirical studies of romantic relationships in adolescence are burgeoning. Whereas 10 years ago one could count the number of investigators who were interested in this topic on the fingers of one hand, this coterie now includes 10 or 20 times that number. By recognizing that romantic relationships are important in social relations before the third decade and by defining some of the ways in which adolescent relationships differ from those of young adults, these investigators are adding an important developmental dimension to this area. Second, the new work is being conducted mainly by developmental psychologists, that is, persons trained to think about the ways in which age constrains relationships and the ways in which relationships cycle through time to influence ontogeny (and vice versa). Although developmental psychologists can claim no special access to the Revealed Truth, their entry into this research field means a "new look," namely, a developmental perspective on romance and romantic relationships.

What constitutes a developmental perspective on romance? Let me count the ways. First, a developmental perspective suggests that romantic relationships are age-constrained, that is, that their dynamics, functioning, and social significance vary according to the ages of the individuals in the relationship. Second, a developmental perspective implies an interest in continuities and discontinuities over time. This does *not* mean merely an interest in the stability of specific relationships but also an interest in their changeworthiness normatively, as well as the extent to which they do not change. Third, developmental views presuppose an interest in qualitative differences among romantic relationships and the implications of these differences across time for the individuals involved in them. Fourth, a developmental perspective implies interest in the relation between one relationship and another, that is, the assumption that experience in one relationship combines with experience in other relationships to affect the outcome. Fifth, a developmental orientation implies interest in the dialectics between relationship change, on the one hand, and developmental changes in individuals, on the other. These dialectics cannot be ignored in studying either relationship dynamics or their significance for the individuals involved in them.

Age-Related Constraints on Romantic Relationships

Developmental status during childhood and adolescence bears on relationship functioning and outcome in at least three ways. First, chronological age is a social category used by both the "insiders" in a relationship and "outsiders" to make self- and other-attributions. Outsiders attribute different degrees of readiness and responsibility to those involved in romantic relationships on the basis of age, and these must be acknowledged, along with related social and moral implications. Second, chronological age is related to changes in person perception, relationship schemas, and theories of social action held by relationship insiders themselves. Relationship socialization may have different outcomes, depending, for example, on what commitment means to adolescent lovers and the extent to which it is seen as necessary in their relations with each other. Third, chronological age constrains both cognitive processing and its social applications. Cognitive development is not completed during childhood; numerous refinements in reasoning occur afterward. Relationship experiences may have something to do with these refinements, and, in turn, these refinements may change the nature of the interaction between romantic partners across the transition from adolescence to adulthood.

Normative Issues

Developmentally speaking, romantic relationships emerge within the broad stream known as *gender relations,* beginning with the gender-segregated societies of early childhood and ending with the mixture of same- and other-sex relationships in which most adults engage. Gender segregation – in both dyadic and group relations – begins in earliest childhood and extends through preadolescence. The cognitive and emotional underpinnings of gender social-ization occurring during this time have been extensively explored. Cross-sex relationships during childhood have not been intensively studied, although some investigators believe that involvement between other-sex children is a risk factor in social development rather than a protective one. Current think-ing suggests that same-sex relationships during childhood are the develop-mental foundations of adolescent romantic relationships rather than other-sex relationships – at least for individuals whose sexual orientation is heterosex-ual. The developmental progression for gay and lesbian youth may be more likely to begin with cross-sex relationships in childhood, although this is not known and should not be presumed. One can guess, however, that children's relationships and adolescent romantic relationships evince both continuities and discontinuities. The contributors' ideas about these and other normative issues are among the most important matters dealt with in this book.

Differential Issues

Romantic relationships are enormously diverse. Almost everything about adolescent romance varies from individual to individual and from relation-ship to relationship – ranging from the genders of the two individuals involved to what they do together and the circumstances under which they interact. In emphasizing these diversities, the contributors to this book ren-der a much-needed service. Social scientists, like other human beings, are inclined to see simplicity in nature rather than complexity. But overly simplified views of adolescent romantic relationships may actually have held social science back: Only now are research workers beginning to see that there are many roads to Rome, that is, that many different pathways connect childhood experiences to adult outcomes. One who wishes to draw the map of adolescent development must therefore describe many different thoroughfares rather than the main road only (should there even be one). Similar lessons have been learned about same-sex relationships during childhood: Supportive and intimate friendships have different implications from negative and conflict-ridden ones. Childhood intimacy, for example, bears on success in establishing romantic relationships during adolescence, and, in turn, supportive romantic relationships between adolescents (especially when one partner is socially mature) minimize the chances that vulnerable individuals will experience interpersonal difficulties in early adulthood and beyond. One cannot overestimate the importance of diversity among romantic relationships in adolescence or the need to document their antecedents and consequences.

Relations Among Relationships

Whether an adolescent establishes a romantic relationship and the nature of that relationship are determined by a concatenation of developmental conditions and events. Both biological and social determinants are involved. Among the early experiences that are relevant to the establishment of romantic relationships in adolescence are transactions with both parents and peers. According to evidence discussed in this volume, parent–child relationships before adolescence have both direct and indirect effects on romantic experience, the indirect effects being mediated mainly through peer relations. Both parent–child and peer relationships are believed to contribute to adolescent experience through carryover effects from childhood and through socialization that continues during the teen years themselves.

Some social scientists believe that their main goal is to partition these sources of variance as precisely as possible so that one can assert the primacy of one relationship (or developmental stage) over others in accounting for romantic experience in adolescence. Our best guess, however, is that many different relationships over many years determine *together* whether romantic relationships are established during the teen years and what they are like. Similarly, romantic experience in adolescence combines with experiences in other relationships to determine self-esteem, attitudes toward others, and other skills that determine success or failure in later adaptations. The contributors to this book acknowledge that these pathways are not well specified at present, mostly because the necessary studies have not been done. Most developmentalists are convinced, however, that combinations and perturbations within the adolescent's entire social network must be taken into account in order to establish the developmental significance of romantic relationships themselves.

Changing Individuals in Changing Relationships

Romantic relationships have beginnings, middles, and, often, ends. During the same time that these transitions are occurring in the relationships themselves, the individuals involved are changing developmentally. Romances that begin before pubescence and extend into the adolescent period, romances that extend from early to late adolescence, or those that extend from adolescence to adulthood and middle age involve complex interconnections between the development of relationships, on the one hand, and the development of individual human beings, on the other. One must remember, too, that the dialectics involving developmental change and relationship change are complicated by the fact that two individuals are developing in every relationship. Because disentangling these dialectics is a very complex process, it is not surprising that little attention is given to them in this book. Nevertheless, these complexities must be addressed in creating a thoroughly developmental view of romantic relationships.

General Comment

Developmental concerns run throughout this book. The authors go considerably beyond developmental analysis, however, in describing the structure and content of romantic relationships, their complexity and diversity, the processes through which they are established, and their significance to the individuals involved. Most impressive is the extent to which these chapters remain consistently focused on conceptual and theoretical matters. The authors have been careful not to turn their contributions into reports of original research or literature reviews. The editors also provide an interesting, integrative guide at the beginning that is quite different from the introductory essays found in most edited volumes. By emphasizing conceptual and theoretical issues relating to romance among adolescents, the editors and contributors have maximized their effectiveness and created a product that enormously benefits relationships research as a whole.

Willard W. Hartup

Acknowledgments

Several other individuals provided important contributions to the preparation of this book. The cover art was designed and produced by Jerry Hirniak, head of the Art Department at Princeton Day School, and his class of advanced art minors – Jake Dickson, Leis Forer, Richard Fox, Annie Jamieson, Emily O'Hara, Amulya Pasupuleti, Benjamin Petrick, Stephanie Sanders, Louis Sparre, Amanda Suomi, and Andrew Warren. Ritch Savin-Williams kindly reviewed most of the chapters in the volume. Marilyn Pelot assisted in preparing the volume for publication. Preparation of the volume was also facilitated by Grant 50106 from the National Institute of Mental Health.

1   Missing the Love Boat

Why Researchers Have Shied Away from Adolescent Romance

*B. Bradford Brown, Candice Feiring,
and Wyndol Furman*

For most American adolescents, romantic relationships begin as a remarkable mystery. What's this weird feeling deep in the pit of my stomach? How do I get someone to like me? How do I know if someone I like likes me back? What should we do together? What can we talk about? How can I tell if someone really loves me or is just trying to take advantage of me? If we start having sex, will it change the relationship? Why don't my parents understand that my boyfriend/girlfriend and I need to spend lots of time together? These arc mysteries that nearly all American adolescents must confront; they are a part of growing up. For help with such issues, adolescents may turn to friends or family members or even television shows. But at present there is little reason for them to turn to social scientists for insights because research on this topic has been surprisingly sparse.

Investigators have not ignored the topic entirely. Descriptive information on dating has been gathered periodically (e.g., Gordon & Miller, 1984; Hansen, 1977; Roscoe, Cavanaugh, & Kennedy, 1988), and some ethnographers have studied peer group processes and romantic relationships (Dunphy, 1969; Eder, 1985). A few theories of adolescent dating and romantic relationships have been proposed (e.g., Dunphy, 1969; Feinstein & Ardon, 1973; McCabe, 1984; Skipper & Naas, 1966). In addition, a substantial amount of research has been conducted on college students, who are sometimes described as late adolescents and sometimes as young adults. Most of that work, however, was not derived from developmental theories, nor was it conducted by adolescent researchers. Instead, the research has stemmed from theories of adult relationships, and the investigators intend them to be studies of adult relationships.

Preparation of this chapter was supported by Grant 50106 from the National Institute of Mental Health (W. Furman, P.I.).

1

Accordingly, we believe it is accurate to say that issues concerning adolescent romance are as mysterious to social scientists as they are to each successive generation of teenagers. That state of affairs spawns the major mystery to be explored in this chapter: Why has there been such limited research and theory over the past half century on a topic of such obvious, enduring importance to adolescent development and behavior? Thus, our agenda for this chapter deviates from the standard introduction in edited volumes, which states the purpose, scope, and organization of the volume and then briefly summarizes the contents of each chapter. We believe that such a deviation is necessary, as the question is not how to extend existing knowledge but how best to venture into the unknown. Understanding the reasons for our limited knowledge about romantic relationships is necessary to appreciate the task we set before the authors in this volume.

We begin with a discussion of the arena of adolescent romance and then describe how romantic relationships are central to adolescent development and behavior. We offer five major reasons for the dearth of work in this area. Finally, we overview the task that we gave to the contributors to this volume.

Romantic Life

What are the essential features of adolescent romance? The challenge of this question quickly becomes apparent by reflecting upon the variety of experiences that are relevant to the development of romance in adolescence. One adolescent daydreams about the person sitting behind him in math class with whom he has never spoken, whereas another goes steady with someone for three years and describes their relationship as the "real thing"; still another couple is inseparable for two straight weeks, then suddenly breaks up. A teenager claims to have a boyfriend but, when asked, the boy denies the connection. Two adolescents acknowledge that they are going together but never spend time with each other apart from other members of their crowd. Another pair of adolescents talk with each other every night but never display any affection for each other in public for fear of being ridiculed by their peers.

All of these forms of romantic experiences, from fantasies to interactions to relationships of short and long duration, must be considered in order to fully understand the development of adolescent romance. It is essential to recognize that not all of an adolescent's romantic experiences stem from romantic relationships. Critical components of adolescent romance exist outside of a concrete relationship with a specific romantic partner (see Brown, this volume; Feiring, this volume; Furman & Wehner, 1997; Larson, Clore, & Wood, this volume). Thus, we distinguish between the individual's romantic experiences and romantic relationships as dyadic phenomena (see the discussion in Furman, Feiring, & Brown, this volume). Early adolescent crushes on *impossible others* (professional athletes, models, pop music stars, famous actors, or even a popular schoolmate who is far above oneself in the social hierarchy) may be critical learning experiences even when no concrete relationship transpires. Individuals can explore romantic feelings in conversations with friends, learning a great deal about the cultural, gender, or sexual scripts that are expected in romantic relationships without negotiating the relationship itself (see the chapters by Coates, this volume; Feiring, this volume; Larson et al., this volume; Miller & Benson, this volume).

Of course, romantic relationships are a particularly important class of romantic experience. There have been efforts to provide explicit definitions of romantic relationships (e.g., Tennov, 1979), but we regard it as premature to place such tight constraints on the construct. Rather, we will point to characteristics or features that are prototypic of these relationships and thus could be included in a definition.

First, romance involves a *relationship,* an ongoing pattern of association and interaction between two individuals who acknowledge some connection with each other. Short-term dating relationships as well as long-term committed relationships are included in this criterion, although some authors in this volume differentiate further between them (see Diamond, Savin-Williams, & Dube, this volume; Graber, Britto, & Brooks-Gunn, this volume).

Second, romantic relationships are voluntary in most Western cultures. Thus, romance is a matter of personal choice, which means that such relationships are tenuous. They may be ended at the discretion of either partner even if a relationship between the couple continues in some other form. In cultures where the relationships are arranged, the romantic feelings one has toward the other are still voluntary, even if the relationship is not.

Third, there is some form of attraction, often (but not necessarily) intense or passionate in nature. This attraction typically includes a sexual component. The sexual attraction is often manifested in some form of sexual behavior, but not always. Personal, religious, or cultural values may constrain such behavior. In certain ethnic groups, opportunities for sexual activity among romantic partners are impeded by the mandatory presence of a chaperone each time the couple meets; some sexual minority youth may feel unable to act on their sexual desires because of societal norms. In some cases, sexual feeling may not be present at all. Adolescents can have relationships for the sake of convenience or status or perhaps as a cover for their sexual orientation. These relationships would not be prototypic romantic relationships, however.

Yet, the attraction toward a romantic partner involves passion or feelings of love beyond those of a sexual nature. There are usually some manifestations of companionship, intimacy, and caring, and many are characterized as a special kind of friendship. As they become long-term, the relationships usually involve some level of commitment and exclusivity, and attachment and caregiving processes become salient (see Collins & Sroufe, this volume; Furman & Simon, this volume).

Collectively, these features differentiate romantic relationships from virtually all other close relationships an adolescent is likely to have. However, the particular way in which these features are manifest or the degree to which they are central to the relationship is likely to vary over the course of a particular relationship, from one relationship to another, from one developmental segment of adolescence or young adulthood to another, from one cultural context to another, and from one historical era to another. The individual, developmental, cultural, and historical variability is what makes it unwise to *fix* a definition or to confine the field to relationships alone. Romantic fantasies, infatuations, conversations with friends about romance and potential partners, preromantic "posturing," and relationships that last for periods ranging from 2 days to several years – all of these are part of the romantic lives of adolescents, and all need to be addressed in theory and research on the topic.

The Importance of Studying Adolescent Romance

It can be argued that a phenomenon that cannot even be easily defined is hardly worth social scientists' close attention. Is there evidence that researchers have truly "missed the boat" by devoting so little effort to theoretical or empirical assessment of adolescent romance? Clearly, romance is central in adolescent pop culture of most Western countries. Love or romance is the central theme in 73% of popular ("Top 40") rock music songs in the United States (Christenson & Roberts, 1998); no other theme or issue is nearly as dominant. Sex, dating, and romantic interests or relationships are one of the most common script themes for adolescent characters featured in television serials (Ward, 1995). Within American popular culture, then, romantic issues are portrayed as in the forefront of adolescents' lives.

Romance is also in the forefront of adolescents' minds. Wilson-Shockley (1995) reported that adolescent girls attribute 34% of their strong emotions to real or fantasized heterosexual relationships, and boys gave this reason for 25%. These proportions are substantially higher than those on any other topic, including school, peers, and family. Ethnographers and anthropologists echo this sentiment in confirming that dating and romance form one of the organizing principles of adolescent peer structure (Dunphy, 1969; Eder, 1985; Mead, 1928); they also are a focal topic of conversation among adolescents in their leisure time (Eder, 1993; Thompson, 1994). Across adolescence the amount of companionship and intimacy with other-sex peers increases substantially (Richards, Crowe, Larson, & Swarr, 1998; Sharabani, Gershoni, & Hofman, 1981) as well as the support received from them (Furman & Buhrmester, 1992). In fact, late adolescents who are in college rate their romantic partners as just as supportive as anyone else in their social network.

The consequences of romantic activity underscore the importance of studying it more closely. Several chapters delineate some of these consequences in detail (see especially Connolly & Goldberg, this volume; Downey, Bonica, & Rincon, this volume; Larson et al., this volume). Briefly, romantic involvement is associated with social competence (Neeman, Hubbard, & Masten, 1995) and positive self-esteem (Samet & Kelly, 1987). On the other hand, adolescents who are involved in romantic relationships at an early age have higher rates of drug use, minor delinquency, and psychological or behavioral difficulties, as well as lower levels of academic achievement than those who are not currently involved in a relationship or who delay romantic activity until later in adolescence (Brown & Theobald, 1996; Cauffman & Steinberg, 1996; Grinder, 1996; Konings et al., 1995: Neeman et al, 1995; Wright, 1982). Whether romantic involvement or involvement at early age is a cause or an effect of these various positive or negative correlates is currently unclear. We suspect that the nature of the romantic experiences and relationships may markedly affect the kind of impact they have on individuals.

From a more distal perspective, adolescent romantic relationships are hypothesized to be a major vehicle for working through issues of identity and individuation and other components of self-concept (see Coates, this volume; Connolly & Goldberg, this volume; Erikson, 1968; Downey et al., this volume; Feiring, this volume; Gray & Steinberg, this volume). Adolescents may also be learning relational patterns that influence the course of subsequent relationships, perhaps even marriages (Erikson, 1968; Furman & Flanagan, 1997; Sullivan, 1953).

To be sure, romance is not the *only* thing on adolescents' minds, but it more than competes for adolescents' attention with school or achievement, career development, and relationships with family or friends. Why, then, is social scientific research and theory in each of these other domains so much more extensive?

Why Adolescent Romance Has Been Ignored

We can think of five reasons why researchers have shied away from studying adolescent romance. These are offered not as an attempt to justify the neglect of the topic, but simply to explain the lack of scientific study in this field. Although scientific efforts to understand adolescent romance may be limited, the same cannot be said of songwriters. From the vast library of popular music about teenage love we easily located a song title that provided an appropriate introduction to each reason.

1. *"Who wrote the book of love?"* Good research, it is said, is theoretically driven, and devotees of a particular theory are constantly looking for phenomena to study that will test or support their theory. Phenomena that lie outside the theory's purview, however, are routinely ignored (Kuhn, 1962). Throughout the middle portion of this century, romantic relations were a source of intrigue to social psychologists studying processes of mate selection – but only to the extent that romantic partners were considering a long-term commitment to each other. Because such concerns come rather late in the typical developmental sequence of adolescent romantic interests and activities (see Brown, this volume; Connolly & Goldberg, this volume; Furman & Simon, this volume), researchers concerned with theories of mate selection had only a circumscribed interest in adolescent romance. Understandably, most of this work was conducted on college students, who were more likely to be involved in relationships with genuine potential for marriage or a lifelong commitment. Studies of a younger population would have been suspect, as it seems questionable that adolescents select dating partners on the same basis as they would marital partners. Thus, mate-selection theories offer a poor fit with the realities of most adolescents' romantic ventures. The fit worsened in recent decades as the median age at first marriage moved well beyond the college years, so that even college students are no longer routinely preoccupied with mate selection in their romantic relationships. Of course, a significant proportion of teenagers do get married or cohabit, but these teenagers are harder to access, a reason discussed subsequently.

Other theories of interpersonal attraction are better suited to exploring the selection of dating partners. For example, balance theory (Heider,

1958), equity theory (Adams, 1965), or exchange theory (see Laursen & Jensen-Campbell, this volume) should be useful for examining adolescents' decisions about initiating, pursuing, or abandoning relationships with particular romantic partners. Although the rapid turnover in romantic alliances during early adolescence should be especially intriguing to theorists from these traditions, their emphasis has been on friendships rather than romantic relationships. In part, this is because friendship lent itself more easily than romantic relationships to the laboratory paradigms that dominated this field for several decades. In part, the explanation may lie in other reasons for ignoring adolescent romance that we review later.

Another framework with a strong interest in romantic relationships is attachment theory. Drawing from Bowlby's conceptualization, Hazan and Shaver (1987) proposed that romantic love involves the integration of the attachment, caregiving, and sexual/reproductive behavioral systems. Furthermore, they suggested that individual differences in how romantic love is experienced may be due to differences in past attachment history; they proposed three main types of love styles that parallel the three infant attachment classifications. Since that time, literally hundreds of studies have been conducted (see Shaver & Hazan, 1993). Most have employed college student samples, partly because of the ease with which these individuals could be studied, but also because one is more likely to find in this age group the serious, intimate, long-term relationships in which an attachment bond develops. The short-term relationships that are characteristic of most young people's romantic experiences and endeavors in early and middle adolescence struck many researchers as unsuitable to this theoretical framework. Several of the current chapters, however, illustrate how an attachment perspective can be applied very effectively to this earlier period of adolescence (see Collins & Sroufe, this volume; Furman & Simon, this volume; Gray & Steinberg, this volume).

Neoanalytic theories (Erikson, 1968; Sullivan, 1953) actually emphasize romantic relationships in their depiction of adolescent development. Sullivan, in particular, placed romantic interests and encounters at the center of one stage in his theory. He argued that, in early adolescence, there is a shift in intimacy needs from an *isophilic* choice (seeking someone quite like the self) to a *heterophilic* choice (seeking someone quite different from the self – intimacy with a member of the other sex); integrating this shift in intimacy needs with the demands of the *lust dynamism* crystallized an adolescent's interest in romantic relationships. Nevertheless, most researchers who have applied Sullivan's theory to adolescent social relationships have focused on friendship. It is difficult to account for this.

In the field of psychology, most of the contemporary theoretical work on love is being done by social psychologists. Sadly, the fields of social psychology and social development are quite distinct from one another. Despite several noteworthy integrative efforts (Brehm, Kassin, & Gibbons, 1981; Masters & Yarkin-Levin, 1984), investigators in each field know relatively little about the work being conducted in the other field. This has hampered the derivation of theories or conceptual models that integrate social/situational factors with the individual/developmental factors that are crucial to understanding the dynamics of adolescent romance. A number of the chapters in this volume, however, illustrate promising ways of integrating theories from these two perspectives and applying them to adolescent romance (e.g., Larson et al., this volume; Laurson & Jensen-Campbell, this volume).

To be fair, adolescents have not made the task easy for theorists. A major source for the development of ideas and theory is personal observations. As most parents know, adolescents are reluctant to discuss their romantic interests and relationships with adults. This reticence is especially characteristic of early to middle adolescence, when self-consciousness and uncertainty about how to behave in a new, emotionally charged role are apt to be high. Friends, rather than social scientists (even those who are parents of teens), are more likely to learn about the ups and downs of romantic life. Social scientists could rely on their own memories of this period, but easy access to more immediate knowledge of adolescent romance may be lacking.

In any case, one explanation for the dearth of research on adolescent romance is that teenagers' romantic ventures do not fit well within the basic constructs or foci of dominant theories of social or interpersonal development. Rather than extend the theories to encompass the broader scope of adolescent romance or evolve new theories for this purpose, social scientists have preferred to wait until romantic relationships evolved to the point where they became more compatible with existing theoretical models of social roles or interpersonal relationships.

2. *"They say it's only puppy love."* In addition to their poor fit with principles of dominant theories in the field, adolescents' romantic ventures struck many investigators as too frivolous for serious study. Certainly, in comparison to the sobering business of mate selection and the formation of lasting relationships in later adolescence, younger people's steady cavalcade of short-term relationships and endless babble about who likes whom and who broke up last weekend can seem trivial to adult researchers. Thus, it may seem wiser to defer scientific inquiry until adolescents have matured into a serious, genuine capacity for romance. One could argue that romantic

encounters prior to this time lack the psychological and social depth to be taken seriously, to be considered as genuine relationships. As our previous discussion of the importance of these relationships indicates, however, this perspective seems shortsighted.

Ironically, concern over the "trivial" interests of youth in their romantic affairs spawned one of the most extensive and intriguing debates among early investigators. Willard Waller (1937) initiated this debate with an article based on his observations of romantic ventures among undergraduates at Pennsylvania State University. He suggested that a substantial number of these late adolescents seemed distracted from the critical mission of mate selection by a concern with the *status* of their dating partners or the status that dating a particular person brought to themselves. He labeled this preoccupation the *rating/dating complex*. It spawned a series of studies that stretched over several decades as investigators debated the existence or predominance of this phenomenon (see Brown, this volume; Gordon, 1981; Herold, 1974). Rather than approaching adolescents' status seeking through romantic relationships with the dispassionate fascination of a social scientist, however, many investigators adopted a moralistic tone, chiding adolescents for their frivolous pursuits or remonstrating their colleagues for mistaking status seeking for "genuine" romance.

In sum, many investigators seemed reluctant to venture into the morass of adolescent romance before the point at which young people displayed the maturity to pursue such relationships with an earnest eye toward intimate, stable, enduring relationships, which were a suitable basis for the assumption of adult family roles. All romantic activity prior to this point was regarded as "puppy love" or an unimportant digression from meaningful socialization into adult roles.

3. *"But that was yesterday, and yesterday's gone."* Our first two reasons for the limited research on adolescent romance fault social scientists for their narrow perspective on romantic relationships, but there is also reason to be sympathetic to their plight. Studying adolescents' romantic ventures is something like chasing a greased pig. It requires researchers to embrace teenage peer culture, which is notoriously evanescent. Romantic ties in this context can be remarkably short, lasting a matter of weeks, if not days. By the time researchers are geared up to study the relationship, it's over! Then, several weeks later, it's back on again, but only for another month. How are researchers supposed to measure such rapidly changing phenomena?

Teenagers also seem to keep changing the rules. In one generation, dating was de rigueur; an identifiable twosome was the basic unit of social interaction (Douvan & Adelson, 1966; Gordon & Miller, 1984); going places and doing things just with a group of friends was a sure sign that one was "out of it" – at least until a new romantic partner could be secured. In the next generation, much of formal dating was replaced by a pattern of socializing in mixed-gender groups that contained some identifiable romantic couples, some who might become couples, and a cadre who were just friends (Miller & Gordon, 1986). Furthermore, the rules vary in different segments of the peer culture. The fluidity of the context makes it difficult to conduct meaningful research, especially work that is longitudinal or that compares one generation to another.

More generally, it is pragmatically difficult to study adolescent romance. Parents, whose consent is usually required, are often reluctant to let researchers delve into their children's love lives, even when issues of sexuality are excluded. Many school administrators are not enthusiastic about giving up precious school time for such a potentially volatile research topic. Adolescents may be reluctant to discuss their romantic interests unless the relationship is secure and longstanding.

It is tempting to avoid these methodological and logistical nightmares by studying college students or married couples. One ought to wait, investigators can argue, until youth are old enough to be readily accessible and follow adult rules of romance, which are far more stable and reliable. The chapters in this volume, however, provide a succession of reasons for resisting this temptation.

4. *"Why don't we do it in the road?"* Another reason for the dearth of studies of adolescent romance is that this work has been overshadowed by research on sexuality. Understandably, sexual attitudes and behavior are of strong interest to researchers of adolescent development. A surge in sexual drives and the emergence of reproductive capabilities are key elements in the process of puberty, and puberty itself is often regarded as the event that initiates and defines adolescence (Steinberg, 1999). Thus, some may perceive adolescent romance simply as an interpersonal context for sexual activity.

From a health policy perspective, adolescent sexual behavior is of vast importance. The rapid rise in sexually transmitted diseases among young people, and the high rates of pregnancy and abortion among American youth (compared to their counterparts in other technologically advanced nations), are persistent causes for concern. Thus, adolescent sexuality is one of the most, if not the most, pressing and consequential facets of adolescents' romantic activities. The result is that there has been far more support and encouragement for research on teenage sexuality than other aspects of teenage romance.

The irony is that in focusing on adolescent sexuality, investigators often forget about romantic relationships altogether. Although studies examine associations between adolescent sexual behavior and various features of parent–child or friendship relationships, rarely do they consider facets of the romantic relationship in which the behavior occurred. Most of the vast research on adolescent sexual activity does not consider the idea that romantic liaisons or relationships are primary contexts for adolescent sexual activity (see Graber et al., this volume; Miller & Benson, this volume). If we are to understand why and when adolescents engage in different forms of sexual behavior, it seems essential to consider their partner in sexual activity and the nature of their relationship.

The most troublesome outcome of this overshadowing of romance by sex is the tendency to equate romance with sexuality or to subsume romantic activity under sexual activity. Adolescent sexual activity can occur in other contexts (see Diamond et al., this volume), and there is much more to romantic relationships than sex. Approximately half of the adolescents in the United States have never engaged in sexual intercourse. Most of them engage in some forms of sexual activity, but the point is that there is diversity in their experiences and their relationships entail more than sex. Our prior discussion of the importance of romantic experience delineates some of these other important elements of romantic relationships, and the chapters that follow point out many other new and interesting elements of adolescent romantic life.

5. *"Don't know much about history."* Historical trends over the last half century in the field of child development provide another possible explanation for the absence of work on adolescent romantic relationships. In general, theory and research have proceeded from the mother–infant dyad outward to other social partners and groups, and from infancy to childhood and adolescence. From the 1950s to the middle 1970s, the focus of social developmental research was on the mother–infant and mother–child relationships (Lamb, 1981). Toward the end of the 1970s, work on fathers began to emerge, as well as research on peer and sibling relationships in childhood. In the 1980s, interest in adolescence as an important developmental period increased and the Society for Research in Adolescence was formed (Dornbusch, Petersen, & Hetherington, 1991). From this perspective, adolescent romance is at the end of a historical trajectory because it concerns relationships outside the parent–offspring dyad and deals with adolescence.

Closely allied to this historical focus on parent–child relationships and childhood socialization is a pattern of federal research funding that gave little impetus to studies of adolescent romance. Without a clear connection to prominent theories of social development and without a direct link to pressing social issues that could affect policy decisions, the field of romantic relationships did not seem to be a high priority in the funded grants programs of various federal agencies or private research foundations. Indeed, researchers bold enough to study issues of romance could be subjected to public ridicule for their "frivolous" expenditure of public tax dollars, as one investigator discovered when Senator William Proxmire gave her one of his infamous "golden fleece" awards for her federally funded research on love. Understandably, investigators followed the flow of federal research dollars into more lucrative facets of adolescent social development.

In sum, we argue that most researchers have overlooked adolescent romance because it did not fit neatly into their theoretical frameworks or provide a reliable source of research funding, or because they felt that related topics such as teenage sexuality and pregnancy were more pressing, or because adolescent romance just did not seem to be important – particularly in view of the challenges of defining and measuring its various manifestations. Adolescents may belabor the intricacies of teenage romance hour after hour in songs on the radio or shows on television, but most adult researchers seem to be tuned to a different channel.

"Why Must I Be a Teenager in Love?"

Particularly with reference to matters of love and romance, parents often hear their teenage offspring's plaintive assertion, "You just don't understand!" We're inclined to take the teenager's side in this debate. At least from the perspective of social scientific research and theory, adults' understanding of adolescent romance extends little beyond their unreliable memories of their own experiences with it. We believe it is time to address this situation, to give social scientists much needed direction and encouragement to explore adolescent romance.

In this volume, we have asked a set of well-established and highly regarded scholars to offer insights into adolescent romantic relationships. Their task was *not* to summarize research to date or to present results of their own recent work. Rather, we asked them to lay the conceptual groundwork for serious research in the field. We chose to solicit conceptual chapters because of the nascent nature of the field; we believed that the field can benefit more from a series of theoretical pieces that suggest systematic directions for research than from initial reports of the work that has just started. In some instances, the authors have borrowed from existing theory about adolescent development, social adjustment, or interpersonal relationships; in other cases, they have derived a new conceptual scheme that seems more suitable to the particular facet of adolescent romance on which they focus.

We asked contributors to be mindful of the diversity of individuals within the adolescent population of North America. In particular, we asked them to be sensitive to cultural and ethnic differences among adolescents that might have an impact on romantic experiences. We also admonished them to bear in mind that not all adolescents are heterosexual and to consider how sexual orientation would influence and be influenced by romantic relationships. We also urged them to consider the broad arena of romantic experiences that include but are not limited to long-term relationships.

The volume is divided into three major parts. The first focuses on *processes* in romantic relationships, that is, on how romantic interests and relationships unfold, both over the course of a specific relationship and over the period of adolescence as a developmental stage. Larson et al. consider the regulation of emotions in adolescents' romantic relationships. Laursen and Jensen-Campbell describe proximal and distal processes in interpersonal interactions. Furman and Simon discuss the nature and role of cognitive views of romantic relationships. Miller and Benson focus on sexuality in romantic relationships. Collectively, these contributions underscore the fact that adolescent romance is neither a singular event nor a stable feature of adolescence, but entails complex processes that unfold in a variety of ways across this period of life.

The second part illuminates how individual differences contribute to the diversity of adolescents' experiences in romantic relationships. Collins and Sroufe consider how the capacity for intimacy in romantic relationships may vary, drawing particularly on the role of relational experiences in childhood. Downey et al. explore how sensitivity to rejection affects adolescents' willingness to engage in romantic activity, as well as their decision making once in a romantic relationship. Diamond et al. discuss the experiences of sexual minority youth (lesbian, gay, and bisexual adolescents) in different kinds of relationships in adolescence. Feiring examines how individual differences in gender identity affect romantic inclinations and encounters, and how these, in turn, can restructure gender identity. Each of these chapters emphasizes the need to move beyond a normative or singular portrait of adolescents' romantic experiences.

In the third part, contributors comment on how forces outside the individual shape and are shaped by adolescent romance. These include the family (Gray and Steinberg), their friendship network (Connolly and Goldberg), and the peer group (Brown), as well as culture (Coates) and society (Graber et al.). These contributors help identify ways to explore the reciprocal relationships between the individual and social forces as they relate to adolescent romance.

In the final chapter (Furman, Feiring, and Brown), we again deviate from the norm for edited volumes by eschewing the standard task of simply summarizing the major points made by each contributor in favor of a broader commentary on the most pressing issues and promising approaches for investigators to consider in the next generation of research on adolescent romance. Our intent is to provide a more integrative evaluation of the chapters in this volume, pointing out intersecting ideas and approaches, as well as facets of adolescent romance that this volume does not attend to adequately. Taken together, the contributions in this volume should provide a choice of perspectives and a variety of ideas from which to approach the understanding and study of adolescent romance.

Adolescence is often regarded as a time of deep and diverse emotions. Few phenomena reflect the euphoria and the despair of this stage of life more poignantly than romantic relationships. Few phenomena have as profound an impact on the young person – both in the immediate and the long term. It is high time that social scientists dive into this intense, emotional, and fascinating aspect of the adolescent experience. We hope that this volume will provide scholars with the motivation and the direction to do so. "Why must I be a teenager in love?" It's a question that deserves a better answer than researchers have provided over the past 50 years.

References

Adams, J. S. (1965). Inequality in social exchange. In L. Berkowitz (Ed.), *Advances in experimental social psychology* (Vol. 2, pp. 267–299). New York: Academic Press.

Brehm, S. S., Kassin, S. M., & Gibbons, S. X. (1981). *Developmental social psychology: Theory and research.* New York: Oxford University Press.

Brooks-Gunn, J., & Furstenberg, F. F., Jr. (1989). Adolescent sexual behavior. *American Psychologist, 44,* 249–257.

Brown, B. B., & Theobald, W. (1996, March). *Is teenage romance hazardous to adolescent health?* Paper presented at the biennial meetings of the Society for Research on Adolescence, Boston.

Cauffman, E., & Steinberg, L. (1996). Interactive effects of menarcheal status and dating on diet and disordered eating among adolescent girls. *Developmental Psychology, 32,* 631–635.

Christenson, P. G., & Roberts, D. F. (1998). *It's not only rock & roll.* Cresskill, NJ: Hampton Press.

Dornbusch, S. M., Petersen, A. C., & Hetherington, E. M. (1991). Projecting the future of research on adolescence. *Journal of Research on Adolescence, 1,* 7–17.

Douvan, E., & Adelson, J. (1966). *The adolescent experience.* New York: Wiley.

Dunphy, D. C. (1969). *Cliques, crowds, and gangs.* Melbourne: Chesire.

Eder, D. (1985). The cycle of popularity: Interpersonal relations among female adolescents. *Sociology of Education, 58,* 154–165.

Eder, D. (1993). "Go get ya a French!": Romantic and sexual teasing among adolescent girls. In D. Tannen (Ed.), *Gender and conversational interaction* (pp. 17–31). New York: Oxford University Press.

Erikson, E. H. (1968). *Identity, youth, and crisis.* New York: Norton.

Feinstein, S. C., & Ardon, M. S. (1973). Trends in dating patterns and adolescent development. *Journal of Youth and Adolescence, 2,* 157–166.

Furman, W., & Buhrmester, D. (1992). Age and sex differences in perceptions of networks of personal relationships. *Child Development, 63,* 103–115.

Furman, W., & Flanagan, A. (1997). The influence of earlier relationships on marriage: An attachment perspective. In W. K. Hafford & H. J. Markman (Eds.), *Clinical handbook of marriage and couples interventions* (pp. 179–202). Chichester, U.K.: Wiley.

Furman, W., & Wehner, E. A. (1997). Adolescent romantic relationships: A developmental perspective. In S. Shulman & W. A. Collins (Eds.), *Romantic relationships in adolescence: Developmental perspectives* (pp. 21–36). San Francisco: Jossey-Bass.

Gordon, M. (1981). Was Waller ever right?: The rating and dating complex reconsidered. *Journal of Marriage and the Family, 43,* 67–76.

Gordon, M., & Miller, R. L. (1984). Going steady in the 1980s: Exclusive relationships in six Connecticut high schools. *Sociology and Social Research, 68,* 463–479.

Grinder, R. E. (1966). Relations of social dating attractions to academic orientation and peer relations. *Journal of Educational Psychology, 57,* 27–34.

Hansen, S. L.(1977). Dating choices of high school students. *The Family Coordinator, 26,* 133–138.

Hazan, C., & Shaver, P. (1987). Conceptualizing romantic love as an attachment process. *Journal of Personality and Social Psychology, 52,* 511–524.

Heider, F. (1958). *The psychology of interpersonal relations.* New York: Wiley.

Herold, E. S. (1974). Stages of date selection: A reconciliation of divergent findings on campus values in dating. *Adolescence, 9,* 113–120.

Konings, E., Dubois-Arber, F., Narring, F., & Michaud, P.-A. (1995). Identifying adolescent drug users: Results of a national survey on adolescent health in Switzerland. *Journal of Adolescent Health, 16,* 240–247.

Kuhn, T. S. (1962). *The structure of scientific revolutions.* Chicago: University of Chicago Press.

Lamb, M. E. (1981). Fathers and child development: An integrative overview. In M. E. Lamb (Ed.), *The role of the father in child development* (2nd ed., pp. 1–70). New York: Wiley.

Masters, J. C., & Yarkin-Levin, K. (Eds.). (1984). *Interfaces between developmental and social psychology.* New York: Academic Press.

McCabe, M. P. (1984). Toward a theory of adolescent dating. *Adolescence, 19,* 159–170.

Mead, M. (1928). *Coming of age in Samoa.* New York: William Morrow.

Miller, R. L., & Gordon, M. (1986). The decline in formal dating: A study in six Connecticut high schools. *Marriage and Family Review, 10,* 139–156.

Neeman, J., Hubbard, J., & Masten, A. S. (1995). The changing importance of romantic relationship involvement to competence from late childhood to late adolescence. *Development and Psychopathology, 7,* 727–750.

Richards, M. H., Crowe, P. A., Larson, R., & Swarr, A. (1998). Developmental patterns and gender differences in the experience of peer companionship during adolescence. *Child Development, 69,* 154–163.

Roscoe, B., Cavanaugh, L. E., & Kennedy, D. R. (1988). Dating infidelity: Behaviors, reasons and consequences. *Adolescence, 23,* 35–43.

Samet, N., & Kelly, E. W. (1987). The relationship of steady dating to self-esteem and sex role identity among adolescents. *Adolescence, 22,* 231–245.

Sharabani, R., Gershoni, R., & Hofman, J. E. (1981). Girlfriend, boyfriend: Age and sex differences in intimate friendship. *Developmental Psychology, 17,* 800–808.

Shaver, P. R., & Hazan, C. (1993). Adult romantic attachment: Theory and evidence. In D. Perlman & W. Jones (Eds.), *Advances in personal relationships* (Vol. 4, pp. 29–70). London: Jessica Kingsley.

Skipper, J. K., & Naas, G. (1966). Dating behavior: A framework for analysis and an illustration. *Journal of Marriage and the Family, 28,* 412–420.

Steinberg, L. (1999). *Adolescence* (5th ed.). New York: McGraw-Hill.

Sullivan, H. S. (1953). *The interpersonal theory of psychiatry.* New York: Norton.

Tennov, D. (1979). *Love and limerence: The experience of being in love.* New York: Stein and Day.

Thompson, S. (1994). Changing lives, changing genres: Teenage girls' narratives about sex and romance, 1978–1986. In A. S. Rossi (Ed.), *Sexuality across the life course* (pp. 209–232). Chicago: University of Chicago Press.

Waller, W. (1937). The rating and dating complex. *American Sociological Review, 2,* 727–734.

Ward, L. M. (1995). Talking about sex: Common themes about sexuality in the prime time television programs children and adolescents view most. *Journal of Youth and Adolescence, 24,* 595–615.

Wilson-Shockley, S. (1995). *Gender differences in adolescent depression: The contribution of negative affect.* Unpublished master's thesis. University of Illinois at Urbana-Champaign.

Wright, L. S. (1982). Parental permission to date and its relationship to drug use and suicidal thoughts among adolescents. *Adolescence, 17,* 409–418.

PART I

Processes in Romantic Relationships

2   The Emotions of Romantic Relationships
Do They Wreak Havoc on Adolescents?

Reed W. Larson, Gerald L. Clore,
and Gretchen A. Wood

Romantic emotions can grip adolescents' lives. A 14-year-old reports feeling so in love that he can think of nothing else. A 15-year-old is distressed that "everyone has a boyfriend but me" and broods for hours in her room. Another girl finds herself in a passionate lesbian relationship and feels elated, affirmed, and "chosen." And a boy reports feeling so enraged by the betrayal of his girlfriend that he is obsessed with thinking up ways to hurt her.

Western thought has long been ambivalent about the role of emotion in human behavior. On the one hand, we have praised and idealized deep feeling. It is the motif for much of our entertainment in novels, television, and film. On the other hand, we have been suspicious about emotions and the disruptive effects they are believed to inflict upon rational thought and action; Kant (1798/1978), for example, referred to emotions as "diseases of the mind." This same ambivalence is manifest in our society's attitudes toward adolescent romance and the emotions that surround it. We sentimentalize young love and the joys and pains that accompany it, yet we also view it with suspicion as a set of affairs that can play havoc with young people's lives.

What is indisputable is that emotions related to romantic relationships constitute a substantial part of adolescents' day-to-day emotional lives, at least in the United States. We have found that adolescents experience much wider swings of emotion than adults (Larson, Csikszentmihalyi, & Graef, 1980; Larson & Richards, 1994b) and that a substantial proportion of these emotional swings are attributable to romantic relationships, including

The authors express thanks to Jennifer Parkhurst, Ritch Savin-Williams, Jasna Jovanovic, and the editors of the volume for useful comments. Reed Larson's work on this chapter was partly supported by NIMH grants MH38324 and MH53846. Gerald Clore wishes to credit NSF grant SBR-93-11879 and NIMH grant MH-50074 for support.

19

actual and fantasized ones (Larson & Asmussen, 1991; Larson & Richards, 1994a). In addition to the emotion of love, the romantic emotions of American adolescents include anxiety, anger, jealousy, and despair. Romantic relationships are both a frequent source of positive feelings and motivation and a frequent source of anguish and distress. In the words of Fisher and Alapack (1987, p. 95), adolescents' experience of first love is a "veritable delivery room of unprecedented emotions."

Given this prevalence of romantic emotions, it is essential that discussions of adolescent personality development, stress, and mental health address the impact these strong feelings have upon adolescents' daily lives. On a trip to India, the first author discovered that many Indian developmental scholars look critically on American adolescents for the large distraction and disruption that romantic relationships create in their lives. In India, even most college students have remarkably little interaction with the other sex (Verma, 1995), and this arrangement is justified as allowing teens to devote more of their psychic energies to the business of learning and development. The central issue of this chapter is how we respond to this critique. Do the strong emotions of romantic relationships wreak havoc upon teenagers' lives? Are teens swept away before they are developmentally ready? Or might these emotions in some circumstances be a stimulus for development? Might teens be able to learn and grow from them?

The first parts of this chapter examine ways in which romantic emotions might be untoward and disruptive. We consider avenues by which biological, social, and psychological factors may lead adolescents into premature romantic emotions, and we evaluate ways in which these emotions can be a source of disturbance and stress. In later parts of the chapter, we discuss a conception of emotional intelligence with regard to romantic emotions, speculating on how adolescents might develop skills to regulate and benefit from these emotions.

Our orientation in this chapter is phenomenological. We are interested in getting inside individual adolescents' skins to understand their hour-to-hour experience and how it shapes their thought and action. Adolescents live their lives in the first person and usually in the present moment. To understand their romantic emotions, we need to adopt an "experience-near" perspective that examines the qualities of this "delivery room" of romantic feelings.

What Are Emotions? Relevant Theories

Fortunately, there has been a recent growth of scholarship on emotion – by psychologists, sociologists, anthropologists, and philosophers – that helps us begin to think about emotional processes in systematic ways. This scholarship provides a set of conceptual frameworks for analyzing when emotions occur, their effects on consciousness, and what differentiates healthy from disruptive emotion. We will draw upon three theoretical perspectives on emotion.

Emotions as Evolved Biological Programs

The earliest theory of emotions came from Darwin, who conceived of them as specialized biological responses evolved to serve the survival and reproductive needs of the organism. Emotions, according to this view, prepare a person physiologically for vital actions, such as fight or flight. Contemporary proponents of this approach have expanded their purview beyond early psychologists' focus on immediate survival, recognizing that many human emotions, such as guilt, jealousy, and love, serve functions of social regulation. And current scholars have demonstrated a long list of ways in which emotions prepare an individual to respond to a situation. In the words of Levenson (1994, p. 123):

> Emotions are short-lived psycho-physiological phenomena that alter attention, shift certain behaviors upwards in response hierarchies, activate relevant associative networks in memory, and rapidly organize the responses of different biological systems including facial expressions, muscular tonus, voice, autonomic nervous system activity, and endocrine activity to produce a bodily milieu that is optimal for effective response.

The beauty of emotions from a biological viewpoint is that, compared to the fixed action patterns prevalent in other species, they allow the organism greater response flexibility. Emotions produce feelings, motivation, and desires rather than triggering behavior directly, thus giving the individual latitude to modify or inhibit an impulse according to exigencies of the situation.

The emotions of romance can easily be conceptualized in these evolutionary terms. Shaver, Hazan, and Bradshaw (1988) see the emotion of love as a functional element of the evolved attachment system and the interrelated systems for caregiving and procreation. Love and sexual desire are psychological states that direct attention to the basic organismic objectives of security, caring, and reproduction. For these reasons, it has been argued that the inclination for passionate love is "prewired" (Hatfield, Brinton, & Cornelius, 1989). The negative emotions related to romantic relationships, such as anger, jealousy, and contempt, may also serve these systems and have the role of mobilizing the organism to protect threatened romantic attachments or discouraging undesirable attachments. Bowlby (1979) asserts that, because of the vital evolutionary function of relationships, "Many of the most intense of all human emotions arise during the formation, the maintenance, the disruption and the renewal of affectional bonds" (p. 69).

A useful concern raised by this evolutionary view, however, is whether many emotional systems, including possibly those surrounding romantic attachment, may be outmoded. Might emotional systems that were shaped for our evolutionary past be ill-suited for the conditions of contemporary life, particularly adolescent life? There is clear evidence that some emotional systems regularly malfunction, as in the example of anxiety and depressive disorders (Watson & Clark, 1994). Possibly the intensity of love (and sexual attraction) may distract adolescents' attention from important but historically newer activities, such as learning algebra.

Emotions as Cultural Scripts

Two other groups of scholars have argued that a biological view of emotions is incomplete if it fails to recognize learned, cognitive components of emotions. One group, consisting of anthropologists and sociologists, has demonstrated that emotions are shaped by cultural and social processes (Hochschild, 1979; Lutz, 1988; Shweder, 1994). The role of the macrosystem is apparent in differences between cultures in the prevalence, meaning, and eliciting conditions for specific emotions. For example, loneliness is not present in some cultures (Peplau, Miceli, & Morasch, 1982), happiness is viewed as amoral among the Ifaluk of Micronesia (Lutz, 1988), and social norms governing the experience and expression of anger have changed dramatically within our society over the last 200 years (Stearns, 1992). Emotions, these scholars argue, are culturally constructed scripts. Societies define when an emotion is to be felt, what one should feel, and how one should act when feeling that emotion. The social practices of a cultural group also shape the array of daily situations that members are placed in – for example, whom they interact with and the nature of these interactions – and this shapes their probability of experiencing differing emotions.

Romantic emotions clearly have this cultural component. Scholars have demonstrated that the definition of passionate love and expectations for managing this emotion vary across cultures and historic periods (de

Rougemont, 1974; Jankowiak & Fischer, 1992). Likewise, the prevalence and nature of jealousy have been shown to vary from one society to another (Buunk, Angleitner, Oubaid, & Buss, 1996). Societies provide the individual with a set of romantic scripts, and they regulate opportunities for contact with potential partners for enacting these scripts. The question posed for our analysis is how contemporary Western culture and the daily organization of adolescents' lives shape their experience of romantic emotions.

Emotions as Judgments

A third group of scholars, mainly psychologists, has emphasized the immediate cognitive processes that lead to the experience of an emotion. This view recognizes that emotions are not automatic; they are preceded by cognitive appraisals. Emotions result from assessments of what may be complex situations (Lazarus, 1991); and they involve evaluation of these situations in relation to a person's goals, standards, and tastes or attitudes (Ortony, Clore, & Collins, 1988). The philosopher Solomon (1976) argues that emotions are "judgments": "My embarrassment is my judgment that I am in an exceedingly awkward situation. My shame is my judgment to the effect that I am responsible for an untoward situation or incident" (p. 186).

Recognition of these cognitive processes is indispensable to understanding the emotions of romantic relationships. Feeling "in love" is an appraisal of one's dispositions toward another person (Frijda, 1986) – it is a judgment that the person meets or exceeds one's tastes and standards. Likewise, feeling jealous, humiliated, or shamed involves interpretation of events. The daily oscillations people often show in romantic feelings illustrate how deliberative these emotions can be: One day a lover feels wronged; the next day she reaches the conclusion that he was not right for her anyway. The appraisal processes that go into romantic emotions, as we all know, may involve rash and sudden judgments or reasoned analysis of information gathered from a large number of interactions.

The latter two perspectives on emotions – as cultural scripts and as judgments – can be integrated with the biological perspective by conceptualizing them developmentally. Fischer, Shaver, and Carnochan (1989) suggest that the course of maturation is one in which cognitive complexity is *added to* the foundation provided by early-appearing, biologically based emotional systems. Indeed, the openness and flexibility of biological emotional systems in humans would appear to be designed so that individuals can refine and adapt these systems as they are socialized into a culture and gain greater skill in making appraisals (Meerum Terwogt & Olthof, 1989). The question posed by the view of emotions as judgments is whether adolescents have yet acquired the necessary level of knowledge and skill to make accurate inferences in the complex domain of romantic emotions. Might their developmental stage make them more susceptible to attributional errors?

Causes of Adolescents' Romantic Emotions

These three theoretical perspectives allow us to evaluate some of the factors leading teenagers to experience romantic emotions. What role might biology, social scripts, and cognitive misattributions play in evoking romantic emotions among adolescents? The underlying issue is, to what extent might the occurrence of these emotions be outside adolescents' control? After addressing this topic, we consider the effects of these emotions on adolescents' thought and behavior.

Puberty

Evidence shows that entrance into the world of romantic feeling is partly instigated by the biological change of puberty. Richards and Larson (1993) found a direct relationship between pubertal status and higher rates of feeling in love. This relationship was evident for both boys and girls and was independent of age. These findings suggests that puberty may be related to the "kicking in" of the biologically based romantic attachment systems, which we have already described. Other research demonstrates connections between puberty and the onset of sexual behavior (Savin-Williams, 1996; Smith, Udry, & Morris, 1985), confirming that it is not just romantic desires, but also the companion system of sexual desire, that kicks in at puberty. "I swear I woke up one day and everything changed," said one boy. "It was like somebody put up a big flashing neon-light sign in my head that said SEX. I was always turned on" (Bell, 1980, p. 6). From an evolutionary perspective, it is logical that puberty, a biological change that makes one capable of reproduction, would be accompanied by changes in the brain that motivate a person to form attachments and use these reproductive tools. The issue, however, is that puberty is occurring 5 years earlier than in our evolutionary past, subjecting adolescents to the emotions of romance at a much earlier age.

Not only do they feel in love more often, pubertal adolescents also experience higher rates of negative emotions (Brooks-Gunn, Graber, & Paikoff, 1994; Buchanan, Eccles, & Becker, 1992; Richards & Larson, 1993), some of which are related to real and fantasized romantic relationships (Larson & Asmussen, 1991). Adolescents spend time thinking about romantic involvement long before they spend time with romantic partners, and negative feelings such as worry, disappointment, and jealousy are often associated with these thoughts (Richards, Crowe, Larson, & Swarr, 1998). Some of the negative emotions following puberty may also be due to unwanted and confusing sexual attention, including sexual harassment, resulting from other people's reactions to one's adult body.

In sum, adolescents' entrance into the world of romantic emotions, including positive and negative emotions, is partly attributable to biological changes that are beyond their control and that are occurring quite a bit earlier than in our evolutionary past. This path of causality from biology to romantic emotions is not only hormonal. In many cases these emotions probably result from "indirect effects" – from one's own and others' reactions to one's changed body (Richards & Larson, 1993). We suspect that biological dispositions toward romantic feelings can also be magnified or subdued by an adolescent's social milieu. This leads us to the role of culture and social processes in shaping adolescent's romantic emotions.

Romantic Scripts

The social-cultural perspective on emotions encourages us to weigh how cultural scripts and daily social opportunities affect adolescents' feelings. Compared to many other cultures, the U.S. culture is permissive, not only in allowing substantial interaction between boys and girls, but also in tolerating and even encouraging heterosexual romantic interactions among teens. A characteristic of Western adolescence, particularly in Anglo culture, is the comparatively early age at which parents grant youth freedom to be away from home and engaged in dating activities (Feldman & Quatman, 1988). The amount of time European American adolescents spend with the family falls by 60% between 5th and 12th grade (Larson, Richards, Moneta, Holmbeck, & Duckett, 1996), and this time is partly replaced by interactions with peers, including cross-sex groups and dyads (Richards, Crowe, Larson, & Swarr, 1998). It seems likely that this frequent interaction intensifies romantic and sexual feelings.

Beginning around the sixth or seventh grade, American adolescents find themselves spending much time in a world of peers where romantic involvement is increasingly expected. Simon, Eder, and Evans (1992) discovered a norm among sixth- to eighth-grade girls whom they studied that "one should always be in love." Daily participation in this social milieu is likely to promote and intensify attributions of love, as well as leading to experiences of frustration, disappointment, and hurt when one's experiences do not live up to expectations.

Our research has provided numerous examples of positive romantic emotions that appear to have been influenced by social scripts. One of our participants reported elation because "I walked home with the most popular boy in school," and another reported feeling in love because "I saw a hot babe." Enacting the cultural script for romance is often emotionally rewarding: We found that high school students reported quite positive average feelings during interactions with the other sex (Richards et al., 1998). Adolescent society designates Friday and Saturday nights as a period for romantic interactions, and this is a time when the positive emotional scripts of love are often fulfilled (Larson & Richards, 1998).

Social scripts, however, also create and intensify negative emotions. Teenagers experience shame, anxiety, or humiliation when their romantic experiences violate perceived peer expectations. Adolescence is a period of heightened sensitivity to peer influence, and romantic relationships are a domain where this sensitivity is particularly acute (Savin-Williams & Berndt, 1990). Romantic involvement with someone of the wrong crowd – or someone of the same sex – may generate intensely negative reactions from others. In some cases, anxiety and emotional confusion are generated when adolescents' actual feelings do not conform to what they think they are supposed to feel (Simon et al., 1992). Another circumstance is when adolescents find themselves the target of unwanted romantic feeling from someone else, a situation that can be more painful than one's own disappointments in love (Baumeister, Wotman, & Stillwell, 1993). And high school adolescents who do not live up to the script for Friday and Saturday night – who find themselves alone at home – report intense loneliness and other negative emotions (Larson & Richards, 1998).

The point we wish to make is that adolescents do not have full control over many of these daily scenarios and thus may have their emotions bandied about. Pressures from others can be particularly acute in early adolescence, a time when the desire to conform to peers is especially strong (Costanzo, 1970). But even in late adolescence, teens deal with a strong ideology that attributes one's worth as a human being to one's success in achieving a romantic ideal (Douvan & Adelson, 1966). Across adolescence, teens are affected by cultural scripts from television and films that reinforce ideals for romantic engagements. And powerful visceral emotional images from music – which the average teen listens to several hours per day (Arnett, 1995) – may intensify feelings of love or rejection.

In these ways, then, Western adolescents are "set up" to be involved in a world of romantic relationships and to encounter a range of emotions around these relationships. Of course, individual adolescents differ greatly in how they respond to the social milieu. Many may be conscious of social pressures, and some may be aware of the arbitrariness of cultural scripts. Supportive friends or parents can help an adolescent chart a more independent course with less emotional distress. Sorting through cultural messages, however, requires maturity of judgment, which is our next area of concern.

Cognitive Attributions and Misattributions

The view of emotions as judgments leads us to inquire about the appraisal processes that go into adolescents' romantic emotions. How well can adolescents sort out all of the factors that affect their romantic feelings? A large body of research shows that misattributions are most likely under conditions in which the cues entering into a judgment are hidden, vague, or undifferentiated (e.g., Keltner, Locke, & Audrain, 1993). Even among adults, many attributions of love probably occur under these conditions, as is suggested by the fact that a large segment of the world's literature, poetry, and song entails attempts of lovers to capture the elusive nature and cause of their romantic feelings. The ease with which irrelevant factors can affect these attributions is demonstrated by controlled studies showing that feelings of attraction to a stranger can be increased by feelings left over from watching an emotional film (Gouaux, 1971), anxiety from crossing a dangerous bridge (Dutton & Aron, 1974), and even physiological arousal due to riding an exercise bicycle (Zillman, 1978) or even bogus feedback that one's heart rate is speeded up (Graziano & Bryant, 1998). The question is whether adolescents – with less developed cognitive skills than adults – might be particularly susceptible to distortion and misattribution in determining their romantic feelings.

To address this question, we might begin by examining adolescents' skill level for emotional reasoning. Research shows that a number of basic elements of emotional cognition are grasped just before or during early adolescence, including:

- Ability to differentiate emotions from the situations that elicit them (Harris, Olthof, & Meerum Terwogt, 1981; Wolman, Lewis, & King, 1971).
- Ability to differentiate one's own emotions from those of others (Nannis & Cowan, 1987).

- Ability to differentiate the intentions of others and to consider them in emotional appraisals (Weiner & Graham, 1984).
- Recognition that two conflicting emotions can occur simultaneously (Harter & Buddin, 1987).
- Differentiation of complex emotional states and blends, such as bliss, contentment, annoyance, and resentment (Fischer, Shaver, & Carnochan, 1990).

As with other domains of reasoning, we cannot expect young adolescents to use these differentiations very consistently (Keating, 1990), especially in a domain as complex as romantic relationships, where their experiential base is limited (Furman & Simon, this volume).

With limited ability to distinguish emotional reactions from the situation, a young adolescent may not be good at determining the extent to which flutters in one's stomach are due to genuine compatibility versus sexual feelings, shameless flattery, one's own needs, lack of sleep, or dozens of other factors that may create arousal. Thus Hatfield et al. (1989) found positive associations between young adolescents' levels of anxiety and their experience of passionate love. With limited ability to separate one's feelings from those of others, it may be hard to separate one's own emotions from passions avowed by a romantic partner. In many cases, too, the reactions of peers may be more significant to young adolescents' attributions than their own feelings. Douvan and Adelson (1966) found that young adolescents' conception of a good romantic partner focused on concrete external qualities valued by peers, such as looks and social prestige, with little sensitivity to interpersonal qualities.

Therefore, we suspect that young adolescents, and even older adolescents, are easily misled by extraneous factors in their attributions of love and other romantic emotions. Research shows that the ability to factor personality into attributions and make fine differentiations between types of intentions comes only in later adolescence; and gaining the skill to sort out the multiplicity of one's feelings in a complex situation is a lifelong task (Fischer et al., 1990). Like Romeo and Juliet, teens may fall in love with little critical analysis of what lies behind their emotion; the emotions elicited by their family's disapproval, for example, may strengthen their level of feeling. Adolescents may be more likely to base an attribution of love on only one or two traits of a potential partner, a characteristic that Noller (1996) relates to immature love. Likewise, teens may be susceptible to becoming jealous or angry based on misleading cues. And their lack of experience in recognizing simultaneous conflicting emotions may lead them to suppress information and feelings that are not in line with a dominant emotion, whether anger or love.

As teens gain experience, they undoubtedly become better able to use these basic emotional skills and avoid some of the "illusions of love." However, there are a number of new factors in middle adolescence that can also distort attributional processes.

Consolidation of formal operational reasoning in middle adolescence is likely to give adolescents greater insight into their feelings, but it may also intensify romantic passions and fuel projection. Inhelder and Piaget (1958) suggest that adolescents' abstract idealism can lead to extremism, and they refer to complications that can be created by adolescents "constructing" a romance (p. 336). In Western society, love is a powerful abstraction from which unrealistic implications are readily deduced. Fisher and Alapack (1987) found the cognitions of adolescent first love to involve many absolutes, eternals, and what they call "rampant idealism." Examples of this kind of reasoning include "I love everything about you," "We'll never part," and "There's nothing I wouldn't do for you." Use of idealistic reasoning of adolescents can easily generate unrealistic deductions about love or love lost, as illustrated in the extreme by Romeo's and Juliet's deductions that death was the only solution to the perceived loss of the other.

Middle adolescence is also a period when issues of identity become salient, and these can magnify and skew romantic emotions. Douvan and Adelson (1966) found that middle adolescents had a greater tendency to project their deep needs into romantic relationships. For example, a ninth-grade girl in our research reported that "when Mike and I fought last night, I felt like I was losing a piece of myself." Being the center of someone else's attention can also extremely inflate one's ego. Douvan and Adelson contend that romance in middle adolescence often has more to do with "love of being in love" than with a genuine relationship between two people. Romantic feelings can be a fantasy, "a projection of the individual's ego-ideal onto the often undeserving object" (Murstein, 1988, p. 31), and with limited relevant experience and limited skills for self-analysis, adolescents may be particularly vulnerable to making these projections. An important finding from laboratory research is that when people have simpler, less complex, and diversified conceptions of themselves – as we might expect of adolescents – they are more prone to strong and intense emotional swings (Linville, 1985). The relatively undeveloped selves of adolescents may make them more susceptible to strong emotions resulting from perceived affirmation or disaffirmation of their tentative and fragile identities.

In these cognitive ways too, then, adolescents may not be in full control of their romantic emotions. How often does this happen? How often do adolescents fall in love with someone with whom they later discover they have nothing in common? How often do they go into a jag of jealousy, anger, or anxiety based on what should be small things? No one knows. We find the arguments compelling – that adolescents' romantic emotions may be easily skewed by misattributions, their novice reasoning skills, idealistic construction of a romance, and self-projection. But there is little research to help us gauge how often and for whom they are a factor or how much more frequently they affect adolescents' than adults' romantic emotions. What we do know, however, is that adolescents experience a high rate of strong emotions in their daily lives and that a substantial number of these involve romantic affairs.

A Topsy-Turvy World

Our window on adolescents' emotional experience comes from thousands of "time samples" obtained from their daily lives. In research with Maryse Richards and Mihaly Csikszentmihalyi, the first author has had teenagers and adults carry electronic pagers for a week and give reports on their activities and feelings at random times when signaled by the pagers. This procedure, called the *experience sampling method,* provides immediate in situ data on daily emotional experience. The goal has been to find out what teens' daily lives feel like to them.

To begin with, these studies have shown that adolescence is a period of frequent and strong emotion. Adolescents report significantly higher rates of negative emotions than preadolescents (Larson & Lampman-Petraitis, 1989) and higher rates of *both* extremely positive and extremely negative emotions than adults (Larson et al., 1980; Larson & Richards, 1994b). From hour to hour, teens experience wide variability in their emotional states.

Romantic affairs, we find, make a major contribution to adolescents' emotionality. In recent studies we have asked participants to provide explanations on those occasions when they experienced a strong feeling. We found that the attribution of emotions to romantic relationships increased dramatically from preadolescence to early adolescence (Larson & Asmussen, 1991), and these rates increased still more into middle adolescence. Among a sample of 9th to 12th graders (Wilson-Shockley, 1995), girls gave real and fantasized heterosexual relationships as the explanation for 34% of their strong emotions, and boys gave this reason for 25%. Of course, these estimates are imprecise: They are based on self-report data, and they leave out same-gender romantic feelings. Nonetheless, they suggest that romantic affairs account for about a quarter to a third of all middle teens' strong emotional states. These rates are higher than attributions of strong emotions to school (13%), family (9%), and same-sex peer relationships (8%). Whereas a majority of the emotions attributed to heterosexual relationships were positive, a substantial minority, 42%, were negative, including feelings of anxiety, anger, jealousy, and depression.

In sum, adolescence is a time of emotional variability, and romantic relationships are a major contributor to this emotionality. The consequence of these strong romantic emotions is that adolescents can live in an unstable and constantly changing world. We found in two studies that teens who had a boyfriend or girlfriend during the week of sampling reported wider daily emotional swings than those who did not (Larson et al., 1980; Richards & Larson, 1990). Some youth reported strong romantic feelings on almost every self-report. In a period of 3 days, one 11th-grade girl went from feeling "happy because I'm with Dan," to upset because they had a "huge fight" and he "won't listen to me and keeps hanging up on me," to feeling "suicidal" because of the fight, to feeling "happy because everything between me and Dan is fine." Savin-Williams (1996) describes similar swings in emotion among gay, lesbian, and bisexual youth. In a short period of time, teens can swing between manic states of elation – a feeling that "we are great" and "the world is perfect" – to raw feelings of anguish, humiliation, or despair.

This delivery room of romantic emotions, we think, is fed by the biological, social, and cognitive factors discussed earlier. The fact that teenagers' romantic relationships are often quite changeable may also contribute. Feiring (1996) found that 15-year-olds' romantic relationships are typically intense and brief, averaging only a few months. We found numerous instances in which teens broke up with one partner and started with a new partner within a few days – circumstances that would have anyone's emotions reeling. Furman and Simon (this volume) discuss how adolescents' lack of experience means that their romantic relationships are inevitably experimental and ad hoc, creating a wide range of experiences including dramatic failures. From adolescents' point of view, these changes in affect and relationships must feel like riding an emotional roller coaster.

Consequences of the Emotions of Romantic Relations

The conclusion that young adolescents may often be over their heads in the domain of romantic emotions would be of little importance if the effects of these emotions were benign. After all, much of children's learning occurs from diving into seas over their heads. However, the consequences are not always benign. For some teens this roller coaster of emotions can have serious effects on their lives. To understand why, we need to understand how emotions affect consciousness.

Emotions as States of Consciousness

The influence of emotions on thought, perception, and, ultimately, action can be understood in terms of our first two theoretical viewpoints on emotion. From the evolutionary perspective, one of the functions of emotion is to interrupt attention and redirect it toward fundamental organismic concerns, including attachments and threats to one's well-being. Like bright lights and loud noises, emotions serve to focus attention on the object of concern (Clore, 1992; Simon, 1967). A corollary of this is that strong emotions diminish the salience of other information in a person's perceptual field, and, as a result, they create "tunnel vision." The organism becomes bodily, cognitively, and motivationally dedicated to the object of the emotion.

Effects of emotions on consciousness also stem from social scripts that dictate how one should feel and act when in a given state (Averill, 1980; Harré, 1986; Hochschild, 1979). The cultural script for an emotion – outrage, for example – commits a person to a certain way of interpreting events and acting upon them. Shweder (1994) argues that emotions "represent somatic and affective experience not simply as a feeling but as a perception (e.g., betrayal by trusted allies) and a plan (e.g., retaliation, realignment, withdrawal, and so forth)" (p. 39). Emotions are constitutive: They label and define a person's relationship to the world. Strong emotions validate what is real and important.

Romantic emotions clearly alter people's state of consciousness in these ways. A number of researchers have described love as a druglike state because it can affect attention, heighten sensory acuity, and create a sense of intoxication (Berscheid & Walster, 1974; Hatfield, 1988; Tennov, 1979). Liebowitz (1983) sees close similarities between passionate love and an amphetamine high, including similarities between the crash that can follow love and amphetamine withdrawal. But these effects are not just physiological. The Western conception of romantic love entails a set of abstract, idealistic cognitions that can have powerful effects on reasoning. The cultural script for this emotion suggests how one should think and act. Likewise, the cultural scripts for negative emotions of romance, such as jealousy, despair, and humiliation, carry strong expectations for thought and action.

What consequences do the fluctuating romantic emotions of adolescence – the roller coaster – have on teenagers' thought and behavior? We will consider the effects of positive and negative emotions separately.

Effects of Positive Romantic Emotions: The "Falling" of Love

Perhaps the more frequent positive romantic emotions should be less of a concern. In the extreme, elation may distract attention, but positive states can have beneficial effects on thinking and problem solving. Positive affect elicits *heuristic thinking,* involving the use of intuition, expectation, and generalizations. People in a happy state tend to be more generous and make decisions faster and more efficiently (Isen & Means, 1983). Good moods lead to confidence in using existing knowledge or using new hunches for integrative thought (Isen, 1987). Thus, adolescents who are in love may benefit from these positive effects. They may be able to think more quickly and see larger, more global patterns, as well as responding more altruistically to others (Isen, 1987).

The excitement of romance may also provide an important motivater for young people. Boredom is frequent in adolescence (Larson & Richards, 1991), and romantic emotions may be one of the things that makes them feel alive and that life is worthwhile. A related feature of positive emotions is that they create greater tolerance of noxious experience (Carlson & Masters, 1986) and more perseverance under certain conditions (Clore, Schwarz, & Conway, 1994). Romance, or even the possibility of romance, may play a valuable role in getting adolescents out of bed in the morning and helping them get through the daily round of boredom in school and hassles with parents.

Positive emotions, however, can also cloud judgment. In happy moods, people tend not to discriminate strong from weak arguments (Schwarz, Bless, & Bohner, 1991), and extreme emotions often reduce reality testing. The experience of "falling" in falling in love can create a detachment from ordinary reality and ordinary concerns. In addition, the use of absolutes that come with adolescent first love may interfere with practical reasoning. The elated feeling that "he's the greatest guy on earth" (from a girl in our research) may prevent one from seeing a partner's faults. Cultural scripts about love and "living happily ever after" may block appropriate apprehension and rational planning for the future.

A domain of particular importance is adolescents' decision making about sexual behavior. Research shows that positive emotions are associated with lower estimates of the likelihood of negative outcomes (Gasper & Clore,

1996). It follows that the elation many teens experience when with a romantic partner might contribute to their underestimating the possibility of pregnancy and sexual disease. Feeling enraptured may cloud adolescents' ability to reason about contraception. Research with college undergraduates shows that the combination of sexual arousal and positive mood reduces estimates of risk for engaging in unsafe sexual behavior (Harris & Young, 1996).

Of course, we are not so Panglossian as to believe that all adolescent sexual behavior occurs in a state of romantic elation. In some cases, adolescents may be faking the script for rapture – with similar behavioral consequences. Or anxiety about what others will think may prevent them from consistent use of contraception. Limited experience and emotional skills may make teens particularly vulnerable to emotional manipulation. Since adolescents are just beginning to learn about the effects of emotion on thought and behavior (Harris et al., 1981), it may be easy for others to take advantage of their positive states or use guilt or shame to manipulate their behavior.

Effects of Negative Emotions: Postromantic Distress Syndrome

The negative emotions generated both during and after romantic relationships definitely deserve to be a concern. Encounters with jealousy, anger, longing, and grief are probably unavoidable, especially when relationships are so short-lived, and negative emotions *do* disrupt ordinary daily functioning. Research shows that people in an unhappy state, although more systematic in their thinking (Sinclair, Mark, & Clore, 1994), tend to fixate on details (Isbell, Clore, & Wyer, 1997) and overestimate the likelihood of negative outcomes (Gasper & Clore, 1997). Depression is associated with more self-focused attention, deficits in initiative, and less active processing and encoding of information (Clore et al., 1994). In the words of Bower (1994, p. 305), "Anxious and depressed people are notoriously poor learners because their working memory is so preoccupied or 'filled' with upsetting ruminations that few attentional resources are devoted to the learning or recall tasks being measured." The belief of our Indian colleagues that romantic emotions – particularly distress – disrupt the schoolwork of American adolescents is a plausible hypothesis. Even at the college level, we often see transcripts of students whose grades fell off for a semester or two because they were dealing with a difficult romantic relationship.

Beyond these disruptions, negative romantic emotions can have more extreme effects on well-being and behavior. Scholarship on personal relationships concludes that the breaking up of a close relationship is a particularly stressful experience (Sprecher, 1994). In our society, romantic involvement is a way of measuring the self, and disappointments in love can be taken as a portent of one's entire romantic destiny (Douvan & Adelson, 1966). One adolescent reported that her decision to break up with a boyfriend led him to smash the car windshield and threaten suicide. A girl indicated that she had been "tormented daily with negative and confusing emotions." The first author asked college juniors and seniors in his seminar to describe their romantic experiences in adolescence, and quite a number reported clinical symptoms from breaking off a relationship, such as loss of appetite, inability to keep food down, irritability, inability to sleep, prolonged crying spells, suicidal thoughts, and withdrawal from friends. In several cases these symptoms lasted for 3 months or more.

The negative emotions surrounding romantic issues may be particularly strong and difficult for lesbian, gay, and bisexual adolescents. Heterosexual adolescents see images of love and sex on television and in movies and know that, even if the images are not quite true to the reality of a relationship, their feelings for the opposite sex are normal. Sexual minority adolescents, in contrast, witness portraits of same-sex love as deviant and unnatural. Because lesbian, gay, and bisexual adolescents are also likely to have underdeveloped cognitive and affective skills for dealing with romantic affairs (Anderson, 1995), their feelings can be hidden in heterosexual relationships or in "sheer will and self-recrimination to suppress homoerotic thoughts and feelings" (Anderson, 1995, p. 22). Not knowing what to do with their feelings and, even if they do, not feeling safe or natural to express them in public can produce "feelings of rage and sadness that are difficult to resolve" (Anderson, 1995, p. 25). Depression, low self-esteem, truancy, substance abuse, and suicidal thoughts or actions can result (Anderson, 1995; Mercier & Berger, 1989; Savin-Williams, 1994).

The frequency with which the negative emotions of love lead to depression, suicide, and interpersonal violence has been all but ignored in the research literature. Bell and Weinberg (1978) found that difficulties in romantic relationships were the single most common reason for suicide attempts by lesbians and gay men, and this may be equally true for heterosexuals. We also suspect that jealousy and anger generated by romantic relationships are leading causes of assault and homicide among adolescents. We have argued elsewhere that, because of the strong and powerful feelings they generate, romantic relationships deserve to be identified as the single largest source of stress for adolescents (Larson & Asmussen, 1991).

Being Swept Away

Thus, both the positive and negative emotions that come with adolescents' romantic affairs may alter thought and behavior. For some teens these effects may be mild and short-lived, but for others they may be extreme and enduring. The tunnel vision created by strong emotions can also perpetuate emotional intensity for some adolescents. An effect of emotion on consciousness, as we have discussed, is to focus attention and limit one's field of vision. The effect of love can be to crowd everything else out of one's consciousness – and one's life. In a self-perpetuating feedback loop, the limited sense of self of some adolescents may intensify their romantic emotions (see, for example, Linville, 1985), which narrows their focus of attention, in turn, further limiting their sense of self. The result, as dramatically illustrated in the film *Endless Love,* can be an imploding world in which a teen becomes increasingly preoccupied with the romantic relationship and increasingly vulnerable to its changing currents. Peele (1988) demonstrates the similarity between romantic involvement and many features of addictive disorders, including craving, obsessive attention, and emotional swings. Peele speculates that adolescents are particularly prone to this syndrome and we agree, but we also believe that the majority of adolescents develop skills that help them be more resilient.

Emotional Growth in Adolescent Romantic Relationships?

In this chapter we have argued, first, that romantic emotions are partly induced by factors outside adolescents' control, such as puberty and a romantically focused social milieu, and that these emotions occur at an age before many adolescents are cognitively able to make reliable attributions about them. Second, although these emotions are not intrinsically bad, they have strong effects on consciousness that can adversely affect decision making and behavior: In some cases, they *can* wreak havoc on adolescents' lives.

One conclusion to this line of reasoning would be to ask what can be done to shield youth from this disruptive set of affairs. For many adolescents, particularly young adolescents, closer monitoring by parents could be beneficial in reducing their likelihood of getting into the web of complex romantic feelings. But isolating teens from contact with potential romantic partners – the traditional Indian tack – is at best a temporary solution in the Western social milieu.

An alternative is to ask what skills teens develop – and can be encouraged to develop – that make them able to understand and manage their romantic emotions. The foundations of these skills undoubtedly originate in early childhood. Young children begin learning impulse control and the ability to elicit comfort from others (Camras, 1994). Dunn, Brown, and Beardsall (1991) show that children who have experience in discussing and expressing emotions in early childhood are better able to judge emotions in middle childhood. Downey and colleagues (this volume) demonstrate that some cases of pathology in adolescents' romantic relationships are related to deficits in these earlier experiences.

As children move into adolescence, we believe, inquiry needs to focus on a new set of processes and skills. Acquisition of these skills, we think, can be important not only in limiting some of the havoc of romantic emotions, but also in providing a valuable arena of personal growth.

Emotional Intelligence

The new processes and skills of adolescence have to do with reasoning about emotions, with what has been called *emotional intelligence.* Salovey and Mayer (1989–1990; Mayer & Salovey, 1997) define this construct as the ability to detect emotion in self and others and to use this information to solve problems and regulate thought and behavior. Our previous analysis leads us to highlight several components of emotional intelligence relevant to adolescents' romantic emotions:

1. The ability to consider the full range of external and internal situational factors in appraisals leading to romantic emotions. Becoming sensitive to the possible role of biology and social scripts in shaping one's feelings.
2. The ability to recognize common misattributions in romantic emotions. Identifying how extraneous features of the situation, the other person, or one's own states and needs can distort feelings.
3. Awareness of how emotions alter consciousness, including perception, reasoning, and behavior. Recognizing the effect of tunnel vision in intensifying emotions.

As with other cognitive skills, we do not expect young adolescents to grasp and deploy these emotional insights immediately. Their application should become easier across adolescence as teens acquire a greater base of knowledge, increased capacity for multidimensional thinking, and an ability to understand and analyze interpersonal systems. Older adolescents develop greater ability to bracket a set of thoughts and evaluate them against other information (Keating, 1990), skills that might help keep them from being carried away by sudden infatuations. Older adolescents also learn to temper idealism with greater realism (Labouvie-Vief, 1980), which may reduce the tendency to construct a romance. All of these skills may diminish misattributions about romantic relationships and help teens regulate their strong emotions. Research shows that people who perceive the causes of their emotions are less likely to show the kinds of misattribution effects that we have discussed (Keltner et al., 1993).

Limiting and controlling emotion, however, is only half of emotional intelligence. Although our focus has been upon ways in which emotion can disrupt consciousness, we would like to be clear that we do not share Kant's view that emotions are diseases of the mind. The *affect-as-information* hypothesis, developed by the second author, maintains that emotions serve the important function of making us aware of our innermost goals and desires (Schwarz & Clore, 1983). Emotions can be seen as efficient sources of information that, when properly heeded, ensure that a person's decisions and actions are congruent with his or her innermost goals and desires. Part of the task for adolescents is to learn to make effective use of this information.

The developmental challenge in using emotions as information is learning to sort out feeling from reality. On the one hand, emotions are bright flashing lights that provide urgent information about our instinctual and self-needs. They tell us that something is very important and thrust it into the center of consciousness. Even fear, envy, and disgust may draw attention to important issues. Thus, failing to heed one's emotions – for example, by coping in ways that deny or suppress emotional information – can have negative implications for one's well-being (Mayer & Salovey, 1995; Pennebaker & Beall, 1986). On the other hand, a person must be able to put the seeming urgency of these emotions into perspective against less salient information that might be drowned out by the strong feelings. In some situations, the information from an emotion may be like a phantom pain: It seems very real, conveying the message that one should cease all other activity and focus on dealing with a bodily injury; yet one needs to be able to ignore what can be deceptive or even false information. One needs to be able to decenter from emotions enough to view them as one source of information among others. Positive mental health requires a delicate balance between emotional spontaneity and reflection, between following affective intuition and maintaining an awareness that emotions present only a partial view of reality.

When adolescents fall in love, then, or feel powerful jealousy, they need to be critical of their attributional processes but also attend to the information that those emotions convey: Is this love or lust? Are these feelings emanating from parts of myself that I value? Might my repeated anxiety be telling me something important about the dynamics of this relationship? Emotional intelligence involves not just debunking illusionary infatuations, it involves learning to accept and take the lead from emotions that are well grounded.

Opportunities for Growth

Once we move beyond a view of emotions as havoc, it becomes useful to ask about the conditions under which romantic emotions can be an arena for psychological maturation. The potential for growth within the world of romantic feelings resides in features of emotions both as states of consciousness and as sources of information.

First, we think that the excitement and positive emotion of romance may often stimulate productive trains of thought for adolescents. The feelings of being in love and being loved can provide rich and poignant information about one's self and one's self-worth; and, as we have discussed, positive emotions bring more expansive and global thinking. Might not this combination sometimes create moments of epiphany in which valuable integrative thinking occurs, not just about one's romantic partner but about one's own life and future? A recent line of speculation recognizes that positive emotions can be "organizers of development" (Collins & Gunnar, 1990; Hauser & Smith, 1991), and this may certainly be true of positive romantic emotions. Perhaps the positive states of love can drive adolescents to seek personal growth, both for their relationship and for themselves.

In some cases, the negative emotions of romance may also be beneficial. Whereas positive affect promotes heuristic thinking, moderately negative affect promotes more *methodical* thinking. People experiencing moderately negative emotion use more logical analysis and observation and focus on detail; they are more realistic, deliberative, and skeptical (Clore et al., 1994). When confronted with persuasive arguments from others, unhappy individuals are also more likely to discriminate strong from weak arguments. Thus, adolescents' swings into negative romantic affect may be useful in tempering the expansiveness and carelessness of cognition under the influence of positive affect.

Even extremely negative emotion may be a touchstone for insight and growth. In the peer literature, it is accepted that conflict between friends can stimulate knowledge about interpersonal relationships (e.g., Shantz & Hobart, 1989). In parallel ways, the experiences of frustration, anger, and disappointment in love may also trigger deeper understanding. Affect is information: Negative emotion can provide a powerful message that one should avoid getting into similar circumstances in the future. Looking back on mistakes may provide an adolescent with fundamental insights about attributional fallacies and human foibles. Reflecting on an unhappy, tempestuous love affair with an emotionally manipulative partner, one teen said, "It was an awful thing to go through, but I did learn a great deal from it."

We would like to emphasize that gaining insight into romantic emotions is not necessarily a solitary enterprise. In many cases, teens may learn these lessens vicariously – from observing friends' experiences – or through discussion of their own experiences with others. Since the challenge of figuring out romantic emotions is partly a task of getting enough distance to separate information from feeling and overcoming tunnel vision, conversation with friends, family members, teachers, or others with a more detached perspective can be extremely beneficial.

Romantic Emotion and Identity Development

Numerous authors have speculated that romantic relationships can be an important arena for development of the self (Douvan & Adelson, 1966; Feiring, 1996; Savin-Williams, 1996). We suspect that much of this growth has to do with sorting out and mastering the delivery room of emotions. Emotions are often directly related to the self – they reflect things that matter most; thus, emotion and identity are inevitably interwoven.

At one level, strong emotions can help orient identity. Haviland and colleagues (1994) theorize that emotion can be the "glue" to adolescents' identity. One boy told us that the happiness and confidence he gained from his first relationship in eighth grade dramatically changed his sense of self. Savin-Williams (1996) described the positive feelings that sexual minority youth experienced in their first gay or lesbian relationship as having a powerful effect in affirming their gay or lesbian identity. Affect is information that provides valuable clues about identity. At the same time, an identity built solely on a feeling is inevitably fragile, and we have argued that the adolescent with an identity based only on a romantic attachment is extremely vulnerable.

At a more advanced level, learning to weather the ups and downs of romantic emotions may be valuable in achieving the sense of "continuity and sameness" that Erikson (1968) saw as central to identity. The adolescent who comes to understand that love does not "conquer all" and that today's disappointment does not portend one's whole future is a step closer to identity attainment. Learning to gain information from emotion, but also seeing beyond the current emotional peak or valley, is critical to achieving a secure sense of self. Emotional knowledge and the capacity for emotional regulation, we think, are closely related to development of a stable identity.

As an arena of growth, then, romantic emotions not only provide a learning ground for attributional insights, they are a domain for achieving compatibility between emotion and self. Maturity requires modifying one's sense of self to be consistent with one's emotions, as well as regulating emotions to be in line with one's sense of self.

Need for Research

Much of what we have said in this chapter is speculative and open to argument. What is badly needed is research to put meat on the bones of our speculations. We recommend a focus upon a number of topics that address and go beyond what we have discussed:

1. Baseline data on the prevalence and course of adolescents' romantic emotions is critical. Research is needed to chart adolescents' feelings as they fantasize about, enter, experience, and leave romantic relationships. With the right techniques, these data could begin to gauge the influence of biology, social scripts, and attributional processes in affecting these feelings.
2. We have given little attention to individual differences, but they are clearly important. There is strong evidence that romantic relationships are shaped by personality dispositions (Berscheid, 1983; Feeney, 1995), gender (Feiring, this volume), and culture (Coates, this volume). We need to examine how adolescents' attributions of romantic emotions and their response to emotions differ as a function of these factors. A particular interest, stemming from this chapter, is what dispositions make adolescents more or less susceptible to being swept away by strong romantic feelings.
3. This leads to the question of skills. Research is needed to evaluate the association between acquisition of emotional regulation in childhood and how adolescents manage romantic emotions: Was there a critical deficit in Romeo's and Juliet's early experience that made them susceptible to distorted romantic logic? Similarly, research is needed to evaluate the link between our

list of hypothetical emotional skills and the daily experience of real emotions.

4. We have focused on emotions as events inside one person. However, once teens become involved in actual relationships, dyadic emotional processes come into play, and we need to examine issues such as emotional communication and emotional boundaries. Here the field might draw upon models from research on other relationships and at other points in the life span. It seems likely that the kinds of "cycles of irritability" that Patterson (1986) describes in mother–child relationships may occur in adolescent romantic relationships. Drawing on research from adult marital relationships, we can also ask whether antecedents of Gottman's (1994) "Four Horsemen of the Apocalypse" occur in the interactions of adolescent romantic partners.

5. Models for education and intervention deserve to be tested. Although much programming has been aimed at adolescent drug use, little has been done to help teens manage the often more powerful druglike states of romance. Can we provide children and adolescents with healthier cultural scripts for romantic emotions? Can we teach adolescents skills of critical thinking that will make them more discriminating about their romantic feelings and better able to use romantic affect as information?

Conclusion

The strong emotions of romantic relationships can thrust an adolescent into a hyperspace: Where things are turned upside down, ordinary reality recedes from view, and he or she leaves the envelope of routine daily life. Biological drives and cultural scripts can have strong effects in creating feelings. Inexperience and lack of emotional knowledge, tunnel vision, and reduced reality testing can easily skew attributions about romantic emotions. For adolescents, this is a domain of non-Euclidean reasoning, Möbius strips, catastrophe theory, and Escher-like phenomena that do not lend themselves to ordinary logic, certainly not the concrete logic of childhood. The daily fluctuations they sometimes encounter between strong positive and negative romantic emotions can undoubtedly make the world seem surreal.

Although these strong emotions may have disruptive effects on adolescents' thought and behavior, they also are an important domain for mastery and growth. Learning to manage and "go with" these strong feelings can bring positive energy to adolescents' lives and create a vital arena for personal development. This can be a domain where teens gain fundamental insights into emotional processes and where the interregulation between emotion and identity is honed.

Perhaps because of this growth, evidence suggests that older adolescents become more competent in managing romantic emotions. We found that older teens reported more positive average emotional states when with the other sex, suggesting that they are acquiring greater skills for regulating the experience (Csikszentmihalyi & Larson, 1984). Douvan and Adelson (1966) found that older adolescents were less bowled over by love than youth in middle adolescence. And Furman and Wehner (1994) report that college-age youth were more likely to have secure romantic relationships than high school adolescents. We suspect that with age, teens become more intelligent about romantic emotions and better able to use affect as information to help them manage their feelings.

Regardless of knowledge and experience, of course, romantic relationships will continue to generate strong emotions. Even in adulthood, they are anything but a placid affair. Romantic relationships involve extremely high stakes in terms of both evolutionary needs and individual requirements for self-affirmation. As a result, at any age they can lead to powerful, and sometimes untoward, emotions. The fact that so many marriages end in divorce suggests that, despite much experience in adolescence, adults are not masters of romantic feelings. This fact, however, only underscores the need for greater knowledge of the powerful, enthralling, complex, and destabilizing dynamics that romantic emotions interject into the lives of adolescents – and the importance of finding ways to help teens manage, learn, and grow from these emotions.

References

Anderson, D. A. (1995). Lesbian and gay adolescents: Social and developmental considerations. In G. Unks (Ed.), *Educational practice and theory for lesbian, gay, and bisexual adolescents.* New York: Routledge.

Arnett, J. (1995). Adolescents' uses of media for self-socialization. *Journal of Youth and Adolescence, 24*(5), 519–534.

Averill, J. R. (1980). Emotion and anxiety: Sociocultural biological, and psychological determinants. In A. O. Rorty (Ed.), *Explaining emotions* (pp. 37–72). Berkeley: University of California Press.

Baumeister, R. F., Wotman, S. R., & Stillwell, A. M. (1993). Unrequited love: On heartbreak, anger, guilt, scriptlessness, and humiliation. *Journal of Personality and Social Psychology, 64,* 377–394.

Bell, A., & Weinberg, M. S. (1978). *Homosexualities: A study of diversity among men and women.* New York: Simon & Schuster.

Bell, R. (1980). *Changing bodies, changing lives.* New York: Random House.

Berscheid, E. (1983). Emotion. In H. H. Kelley, E. Berscheid, A. Christensen, J. H. Harvey, T. L. Huston, G. Levinger, E. McClintock, L. A. Peplau, & D. R. Peterson (Eds.), *Close relationships* (pp. 110–168). New York: W. H. Freeman.

Berscheid, E., & Walster, E. (1974). A little bit about love. In T. L. Huston (Ed.), *Foundations of interpersonal attraction* (pp. 356–381). New York: Academic Press.

Bower, G. H. (1994). Some relations between emotions and memory. In P. Ekman & R. Davidson (Eds.), *The nature of emotion: Fundamental questions* (pp. 303–305). New York: Oxford University Press.

Bowlby, J. (1979). *The making and breaking of affectional bonds.* London: Tavistock.

Brooks-Gunn, J., Graber, J. A., & Paikoff, R. L. (1994). Studying links between hormones and negative affect: Models and measures. *Journal of Research on Adolescence, 4*(4), 469–486.

Buchanan, C. M., Eccles, J. S., & Becker, J. (1992). Are adolescents the victims of raging hormones? *Psychological Bulletin, 111,* 62–107.

Buunk, B. P., Angleitner, A., Oubaid, V., & Buss, D. M. (1996). Sex differences in jealousy in evolutionary and cultural perspective: Tests from the Netherlands, Germany, and the United States. *Psychological Sciences, 7,* 359–263.

Camras, L. A. (1994). Two aspects of emotional development: Expression and elicitation. In P. Ekman & R. Davidson (Eds.), *The nature of emotion: Fundamental questions* (pp. 347–351). New York: Oxford University Press.

Carlson, C. R., & Masters, J. C. (1986). Inoculation by emotion: Effects of positive emotional states on children's reactions to social comparison. *Developmental Psychology, 22*(6), 760–765.

Clore, G. L. (1992). Cognitive phenomenology: Feelings and the construction of judgement. In L. L. Martin & A. Tesser (Eds.), *The construction of social judgement* (pp. 133–164). Hillsdale, NJ: Erlbaum.

Clore, G. L., Schwarz, N., & Conway, M. (1994). Affective causes and consequences of social information processing. In R. S. Wyer & T. K. Srull (Eds.), *Handbook of social cognition* (2nd ed., pp. 323–417). Hillsdale, NJ: Erlbaum.

Collins, W. A., & Gunnar, M. R. (1990). Social and personality development. *American Review of Psychology, 41,* 387–416.

Costanzo, P. (1970). Conformity development as a function of self-blame. *Journal of Personality and Social Psychology, 14,* 366–374.

Csikszentmihalyi, M., & Larson, R. (1984). *Being adolescent: Conflict and growth in the teenage years.* New York: Basic Books.

de Rougemont, D. (1974). *Love in the Western world.* New York: Fawcett.

Douvan, E., & Adelson, J. (1966). *The adolescent experience.* New York: Wiley.

Dunn, J., Brown, J., & Beardsall. (1991). Family talk about feeling states and children's later understanding of others' emotions. *Developmental Psychology, 27*(3), 448–455.

Dutton, D., & Aron, A. (1974). Some evidence for heightened sexual attraction under conditions of high anxiety. *Journal of Personality and Social Psychology, 30,* 510–517.

Erikson, E. H. (1968). *Identity: Youth and crisis.* New York: Norton.

Feeney, J. (1995). Adult attachment and emotional control. *Personal Relationships, 2,* 143–159.

Feiring, C. (1996). Concepts of romance in 15-year-old adolescents. *Journal of Research on Adolescence, 6*(2), 181–200.

Feldman, S. S., & Quatman, T. (1988). Factors influencing age expectations for adolescent autonomy: A study of early adolescence and parents. *Journal of Early Adolescence, 8,* 325–343.

Fischer, C., & Alapack, R. J. (1987). A phenomenological approach to adolescence. In V. V. Hasselt & J. M. Herson (Eds.), *Handbook of adolescent psychology* (pp. 91–107). New York: Pergamon.

Fischer, K. W., Shaver, P. R., & Carnochan, P. (1989). A skill approach to emotional development: From basic- to subordinate-category emotions. In W. Damon (Ed.), *Child development today and tomorrow* (pp. 107–136). San Francisco: Jossey-Bass.

Fischer, K. W., Shaver, P. R., & Carnochan, P. (1990). How emotions develop and how they organize development. *Cognition and Emotion, 4*(2), 81–127.

Frijda, N. H. (1986). *The emotions: Studies in emotions and social interaction.* Cambridge: Cambridge University Press.

Furman, W., & Wehner, E. A. (1994). Romantic views: Toward a theory of adolescent romantic relationships. In M. Montemayor, G. R., Adams, & T. P. Gullotta (Eds.), *Personal relationships during adolescence* (pp. 168–195). Thousand Oaks, CA: Sage.

Gasper, K., & Clore, G. L. (1996). *Mood, mood monitoring, and judgement.* Unpublished manuscript.

Gasper, K., & Clore, G. L. (1997). *The persistent use of negative affect by anxious individuals to estimate risk.* Unpublished manuscript.

Gottman, J., with Silver, N. (1994). *Why marriages succeed or fail.* New York: Simon & Schuster.

Gouaux, K. (1971). Induced affective states and interpersonal attraction. *Journal of Personality and Social Psychology, 20,* 37–43.

Graziano, W. G., & Bryant, W. H. M. (1998) Self-monitoring and the self-attribution of positive emotions. *Journal of Personality and Social Psychology, 74*(1), 250–261.

Harré, R. (1986). An outline of constructionist viewpoint. In R. Harré (Ed.), *The social construction of emotions* (pp. 2–14). New York: Basil Blackwell.

Harris, P. L., Olthof, T., & Meerum Terwogt, M. (1981). Children's knowledge of emotion. *Journal of Child Psychology and Psychiatry, 22,* 247–261.

Harris, J. L., & Young, J. (1996, July). *How sexual arousal and mood affect decision making in risky sexual behavior.* Paper presented at the meetings of the American Psychological Society, San Francisco.

Harter, S., & Buddin, B. J. (1987). Children's understanding of the simultaneity of two emotions: A five-stage developmental acquisition sequence. *Developmental Psychology, 23*(3), 388–399.

Hatfield, E. (1988). Passionate and companionate love. In R. J. Sternberg & M. L. Barnes (Eds.), *The psychology of love* (pp. 191–217. New Haven: Yale University Press.

Hatfield, E., Brinton, C., & Cornelius, J. (1989). Passionate love and anxiety in young adolescents. *Motivation and Emotion, 13*(4), 271–289.

Hauser, S. T., & Smith, H. F. (1991). The development and experience of affect in adolescence. *Journal of the American Psychoanalytic Association, 39,* 131–165.

Haviland, J. M., Davidson, R. B., Ruetsch, C., Gebelt, J. L., & Lancelot, C. (1994). The place of emotion in identity. *Journal of Research on Adolescence, 4*(4), 503–518.

Hochschild, A. R. (1979). Emotion work, feeling rules, and social structure. *American Journal of Sociology, 85,* 551–575.

Inhelder, B., & Piaget, J. (1958). *The growth of logical thinking.* Trans. by A. Parsons & S. Milgram. New York: Basic Books.

Isbell, L., Clore, G. L., & Wyer, R. S. (1997). *Mood-mediated uses of stereotypes in impression formation.* Unpublished manuscript.

Isen, A. M. (1987). Positive affect, cognitive processes, and social behavior. In L. Berkowitz (Ed.), *Advances in experimental social psychology* (Vol. 20, pp. 203–253). New York: Academic Press.

Isen, A. M., & Means, B. (1983). The influence of positive affect on decision-making strategy. *Social Cognition, 2,* 18–31.

Jankowiak, W. R., & Fischer, E. F. (1992). A cross-cultural perspective on romantic love. *Ethnology, 31*(2), 149–155.

Kant, I. (1978). *Anthropology.* Carbondale: Southern Illinois University Press. (Original work published 1798)

Keating, D. P. (1990). Adolescent thinking. In S. S. Feldman & G. R. Elliott (Eds.), *At the threshold: The developing adolescent* (pp. 54–89). Cambridge, MA: Harvard University Press.

Keltner, D., Locke, K. D., & Audrain, P. C. (1993). The influence of attributions on the relevance of negative feelings to personal satisfaction. *Personality and Social Psychology Bulletin, 19*(1), 21–29.

Labouvie-Vief, G. (1980). Beyond formal operations: Uses and limits of pure logic in life-span development. *Human Development, 23,* 141–161.

Larson, R., & Asmussen, L. (1991). Anger, worry, and hurt in early adolescence: An enlarging world of negative emotions. In M. E. Colten & S. Gore (Eds.), *Adolescent stress: Causes and consequences* (pp. 21–41). New York: Aldine de Gruyter.

Larson, R., Csikszentmihalyi, M., & Graef, R. (1980). Mood variability and the psychosocial adjustment of adolescents. *Journal of Youth and Adolescence, 9*(6), 469–490.

Larson, R., & Lampman-Petraitis, C. (1989). Daily emotional states reported by children and adolescents. *Child Development, 60,* 1250–1260.

Larson, R., & Richards, M. (1991). Boredom in the middle school years: Blaming schools versus blaming students. *American Journal of Education, 91,* 418–443.

Larson, R., & Richards, M. (1994a). *Divergent realities: The emotional lives of mothers, fathers, and adolescents.* New York: Basic Books.

Larson, R., & Richards, M. (1994b). Family emotions: Do young adolescents and their parents experience the same states? *Journal of Research on Adolescence, 4*(4), 567–583.

Larson, R., & Richards, M. (1998). Waiting for the weekend: The development of Friday and Saturday nights as the emotional climax of the week. In R. W. Larson & A. C. Crouter (Eds.), *Temporal rhythms in the lives of adolescents: Themes and variations.* New Directions for Child Development (Vol. 82). San Francisco: Jossey-Bass.

Larson, R., Richards, M. H., Moneta, G., Holmbeck, G., & Duckett, E. (1996). Changes in adolescents' daily interactions with their families from ages 10 to 18: Disengagement and transformation. *Child Development, 32,* 744–754.

Lazarus, R. S. (1991). *Emotion and adaptation.* New York: Oxford University Press.

Levenson, R. W. (1994). Human emotion: A functional view. In P. Ekman & R. Davidson (Eds.), *The nature of emotion: Fundamental questions* (pp. 123–126). New York: Oxford University Press.

Liebowitz, M. R. (1983). *The chemistry of love.* Boston: Little, Brown.

Linville, P. (1985). Self-complexity and affective extremity: Don't put all your eggs in one cognitive basket. *Social Cognition, 3,* 94–120.

Lutz, C. A. (1988). *Unnatural emotions: Everyday sentiments on a Micronesian atoll and their challenge to Western theory.* Chicago: University of Chicago Press.

Mayer, J. D., & Salovey, P. (1995). Emotional intelligence and the construction and regulation of feelings. *Applied and Preventive Psychology, 4,* 197–208.

Mayer, J. D., & Salovey, P. (1997). What is emotional intelligence? In P. Salovey & D. Sluyter (Eds.), *Emotional development and emotional intelligence: Educational implications* (pp. 3–34). New York: Basic Books.

Meerum Terwogt, M., & Olthof, T. (1989). Awareness and self-regulation of emotion in young children. In C. Saarni & P Harris (Eds.), *Children's understanding of emotion* (pp. 209–237). Cambridge: Cambridge University Press.

Mercier, L. R., & Berger, R. M. (1989). Social service needs of lesbian and gay adolescents: Telling it their way. In P. Allen-Meares & C. Shapiro (Eds.), *Adolescent sexuality: New challenges for social work* (pp. 75–95). New York: Haworth Press.

Murstein, B. I. (1988). A taxonomy of love. In R. J. Sternberg & M. L. Barnes (Eds.), *The psychology of love* (pp. 13–37). New Haven: Yale University Press.

Nannis, E. D., & Cowan, P. A. (1987). Emotional understanding: A matter of age, dimension, and point of view. *Journal of Applied Developmental Psychology, 8,* 289–304.

Noller, P. (1996). What is this thing called love? Defining the love that supports marriage and family. *Personal Relationships, 3*(1), 97–115.

Ortony, A., Clore, G. L., & Collins, A. (1988). *The cognitive structure of emotions.* New York: Cambridge University Press.

Patterson, G. R. (1986). Performance models for antisocial boys. *American Psychologist, 41,* 432–444.

Peele, S. (1988). Fools for love. In R. J. Sternberg & M. L. Barnes (Eds.), *The psychology of love* (pp. 159–188). New Haven: Yale University Press.

Pennebaker, J. W., & Beall, S. K. (1986). Confronting a traumatic event: Towards an understanding of inhibition and disease. *Journal of Abnormal Psychology, 95,* 274–281.

Peplau, L. A., Miceli, M., & Morasch, B. (1982). Loneliness and self-evaluation. In L. A. Peplau & D. Perlman (Eds.), *Loneliness: A sourcebook of current theory, research and therapy* (pp. 135–151). New York: Wiley.

Richards, M. H., Crowe, P. A., Larson, R., & Swarr, A. (1998). Developmental patterns and gender differences in the experience of peer companionship during adolescence. *Developmental Psychology, 69,* 154–163.

Richards, M. H., & Larson, R. (1990, July). *Romantic relations in early adolescence.* Paper presented at the Fifth International Conference on Personal Relations. Oxford, U.K.

Richards, M. H., & Larson, R. (1993). Pubertal development and the daily subjective states of young adolescents. *Journal of Research on Adolescence, 32*(2), 145–169.

Salovey, P., & Mayer, J. D. (1989–1990). Emotional intelligence. *Imagination, Cognition and Personality, 9*(3), 185–211.

Savin-Williams, R. C. (1994). Verbal and physical abuse as stressors in the lives of lesbian, gay male, and bisexual youths: Associations with school problems, running away, substance abuse, prostitution, and suicide. *Journal of Consulting and Clinical Psychology, 62*(2), 261–269.

Savin-Williams, R. C. (1996). Dating and romantic relationships among gay, lesbian, and bisexual youths. In R. C. Savin-Williams & K. M. Cohen (Eds.), *The lives of lesbians, gays, and bisexuals: Children to adults* (pp. 166–180). Ft. Worth, TX: Harcourt Brace College Publishers.

Savin-Williams, R. C., & Berndt, T. J. (1990). Friendship and peer relations. In S. S. Feldman & G. R. Elliott (Eds.), *At the threshold: The developing adolescent* (pp. 277–309). Cambridge, MA: Harvard University Press.

Schwarz, N., Bless, H., & Bohner, G. (1991). Mood and persuasion: Affective states influence the processing of persuasive communications. *Advances in Experimental Social Psychology, 24,* 161–199.

Schwarz, N., & Clore, G. L. (1983). Mood, misattribution, and judgements of well-being: Informative and directive functions of affective states. *Journal of Personality and Social Psychology, 45,* 513–523.

Shantz, C. U., & Hobart, C. J. (1989). Social conflict and development: Peers and siblings. In T. J. Berndt & G. W. Ladd (Eds.), *Peer relationships in child development* (pp. 71–94). New York: Wiley.

Shaver, P. R., Hazan, C., & Bradshaw, D. (1988). Love as attachment: The integration of three behavioral systems. In R. J. Sternberg & M. L. Barnes (Eds.), *The psychology of love* (pp. 68–99). New Haven, CT: Yale University Press.

Shweder, R. A. (1994). "You're not sick, you're just in love": Emotion as an interpretive system. In P. Ekman & R. J. Davidson (Eds.), *The nature of emotion: Fundamental questions* (pp. 32–44). New York: Oxford University Press.

Simon, H. (1967). Motivational and emotional controls of cognition. *Psychological Review, 74,* 29–39.

Simon, R. W., Eder, D., & Evans, C. (1992). The development of feeling norms underlying romantic love among adolescent females. *Social Psychology Quarterly, 55*(1), 29–46.

Sinclair, R. C., Mark, M. M., & Clore, G. L. (1994). Mood-related persuasion depends on (mis)attributions. *Social Cognition, 12,* 309–326.

Smith, E., Udry, J. R., & Morris, N. M. (1985). Pubertal development and friends: A biosocial explanation of adolescent sexual behavior. *Journal of Health and Social Behavior, 26,* 183–192.

Solomon, R. C. (1976). *The passions: The myth and nature of human emotion.* Notre Dame, IN: University of Notre Dame Press.

Sprecher, S. (1994). Two sides to the breakup of dating relationships. *Personal Relationships, 1,* 199–222.

Stearns, P. N. (1992). Gender and emotion: A twentieth-century transition. In V. Gecas & D. D. Franks (Eds.), *Social perspectives on emotion* (Vol. 1, pp. 127–160). Greenwich CT: Jai Press.

Tennov, D. (1979). *Love and limerence.* New York: Stein and Day.

Verma, S. (1995). *Expanding time awareness.* Chandigarh, India: Government Home Science College.

Watson, D., & Clark, L. A. (1994). The vicissitudes of mood: A schematic model. In P. Ekman & R. Davidson (Eds.), *The nature of emotion: Fundamental questions* (pp. 400–405). New York: Oxford University Press.

Weiner, B., & Graham, S. (1984). An attributional approach to emotional development. In C. Izard, J. Kagan & R. Zajonc (Eds.), *Emotions, cognition, and behavior* (pp. 167–191). Cambridge: Cambridge University Press.

Wilson-Shockley, S. (1995). *Gender differences in adolescent depression: The contribution of negative affect.* M.S. thesis. University of Illinois at Urbana–Champaign.

Wolman, R., Lewis, W., & King, M. (1971). The development of the language of emotions: Conditions of emotional arousal. *Child Development, 42,* 1288–1293.

Zillman, D. (1978). Attribution and misattribution of excitatory reactions. In. J. H. Harvey, W. I. Ickes, & R. F. Kidd (Eds.), *New directions in attribution research, Vol. 2,* 335–368. New York: Erlbaum.

3 The Nature and Functions of Social Exchange in Adolescent Romantic Relationships

Brett Laursen and Lauri A. Jensen-Campbell

For several decades, social psychologists have tilled the fertile fields of interpersonal attraction and close relationships, with impressive results. It is now possible to predict with some certainty the course and future of an adult romantic relationship on the basis of the behaviors and attitudes of the participants (Fletcher & Fincham, 1991; Gottman, 1994). Unfortunately, the study of adolescent romantic relationships has not kept apace with these advances; models generated to describe adult relationships have not been applied systematically to those during adolescence. In this chapter we discuss the nature and functions of adolescent romantic relationships, integrating prevailing theories of social exchange with a developmental perspective on close relationships.

Social exchange theory (Kelley & Thibaut, 1978; Thibaut & Kelley, 1959) provides a popular and compelling framework for understanding adult romantic relationships (Clark & Reis, 1988). Economic principles are extended to interpersonal behavior: Individuals establish and maintain relationships that proffer optimal rewards relative to costs. Widely recognized by social psychologists, exchange theory awaits developmental applications (Graziano, 1984; Laursen, 1996). This oversight is not an indictment of the theory but a manifestation of conceptual neglect in the area of adolescent close peer relationships (Furman, 1993).

We plunge into this void with three goals. First, models of close relationships derived from social exchange theory are reviewed, with particular emphasis on principles applicable to adolescents. Second, developmental processes that shape social exchanges are discussed. Adolescent romantic

Support for preparation of this chapter was provided, in part, by a grant from the U.S. National Institute of Child Health and Human Development (R29-HD33006) to Brett Laursen.

relationships may differ from those during other age periods due to alterations in resources attributed to proximal and distal mechanisms. Third, a framework for understanding adolescent romantic relationships is proposed that elaborates developmental variations in exchange processes and resources. Our aim is to apply models of adult social exchange to adolescent romantic relationships, advancing an account designed to stimulate research on the subject.

Social Exchange in Romantic Relationships

Social interaction captures the essence of an interpersonal relationship (Bales, 1950). Indeed, Hinde (1979) defines a relationship as a series of interactions across time. Romantic relationships, like other close relationships, contain interactions that reflect the nature and functions of the relationship. First, social interactions are reciprocally significant; participants attach value and priority to mutually influential behavior. Second, social interactions reflect interdependence: "This means that a change in the state of any subpart changes the state of any other subpart" (Lewin, 1948, p. 84). Third, social interactions represent social exchanges in the sense that they provide rewards and costs to each participant (Goffman, 1961). The following account describes romantic relationships in terms of the processes and outcomes of social interaction and the interdependencies that arise from favorable social exchanges.

Theoretical Accounts of Social Exchange

Social exchange theory, in its original form, postulated that individuals are motivated by a mental accounting aimed at maximizing rewards and minimizing costs (Thibaut & Kelley, 1959). Individuals interpret rewards (positive outcomes) and costs (negative outcomes or investments) as pleasurable or inhibitory (Homans, 1961). Each relationship participant seeks preferential outcomes (i.e., more rewards than costs) from social interactions. Interdependence is central to relationship maintenance; when both parties are satisfied with benefits from social exchanges, each comes to depend upon the relationship to provide the anticipated outcomes.

Expressions of interdependence differ because standards for evaluating outcomes vary (Thibaut & Kelley, 1959). Individuals maintain a comparison level against which the attractiveness of a relationship is evaluated according to the outcomes desired. Comparison levels are relative rather than fixed; they depend on potential benefits available from alternative relationships. Given attractive alternatives, standards for evaluating a relationship may be higher than they would be given few or no desirable relationship options. It follows that comparison levels shape social interactions, producing distinct outcomes across different relationships and within the same relationship over time.

Later revisions to the theory suggested that social exchanges are altered as participants grow increasingly interdependent (Kelley & Thibaut, 1978). Acquaintances adhere to principles designed to maximize individual outcomes. As interdependence develops, new patterns of social exchange emerge. Two are prevalent. Participants in some relationships strive for equality by minimizing differences between each partner's outcomes. Participants in other relationships strive to maximize joint outcomes by expanding rewards for either participant. Both pathways abandon strict pursuit of individual benefits in favor of optimizing dyadic outcomes: Personal gain is subsumed by relationship advantage. Typically, romantic relationships are organized around maximizing mutual benefits (Berscheid & Reis, 1998). As self-orientation wanes, benefits received by the partner are welcomed as benefits received by the self; outcomes usually balance out over time, and this strategy efficiently secures the greatest number of total benefits.

Social exchange theory differs from learning theory accounts of social interaction in that there is no direct causal correspondence between behavior and relationship outcomes. Dyadic interchanges are mediated by individual representations of the social world in a manner reminiscent of Lewin's (1946) cognitive restructuring of the field. In gauging the impact of a social interaction, rewards tend to improve opinions about an interdependent relationship incrementally, whereas minor costs exert little detrimental influence until a critical threshold of negativity is reached (Rusbult, 1983). Exchanges are colored by perceptions such that large investments and few alternatives may ensure continued interdependence, regardless of benefits (Rusbult & Martz, 1995). Thus, relationship outcomes are shaped by cognitive transformations that interpret external contingencies and feedback in terms of personal needs and preferences.

Equity emphasizes relative individual outcomes in that benefits from interactions are expected to be proportional to personal contributions (Walster, Berscheid, & Walster, 1973). Equity is attained when investments and the ratio of rewards to costs are the same for both participants. In general, equitable and mutually beneficial social exchanges promote interdependence, whereas inequity disrupts interactions and threatens interdependence (Berscheid & Walster, 1969). Short-term inequities are tolerated (and even interpreted as rewarding) so long as relationship interdependence and long-term equity are maintained.

Close relationship models of social exchange characterize interdependence as causal interconnections in the thoughts, behaviors, and emotions of participants; these interconnections are manifest in a strong, recurring, and diverse set of mutually beneficial exchanges (Kelley et al., 1983). Relationships are organized around interdependencies, rather than outcomes, because the extent to which exchanges attain (real or perceived) equality and equity varies across individuals and relationships. Behaviors and outcomes may differ as a result of cognitive transformations, but all close relationships are similar in that participants are connected by an elaborate web of social exchanges that foster and maintain interdependence.

Processes and Properties of Social Exchange

Systematic relationship differences, such as those between communal and exchange relationships, have been identified (Clark & Mills, 1979). In a communal relationship, participants are oriented toward maximizing mutual relationship rewards. In an exchange relationship, participants behave so as to maximize individual rewards. Distinctions between open-field and closed-field relationships also have been identified (Berscheid, 1986). Participants in open-field or voluntary relationships are free to dissolve the affiliation whenever social exchanges become inequitable. Closed-field or obligatory relationships are bound together by bonds difficult to dissolve, so participants must endure inequitable social exchanges.

Close relationships develop over time with the progressive reorganization of interaction processes (Hinde, 1979). In their earliest stages, adult romances are open-field exchange relationships (Berscheid & Walster, 1969). Should initial social exchanges prove mutually beneficial, interdependence may develop: Interconnected behaviors expand as participants become dependent on benefits provided exclusively by the relationship. Interdependence deepens with the shift from an exchange to a communal relationship, and participants may make these relationships less voluntary in order to protect investments and avoid disruption of beneficial exchanges (Thibaut & Kelley, 1959). Western culture offers social norms designed to shift publicly proclaimed romantic relationships from the open field to the closed field: Exclusive dating, becoming engaged, and getting married represent a succession of relationship steps that are increasingly difficult to retrace.

The full potential of social exchange theory has yet to be realized. Most research on romantic social exchange involves university students, so the model describes relationships during late adolescence and young adulthood with some precision. Less is known about earlier age periods, although it is clear that equality and equity form the basis for interpersonal relationships among all but the very youngest children (Hartup & Laursen, 1991). Brown (this volume), Dunphy (1969), and Furman (1989) contend that peer relationships encompass greater closeness and reciprocity with age, and research on adolescent romantic relationships attests to the significance of these characteristics of interdependence (Furman & Burhmester, 1992; Laursen & Williams, 1997). Yet, despite its obvious significance, developmental applications of social exchange theory remain to be elaborated, as few studies have directly examined interdependence in adolescent romantic relationships.

The absence of a developmental perspective raises questions as to how assumptions about adult social exchange should be applied to adolescent romantic relationships. Do romantic relationships progress normatively across adolescence from exchange to communal and from open field to closed field? Do cognitive transformations differ across stages of adolescent development and stages of adolescent romantic relationships? Adolescents experience profound changes likely to shape behavior in romantic relationships. It seems reasonable to assume that romantic relationships are transformed by individual development, as intellectual advances improve interpersonal skills (Selman, 1980) and physical maturity increases the salience of romantic interactions (Stattin & Magnusson, 1990). Adolescent romantic relationships also are influenced by environmental factors, such as the values and expectations of parents and peers (Billy & Udry, 1985; Inazu & Fox, 1980). Some cultures encourage early participation in romantic relationships, whereas others require the emancipation of adulthood. This line of study, and others that cut across similar subfields of psychology, may signal an impending paradigm shift as the science of close relationships broadens its scope of inquiry (Berscheid, 1999).

To summarize, social exchange theories assume that adult romantic relationships are organized around interdependent behaviors and outcomes. Interactions between romantic partners become exclusive and committed as interdependence deepens, increasing each participant's investment in the continuation of social exchanges. As the relationship develops, participants adopt a communal rather than an exchange orientation, which may ultimately lead to a shift from open-field to closed-field relationship conditions. Extending this framework to adolescent romantic relationships is an important challenge confronting developmental scholars. In the next section, we turn our attention to this task.

Developmental Variations in Social Exchange Processes

From a developmental perspective, social exchange theory depictions of romantic relationships suffer from two weaknesses. First, the theory is adevelopmental in that the same principles apply regardless of participant age, maturity, and experience (Berscheid, 1986). No allowance is made for the fact that adolescents differ socially, cognitively, and physically, both from one another and from adults. Second, the theory is excessively rational in that interpersonal behavior is the result of calculations concerning investments, outcomes, and available alternatives (Graziano, 1984). Love and passion are not easily captured by social interactions and cognitive transformations. The successful application of social exchange theory to adolescent romantic relationships must incorporate models that address individual changes unique to this age period, as well as the perception that youthful romantic behavior reflects precious little conscious consideration. As a prelude to our nascent developmental model of adolescent romantic relationships, two sources of variance in social exchange are reviewed: (1) differences ascribed to proximal mechanisms and (2) differences ascribed to distal mechanisms.

Proximal Mechanisms Influencing Resource Exchange

All exchanges are not created equal: Similar social interactions and outcomes may be interpreted in a profoundly different manner (Foa, 1971). The hungry may value food above companionship, whereas the lonely may prefer the company of friends to dinner alone. An understanding of social exchange requires an examination of the meaning attributed to interpersonal behavior; such an accounting reveals that the relative value of different types of social exchange varies according to individual, relationship, and setting characteristics.

Two orthogonal dimensions distinguish resources provided by social exchanges according to their value to participants (Foa, 1971): particularism and concreteness. *Particularism* describes the significance of the relationship providing the resource and the value attached to receiving it from a specific source. Resources low in particularism have value regardless of their origin, whereas resources high in particularism usually are cherished only if received from certain individuals. *Concreteness* describes the type of social exchange and the outcome provided. Concrete commodities and behaviors differ from symbolic ones in that the latter afford meaning beyond the material value of the item or act. On the basis of these distinctions, Foa (1971) identified six types of resources: status, love, service, goods, money, and information. Those that are particular range from the concrete (service) to the symbolic (status) and points in between (love). Those low in particularism also vary from the concrete (goods) to the symbolic (information) and points in between (money).

Different resources are salient in different relationships (Foa & Foa, 1974). Particularistic exchanges are limited to a few close relationships: Resources valued for their origins usually come from family members, friends, and romantic partners. Concrete resources, in contrast, are exchanged in all relationships. As interconnections between participants increase, so does the variety of resources exchanged and their relative significance (Berg & Clark, 1986). Relationships that are not close tend to be linked to a specific resource: Teachers provide information; beauticians render a service; clothiers furnish goods. Close relationships include most resources, each with a differing value. Love tends to be the most important resource in a romantic relationship, followed by information and service (Berg & McQuinn, 1986).

Principles that govern social exchanges depend on the resources exchanged (Törnblom & Foa, 1983). Most resource exchanges invoke equality, although status is governed by merit and equity. Monetary exchanges also entail equity, and those involving information may be defined by need. In relationships with few resources, behavior is typically the product of a single exchange rule. Close relationships, in contrast, involve a variety of resource transactions, each accompanied by special provisions. For instance, romantic relationships are built on love, which is guided by equality, but in financial matters couples reorient to equity. Adolescents learning the rules of romantic engagement undoubtedly struggle to match social exchanges to resources and relationships; anecdotal evidence suggests that some adults remain challenged by this task.

The relative significance of a relationship resource may be specific to an age period. Peer social exchanges become increasingly important across adolescence: Resources provided by friends and romantic partners expand or remain constant from childhood through adulthood, whereas those provided by parents and siblings decline (Teichman, Glaubman, & Garner, 1993). Interpretations of social interactions also differ with age, as behaviors with identical outcomes carry different meanings. Consider romantic relationships: The signification of an affectionate hug differs for grade school children on a playground, early teens on a first date, college students in singles bars, married couples retiring to bed, or jaded divorcees on a lonely hearts cruise.

These developmental differences are reflected in resources exchanged. Love is manifest as companionship in early adolescence, lust in mid-adolescence, and commitment in late adolescence (Sullivan, 1953). The salience of service and information increases with age, as romantic inter-connections expand from transportation and gossip to interchanges that range from chores to future aspirations (Brown, Mory, & Kinney, 1994). The relative value of status declines from early adolescence, when prestige is linked to peer group affiliation (Waller, 1937), so that by late adolescence it rivals money and goods as the least valued resource in romantic relation-ships (Berg & McQuinn, 1986). Some social exchanges in romantic rela-tionships cut across resource categories: Sex is an act of love for some adolescents, a status symbol for others, and an exchange of goods and ser-vices for a few (Katchandourian, 1990). Adolescent maturity and experi-ence alter the resource value of sex in ways that have yet to be specified.

To summarize, proximal mechanisms exert a powerful influence on romantic social interactions. Interpersonal behavior is driven by the value of a social exchange, which depends on the resource and its meaning to participants. Resources prominent in adult romantic relationships are not the same as those in adolescent romantic relationships, and as resources change with development, so do the principles that govern their exchange.

Distal Mechanisms Influencing Resource Exchange

Taking a somewhat longer view of interpersonal relationships, evolu-tionary psychology (Buss, 1995; Kenrick & Trost, 1989) also addresses variation in social exchange processes. Describing the origins of human reproductive behavior, this perspective describes specific social interactions in terms of tendencies that once facilitated human survival. Contemporary romantic exchanges are assumed to be proximal expressions of some of these distal influences.

Like theories of proximal influence mechanisms, evolutionary psychol-ogy describes individuals who seek to maximize personal gain from roman-tic relationships. Evolutionary accounts also assume that resource exchange is the objective of heterosexual relationships. Exchange theory and evolu-tionary psychology differ, however, in depictions of the resources exchanged. The former focuses on socially defined rewards, whereas the latter emphasizes rewards based on psychological mechanisms that evolved over time to ensure adaptation and survival (Buss, 1990). These processes need not be considered mutually exclusive: The ultimate goal of romantic relationships from an evolutionary perspective is reproduction, which entails an exchange of resources on both proximal and distal levels (Brewer, 1997).

Preferential mate choices may be linked to evolutionary pressures. Sexual selection describes the tendency of members of one sex to compete for members of the other sex, with mating decisions made on the basis of characteristic preferences (Darwin, 1871). Sometimes the preferences of males and females overlap, presumably because of similar adaptive demands. For instance, men and women place a premium on cooperation and compassion (Jensen-Campbell, Graziano, & West, 1995). Some reproductive strategies, however, suggest different adaptive pressures on men and women. The parental investment model (Trivers, 1972) assumes that distinct strategies optimize reproductive success: Females seek mates with the resources to support offspring, whereas males seek mates that display physical cues to reproductive capacity (Feingold, 1992). In this manner, prehistoric social exchanges between males and females may have contributed to contemporary psychological preferences for romantic partners.

Evolutionary psychology may account for some of the illogical and emotional behavior in romantic relationships. A habit of depending on one's partner for important resources is well and good, as are sanctions to inhibit relationship dissolution, but a strong physiological attachment between mates maximizes reproductive fitness by cementing the relationship. This suggests that intense affective arousal (sometimes responsible for concomitant irrational behavior) facilitates pair bonding and, as such, may be a product of natural selection (Kenrick & Trost, 1989).

Evolved psychological mechanisms exert an indirect rather than a deterministic influence on romantic social exchanges. Distal processes are mediated by proximal constraints that reflect characteristics of the individual, the relationship, and the setting. Three points require consideration. First, evolutionary mechanisms represent broad solutions to specific adaptive problems that originated in a particular historical context. The result is a psychological tendency that affords diverse behavioral responses. For instance, male risk-taking propensities may have evolved because of competition for females who make preferential choices among potential mates (Darwin, 1871). When physical prowess was paramount, males who took risks were most apt to secure mates. Males evince this tendency still: The height of intrasexual competition for mates coincides with risk-taking that produces a mortality rate 200% higher among adolescent males than among adolescent females (Trivers, 1985). Manhood may be expressed differently nowadays, on playing fields rather than on killing fields, but the results are similar: To the risk-taker go the spoils of victory. Thus, distal demands created flexible tendencies adaptive to proximal challenges.

Second, evolved psychological mechanisms are influenced by ontogenetic context (Oyama, 1989). Critical experiences during early developmental stages may elicit strategies that encourage different life trajectories. For example, girls without fathers may mature earlier and adopt less discriminating mating strategies than those raised with fathers (Draper & Harpending, 1982). Childhood father absence may prompt adaptive mechanisms that assume that males are absent, unreliable, or lack resources. To maximize the survival of offspring in these challenging circumstances, females may bear children early and often (Belsky, Steinberg, & Draper, 1991). Adolescent reproduction may also prompt matrilineal parenting, an adaptive response ensuring efficient allocation of resources to offspring given that adolescent males tend to be unreliable fathers (Maccoby, 1991). These examples illustrate how different evolved mechanisms may be triggered by crucial proximal developmental experiences.

Finally, evolved psychological mechanisms may be subsumed by environmental or developmental demands (DeKay & Buss, 1992). Exaptations describe instances in which tendencies designed to address a particular historical problem are applied unexpectedly by succeeding generations (Buss, Haselton, Shackelford, Bleske, & Wakefield, 1998). Opposable thumbs did not evolve so that toxins could be self-administered efficiently any more than sex evolved as a recreational activity divorced from reproduction. Yet present-day adolescents tend to practice short-term sexual behavior instead of long-term pair bonding; contemporary conventions have altered past propensities so that adolescence is no longer a period of reproduction but rather one of sexual experimentation (Buss, 1994). Sexual capabilities were uncoupled from reproductive fitness when advances in health and nutrition brought about a decline in the age of menarche (Eveleth & Tanner, 1976) at the same time that economic and social demands delayed the onset of adulthood (Bakan, 1972). Thus, behaviors with evolutionary origins may be expressed in a manner that has more to do with proximal demands than with distal adaptive pressures.

Human pair bonding is a complicated enterprise. Quite probably a variety of strategies evolved for choosing mates (Cunningham, Druen, & Barbee, 1997). Despite the current emphasis on love, it is clear that more than one type of resource will secure a mate. This multiple fitness model is consistent with resource theory in stressing that human pair bonding may originate from many forms of exchange, each providing a basis for interpersonal attraction. Varied strategies for mate selection are a healthy form of behavioral diversity in that proximal variations in romantic social exchange represent different routes to the same goal – reproduction.

The multiple fitness model implies that reproductive exchanges differ across the life span (Cunningham et al., 1997). Young adult females at the height of reproductive fitness need not offer different resources to entice potential mates. Young adult males, who command few concrete resources, need to cultivate particularistic resources to attract mates. Female reproductive fitness declines with age, and attracting mates on the basis of physical appearance is increasingly difficult; successful reproductive strategies involve securing additional resources. Male dominance increases with age, making it easier to attract mates with status, money, goods, information, and service. Other psychological mechanisms at work in the selection process are less sensitive to developmental variation. From early adolescence through adulthood, males and females report that kindness is the most important attribute in a potential mate (Buss & Barnes, 1986; Roscoe, Diana, & Brooks, 1987). The salience of some resources remains the same across the life span, whereas the salience of others differs as a function of maturation and gender.

To summarize, distal mechanisms, tempered by proximal constraints, influence romantic exchanges. Capabilities and propensities may be products of evolutionary history, but behavior is an expression of immediate environmental pressures. Reproductive fitness and the resources available for sexual selection change across the life cycle, with trajectories that differ for males and females. As a result, romantic exchanges may undergo developmental transformations, reflecting alterations in the extent to which distal processes impact contemporary behavior.

The Generalizability of Proximal and Distal Mechanisms

Our discussion to this point assumes consistency in mechanisms of influence that shape adolescent romantic relationships. This assumption should be qualified: Proximal and distal influences probably vary according to participants and contexts. Certainly all adolescent romantic relationships are swayed by some pressures that may be attributed to environment and evolution, but the exact nature and relative strength of these influences are not fixed. What circumstances alter proximal and distal pressures on adolescent romantic relationships? Three potential moderating forces are considered: (1) differences in social exchange orientation; (2) differences in relationship organization; and (3) differences in resources exchanged.

Diversity in social exchange orientation cuts across individuals and cultures. Although most people favor communal romantic relationships, a few prefer exchange relationships (Mills & Clark, 1994). These orientations shape affective responses to resource exchanges. For example, reactions to providing assistance depend on the relationship expected (Williamson & Clark, 1989). Helping increases positive affect when a communal relationship is desired but not when an exchange relationship is anticipated. Cultures also differ in the value placed on social exchange orientations. Collectivism emphasizes the partnership over the self, whereas individualism stresses the self over the relationship (Triandis, Bontempo, & Villareal, 1988). Resource distribution behaviors illustrate the distinction: College students from collectivistic societies allocate more resources to friends than those from individualistic societies; resource scarcity increases generosity among the former group, but the latter maintain their preference for equity (Hui, Triandis, & Yee, 1991). Despite a general tendency for exchange orientations in close relationships, specific behaviors vary with individual preferences and cultural norms, variations that alter the relative impact of proximal and distal influences on romantic interactions.

Exchange processes reflect the organization of a relationship. Individual differences in sexual attraction contribute to romantic orientations that, in turn, guide social interactions. Although the same principles of social exchange apply to same-sex and cross-sex romantic relationships, the pattern and availability of rewards may differ (Duffy & Rusbult, 1986). Relationship satisfaction and commitment predict outcomes and investments regardless of sexual orientation. Even so, homosexual relationships differ from heterosexual relationships in terms of mate selection characteristics and resource exchanges; gender-specific preferences for status and beauty are less evident in same-sex than in cross-sex romantic relationships (Deaux & Hanna, 1984). Adolescents, in particular, have difficulty identifying homosexual partners, which limits opportunities for romantic exchange (Diamond et al., this volume). The structure of romantic relationships reflects cultural as well as individual imperatives. In societies with flexible romantic roles, personal preferences determine mate selection, but in societies with fixed romantic roles, the individual has little power over partner selection (Blood, 1967). Taken together, the evidence suggests that the organization of a romantic relationship defines exchanges between participants. Proximal and distal influences differ across relationship types as a function of their relevance to the interconnections that comprise dyadic interdependence.

The relative value of a given resource differs across relationships. Individual preferences are expressed in patterns of romantic social exchange such that resources salient in one relationship may be less relevant in another. Some romantic relationships emphasize intimacy and closeness, others demand passion and sexual attraction, and still others require predictability and quietude (Sternberg, 1986). Just as individuals differ in romantic resource expectations, so do cultures. In some societies passion is desired and love is requisite for marital commitment, whereas in other societies passion is considered troublesome and love unnecessary (Sprecher et al., 1994). Given that romantic relationships traffic in different resources, the extent to which proximal and distal mechanisms influence social exchanges depends upon individual preferences, cultural norms, and the type of resource exchanged.

Social exchange theory encompasses most forms of romantic interdependence, regardless of individual, relationship, and cultural variation. There is considerable diversity, however, in the relative influence that proximal and distal mechanisms exert over social exchanges. Romantic orientations, organizations, and resources vary according to individual preferences, social settings, and developmental timetables. These moderating factors may be strong enough to curb evolved pressures and environmental influences; alternatively, they may create conditions that enhance the significance of proximal and distal pressures.

Social Exchange in Adolescent Romantic Relationships

The aphorism proclaiming nothing to be as practical as a good theory (Lewin, 1944) leaves unspecified the standards against which the theory ought to be measured. Minimally, a good theory must account for the empirical data. When considering adolescent romantic relationships, three distinctions emerge from the available evidence. First, adolescent romantic relationships differ from other adolescent relationships. Second, adolescent romantic relationships differ from adult romantic relationships. Third, characteristics of romantic relationships change across adolescence. This section reviews distinguishing characteristics of adolescent romantic relationships and outlines a social exchange model to account for the evidence.

Characteristics of Adolescent Romantic Relationships

Adolescent relationships are not monolithic entities; romantic relationships differ from family and friend relationships in their specific processes and global properties. Adolescents consistently rate romantic relationships as significant sources of affection, companionship, and support; mothers or friends may rival romantic partners on specific attributes, but the latter prevail on most overall indices of closeness (Zani, 1993). Few studies directly compare social exchanges in different adolescent relationships, but those that do indicate that interdependence cuts across romantic resources, whereas friendships offer companionship but not influence, and parent–child relationships encompass influence but not companionship (Laursen & Williams, 1997).

Unique features of romantic relationships produce exceptional patterns of exchange. Like friendships, romantic relationships in their initial stages are communal and voluntary; exchanges in these open-field relationships are designed to minimize threats to mutual benefits (Laursen, 1996). Friendships and romantic relationships are also reciprocal or horizontal (Youniss, 1980); participants wield similar social power and are relatively egalitarian. Romances differ from friendships, however, in the manner in which social exchanges are transformed over the course of the relationship: The greater the investment in a romantic relationship, the more it resembles a closed-field relationship. Like family relationships, committed romantic relationships include interconnections that are obligatory (publicly proclaimed bonds are difficult to abrogate) and vertical (interactions are not normatively egalitarian), but unlike family relationships these interconnections are not indissoluble (Rusbult, 1983). These distinctions suggest that romantic relationships are a class of interdependent relationships unto themselves: Sharing some features of open-field relationships and other features of closed-field relationships, romantic relationships also proffer a singular set of social exchanges unavailable in most close relationships.

Few studies directly contrast romantic relationships during adolescence with those during adulthood, but the available evidence suggests differences in manifestations of interdependence. Compared with adult affiliations, adolescent romantic relationships are transitory and fleeting, as well as less exclusive and intimate (Fraysner, 1985; Reis & Shaver, 1988). Greater closeness in romantic relationships often comes at the expense of friendships, which suggests that romantic interconnections supplant those between friends (Rusbult, 1983). Although this process begins during adolescence, alterations in social exchanges accelerate during adulthood as pair bonding emerges as an important life task (Coleman & Hendry, 1989). Motives and goals for romantic relationships also differ with age: Career and self-development tasks during adolescence give way to interpersonal tasks during adulthood, and vice versa (Cantor & Malley, 1991).

Eventually, social exchanges are revised so that the romantic relationships of adolescents resemble those of adults. Intimacy, companionship, support, and affection increase in cross-sex relationships across adolescence (Furman & Buhrmester, 1992; Sharabany, Gershoni, & Hofman, 1981). Romantic interdependence expands from early adolescence to late adolescence (Laursen & Williams, 1997) and from late adolescence to young adulthood (Argyle & Furnham, 1983). Thus, burgeoning interconnections with romantic partners during adolescence and young adulthood accompany declining interdependence with family members and friends.

Interdependence alters the organization of romantic relationships. Adult romantic relationships contain an array of interconnected behaviors and exclusive benefits that encourage commitment, whereas adolescent romantic relationships are surrounded by social sanctions and a large pool of available alternatives that inhibit commitment. Brief romantic encounters provide adolescents with opportunities to practice exchange rules and refine personal resources prior to initiating relationships that entail commitment and reproduction. Functional significance may be embedded within these developmental differences: Social experience and cognitive maturation should improve mate selection, pair bonding, and child rearing (Buss, 1994). This system of incrementally revising and expanding interconnections in romantic relationships encourages experimentation and permits a graduated entry into the mating arena.

Individual development and cultural expectations prompt changes in adolescent romantic relationships. Romantic interconnections become more attractive and unfettered with age: Physical and social maturity enhance available outcomes at the same time that environmental constraints on social interactions are loosened (Laursen, 1996). The relative significance of particularistic resources increases across adolescence so that love and service emerge as two of the most important exchanges in close relationships (Teichman et al., 1993). Dating patterns reflect these developmental trends: Age and cultural norms determine the onset of dating (Dornbusch et al., 1981) and shift the orientation of social exchanges from self-centered goals (e.g., peer and parent approval, physical appearance) during early adolescence to relationship-centered goals (e.g., reciprocity, compatibility) during late adolescence (Roscoe et al., 1987).

To summarize, romantic interdependence and commitment, hallmarks of adult pair bonds, gradually emerge with adolescent development. As interconnections increase, distinct social exchange rules set romantic relationships apart from family and friend relationships.

A Developmental Model of Social Exchange in Adolescent Romantic Relationships

To account for different patterns of interdependence across adolescence, we propose a developmental model of romantic relationships based on principles of social exchange. This model holds that exchanges serve as points around which romantic relationships are organized. Across adolescence, social exchanges are transformed by maturation and development, by changes in the nature of the relationship and in the resources available from it, and by age-related alterations in social norms and expectations. Environmental and evolutionary pressures eventually give way to individual preferences and niche-picking. During early adolescence, cultural and distal influences have a heavy hand in shaping romantic interactions. Aside from variation ascribed to developmental timetables, the romantic relationships of young adolescents contain few degrees of individual freedom; physical, social, and cognitive limitations restrict romantic interactions to exchange relationships promoting personal gain. External and distal forces abate by late adolescence, and proximal psychological influences derived from personal experiences assert themselves, rewriting the rules of romantic social exchange to encourage communal relationships and mutual gain. These proximal mechanisms diversify social interactions as participants establish interconnections that match their tastes and temperaments.

External influences curtail early adolescent romantic exchanges. Laws forbid sexual contact, curfews restrict opportunities for social interaction, schools prohibit public displays of affection, religious organizations condemn romantic behaviors, and parents regulate resources and the manner in which they are exchanged. Mobility is constrained and access to services, goods, and information is limited, both of which indirectly inhibit romantic interconnections. Peers represent another form of external influence, shaping norms and opportunities to initiate relationships, select partners, and exchange resources. These environmental constraints appear to have a common purpose: Restrict social interactions so that peer pressure and adolescent naiveté do not result in premature procreation that may threaten long-term pair bonding.

Developmental factors also inhibit early adolescent romantic relationships. First, biological immaturity limits the exchange of sexual resources. Circumscribed physical capabilities and a lack of secondary sexual characteristics hinder young adolescents in the competition for romantic partners. Second, social immaturity and inexperience limit rewards from romantic exchanges. Prior to the onset of romantic relationships, open-field interdependent relationships with same-sex best friends discourage cross-sex relationships; potential romantic partners are treated with ambivalence or hostility. Personal history offers little guidance to those initiating romantic exchanges, so old scripts must be discarded without the benefit of new ones. Third, cognitive immaturity limits mental transformations of exchanges in close relationships. Representations of romantic partners and relationships tend to be driven by stereotypes, fostering inaccurate and unrealistic expectations. These difficulties are compounded by adolescent egocentrism and concrete thought, which conspire to promote interactions with short-term individual gains at the expense of long-term relationship objectives. Taken together, physical, social, and cognitive limitations dampen the contribution of individual psychological preferences to the construction and maintenance of early adolescent romantic relationships.

The suppression of psychological preferences by external forces gives rise to a period in which distal influences have a strong and unprecedented sway over romantic relationships. Early adolescents, unable to base mental representations of romantic relationships on personal experience because of environmental strictures and developmental limitations, have few internal resources to guide them except evolved tendencies. In other words, because young adolescents lack wisdom, they must rely on their instincts. The manner in which distal mechanisms are expressed and their relative influence is a matter of social convention. Evolved preferences in pair bonding may be manifest directly through the individual or indirectly through the clan.

In cultures that emphasize familialism and collectivism, kin are intimately involved with mate selection; pair bonding in the absence of parent approval is atypical. Distal pressures on romantic relationships are expressed through family members (acting for personal gain and to perpetuate the gene pool) who select prospective mates demonstrating reproductive fitness with displays of physical attractiveness, goods, money, and status. In these circumstances, development affords few opportunities for the expression of individual psychological preferences in sanctioned romantic relationships: Late adolescents may attempt to influence family decisions on mate selection or defy family dictates and risk alienation from the collective support system.

In societies that emphasize individualism, some distal pressures on early adolescents are maintained by the family but most are expressed through the individual. Lacking direct control over pair bonding, parents influence interconnections by attempting to define the parameters of romantic exchanges. Rather than proscribe social interactions, parents establish the boundaries of acceptable resource exchanges by creating sanctions against specific interconnections and particular partners. Unable to dictate consorts and activities, parents must settle for expressing a preference for nice, attractive, and affluent mates. Of course, parents indirectly influence romantic relationships, narrowing the cast of prospective mates by their choice of neighborhoods, schools, and cultural and leisure activities. Yet despite the exhortations and exertions of kin, decisions concerning romantic relationships ultimately fall to the individual. What guides early adolescents in their choice of romantic partners? Distal mechanisms appear to play an important role. Consistent with evolutionary theory, young adolescents place priority on status and physical appearance; the relative importance of these romantic resources is at an apex during this age period. Stereotypes, peer approval, and media depictions that glorify power and beauty strengthen these evolved tendencies. Thus, distal pressures are reinforced in individualistic societies by cultural and familial messages that stress characteristics of reproductive fitness in romantic exchanges.

Most cultures that promote individualism recognize adolescence as a period of prolonged experimentation. Spanning the second decade of life and beyond, contemporary adolescence offers the individual opportunities to explore life trajectory options before committing to a career, a family, and a lifestyle. Romantic relationships are but one arena in which adolescent experimentation is implicitly condoned. Primogenial romantic experiences enable individuals to estimate their relative attractiveness as a partner, to experiment with different strategies for securing and retaining mates, and to clarify preferences in relationships and resources. During early adolescence, a safety net (of sorts) is in place to catch those whose exploration takes them beyond the established boundaries. Strong interconnections with family members cushion the blow of temporary teen trifles (and those of a more serious nature), demand respect from potential suitors, and bear the costs of carrying through or terminating a premature pregnancy. By late adolescence, diminished interdependence with family members opens the way for children to assume responsibility for their own romantic exchanges. In individualistic cultures, adolescents are expected to explore the social world before acquiring adult roles; romantic relationships are one of many arenas in which experimentation is tolerated and sanctioned.

One by one, properties of social exchange that may have origins in evolutionary history are rehearsed and considered by adolescents in individualistic societies; some are rejected, and others are incorporated into a set of personal preferences that guide romantic relationships. Distal mechanisms that initially exert similar pressures on all young adolescents are transformed by individual experience, producing expectations about romantic relationships during late adolescence that reflect proximal psychological concerns. As environmental constraints are lifted, adolescents are better able to select relationship niches that suit their predilections and predispositions. Consistent with this developmental trend, the significance of status and physical attraction in adolescent romantic relationships declines in relation to kindness and reciprocity. The romantic resources preferred most by early adolescents provide for expressions of evolved mechanisms or external influences; social exchanges between participants are typically selfish, maximizing personal gain and reproductive success. The romantic resources preferred most by late adolescents and young adults provide for expressions of individuality and experience; social exchanges between participants typically proffer mutual gain, thereby maximizing interdependence and relationship stability. Thus, the relative importance of distal mechanisms on romantic social exchange diminishes for adolescents in individualistic societies; as environmental constraints on social interactions are removed, they are replaced by proximal psychological preferences created from a widening base of social experiences.

To summarize, romantic relationships during adolescence are distinct from other adolescent close relationships and from romantic relationships during other age periods. A model of romantic relationships is proposed in which social exchange alterations reflect a shift in the resources attributed to proximal and distal influences. With social interactions restricted by family and culture, young adolescent mating preferences are heavily influenced by pressures attributed to the immediate environment and to evolutionary history. In societies that espouse individualism, age and maturation prompt the lifting of external constraints. This new behavioral latitude affords opportunities for experience in romantic relationships, enhancing the role of personal psychological preferences in late adolescent mate selection at the expense of distal and environmental influences. As a result, the rules of social exchange are altered along with the resources, and exchange romantic relationships give way to communal romantic relationships.

Predicting Social Exchanges in Adolescent Romantic Relationships

Exchange theory may be criticized for being overly descriptive, lacking predictive validity and falsifiability (Graziano, 1984). Much the same can be said about the mechanisms inherent in evolutionary psychology. It is difficult to experimentally manipulate interdependence and preserve ecological validity; it is even harder to isolate sources of influence and trace their origins to proximal and distal pressures. Despite these limitations, social exchange remains a powerful framework for the empirical study of close relationships. Much of the theory's success stems from its ability to expand and accommodate new evidence. In this spirit, we offer several prospective research directions designed to elaborate critical tenets of the proposed social exchange model of adolescent romantic relationships.

Adolescent romantic relationships are assumed to be characterized by patterns of social exchange that differ from those in family relationships and friendships. Although questionnaire data (Furman & Buhrmester, 1992; Laursen & Williams, 1997) indicate that adolescents perceive relationship differences consistent with social exchange theory suppositions, support from observational data is scarce. The dearth of research calls into question the assumption that principles of exchange guide adolescent interactions and organize relationships. Classic laboratory studies demonstrating social exchange in adult relationships (Kelley & Thibaut, 1978) must be replicated with younger subjects to determine the veracity of adolescent self-reports and the applicability of the theory to adolescent close relationships.

Differences between adults and adolescents in romantic exchanges also are assumed to reflect variations in proximal and distal influences. Isolated studies of adolescent relationships are consistent with this assertion (Buss, 1995; Teichman et al., 1993), but cross-sectional work must be supplemented by longitudinal data tracking developmental alterations in social exchange. Three areas of study will advance this research agenda. First, depictions of ideal and real adolescent partners will facilitate identification of developmental characteristics of romantic relationships consistent with proximal and distal influences. Second, observational and interview methodologies must be employed to better understand cognitive transformations that occur within romantic relationships across adolescence. Third, pathways of development should be examined for individual differences in influence mechanisms.

Developmental mechanisms remain to be explicated. Although physical maturity alters available resources, cognitive maturity facilitates long-term relationship assessments, and social maturity affords sustained interdependence, it is not clear which developmental changes prompt which alterations in romantic exchanges. The study of adolescents who attain developmental milestones "off-time" will assist in identifying the normative sequence of romantic interdependence and in isolating maturational components associated with specific patterns of romantic exchange. Longitudinal tracking of adolescents and their romantic relationships should pinpoint the antecedents of change in resources and social exchanges. Even so, the task is formidable. Cohort differences will obscure the picture, as new social experiences and different expectations alter proximal influences on romantic relationships. Contextual variation also will complicate the effort to identify developmental mechanisms; culture, ethnicity, and race shape timetables, define proximal pressures, and perhaps even elicit specific distal influences.

Conclusion

At the outset, we noted that developmental psychologists could learn a great deal about romantic relationships from the field of social psychology. Exchange theory, one of the most successful and influential accounts of adult interpersonal behavior, offers a logical entry point for those interested in the development of adolescent romantic relationships. Presumably, mature patterns of romantic social interaction do not germinate and blossom during adulthood, but rather emerge gradually with experience and maturation acquired during adolescence. The model proposed in the present chapter assumes that romantic relationships are organized according to principles of social exchange but that ontogenesis alters specific patterns of relationship interdependence. Across adolescence, proximal and distal influences systematically modify the exchange of romantic resources. Thus, it would appear that social psychologists could learn something about romantic relationships from the field of developmental psychology. Efforts in this vein may produce something akin to a communal relationship: The application of social exchange theory to the earliest romantic relationships should foster interconnections between social psychology and developmental psychology that increase interdisciplinary interdependence and promote mutually rewarding insights into adolescent romantic behavior.

References

Argyle, M., & Furnham, A. (1983). Sources of satisfaction and conflict in long-term relationships. *Journal of Marriage and the Family, 45,* 481–493.

Bakan, D. (1972). Adolescence in America: From idea to social fact. In J. Kagan & R. Coles (Eds.), *Twelve to sixteen: Early adolescence* (pp. 73–89). New York: Norton.

Bales, R. F. (1950). *Interaction process analysis.* Cambridge, MA: Addison-Wesley.

Belsky, J., Steinberg, L. D., & Draper, P. (1991). Childhood experience, interpersonal development and reproductive strategy: An evolutionary theory of socialization. *Child Development, 62,* 647–670.

Berg, J. H., & Clark, M. S. (1986). Differences in social exchange between intimate and other relationships: Gradually evolving or quickly apparent? In V. J. Derlega & B. A. Winstead (Eds.), *Friendship and social interaction.* New York: Springer-Verlag.

Berg, J. H., & McQuinn, R. D. (1986). Attraction and exchange in continuing and noncontinuing dating relationships. *Journal of Personality and Social Psychology, 50,* 942–952.

Berscheid, E. (1986). Emotional experience in close relationships: Some implications for child development. In W. W. Hartup & Z. Rubin (Eds.), *Relationships and development* (pp. 135–166). Hillsdale, NJ: Erlbaum.

Berscheid, E. (1999). Commentary: Integrating relationship knowledge. In W. A. Collins & B. Laursen (Eds.), *Relationships as developmental contexts: The Minnesota Symposia on Child Psychology* (Vol. 29, pp. 307–314). Hillsdale, NJ: Erlbaum.

Berscheid, E., & Reis, H. T. (1998). Attraction and close relationships. In D. T. Gilbert, S. T. Fiske, & G. Lindzey (Eds.), *The handbook of social psychology* (4th ed., pp. 193–281). New York: McGraw-Hill.

Berscheid, E., & Walster, E. H. (1969). *Interpersonal attraction.* Reading, MA: Addison-Wesley.

Billy, J. O. G., & Udry, J. R. (1985). The influence of male and female best friends on adolescent sexual behavior. *Adolescence, 20,* 21–32.

Blood, R. O., Jr. (1967). *Love-match and arranged marriage.* New York: Free Press.

Brewer, M. B. (1997). On the social origins of human nature. In C. McGarty & S. A. Haslam (Eds.), *The message of social psychology: Perspectives on mind in society* (pp. 54–62). London: Blackwell.

Brown, B. B., Mory, M. S., & Kinney, D. (1994). Casting adolescent crowds in a relational perspective: Caricature, channel, and context. In R. Montemayor, G. R. Adams, & T. P. Gullotta (Eds.), *Personal relationships during adolescence* (pp. 123–167). Thousand Oaks, CA: Sage.

Buss, D. M. (1990). The evolution of anxiety and social exclusion. *Journal of Social and Clinical Psychology, 9,* 196–201.

Buss, D. M. (1994). *The evolution of desire: Strategies of human mating.* New York: Basic Books.

Buss, D. M. (1995). Evolutionary psychology: A new paradigm for psychological sciences. *Psychological Inquiry, 6,* 1–30.

Buss, D. M., & Barnes, M. F. (1986). Preferences in human mate selection. *Journal of Personality and Social Psychology, 50,* 559–570.

Buss, D. M., Haselton, M. G., Shackelford, T. K., Bleske, A. L., & Wakefield, J. C. (1998). Adaptations, exaptations, and spandrels. *American Psychologist, 53,* 533–548.

Cantor, N., & Malley, J. (1991). Life tasks, personal needs, and close relationships. In G. J. O. Fletcher & F. D. Fincham (Eds.), *Cognition in close relationships* (pp. 101–125). Hillsdale, NJ: Erlbaum.

Clark, M. S., & Mills, J. (1979). Interpersonal attraction in exchange and communal relationships. *Journal of Personality and Social Psychology, 37,* 12–24.

Clark, M. S., & Reis, H. T. (1988). Interpersonal processes in close relationships. *Annual Review of Psychology, 39,* 609–672.

Coleman, J. C., & Hendry, L. (1989). *The nature of adolescence.* London: Routledge.

Cunningham, M. R., Druen, P. B., & Barbee, A. P. (1997). Angels, mentors, and friends: Trade-offs among evolutionary, social, and individual variables in physical appearance. In J. A. Simpson & D. T. Kenrick (Eds.), *Evolutionary social psychology* (pp. 109–140). Hillsdale, NJ: Erlbaum.

Darwin, C. (1871). *The descent of man and selection in relation to sex.* New York: Appleton.

Deaux, K., & Hanna, R. (1984). Courtship in the personals column: The influence of gender and sexual orientation. *Sex Roles, 11,* 363–375.

DeKay, W. T., & Buss, D. M. (1992). Human nature, individual differences, and the importance of context: Perspectives from evolutionary psychology. *Current Directions in Psychological Science, 1,* 184–189.

Dornbusch, S. M., Carlsmith, J. M., Gross, R. T., Martin, J. A., Jennings, D., Rosenberg, A., & Duke, P. (1981). Sexual development, age and dating: A comparison of biological and social influences upon one set of behaviors. *Child Development, 52,* 179–185.

Draper, P., & Harpending, H. (1982). Father absence and reproductive strategy: An evolutionary perspective. *Journal of Anthropological Research, 38,* 255–273.

Duffy, S., & Rusbult, C. E. (1986). Satisfaction and commitment in homosexual and heterosexual relationships. *Journal of Homosexuality, 12,* 1–23.

Dunphy, D. C. (1969). *Cliques, crowds, and gangs.* Melbourne, Australia: Chesire.

Eveleth, P., & Tanner, J. (1976). *Worldwide variation in human growth.* New York: Cambridge University Press.

Feingold, A. (1992). Gender differences in mate selection preferences: A test of the parental investment model. *Psychological Bulletin, 112,* 125–139.

Fletcher, G. J. O., & Fincham, F. D. (1991). Attribution processes in close relationships. In G. J. O. Fletcher & F. D. Fincham (Eds.), *Cognition in close relationships* (pp. 7–35). Hillsdale, NJ: Erlbaum.

Foa, U. G. (1971). Interpersonal and economic resources. *Science, 171,* 345–351.

Foa, E. B., & Foa, U. G. (1974). *Social structures of the mind.* Springfield, IL: Thomas.

Fraysner, S. (1985). *Varieties of sexual experience: An anthropological perspective.* New Haven, CT: HRAF Press.

Furman, W. (1989). The development of children's social networks. In D. Belle (Ed.), *Children's social networks and social supports* (pp. 151–172). New York: Wiley.

Furman, W. (1993). Theory is not a four letter word: Needed directions in the study of adolescent friendships. In B. Laursen (Ed.), *Close friendships in adolescence: New Directions for Child Development* (No. 60, pp. 89–103). San Francisco: Jossey-Bass.

Furman, W., & Buhrmester, D. (1992). Age and sex differences in perceptions of networks of personal relationships. *Child Development, 63,* 103–115.

Goffman, E. (1961). *Asylums.* Garden City, NY: Doubleday.

Gottman, J. M. (1994). *What predicts divorce? The relationship between marital processes and marital outcomes.* Hillsdale, NJ: Erlbaum.

Graziano, W. G. (1984). A developmental approach to social exchange processes. In J. C. Masters & K. Yarkin-Levin (Eds.), *Boundary areas in social and developmental psychology* (pp. 161–193). Orlando: Academic Press.

Hartup, W. W., & Laursen, B. (1991). Relationships as developmental contexts. In R. Cohen & A. W. Siegel (Eds.), *Context and development* (pp. 253–279). Hillsdale, NJ: Erlbaum.

Hinde, R. A. (1979). *Towards understanding relationships.* New York: Academic Press.

Homans, G. C. (1961). *Social behavior: Its elementary forms.* New York: Harcourt, Brace, and World.

Hui, C. H., Triandis, H. C., & Yee, C. (1991). Cultural differences in reward allocation: Is collectivism the explanation? *British Journal of Social Psychology, 30,* 145–157.

Inazu, J. K., & Fox, G. L. (1980). Maternal influence on the sexual behavior of teenage daughters. *Journal of Family Issues, 1,* 81–102.

Jensen-Campbell, L. A., Graziano, W. G., & West, S. (1995). Dominance, prosocial orientation, and female preferences: Do nice guys really finish last? *Journal of Personality and Social Psychology, 68,* 427–440.

Katchandourian, H. (1990). Sexuality. In S. S. Feldman & G. R. Elliott (Eds.), *At the threshold: The developing adolescent* (pp. 330–351). Cambridge, MA: Harvard University Press.

Kelley, H. H., Berscheid, E., Christensen, A., Harvey, J. H., Huston, T. L., Levinger, G., McClintock, E., Peplau, L. A., & Peterson, D. R. (Eds.). (1983). *Close relationships.* New York: Freeman.

Kelley, H. H., & Thibaut, J. W. (1978). *Interpersonal relations: A theory of interdependence.* New York: Wiley.

Kenrick, D. T., & Trost, M. R. (1989). A reproductive exchange model of heterosexual relationships: Putting proximate economics in ultimate perspective. In C. Hendrick (Ed.), *Close relationships: Review of personality and social psychology* (Vol. 10, pp. 92–118). Newbury Park, CA: Sage.

Laursen, B. (1996). Closeness and conflict in adolescent peer relationships: Interdependence with friends and romantic partners. In W. M. Bukowski, A. F. Newcomb, & W. W. Hartup (Eds.), *The company they keep: Friendships in childhood and adolescence* (pp. 186–210). New York: Cambridge University Press.

Laursen, B., & Williams, V. (1997). Perceptions of interdependence and closeness in family and peer relationships among adolescents with and without romantic partners. In S. Shulman & W. A. Collins (Eds.), *Romantic relationships in adolescence: New Directions for Child Development* (No. 78, pp. 3–20). San Francisco: Jossey-Bass.

Lewin, K. (1944). Constructs in psychology and psychological ecology. *University of Iowa Studies in Child Welfare, 20,* 23–27.

Lewin, K. (1946). Behavior and development as a function of the total situation. In L. Carmichael (Ed.), *Manual of child psychology* (pp. 918–970). New York: Wiley.

Lewin, K. (1948). *Resolving social conflicts.* New York: Harper.

Maccoby, E. E. (1991). Different reproductive strategies in males and females. *Child Development, 62,* 676–681.

Mills, J., & Clark, M. S. (1994). Communal and exchange relationships: Controversies and research. In R. Erber & R. Gilmour (Eds.), *Theoretical frameworks for personal relationships* (pp. 29–42). Hillsdale, NJ: Erlbaum.

Oyama, S. (1989). Ontogeny and the central dogma: Do we need the concept of genetic programming in order to have an evolutionary perspective? In M. R. Gunnar & E. Thelen (Eds.), *Systems and development: The Minnesota Symposia on Child Psychology* (Vol. 22, pp. 1–34). Hillsdale, NJ: Erlbaum.

Reis, H. T., & Shaver, P. (1988). Intimacy as an interpersonal process. In S. Duck & D. F. Hay (Eds.), *Handbook of personal relationships: Theory, research, and interventions* (pp. 367–389). New York: Wiley.

Roscoe, B., Diana, M. S., & Brooks, R. H. (1987). Early, middle and late adolescents' views on dating and factors influencing partner selection. *Adolescence, 22,* 59–68.

Rusbult, C. E. (1983). A longitudinal test of the investment model: The development (and deterioration) of satisfaction and commitment in heterosexual involvement. *Journal of Personality and Social Psychology, 45,* 101–117.

Rusbult, C. E., & Martz, J. M. (1995). Remaining in an abusive relationship: An investment model analysis of nonvoluntary dependence. *Personality and Social Psychology Bulletin, 21,* 558–571.

Selman, R. (1980). *The growth of interpersonal understanding.* New York: Academic Press.

Sharabany, R., Gershoni, R., & Hofman, J. E. (1981). Girlfriend, boyfriend: Age and sex differences in intimate friendship. *Developmental Psychology, 17,* 800–808.

Sprecher, S., Aron, A., Hatfield, E., Cortese, A., Potapova, E., & Levitskaya, A. (1994). Love: American style, Russian style, and Japanese style. *Personal Relationships, 1,* 349–369.

Stattin, H., & Magnusson, D. (1990). *Pubertal maturation in female development.* Hillsdale, NJ: Erlbaum.

Sternberg, R. J. (1986). A triangular theory of love. *Psychological Review, 93,* 119–135.

Sullivan, H. S. (1953). *The interpersonal theory of psychiatry.* New York: Norton.

Thibaut, J. W., & Kelley, H. H. (1959). *The social psychology of groups.* New York: Wiley.

Teichman, M., Glaubman, H., & Garner, M. (1993). From early adolescence to middle-age adulthood: The perceived need for interpersonal resources in four developmental stages. In U. G. Foa, J. Converse, Jr., K. Y. Törnblom, & E. B. Foa (Eds.), *Resource theory: Explorations and applications* (pp. 157–165). San Diego: Academic Press.

Törnblom, K. Y., & Foa, U. G. (1983). Choice of a distribution principle: Cross-cultural evidence on the effects of resources. *Acta Sociologica, 26,* 161–173.

Triandis, H. C., Bontempo, R., & Villareal, M. J. (1988). Individualism and collectivism: Cross-cultural perspectives on self–in-group relationships. *Journal of Personality and Social Psychology, 54,* 323–338.

Trivers, R. L. (1972). Parental investment and sexual selection. In B. Campbell (Ed.), *Sexual selection and the descent of man: 1871–1971* (pp. 136–179). Chicago: Aldine.

Trivers, R. (1985). *Social evolution.* Menlo Park, CA: Benjamin-Cummings.

Waller, W. (1937). The rating and dating complex. *American Sociological Review, 2,* 727–734.

Walster, E., Berscheid, E., & Walster, W. G. (1973). New directions in equity research. *Journal of Personality and Social Psychology, 25,* 151–176.

Williamson, G. M., & Clark, M. S. (1989). Providing help and desired relationship type as determinants of changes in moods and self-evaluations. *Journal of Personality and Social Psychology, 56,* 722–734.

Youniss, J. (1980). *Parents and peers in social development: A Piaget–Sullivan perspective.* Chicago: University of Chicago Press.

Zani, B. (1993). Dating and interpersonal relationships in adolescence. In S. Jackson & H. Rodriguez-Tomé (Eds.), *Adolescence and its social worlds* (pp. 95–119). Hove, U.K.: Erlbaum.

4   Cognitive Representations of Adolescent Romantic Relationships

Wyndol Furman and Valerie A. Simon

Romantic relationships are a new and exciting arena for adolescents. As they embark on these relationships, they try out unfamiliar behaviors, experiment with different ways of interacting, and acquire new skills. They have to make sense out of many novel, often surprising experiences. Much time is devoted to thinking or talking about their boyfriend or girlfriend and their relationship. They may wonder what a particular interaction meant or how each feels about the other. Sometimes they mentally enact different hypothetical scenarios with romantic partners, using past relationship experiences to anticipate their own and their partner's response to a given situation.

These thoughts, beliefs, and expectations concerning romantic relationships vary from person to person. For example, when faced with a family problem, one adolescent may think that she should turn to her partner to seek comfort and guidance. Another may feel that she should keep the problem to herself, fearing that the other would consider the problem to be insignificant and would not be interested. A third may feel it is important to seek out her partner, yet may think she is likely to be dissatisfied with the other's effort to comfort her. Such thoughts or representations of relationships are expected to guide an individual's behavior and serve as a basis for predicting and interpreting others' behavior. Social scientists have described these representations using terms such as schemas, scripts, prototypes, or working models. In the present chapter, we use the term *views* to refer to such representations of relationships. We are reluctant to introduce another term to the long list of seemingly similar concepts, but have chosen

This work was supported by Grant 50106 from the National Institute of Mental Health. Appreciation is expressed to Anna Flanagan, Amanda Jacobs, Todd Ognibene, Laura Shaffer, and Stephen Shirk for their comments on a draft of this chapter.

75

to do so because of some differences in conceptualization that are discussed subsequently. For the present, suffice it to say that our particular conceptualization of views is based on attachment theory (Bowlby, 1973; Main, Kaplan, & Cassidy, 1985) but is intended to be more general in application. That is, attachment theorists have been principally concerned with working models of attachment figures, the self in attachment relationships, and attachment relationships. We think, however, that the basic concepts of working models and attachment styles can also be applied to other relationships. Just as individuals have sets of rules for the organization and accessibility of information relevant to attachment (Main et al., 1985), they also have sets of rules and expectations for other relational experiences.

In the present chapter, we discuss how these concepts that were originally used to describe attachment relationships can be broadened to apply to adolescent romantic relationships. We begin by comparing and contrasting parent–child relationships and romantic relationships. We suggest that the attachment system is significant in both relationships but that the affiliative, sexual, and caretaking systems also play important roles in romantic relationships. In the second section of the chapter, we discuss how the particular characteristics of relationships influence cognitive representations of them and propose a hierarchical model of views. Whereas the first two sections focus on romantic relationships in general, the third section looks more closely at the distinct features of adolescent romantic relationships and the ways in which they may impact adolescents' romantic behavior, their developing romantic views, and the manner in which these views are expressed. In the fourth section of the chapter, we consider how the cognitive development of adolescents may influence their views and their expression. In the fifth section, we illustrate how these issues influence the measurement of views by describing our measures that were developed from this conceptualization.

Parent–Child and Romantic Relationships

Parent–child relationships and romantic relationships share some critical features and differ on others. With respect to similarities, attachment theorists have proposed that both types of relationships can be conceptualized as attachment relationships (Hazan & Shaver, 1987; Shaver & Hazan, 1988). That is, adults' romantic relationships may serve functions similar to those of children's relationships with parents. For example, both the infant in a parent–child relationship and an adult in a romantic relationship regularly seek proximity to their respective relationship partner. A parent or a romantic partner may function as a safe haven, such that when either an infant or an individual in a romantic relationship experiences discomfort or perceives a potential threat, he or she turns to the parent or partner for comfort and protection. Both an infant and someone in a romantic relationship may also use their respective relationship partners as a secure base from which to explore the environment and take on new challenges. Additionally, each reacts to separations or potential threats to the relationship with demonstrations of protest. Finally, the loss of either a parent or a partner is grieved.

Although parent–child and adult romantic relationships may both be attachment relationships, there are important differences between them. In parent–child relationships, the roles are asymmetrical, with the parent being responsible for taking care of the child but not the reverse (at least not while the latter is a child). Ideally, the attachment behavioral system of the child and the caretaking system of the parent system are coordinated with each other. When in danger or distress, the child may engage in attachment behaviors and seek out the parent; perceptions of danger to the child or the child's distress should activate the caretaking system in the parent.

In romantic relationships, the roles are reciprocal. Each may seek out caretaking from the other on some occasions, and each may provide care for the other in other instances. In effect, each partner becomes attached to the other and serves as an attachment figure to the other. At the same time, it does not seem accurate to argue that each person parents the other, as the symmetrical nature of the relationship makes the caretaking qualitatively different from that a parent provides to a child.

Another obvious difference between romantic and parent–child relationships is the element of sexuality. Sexual attraction plays an important role in the choice of romantic partners. Once a partner is chosen, sexual behavior becomes a central facet of the relationship and may foster an attachment bond (Hazan & Zeifman, 1994).

Shaver, Hazan, and Bradshaw (1988) recognized these differences between parent–child and romantic relationships, and consequently proposed that romantic love involves the integration of the attachment, caregiving, and sexual/reproductive behavioral systems. We believe that not only are these three systems involved, but an affiliative system is as well (Furman, in press; Furman & Wehner, 1994).

By the affiliative system, we refer to humans' biological predisposition to seek out and interact with known others. Throughout evolutionary history, human beings have lived in groups (Foley, 1989). Affiliative behavior afforded protection from predators and provided opportunities for cooperative food sharing, mutualism, reciprocal altruism, and social play (see Caporeal, Dawes, Orbell, & van de Kragt, 1989; Furman, in press). In contemporary societies, affiliative interactions with peers, including romantic partners, continue to serve critical functions. The symmetrical nature of peer relationships provides an egalitarian context in which individuals learn and practice skills of cooperation, mutual exchange, collaboration, intimate self-disclosure, and consensual validation of personal worth. Over the course of development, these peer relationships move from collaborative play to intimate friendships to intimate romance. In this way, the affiliative behavioral system may underlie the mutuality, collaboration, reciprocity, and co-construction that are characteristic of all peer relationships, including romantic relationships.

In summary, attachment processes seem to play central roles in early parent–child relationships and romantic relationships, but romantic relationships also entail elements of affiliation, mutual caretaking, and sexuality. These similarities and differences in the characteristics of the two types of relationships have important implications for how cognitive representations of these relationships should be conceptualized, the topic turned to next.

Views of Parent–Child and Romantic Relationships: A Hierarchical Model

The fact that both parent–child and romantic relationships could be conceptualized as attachment relationships led Shaver and Hazan (1988) to suggest that similar frameworks can be used to describe individual differences in how these relationships are approached. That is, both types of relationships can be classified using the three primary attachment categories – secure, anxious-avoidant (dismissing), and anxious-ambivalent (preoccupied). Like the young child who has a secure relationship with a parent, a person with a secure romantic attachment would be comfortable turning to a partner at times of distress. Someone with an anxious-avoidant attachment would avoid depending on a parent or partner. Finally, an individual with an anxious-ambivalent attachment to a parent or partner would find it difficult to be comforted by the other because of uncertainty concerning the other's availability.

Whereas the same general categories seem appropriate for classifying either infants' or adults' approaches to their attachment relationships, the indices of these categories differ developmentally. In infants' attachment relationships with caretakers, these patterns are manifested in the infant's behavior, whereas in adult romantic relationships, the corresponding patterns are reflected not only in behavior, but also in their expectations or cognitive representations concerning attachment behavior. That is, the nature of infants' representations of parent–child attachment are likely to be event-based, with the degree of representational abstraction being limited to concrete behavioral patterns (Stern, 1985). Adults' representations are more cognitively differentiated and complex. They include not only representations of behavioral patterns, but also abstract knowledge systems about the meaning of behaviors, related affects, and the relationship of these to models of self and others.

In the last decade, numerous investigators have documented differences among the three romantic attachment styles that are consistent with findings concerning differences in parent–child attachment (see Shaver & Hazan, 1993). For example, individuals with secure romantic attachment styles cope with stress by seeking social support (Mikulincer, Florian, & Weller, 1993), whereas those with an avoidant style tend to withdraw from their partners when stressed (Simpson, Rholes, & Nelligan, 1992). Those with an anxious-ambivalent style are preoccupied with their partners' responsiveness (Collins & Read, 1990; Feeny & Noller, 1990).

Differences also exist concerning caretaking, sexuality, and affiliation. With respect to caretaking behavior, securely attached men display more emotional support, reassurance, and concern for their partner's well-being than avoidant men, who show the opposite pattern (Simpson et al., 1992). Anxious-ambivalents (preoccupied individuals) report overinvolvement and insensitive caretaking (Kunce & Shaver, 1994). They often assert their own feelings and needs without adequate regard for those of their partners (Daniels & Shaver, 1991). In terms of sexuality, avoidant individuals are prone to engaging in uncommitted sexual relations (Simpson & Gangstead, 1991). As to affiliation, those with secure styles have romantic relationships characterized by trust, friendship, enjoyment, mutuality, self-disclosure, compromise, and a collaborative problem-solving orientation (Collins & Read, 1990; Feeney & Noller, 1991; Hazan & Shaver, 1987; Keelan, Dion, & Dion, 1994; Lopez et al., 1997). Avoidant individuals are relatively uninvested in romantic relationships (Shaver & Brennan, 1992). They feel bored and distant during interactions (Tidwell, Reis, & Shaver, 1996), scorn self-disclosure (Mikulincer & Nachshon, 1991), and use disengaged communication strategies (Daniels & Shaver, 1991). Preoccupied individuals, on the other hand, are overcontrolling in their interactions (Kunce & Shaver, 1994). They disclose too much or too soon (Mikulincer & Nachshon, 1991) and use self-focused communication strategies (Pistole, 1989).

Taken together, these findings suggest that such individual differences in cognitive representations play an important role in romantic relationships. The fact that differences are found not only in attachment behavior but also in caretaking, sexuality, and affiliation suggests, however, that these are not representations of attachment per se. Instead, they may be better conceptualized as representations of relationships or, in our terminology, *relational views* (Furman & Wehner, 1994). For example, a person with a secure view of a romantic relationship may not only think that she or he should be able to turn to a partner at times of distress, but also may value taking care of the other, desire to invest energy in the process of constructing a mutual relationship, and value the affectionate and caring elements of sexuality. Someone with an avoidant or dismissing view may have little interest in caretaking, little investment in a relationship, see sex as an opportunity for experimentation or self-gratification, and not consider a partner as someone to turn to at times of distress. Finally, someone with an anxious-ambivalent or preoccupied view may not only find it difficult to feel comforted by a partner when distressed, but may also be overly concerned about a partner's problems (i.e., compulsive caretaking), overly invested in relationships in a self-sacrificing manner, and perceive sexual behavior as a way to make oneself feel worthy. Thus, we believe that individuals have views or representations of a romantic relationship that refer to and reflect the functioning of all four behavioral systems. In effect, such views are expectations regarding intimacy and closeness, which may be enacted in terms of attachment, caretaking, sexuality, and affiliation.

We also propose that views are hierarchically organized (see Collins & Read, 1994, for a similar conceptualization). As shown in Figure 4.1, individuals have views of particular relationships, types of relationships (e.g., romantic relationships), and close relationships in general. The views of particular relationships and particular types of relationships center on the behavioral systems and other characteristics that are particularly salient in those relationships. Thus, views of romantic relationships include expectations or beliefs concerning attachment, caretaking, sexuality, and affiliation in romantic relationships, whereas views of relationships with parents may be focused on attachment to a parent.

The different layers of the hierarchy are interdependent. Thus, our views of close relationships in general are based on an integration of our representations and experiences in different relationships, but our general views also influence those concerning particular relationships.

This multilayered organization provides a means of accounting for continuities and discontinuities across views of different relationships. In par-

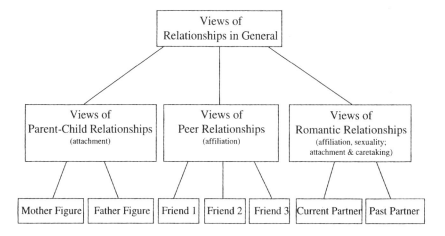

Figure 4.1. Hierarchical model of views.

ticular, early experiences with parents influence not only views of intimacy and closeness in those relationships, but also views of intimacy and closeness in close relationships in general (see Collins & Sroufe, this volume, for a similar perspective). Accordingly, a person with a secure attachment to the primary caretaker is likely to approach other relationships expecting closeness and intimacy, and thus engage in affiliative, caretaking, sexual, and attachment behaviors that promote closeness and intimacy, which in turn reinforce such views. Consistent with these ideas, early attachment relationships have been found to be linked to friendships in childhood and adolescence (see Collins & Sroufe, this volume; Rothbart & Shaver, 1994). By the same reasoning, links are expected between early attachment relationships and romantic relationships. The existing data are consistent with this idea but consist primarily of adults' retrospective reports of their childhood attachment relationships (see Rothbart & Shaver, 1994).

Although early attachment experiences are expected to be key influences in the development of views about romantic relationships, they are not expected to be the exclusive determinant of them. Experiences with peers should also play an important role in shaping views about close relationships in general, which, in turn, should influence views of romantic relationships, especially with regard to expectations about reciprocity, mutuality, and other affiliation-related features. Although the links between friendships and romantic relationships have not been studied as extensively, we have found significant associations in several studies (see Furman, in press; Furman & Wehner, 1997).

One's own experiences in romantic relationships play particularly critical roles in shaping one's views of these relationships (Furman & Flanagan, 1997). After all, to be effective, views should be open to changes or further elaboration that reflect the experiences someone has had. Individuals come into these relationships with expectations derived from past close relationships, and such expectations should influence the pattern of interactions with romantic partners. Yet if the experiences in romantic relationships differ enough from existing expectations, views of these relationships are expected to change. For example, breakups lead some individuals with secure romantic styles to develop insecure styles, whereas some people with avoidant styles become secure when they establish a new relationship (Kirkpatrick & Hazan, 1994). When romantic experiences are similar to those in past relationships, prior expectations are reinforced and further elaborated.

The importance of romantic experiences in shaping romantic views is underscored by the fact that the partner, as well as oneself, influences the course of the interactions that occur. The partner's role is particularly important, as the two individuals' preexisting views do not necessarily correspond with one another. In fact, couples' preexisting internal working models and their self-reports of attachment styles are relatively unrelated or moderately related at most (see Furman & Flanagan, 1997). The relatively modest correspondence is not surprising, as views are expected to play a bigger role in shaping the relationship that does develop than in determining to whom one is attracted. Similarity, physical attraction, infatuation, and availability are expected to play a bigger role in the initiation of relationships than views do.

Consequently, individuals may approach each other with different expectations in the early stages of a romantic relationship. For example, one person may believe that others can be turned to at times of distress, but may have a partner who does not turn to others and who is not particularly responsive to such overtures. One would expect the experiences of at least one person, and probably of both, to be somewhat different from their expectations. The experiences may even be sufficiently different from prior expectations to lead to some reevaluation of their romantic views. In fact, premarital couples' working models of their romantic relationship correspond more than their models of their parent–child relationships, suggesting that their experiences together lead to some changes and convergence in the models of these relationships (Owens et al, 1995).

Because the partners differ, one's experiences in different romantic relationships are likely to vary. Those relationships that are longer or involve more commitment are expected to have a greater impact on romantic views than short-lived liaisons. Similarly, as romantic relationships become more serious and gain increasing importance in the hierarchy, their influence on general views of relationships increases.

Finally, although we have emphasized the role of one's own experiences in close relationships, other factors affect these representations as well. Individuals develop expectations by observing their parents' marriage and, in many cases, divorce and remarriage. Additionally, they see and hear of their peers' and older siblings' adventures in the romantic arena. Cultural norms also exist regarding the timing and nature of such relationships (Simon, Bouchey, & Furman, in press). Images of heterosexual relationships are pervasive in the mass media. Images of gay and lesbian relationships are less common and often stereotypic, but these images, including the fact that they are infrequent, influence expectations and attitudes regarding homosexual relationships.

In summary, we propose a hierarchical model of views as an integrative framework for conceptualizing cognitive representations of close relationships. Such a model takes into account both the similarities and differences among the characteristics of different relationships, as individuals are expected to have views of different types of relationships that reflect the various behavioral systems that are particularly salient in those relationships. Thus, views of parent–child relationships center on the attachment system, whereas those of romantic relationships involve coordinated representations of multiple behavioral systems, including affiliation, sexuality, and caretaking, as well as attachment.

The hierarchical model also includes some mechanism for accounting for continuity across different relationships. Views of particular relationships or types of relationships are expected to influence views of close relationships in general, which, in turn, influence views of other relationships. At the same time, this model recognizes that lawful discontinuities may exist, as the views of particular relationships are influenced by experiences in those relationships, as well as by general views.

Adolescent Romantic Relationships

In the preceding sections, we discussed romantic relationships in general. Most of the comments seem applicable to both heterosexual and homosexual relationships, although gay, lesbian, or bisexual individuals who are in the process of developing a sexual identity may have different views of their same-sex and other-sex romantic relationships. Most of the comments seem applicable to both adult and adolescent romantic relationships, but the differences between adult and adolescent relationships also influence the nature of their views.

In adult romantic relationships, marital and long-term partners are key figures in the functioning of the attachment, caregiving, sexual, and affiliative systems. However, attachment and caregiving processes are not likely to be central in most adolescent relationships. Some features of an attachment relationship may be present, such as proximity-seeking or serving as a source of support or a safe haven; however, other features, such as separation protest or serving as a secure base, are not characteristic of most adolescent relationships (Hazan & Zeifman, 1994). Typically, parents continue to serve as primary attachment and caregiving figures until at least late adolescence. Romantic partners are not expected to emerge as primary attachment figures or major recipients of caretaking until an individual begins to develop long-term relationships.

Sexual and affiliative processes are likely to be more central in adolescent relationships than attachment or caretaking are. Some element of sexuality is involved in almost all, if not all, romantic relationships. The emergence of the sexual behavioral system figures importantly in the developmental shift from intimate friendships to intimate romance. Similarly, affiliative features are also quite prominent in these relationships. In the eyes of a 15-year-old, dating partners are beneficial because of the companionship and intimacy they provide (Feiring, 1996). Much of the time together is spent doing things or simply "hanging out."

The centrality of adolescent affiliative processes implies that friendships play a particularly important role in the development of adolescent romantic relationships (Furman, in press). After all, many of the social competencies learned in establishing friendships, such as those involved in intimacy and companionship, are required for developing romantic relationships as well. Some of the functions of dating, including recreation, autonomy seeking, status seeking, and social skills practice, also overlap with those of friendship (Grinder, 1966; Skipper & Naas, 1966).

By the same line of reasoning, representations of affiliation in peer relationships are likely to influence our representations of affiliation in relationships in general, which, in turn, may serve as a basis for the representations of affiliation in romantic relationships. Consistent with this idea, high school students' views of friendships have been found to be related to their views of romantic relationships (Furman, in press). Interestingly, views of parent–child relationships were not strongly related to views of romantic relationships in middle adolescence, but they were related to such views in late adolescence (Furman & Wehner, 1997). Perhaps the links between parent–child and romantic relationships become stronger as attachment and caretaking processes become more salient features of romantic relationships. The changes may also occur as relationships with parents become more egalitarian in nature, and affiliative or reciprocal features begin to play a bigger role in those relationships as well.

Up to this point, we have focused on the implications of the idea that adolescents are less likely than adults to have attachment relationships with their romantic partners. Of course, many adults may not have a long-term attachment relationship with a romantic partner at a particular time, but even the short-term relationships of adults and adolescents are likely to differ. During adolescence, romantic relationships are newer and less well established, and teens are more likely than adults to expect that their romantic liaisons will be short-lived.

In addition, adolescents' romantic relationships commonly serve functions other than attachment, caretaking, affiliation, or sex, particularly in early adolescence. For example, status grading and status achievement are often accomplished through these early relationships and appear to be normative developmental phenomena (Brown, this volume; Skipper & Naas, 1966). Compared to adults, adolescents are novices in the romantic arena, and they spend much of their teenage years exploring the various facets of romantic life and developing their identities as romantic partners.

Adolescents are also likely to experiment with different types of romantic relationships. In adolescence, there is an emerging capacity to think about future, hypothetical, or ideal selves. Markus and Nurius (1986) propose that these possible selves serve a motivational function in clarifying which selves are to be approached and avoided. From this perspective, role experimentation, either with different types of romantic partners or with different ways of behaving in a relationship, should be viewed as a normative phenomenon. In fact, adolescents state that they often behave falsely in their dating relationships, suggesting that they recognize that their behavior may not reflect who they are (Harter & Lee, 1989).

Just as these relationships are new and experimental to adolescents, so are their corresponding views. Their representations are more limited than those of adults, who have acquired the firsthand experience necessary to articulate and clarify their specific belief systems. Consequently, views of romantic relationships may be less developed in adolescence, and a certain degree of relationship experience (and, perhaps, cognitive development) may be required before these representations become more clearly articulated.

In fact, the novelty of romantic relationships for adolescents may render them particularly open to new information as they explore a variety of romantic relationships and experiment with ways of relating to their romantic partners. Romantic views are likely to be influenced by relationship experiences with parents and peers, but adolescents may also have more opportunities to disconfirm preexisting views. That is, in the course of experimentation and exploration, they may find themselves in relationships that provide experiences that are novel or inconsistent with their expectations. Accordingly, different patterns of relational behavior may be required, and accommodating these experiences with existing views may in some instances result in the development of belief systems that are different from those held about other types of relationships.

One implication of this idea of experimentation is that adolescents' views of romantic experiences and their actual experiences may be less related than when they are more experienced in this arena. Based on our interviews with adolescents, it appears that many have a series of relationships that are often quite different from one another. A substantial number describe at least one anomalous relationship or "mistake." For example, some describe having several supportive relationships but also having one conflictual, perhaps even abusive, relationship. Such anomalies can occur because individuals' selection of dating partners is strongly influenced by factors other than their relationship views; thus, a partner's behavior may not be congruent with one's own views. Such lack of correspondence seems especially likely to occur in adolescence, when individuals are inexperienced, experimenting with different kinds of relationships, and not seeking a long-term relationship. At the same time, we believe that views play an important role in determining what one learns or fails to learn from a relationship, be it a mistake or not. Thus, secure individuals are expected to learn more from their experiences than insecure ones, who may find themselves repeating the same mistakes.

In summary, in the previous section, we concluded that the concept of views can be applied to romantic relationships as well as parent–child relationships, but that the differences between the two types of relationships lead to some differences in the content of the representations of these relationships. In this section, we have shown that the contrast is even more striking when we consider adolescent romantic relationships and the centrality of affiliative and sexual processes to these relationships. The fact that the relationships are not attachment relationships, are frequently short-term, and often contain novel experiences all have implications for the nature of their views.

The contrast between parent–child relationships and adolescent romantic relationships also illustrates why we propose that views are representations of relationships rather than just of attachment. If views are representations of attachment per se, it is not clear why they would be expected to influence relationships in which attachment processes do not play a central role. Yet, working models of parental attachment in childhood are predictive not only of the subsequent course of attachment relationships, but also of relationships with nonattachment figures such as friends or peers (e.g., Collins & Sroufe, this volume; Elicker, Eglund, & Sroufe, 1992; Youngblade & Belsky, 1992). Such links with nonattachment relationships are understandable, however, if children develop not only expectations regarding attachment, but also expectations of intimacy and closeness in general, which may be enacted in terms of affiliation, caretaking, and sexuality as well as attachment. One could think of these as attachment representations if one uses a broad definition of attachment, but such an approach means that one has attachment representations of nonattachment relationships. Any distinction between attachment and nonattachment relationships seems to be blurred. Accordingly, we suggest that they are best thought of as representations of relationships, and not just the attachment system per se.

The Developmental Status of Adolescents

In the previous section, we argued that the romantic views of adolescents and adults differ because of differences in the nature of their romantic relationships and the behavioral systems that are salient in each. Moreover, adolescents and adults are developmentally different, leading to some unique qualities of adolescents' relationship views.

A number of cognitive changes occur during adolescence that impact the nature and organization of relationship views. Thinking and reasoning, for example, become increasingly abstract, multidimensional, and self-reflective (see Keating, 1990). Adolescents become better able to compare several complex mental representations simultaneously. Such growing information processing capabilities allow adolescents to contemplate their own internal worlds of thoughts and feelings and to compare them with those of others, mental activities that were previously unavailable during childhood.

These developments provide adolescents with new cognitive tools for processing relational information and making sense of their relationship experiences. For example, adolescents' increased information processing capabilities, more complex reasoning skills, and better ability to think about abstract aspects of the self and others facilitate the reevaluation and updating of relationship views (Kobak & Cole, 1994). Advances in perspective-taking and self-reflection allow adolescents to compare existing views with potential alternatives and to conceive of their views as changeable rather than static constructions. These developments render adolescent views amenable to change through personal insight and reflection, whereas alterations of childhood views are thought to require concrete changes in relationship experiences (Main et al., 1985).

Although these cognitive developmental advances render adolescents' relationship views qualitatively different from those of children, their representations are not yet comparable to those of adults. In particular, the acquisition of these new cognitive skills does not imply that they are uniformly applied across all domains or contexts. After all, découlage is more characteristic of development than uniformity (Fischer, 1980). One factor that critically influences the use of higher-level reasoning skills is familiarity with the content area about which the person is reasoning (Kuhn, Amsel, & O'Loughlin, 1988; Kuhn, Ho, & Adams, 1979). Similarly the advances in adolescence in working memory, allocation of available resources, and automatizing of these processes are dependent upon one's level of experience in a given area (Chi, 1978; Chi, Glaser, & Rees, 1982; Glaser, 1984). Accordingly, the content, organization, and expression of adolescents' relational views depend on both the development of new cognitive structures and adolescents' experience in a particular type of relationship. In other words, the lack of experience in romantic relationships may restrict the emergence of more developmentally sophisticated reasoning about these particular relationships, even after these cognitive skills have been demonstrated in other, more familiar domains.

A comparison of parent–child and romantic relationship views nicely illustrates the interaction between cognitive development and domain-specific experience. Adolescents' views of parent–child relationships are likely to be relatively well established as the result of years of experience and interactions in these relationships. The developmental task with respect to their views of parent–child relationships is primarily to reexamine and update them as adolescents become more autonomous and their relationships with parents are transformed. Adolescents' familiarity with parent–child relationships facilitates the application of their newly acquired cognitive tools to this domain, making it possible for parent–child relationship views to be reformulated in the absence of actual relationship changes.

Romantic relationships, on the other hand, are new to adolescents. Because they are just learning what to expect in these relationships, the content, organization, and expression of their romantic views are expected to be at a different developmental stage than their views about parental relationships. In effect, the developmental task for adolescents is to gain the requisite experience for elaborating their romantic views and integrating their experiences. Thus, differences in the level of experience in parent–child and romantic relationships should lead us to expect differences in the levels of reasoning or cognitive skills applied to thinking about these relationships. The application of newly acquired cognitive tools should emerge later for romantic views than for parent–child views.

For these reasons, we expect to see a great deal of development in the sophistication and elaboration of romantic views over the course of adolescence. Young adolescents initially enter romantic relationships with primitive views of what these relationships are apt to be like. As previously noted, these early romantic views are likely to be derived from past experiences with parents and peers, as well as from cultural norms, media representations, and observations of others' romantic relationships (e.g., those of parents, older siblings, and peers). The expectations derived from these "raw materials" are then further elaborated through specific romantic experiences with various partners. As adolescents become more familiar with these relationships, they can then begin to compare their experiences across different romantic relationships and form experientially based expectations about what these relationships are apt to be like.

Increased familiarity in the domain of romantic relationships should then facilitate more effective application of emerging abstract reasoning skills. Recursive perspective-taking, or the ability to take a third person's perspective, begins to emerge in early to middle adolescence (Selman, 1980). Initially, adolescents may find it difficult to take such a perspective in their romantic relationships because of their heightened self-consciousness in this unfamiliar and challenging domain. As they become more comfortable, however, they may be able to develop a better understanding of their partners' motivations and behavior. Nevertheless, we expect that such insights into current relationships may lag somewhat, as the benefits of hindsight are not available. Moreover, for better or worse, infatuation and passion can make it hard to view things objectively (see Larson, Clore, & Woods, this volume).

To this point, we have emphasized the developmental advances that occur during adolescence and the corresponding changes in romantic views. However, cognitive advances often bring about certain liabilities, rendering individuals prone to various cognitive errors as they struggle to control the application of new cognitive skills to unfamiliar, emotionally laden, and personally stressful domains (Harter, 1990). Such errors may influence not only how adolescents think about specific types of relationships, but also the consistencies they are able to perceive about themselves across their hierarchy of relationship views. For example, young adolescents may be more likely to engage in "imaginary audience" behavior about romantic relationships, falsely assuming that real or potential romantic partners are as concerned with their behavior and appearance as they are themselves (Elkind, 1967). Accordingly, they may be more likely to overpersonalize their experiences with real or potential romantic partners.

Whereas underdifferentiation may occur in young adolescents' reasoning about romantic relationships, overdifferentiation may be present in their reasoning about parental relationships. As adolescents begin to develop a more autonomous identity, parents may become prime targets of their "personal fable" in which they perceive themselves as unique (Elkind, 1967). That is, they may feel that parents are very different from themselves and could not possibly understand their experiences. Such feelings may lead young adolescents to create overly rigid boundaries between their conscious perceptions of their relationships with parents and those with others. They may fail to appreciate the influence parents have had on their romantic behavior, and may not see the similarities in their behavior toward parents and romantic partners. As the cognitive capacities to integrate aspects of their relational selves through the use of abstract knowledge systems emerge in middle to late adolescence, the capacity to observe and articulate links among various relationships should become more apparent (Harter & Monsour, 1992).

In summary, adolescence is a period in which marked advances in cognitive skills occur. Such advances are expected to have a major impact on the sophistication, organization, and expression of their relationship views. These new cognitive skills require some experience in the romantic domain before they can be fully and effectively applied, but as that experience is acquired, these skills provide adolescents with the tools for integrating their experiences and developing elaborated, abstract representations of their relationships.

Although developmental advances in cognitive reasoning are generally anticipated, adolescents vary in the degree to which they acquire these skills. In fact, those with insecure parental attachments perform more poorly on measures of formal operational reasoning and deductive reasoning than do those with secure attachments (Jacobsen, Edelstein, & Hoffman, 1994). Additionally, insecure individuals may also be less able to take advantage of the cognitive skills they acquire, as insecure models of relationships are believed to be less open to new experiences and reexamination than secure models are (Bowlby, 1988). Thus, variations in the quality of close relationships with parents, other adults, and peers may produce individual differences in both the acquisition of new cognitive skills and adolescents' ability to apply them to their romantic relationships.

Finally, the application of these cognitive skills to the romantic domain may also be delayed for those individuals who have few opportunities for romantic experience because of familial or cultural constraints.

The Measurement of Adolescent Romantic Views

The points raised in this chapter have important implications for the measurement of adolescents' views of romantic relationships. We tried to address these issues in the instruments we developed for assessing such views.

To assess internal working models of romantic relationships, we developed a Romantic Relationship Interview. This instrument was derived from the Berkeley Adult Attachment Interview, the classic measure of working models of parent–child relationships (George, Kaplan, & Main, 1985). Other investigators have adapted that interview to assess romantic relationships (e.g., Crowell & Owens, 1996; Silver & Cohn, 1992), but their interviews focus on a marriage or a committed relationship. Our Romantic Relationship Interview was also derived from Main's seminal work, but was intended for adolescents or young adults who do not necessarily have a committed relationship or, for that matter, a current relationship of any kind. The interview does, however, require that they have a moderate amount of experience in the romantic arena, such that their answers reflect their own experiences and not just stereotypical or cultural expectations.

Whereas the other interviews focus on the marital or premarital relationship, our interview typically assesses experiences in a number of different relationships. Most questions ask about the one or usually two relationships deemed most important, but adolescents commonly refer to other relationships when answering various questions. A married person's working model of romantic relationships is likely to be based on the marriage, but an adolescent's model may be influenced by experiences in a number of different relationships.

Like the other romantic interviews, our interview assesses caretaking as well as attachment features. Thus, questions are asked about how the person responds when the partner is upset, as well as how the partner responds when the subject is upset. The interview also assesses affiliative features, such as mutuality. Ideally, the interview would tap the sexual features as well, but this seems difficult to do in a face-to-face interview with an adolescent. Some adolescents, however, particularly late adolescents, discuss such topics spontaneously.

The coding system for the interview is intended to parallel those of other attachment interviews and includes scales assessing inferred experiences in particular relationships, other scales assessing discourse, and an overall classification. The inferred experiences scales were partially derived from the Current Relationship Interview scoring system (Crowell & Owens, 1996) and include particular indices of attachment, caretaking, and affiliation. Scales are included to assess both the individual's behavior and the behavior of each of the primary partners. Scales for each partner are included, as his or her behavior is expected to have a major impact on the nature of the relationship and the subject's behavior in that relationship.

One of Main's critical contributions was to distinguish between the past relational experiences individuals have had and their current states of mind. Past relational experiences have a major impact on current states of mind with regard to such attachment relationships, but the correspondence is not perfect. Some individuals have had very rejecting, neglecting, or overinvolved parents but manage to develop a secure state of mind with regard to these figures. For that matter, children commonly have a secure relationship with one parent and an insecure relationship with the other (Fox, Kimmerly, & Schafer, 1991) but seem to develop a single state of mind.

The distinction between experiences and states of minds seems particularly important for assessing adolescents' romantic views, as we have suggested that they are often experimenting in these new relationships, and many have diverse experiences across relationships. Thus, we previously suggested that the early romantic experiences per se may not be as critical as what the adolescents learn from them or how they are integrated into a state of mind. Accordingly, our interview uses the same indices of coherence as the other attachment interviews for assessing state of mind. The interview itself, however, was modified to address the idea that adolescents' abstractions, particularly about romantic relationships, may be developmentally and experientially constrained. While still trying to "surprise the unconscious," we provide increased scaffolding in the sequence and manner of questioning in order to facilitate adolescents' discourse about their romantic experiences. Thus, the interview is designed to provide the structure necessary to draw out adolescents' thought processes while preserving opportunities to elucidate individual differences in the nature of their working models about romantic relationships.

Just as in the case of the Berkeley Adult Attachment Interview, the various scales assessing coherence serve as the primary basis for an overall classification of romantic working models. In particular, individuals are categorized as having secure, dismissing, preoccupied, or unresolved/disorganized working models of romantic relationships. Although these categories were originally designed for the classification of representations of attachment relationships, we find that representations of adolescent romantic relationships and friendships can be readily classified into these categories in most instances. The fact that they seem classifiable suggests that these are representations of relationships and not of attachment per se.

The issues raised in the present chapter also influenced the development of a self-report measure of adolescent romantic styles, the Behavioral Systems Questionnaire. Like the Adolescent Romantic Relationship Interview, this questionnaire examines perceptions of romantic relationships in general rather than just one relationship. Questions are included about affiliation, caretaking, and sexuality, as well as attachment. For each of the four domains, scales assessing secure, preoccupied, and dismissing styles are included. Corresponding scales in the four different domains are relatively highly related, suggesting that the perceptions of the different behavioral systems are coordinated. Similar measures also exist for assessing styles of parent–child relationships and friendships. Consistent with a hierarchical model of views, perceptions of different types of relationships have been found to be related, but not so highly as to suggest that individuals have one style for all relationships (see Furman, in press; Furman & Wehner, 1994, 1997).

Finally, it should be noted that we have developed both self-report and interview measures because they appear to assess different aspects of views. The self-report measures tap *conscious styles,* whereas the interview is intended to assess internal, partially unconscious *working models,* which reflect more automated processing (Furman & Wehner, 1994). Conscious and unconscious representations of relationships do not correspond very highly to one another, seemingly because of defensive processes and other factors (Borman-Spurrell, Allen, Hauser, Carter, & Coie-Detke, 1993; Crowell et al. 1993). By examining both styles and working models, however, we should be able to obtain a comprehensive picture of adolescents' representations of these relationships.

Conclusion

In this chapter, we have discussed how the concept of cognitive representations or views can be applied to romantic relationships as well as parent–child relationships. We suggested that long-term adult romantic relationships can be conceptualized as attachment relationships, but that the sexual, caretaking, and affiliative systems are also important features of these relationships that are reflected in individuals' views of these relationships. Accordingly, we proposed a hierarchical model of views to take into account both the similarities and differences among the characteristics of different relationships. The hierarchical model also includes some mechanism for accounting for continuity and discontinuity across different relationships. That is, views of particular relationships or types of relationships are expected to influence views of close relationships in general, which, in turn, influence views of other relationships. The greater the similarity of the different relationships, the more carryover one might expect, underscoring why romantic views may be influenced by friendships and past romantic relationships, as well as by parent–child relationships.

The preceding points seem particularly apposite for adolescents' romantic relationships. The novelty of these relationships and the relatively short-term nature of most of them suggest that aspects other than attachment per se are central in adolescents' views. Affiliative experiences in peer relationships may play particularly important roles in shaping the early representations of relationships. Moreover, because of their limited experience in romantic relationships and their stage of development, adolescents may have less articulated views, which are prone to various cognitive biases.

Thus, representations of adolescent romantic relationships are likely to be somewhat different in nature than the classic ideas of attachment working models or styles. Our intent, however, is not to criticize these classic concepts but rather to point out the ways in which these ideas need to be modified to be applicable to adolescent romantic relationships. With such modifications, these ideas should prove to be valuable in elucidating the nature of adolescent romantic relationships. After all, the concept of attachment styles has already proven quite fruitful in studying adult romantic relationships (see Shaver & Hazan, 1993). Moreover, in many of these studies, a significant proportion of the subjects were not involved in long-term relationships, and yet meaningful differences were found among the three attachment styles; thus, it appears that these concepts can be applied to short-term, nonattachment relationships – that is, the kinds of relationships that adolescents are likely to have.

In fact, we have successfully used the measures of relational styles and working models described in this chapter in our ongoing research on adolescent romantic relationships (see Furman, in press; Furman & Wehner, 1997). It is hoped that this chapter will stimulate further work on adolescents' representations of their relationships so that we may have a better understanding of the factors that shape the nature of their experiences.

References

Borman-Spurrell, E., Allen, J.P., Hauser, S. T., Carter, A., & Coie-Detke, H. (1993). *Assessing adult attachment: A comparison of interview-based and self-report methods.* Manuscript under review.

Bowlby, J. (1973). *Attachment and loss: Volume 2, Separation.* New York: Basic Books.

Bowlby, J. (1988). *A secure base: Parent–child attachment and healthy human development.* New York: Basic Books.

Caporael, L. R., Dawes, R. M., Orbell, J. M., & van de Kragt, A. J. C. (1989). Selfishness examined: Cooperation in the absence of egoistic incentives. *Behavioral and Brain Sciences, 12,* 683–789.

Chi, M. T. H. (1978). Knowledge structures and memory development. In R. Seigler (Ed.), *Children's thinking: What develops?* (pp. 112–147). Hillsdale, NJ: Erlbaum.

Chi, M. T. H., Glaser, R., & Rees, E. (1982). Expertise in problem solving. In R. J. Sternberg (Ed.), *Advances in the psychology of human intelligence* (Vol. 1, pp. 7–75). Hillsdale, NJ: Erlbaum.

Collins, N. L., & Read, S. J. (1990). Adult attachment, working models, and relationship quality in dating couples. *Journal of Personality and Social Psychology, 58,* 644–663.

Collins, W. A., & Read, S. J. (1994). Cognitive representations of attachment: The structure and function of working models. In D. Perlman & W. Jones (Eds.), *Advances in personal relationships: Attachment processes in adulthood* (Vol. 4, pp. 29–70). London: Jessica Kingsley.

Crowell, J. A., Holtzworth-Munroe, A. H., Treboux, D., Waters, E., Stuart, G. L., & Hutchinson, G. (1993). *Assessing working models: A comparison of the Adult Attachment Interview with self-report measures of attachment relationships.* Manuscript under review.

Crowell, J. A., & Owens, G. (1996). *The Current Relationship Interview and Scoring System, Version 2.* Unpublished document, State University of New York at Stony Brook.

Daniels, T., & Shaver, P. R. (1991). *Attachment styles and power strategies in romantic relationships.* Unpublished manuscript, State University of New York at Buffalo, Department of Psychology.

Elicker, J., Eglund, M., & Sroufe, L. A. (1992). Predicting peer competence and peer relationships in childhood from early parent–child relationships. In R. Parke & G. Ladd (Eds.), *Family–peer relationships: Modes of linkage* (pp. 77–106). Hillsdale, NJ: Erlbaum.

Elkind, D. (1967). Egocentrism in adolescence. *Child Development, 38,* 1025–1034.

Feeney, J. A., & Noller, P. (1990). Attachment style as a predictor of adult romantic relationships. *Journal of Personality and Social Psychology, 58,* 281–291.

Feeney, J. A., & Noller, P. (1991). Attachment style and verbal descriptions of romantic partners. *Journal of Social and Personal Relationships, 8,* 187–215.

Feiring, C. (1996). Concepts of romance in 15-year-old adolescents. *Journal of Research on Adolescence, 6,* 181–200.

Fischer, K. W. (1980). A theory of cognitive development: The control and construction of hierarchies of skills. *Psychological Bulletin, 87,* 477–531.

Foley, R. (1989). The evolution of hominid social behaviour. In V. Standen & R. A. Foley (Eds.), *Comparative socioecology* (pp. 473–494). Oxford: Blackwell Scientific.

Fox, N. A., Kimmerly, N. L., & Schafer, W. D. (1991). Attachment to mother/attachment to father: A meta-analysis. *Child Development, 62,* 210–225.

Furman, W. (in press). Friends and lovers: The role of peer relationships in adolescent heterosexual romantic relationships. In W. A. Collins & B. Laursen (Eds.), *Relationships as developmental contexts: Minnesota Symposium on Child Development, Vol. 30.* Hillsdale, NJ: Erlbaum.

Furman, W., & Flanagan, A. (1997). The influence of earlier relationships on marriage: An attachment perspective. In W. K. Halford & H. J. Markman (Eds.), *Clinical handbook of marriage and couples interventions* (pp. 179–202). New York: Wiley.

Furman, W., & Wehner, E. A. (1994). Romantic views: Toward a theory of adolescent romantic relationships. In R. Montemayor, G. R. Adams, & G. P. Gullota (Eds.) *Advances in adolescent development: Volume 6, Relationships during adolescence* (pp. 168–175). Thousand Oaks, CA: Sage.

Furman, W., & Wehner, E. A. (1997). Adolescent romantic relationships: A developmental perspective. In S. Shulman & W. A. Collins (Eds.), *Romantic relationships in adolescence: Developmental perspectives* (pp. 21–36). San Francisco: Jossey-Bass.

George, C., Kaplan, N., & Main, M. (1985). *An adult attachment interview.* Unpublished manuscript, University of California at Berkeley.

Glaser, R. (1984). Education and thinking: The role of knowledge. *American Psychologist, 39,* 193–202.

Grinder, R. E. (1966). Relations of social dating attractions to academic orientation and peer relations. *Journal of Educational Psychology, 57,* 27–34.

Harter, S. (1990). Self and identity development. In S. S. Feldman & G. Elliott (Eds.), *At the threshold: The developing adolescent* (pp. 352–387). Cambridge, MA: Harvard University Press.

Harter, S., & Lee, L. (1989). *Manifestations of true and false selves in early adolescence.* Presented at the meeting of the Society for Research in Child Development, Kansas City, MO.

Harter, S., & Monsour, A. (1992). Developmental analysis of conflict caused by opposing attributes in the adolescent self-portrait. *Developmental Psychology, 28,* 251–260.

Hazan, C., & Shaver, P. (1987). Romantic love conceptualized as an attachment process. *Journal of Personality and Social Psychology, 52,* 511–524.

Hazan, C., & Zeifman, D. (1994). Sex and the psychological tether. In K. Bartholomew & D. Perlman (Eds.), *Advances in personal relationships, Volume 5: Attachment processes in adulthood* (pp. 151–180). London: Jessica Kingsley.

Jacobsen, T., Edelstein, W., & Hoffman, V. (1994). A longitudinal study of the relation between representations of attachment in childhood and cognitive functioning in childhood and adolescence. *Developmental Psychology, 30,* 112–124.

Keating, D. (1990). Adolescent thinking. In S. S. Feldman & G. Elliott (Eds.), *At the threshold: The developing adolescent* (pp. 54–90). Cambridge, MA: Harvard University Press.

Keelan, J. P., Dion, K. L., & Dion K. K. (1994). Attachment style and heterosexual relationships among young adults: A short-term panel study. *Journal of Social and Personal Relationships, 11,* 201–214.

Kirkpatrick, L. A., & Hazan, C. (1994). Attachment styles and close relationships: A four-year prospective study. *Personal Relationships, 1,* 123–142.

Kobak, R., & Cole, P. (1994). Attachment and meta-monitoring: Implications for adolescent autonomy and psychopathology. In D. Cicchetti & S. L. Toth (Eds.), *Rochester Symposium on Development and Psychopathology: Volume 5, Disorders and dysfunctions of the self.* Rochester, NY: University of Rochester Press.

Kuhn, D., Amsel, E., & O'Loughlin, M. (1988). *The development of scientific thinking skills.* San Diego, CA: Academic Press.

Kuhn, D., Ho, V., & Adams, C. (1979). Formal reasoning among pre- and late adolescents. *Child Development, 50,* 1128–1135.

Kunce, L. J., & Shaver, P. R. (1994). An attachment-theoretical approach to caregiving in romantic relationships. In K. Bartholomew & D. Perlman (Eds.), *Attachment processes in adulthood: Advances in personal relationships* (Vol. 5, pp. 205–238) London: Jessica Kingsley.

Lopez, F. G., Gover, M. R., Leskela, J., Sauer, E. M., Schirmer, L., & Wyssmann, J. (1997). Attachment styles, shame, guilt, and collaborative problem-solving orientations. *Personal Relationships, 4,* 187–199.

Main, M., Kaplan, N., & Cassidy, J. (1985). Security in infancy, childhood, and adulthood: A move to the level of representation. In I. Bretherton & E. Waters (Eds.), *Growing points of attachment theory and research* (pp. 66–104). *Monographs of the Society for Research in Child Development, 50* (Serial No. 209, 1–2). Chicago: University of Chicago Press.

Markus, H., & Nurius, P. (1986). Possible selves. *American Psychologist, 41,* 954–969.

Mikulincer, M., Florian, V., & Weller, A. (1993). Attachment styles, coping strategies, and posttraumatic psychological distress: The impact of the Gulf War in Israel. *Journal of Personality and Social Psychology, 64,* 817–826.

Mikulincer, M., & Nachshon, O. (1991). Attachment styles and patterns of self-disclosure. *Journal of Personality and Social Psychology, 61,* 321–331.

Owens, G., Crowell, J. A., Pan, H., Treboux, D., O'Connor, E., & Waters, E. (1995). The prototype hypothesis and the origins of attachment working models: Adult relationships with parents and romantic partners. In E. Waters, B. E. Vaughn, G. Posada, & K. Kondo-Ikemura (Eds.), *Caregiving, cultural, and cognitive perspectives on secure-base behavior and working models* (pp. 216–233). *Monographs of the Society for Research in Child Development, 60* (Serial No. 244).

Pistole, M. C. (1989). Attachment in adult romantic relationships: Style of conflict resolution and relationship satisfaction. *Journal of Social and Personal Relationships, 6,* 505–510.

Rothbart, J. C., & Shaver, P. R. (1994). Continuity of attachment across the life span. In M. B. Sperling & W. H. Berman (Eds.), *Attachment in adults: Clinical and developmental perspectives* (pp. 31–71). New York: Guilford Press.

Selman, R. L. (1980). *The growth of interpersonal understanding: Developmental and clinical analysis.* New York: Academic Press.

Shaver, P. R., & Brennan, K. A. (1992). Attachment styles and the "big five" personality traits: Their connections with each other and with romantic relationship outcomes. *Personality and Social Psychology Bulletin, 18,* 536–545.

Shaver, P. R., & Hazan, C. (1988). A biased overview of the study of love. *Journal of Social and Personal Relationships, 5,* 473–501.

Shaver, P. R., & Hazan, C. (1993). Adult romantic attachment: Theory and evidence. In D. Perlman & W. Jones (Eds.), *Advances in personal relationships* (Vol. 4, pp. 29–70). London: Jessica Kingsley.

Shaver, P. R., Hazan, C., & Bradshaw, D. (1988). Love as attachment: The integration of three behavioral systems. In R. F. Sternberg & M. L. Barnes (Eds.), *The psychology of love* (pp. 68–99). New Haven, CT: Yale University Press.

Silver, D. H., & Cohn, D. A. (1992). *Couple attachment interview.* Unpublished instrument, University of California, Berkeley.

Simon, V. A., Bouchey, H. A., & Furman, W. (in press). The social construction of adolescents' representations of romantic relationships. In S. Larose & G. M. Tarabulsy (Eds.), *Attachment and development: Volume 2, Adolescence.* Quebec: Les Presses de l'Universite du Quebec.

Simpson, J. A., & Gangstead, S. W. (1991). Individual differences in sociosexuality: Evidence for convergent and discriminant validity. *Journal of Personality and Social Psychology, 60,* 870–883.

Simpson, J. A., Rholes, W. S., & Nelligan, J. S. (1992). Support seeking and support giving within couples in an anxiety-provoking situation: The role of attachment styles. *Journal of Personality and Social Psychology, 62,* 434 446.

Skipper, J. K., & Naas, G. (1966). Dating behavior: A framework for analyses and an illustration. *Journal of Marriage and the Family, 28,* 420.

Stern, D. N. (1985). *The interpersonal world of the infant.* New York: Basic Books.

Tidwell, M., Reis, H. T., & Shaver, P. R. (1996). Attachment, attractiveness, and social interactions: A diary study. *Journal of Personality and Social Psychology, 71,* 729–745.

Youngblade, L. M., & Belsky, J. (1992). Parent–child antecedents of 5-year-olds' close friendships: A longitudinal analysis. *Developmental Psychology, 28,* 700–733.

5   Romantic and Sexual Relationship Development During Adolescence

Brent C. Miller and Brad Benson

Romantic and sexual relationships have a unique intensity during the second decade of life. Childhood is widely perceived as a time of relative quiescence compared to the romantic and sexual exuberance of youth. Romantic feelings and sexual behavior are not completely dormant during childhood, but adolescence is qualitatively different; by the early or middle teens, the vast majority of adolescents become preoccupied with romantic feelings (Medora, Goldstein, & Von der Hellen, 1994; Savin-Williams & Berndt, 1990) and begin a lifetime trajectory of overt sexual experiences (Miller, Christopherson, & King, 1993). One study that monitored the daily subjective states of adolescents found that the strongest association between puberty and emotional experience is the specific feeling of being in love (Richards & Larson, 1993).

How is the development of romantic feelings and sexual behaviors related to one another? We conjecture that almost all children and early adolescents have romantic ideas ("crushes") about persons with whom they have no sexual contact. We further conjecture that romantic thoughts and interactions typically precede sexual involvement in the process of normal adolescent development. However, through choice or coercion, some children and adolescents have "body-centered" sexual experiences devoid of romantic meanings. There is a growing awareness that the development of intimate relationships can be profoundly affected by coercive sexual experiences. Although it is clear that romantic ideation and sexual interaction are related and usually co-occur, it also is clear that neither is a *necessary* precondition for the other. In this chapter we further explore ways that romantic and sexual development are similar and different, and how they are related to one another during adolescence.

Appreciation is expressed to Sunhee Ahn, Andrea Hart, Douglas Kjar, and Kenneth Thevenin for their intellectual contributions to this chapter.

Conceptual and Theoretical Perspectives

The biological processes of sexual development are predictably uniform for most teenagers, but the thoughts, feelings, and behaviors that symbolize romantic relationships vary cross-culturally. Romantic love implies an attraction of one individual to another who is perceived as an object of endearment and desire. Attraction may be based on various characteristics, such as physical appearance or personality traits, as well as compatibility of intellect, interests, and abilities. How these characteristics become valued romantically depends largely on socialization. Gender role socialization is one example of enculturation that influences how sex and romance are understood. Studies have shown a tendency for males to emphasize sexual aspects of a relationship, whereas females more often romanticize them (Cimbalo & Novell, 1993; Feingold, 1990; Hong & Faedda, 1994). Similarly, among males and females in homosexual relationships, it is relatively more common for gay men to prioritize sexual relationships than lesbians, who place greater emphasis on emotional bonding. Security, fulfillment, and validation can be viewed as critical developmental needs that adolescent relationships promise to address. Initial stages of romantic relationships revolve around images that are inflated both in terms of what is projected to others and how others are perceived (Aune, Aune, & Buller, 1994). Such unrealistic images lead romantic pairs to form idealized emotions and, at least initially, to experience decreased conflict in their relationship.

No single theoretical template adequately organizes concepts and data about the joint development of adolescent romantic and sexual relationships. In the broadest terms, the two most basic theoretical paradigms are biological and cultural (Miller & Fox, 1987). For example, Sigmund Freud (1920, 1933) explained sexual behavior as being undergirded by the unfolding or emergence of biological drives that begin pressing most urgently for genital expression during adolescence. In contrast to biological and inner-driven views, a social/cultural paradigm explains romantic attraction and sexual behavior as the result of socially shaped and learned patterns that are highly variable across cultural space and time. According to this view, for example, cultural elements constrain "the age, gender, legal, and kin relationships between sexual actors, as well as setting limits on the sites of behavior and the connections between sexual organs" (Gagnon & Simon, 1973, p. 4). Current theories combine elements of both biological and social explanations in understanding the timing and variation of adolescent sexual behavior (Benda & DiBlasio, 1991; Udry & Campbell, 1994). A biosocial approach (Smith, 1989) argues that hormonal changes early in adolescence have both a direct biological influence on sexual interest and motivation and an indirect influence on sexual involvement by altering the adolescent's physical appearance and sexual attractiveness. In addition, social and cultural influences need to be recognized as facilitating or inhibiting romantic and sexual involvement, affecting the forms of sexual expression, and defining appropriate romantic/sexual partners.

Because romance is, at least in part, culturally defined, the pattern and emphasis of romance in sexual relationships would be expected to vary. Cultural variation in romantic patterns does, in fact, characterize human societies. We would expect to find greater emphasis on romantic aspects of dating relationships in cultures where premarital sexual involvement is discouraged; conversely, less emphasis on romantic emotional bonding might be expected in cultures where sexual experimentation is encouraged.

According to evolutionary theories of heterosexual mating, each sex seeks to maximize its opportunity for reproductive success. Although evolution is most often associated with biological adaptation, cultural traditions similarly develop over time, perhaps also for the purpose of optimizing biological succession. In pair bonding, sexual desire becomes a powerful motivator for engaging in sexual behavior. Sexual gratification alone can be relatively transitory in a relationship; romantic ideation, however, has the potential for perpetuating and enhancing sexual attraction and arousal. From an evolutionary perspective the central feature of a mating relationship is reproductive sex, but emotional bonding could also further strengthen pair commitment and cohesion.

Males tend to seek out partners based on physical attraction, whereas females seek mates who can provide for themselves and their offspring. Males are more inclined to pursue low-investment sex, whereas females prioritize high-investment in sexual relationships (Landolet, Lalumiere, & Quinsey, 1995). Although intrasex competition has been linked to mating tactics (Walters & Crawford, 1995), emotions may play an important role in increasing commitment once a relationship is formed (Townsend, Kline, & Wasserman, 1995). Romantic love can be viewed as an evolutionary adaptation to promote commitment in pair bonding, akin to the attachment formed between caregiver and infant. The premise of Bowlby's (1969) attachment theory suggests an innate programming for establishing emotional bonds between humans for the purpose of strengthening relational commitments and optimizing survivability of the species.

Biological Bases of Sex and Romance

The biological facts of sexual differentiation, maturation, and arousal provide a powerful explanation for increased sexual behaviors (and, perhaps, romantic attraction) during the second decade of life. Across human populations there arc marked consistencies in the biological substrate of sexual development. Accelerated sexual maturation and increased libido early in the second decade of life are strongly implicated in the increased sexual behaviors that characterize adolescence.

Puberty is the developmental period when adolescents experience and observe changes in their bodies that prepare them for sexual and reproductive functions. These biological transformations are largely parallel in the sexes in that both males and females experience growth spurts, increased glandular secretions, growth of body hair, and increased hormonal production. Girls experience breast and genital development and begin menstruation, and boys experience comparable development in genital size and function, increased frequency of spontaneous erections, nocturnal emissions, and lowering of the voice.

The hormones estrogen and testosterone are especially important in regulating the timing and outcome of these events. Because hormone production is primarily responsible for the timing and pace of individual sexual development, it is not unreasonable to think that some individuals might experience an earlier and perhaps stronger biological push toward sexual interest and behavior than others. There is, in fact, considerable evidence from human and other primate studies that androgenic hormones are primarily responsible for sexual arousal in both males and females (Morris, 1992; Smith, 1989).

Hormones could influence sexual behavior directly by increasing arousal or indirectly by the social stimulus associated with physical changes (Udry, 1988, 1990; Udry, Billy, Morris, Groff, & Raj, 1985). Early studies by Richard Udry and his colleagues indicated that androgen levels have a direct effect on sexual behavior. That androgen effects were stronger for adolescent males suggests perhaps a threshold level for testosterone effects, or perhaps social factors play a greater role in shaping how girls express sexual arousal (Udry, 1988, 1990). More recent longitudinal analyses (Halpern, Udry, Campbell, & Suchindran, 1993) do not support the interpretation of a simple direct relationship between testosterone level and change over time in sexual motivation or behavior among adolescent males.

Several other lines of evidence support the influence of pubertal development on adolescent sexual behavior. Early-maturing girls tend to have older friends, are granted greater freedom by their parents, and begin to date and engage in sexual behavior at younger ages than their less developed peers (Brooks-Gunn, 1987; Phinney, Jensen, Olsen, & Cundick, 1990). Similarly, adolescent males are more sexually involved if their level of pubertal development is more advanced, regardless of their age. Current thinking is that pubertal maturation is related to the initiation of sexual activity both because of its social stimulus value and as a proxy for increased hormone levels.

Research also indicates that the emotional state of "being in love" is related to a release of chemicals that are similar to amphetamines (Toufexis, 1993). Liebowitz (1983) discussed the role of neurotransmitter levels in regulating emotional states and conceptualized romantic relationships as having two feeling qualities that could be based on biochemical reactions. *Attraction* relates to the initial interest and excitement that develop when two individuals come into contact with one another, and *attachment* is the security bond that develops over the course of early companionship, enabling the relationship to endure for the long term. Higher levels of neurotransmitters and increased sensitivity of chemical receptor sites appear to account for a biological change that causes pleasure and stimulation in sexual and romantic attraction.

Although the biological substrate is fundamental, cultural influences play a key role in defining how and when biologically based sexual urges are expressed. Because hormones and chemistry have been suggested as the basis of emotions (Liebowitz, 1983), perhaps puberty, with its associated hormonal surges, is a critical period for the development of romantic love as well as sexual behavior.

Cultural Influences on Romantic and Sexual Relationships

Cultural norms and proscriptions most clearly shape the development of romantic notions by defining who is perceived to be an eligible partner and what characteristics make particular persons more or less attractive. For the establishment of long-term sexual or marital relationships, romantic attraction is the cultural imperative in North America; that is, partners are expected to develop romantic feelings and affection for each other before having sex (Reiss, 1986; Smith, 1994). By contrast, in traditional cultures, elders or matchmakers arrange unions between partners who might subsequently develop a romantic attachment for one another. Cultural influences in North America link sexual relationships to a history, and a future expectation, of commitment and intimacy.

Levesque (1993) reported that conceptions of romance among adolescents are quite similar to those of adults, suggesting that there might be greater variation in romantic ideas between cultures than between age groups within cultures. Hatfield, Schmitz, Cornelius, and Rapson (1988) also found support for the idea that children had romantic conceptualizations of love similar to those of adults. Other scholars have argued for a cognitive model of romance in which schematics play an important role in the way relationships are conceptualized (Baxter, 1992; Honeycutt, Cantrill, & Greene, 1989).

Much of Western culture is constructed around romantic ideas. Consumer products for both adolescents and adults often are romanticized through marketing strategies in popular media. In Western society, romantic love has taken on a culture of its own in which the seeking for and the attainment of romance becomes an expected part of pairing, if not an end in itself. In popular teen culture, references to movies, books, music, or settings as being "romantic" do not always identify sexual arousal per se, but sometimes convey feelings of affection, tenderness, and love.

In Western societies, individuals also have relatively high control over their choice of mates, and romance has further evolved through the pervasive power of the mass media. Societies that have limited exposure to Western culture and pervasive media influences have different constructions of romance. Arranged marriage, plural marriage, wife stealing, and long-term courting of multiple potential partners are mating rituals carried out in diverse human groups. The process that establishes couple relationships varies by culture, and no single definition of romantic love exists (Beall & Sternberg, 1995). However, Jankowiak and Fischer (1994), who investigated the prevalence of romantic love in non-Western cultures using the Standard Cross-Cultural Sample (SCCS), concluded that romantic love is a nearly universal aspect of human relationships. In their study, romantic love was defined as "any intense attraction that involves the idealization of the other, within an erotic context, with the expectation of enduring for some time into the future" (p. 150); by this definition, romantic love was present in 88.5% of cultures.

Even more than romantic partnerships, the establishment of sexual unions is – without exception – a universal aspect of human cultures. From one perspective, romantic love can be viewed as a mating ritual that serves to bring about sexual pairing in a particular cultural context for the purpose of species reproduction and family formation. In this view, romantic thoughts are cultural inventions linked primarily to the biological sex drive. Although sexual arousal and relationships are universal, the forms of mate selection – including romantic attraction – vary, and the power behind such arrangements could be the more universal human foundations of sexual drives, mating, and reproduction.

Evidence from several studies (Dunphy, 1963; Furman & Wehner, 1994; Van Wel, 1994) supports the importance of peer and friendship influences in forming romantic attachments. Furman and Wehner (1994) presented a four-part behavioral systems conceptualization of adolescent romantic relationships that emphasized the affiliating system since peers, and particularly friends, are central to forming romantic attachments. This supports a line of thinking about peer attachment that links the strengthening of peer ties to a lessening of dependency on parental and family relationships during adolescence (Paterson, Pryor, & Shields, 1995; Shulman, Elicker, & Sroufe, 1994). At the same time that romantic relationships develop, teens are likely to become involved in sexual activity. Compared with classic attachment theory, these perspectives provide a broader understanding of peer and friendship influences on romantic and sexual relationships in adolescence.

Developmental Trajectory of Adolescent Intimate Relationships

In addition to the biological and cultural elements previously considered, adolescence is a period of achieving greater independence from parents and family. In the course of loosening their dependence on parents, adolescents seek other close relationships. Romantic relationships appear to fulfill adolescent needs partly because they simultaneously foster the attainment of independence, identity, and intimacy. Romantic attitudes might be more influenced by peers than by family. Inman-Amos, Hendrick, and Hendrick (1994) found little similarity in love attitudes between parents and children, even though there was a high correlation between the love attitudes of husbands and wives. Additionally, research has provided clear support for the influence of peers on adolescent sexual activity (Benda & DiBlasio, 1994; Benda & Kashner, 1994; Dolcini & Adler, 1994; Rowe & Rodgers, 1994).

Adolescent romantic thoughts and expressions sometimes are directed toward persons who are unlikely or unattainable partners (teachers, movie stars, famous musicians, etc). We conjecture that such unrequited romances and longing are especially common among young adolescents. The more common recipients of adolescent romantic thoughts and sexual expressions are dating partners. Thus, in this section we consider adolescent romantic and sexual development in relation to dating. Pubertal development, dating, and sexual behaviors interact during the second decade of life to effect major changes in the lives of adolescents. Although usually overlapping, these three lines of development are to some extent divisible and can be experienced separately. Occasionally adolescents go through pubertal development and arrive at their late teens without dating; conversely, some preadolescent children begin heteroscxual pairing off (dating) prior to pubertal development, and other children are sexual adventurers (or victims) before either dating or pubertal development is underway. For the large majority, however, pubertal development, dating, and sexual experiences combine to form the primary matrix for early adolescent romantic and sexual development.

Adolescent Dating Behavior

Cultural definitions and norms about dating are continually redefined. In the United States, dating was more formally scripted for previous generations. Males were expected to ask females for dates, and dating proceeded from group dating to casual single dates, going steady, and eventually to engagement and marriage. This progression constituted an institutionalized system of dating and courtship (Burchinal, 1964; Ehrman, 1959). By contrast, contemporary adolescent pairing off is characterized by greater gender equality and less formality. The terms *courtship* and even *dating* have given way to *hanging out* and *going with* someone. However, although courtship norms have relaxed and dating experiences are less formal, adolescent couples still constitute the primary context for contemporary romantic and sexual development.

At young ages, children's peer groups tend to be segregated along gender lines, but during the transition from childhood to adolescence, the gender-based barriers weaken, and cross-gender relationships become increasingly important. The erosion of childhood gender barriers and the development of romantic sexual relationships is usually a gradual, experimental process. "As the biological and social clocks tick onward, young people increasingly relate to those of the other sex . . . become increasingly experienced in dating, and the amount of time young couples spend together increases. . . . This emotional and romantic involvement is often accompanied, and intensified, by expanding levels of sexual involvement" (Thornton, 1990, p. 240).

Although its formality has relaxed, dating still tends to follow a progression from casual associations to a steady relationship, with the potential outcome of relationship permanence. Maturation, social influences, and personal meaning are considered to be primary forces involved in determining a dating orientation. McCabe (1984) asserts that the culmination of experiential and biological factors leads to adolescents acquiring a relationship orientation that is primarily affectional or sexual, and teens who adopt an affectional orientation are thought to experience a greater romantic quality in their relationships.

Dating debut appears to be more strongly related to age norms than to sexual maturation (Dornbusch et al., 1981). Adolescents are socially expected to date, and they generally do, regardless of their individual level of sexual development. However, adolescents who initiate heterosexual dating early and who have steady relationships are more likely to become sexually experienced sooner and to have sexual relations with more partners (Miller, McCoy, & Olson, 1986; Thornton, 1990), including relationships with other boys for gay and bisexual males (Savin-Williams, 1995).

Research in previous decades documented that stages of dating commitment (e.g., casual, steady, engaged) are strongly related to intimacy of sexual behavior (kissing, petting, intercourse). In one longitudinal study it was reported that about 75% of young women first experienced sexual intercourse within a committed interpersonal relationship (steady dating, engagement, or marriage) compared to about 50% of young men (Jessor & Jessor, 1977). Miller et al. (1986) reported that the stage of dating was strongly related to both sexual attitude permissiveness and sexual intercourse experience, and this was more strongly the case for females than for males. In general, however, an increase in relationship commitment is accompanied by increasing sexual involvement for both males and females. Females approach males' level of sexual involvement as they grow older and more committed to the relationship.

These data are consistent with a developmental model for couple romantic and sexual relationships; as partners become increasingly involved with each other emotionally, the range of sexual behavior that is normatively acceptable increases along with their sexual experience. Both the timing of the initiation of dating, and the development of steady dating relationships, have substantial implications for the initiation of sexual intercourse. Those who begin dating early and who develop steady relations early are not only more likely to have sexual intercourse, but also to have sex with more partners and to be more sexually active during their late teenage years (Thornton, 1990).

Sexual Behavior in Adolescent Dating

There is substantial research evidence documenting a developmental pattern in the sequence of adolescent heterosexual behavior. Couples generally embrace and kiss first, then fondle and pet, and subsequently engage in more intimate behaviors that include sexual intercourse. McCabe and Collins (1984) assessed desired and experienced sexual involvement among Australian adolescents during various stages of dating. As dating became more serious and committed, the level of sexual activity increased. Males had more desire for sexual intimacy on a first date than females, but these gender differences decreased with prolonged relationship involvement (McCabe & Collins, 1984).

Smith and Udry (1985) used both cross-sectional analyses and longitudinal linking of behavior separated by 2 years to investigate the sequence of sexual behavior among young adolescents in the United States. At the first round, results for White adolescents 12 to 15 years old showed the expected ordering of heterosexual behavior: Necking occurred most often, then feeling breasts through clothing, feeling breasts directly, feeling female sex organs directly, feeling penis directly, and finally intercourse. The sequence of behaviors for Black adolescents was quite different: A greater percentage of Black teens indicated that they had intercourse than had engaged in the unclothed petting of breasts and feeling of male or female sex organs. Longitudinal data were analyzed to determine if the ordering of sexual behaviors for White and Black adolescents that was found in the cross-sectional data was predictive of subsequent sequences of behavior. Among White adolescents the longitudinal results supported the cross-sectional sequence of sexual behaviors. Among Black adolescents there was no predictable progression in precoital sexual activity over time. White and Black adolescents in the United States apparently have somewhat different normative expectations regarding heterosexual behavior (Furstenberg, Morgan, Moore, & Petersen, 1987). White teens are more likely than Black teens to engage in a series of noncoital behaviors for a period of time before having intercourse.

Demographic Patterns and Trends in Adolescent Sexual Intercourse

In every nationally representative survey, more male than female teens report having had intercourse at every year of age (Moore, Miller, Glei, & Morrison, 1995). About 9% of males and 1% of females have had intercourse by age 13 compared to 76% of females and 80% of males by age 20 (Alan Guttmacher Institute, 1994). The gender difference in teen sexual experience has been declining over time. Still, after the early teens, the proportion of males at each year of age who report having sex is roughly equal to the number of sexually experienced females who are 1 year older.

Race differences in adolescent sexual experience also are substantial, with more Black teenagers having had sex than White or Hispanic teens. More than half of non-Hispanic Black males have had sex by age 15, but Hispanic and non-Hispanic White males do not attain this level of sexual activity until they are age 17. Similarly, 45% of young non-Hispanic Black females have initiated sex by age 16, whereas non-Hispanic White and Hispanic females do not attain this level until age 17 (Alan Guttmacher Institute, 1994). These racial differences are at least partly due to socioeconomic and contextual difference between the races.

Since the 1950s and 1960s, age at first marriage has risen dramatically, from just over age 20 to past age 25 among females. Delayed marriage, combined with an earlier age of first sexual experience, has meant that the likelihood that a White teenage female would have intercourse before marriage more than doubled between the late 1950s and mid-1980s. As a result, 95% of sexually experienced White teenagers in the 1980s were unmarried at first intercourse compared with less than 60% in the late 1950s (Alan Guttmacher Institute, 1994). There have been much smaller changes in the sexual behavior of Black teenagers over the same period of time.

In addition to the increase in premarital sexual intercourse attributed to postponement of marriage, there is widespread agreement that the onset of sexual intercourse is occurring at younger ages. To estimate the younger onset of sexual intercourse over time, tabulations were recently reported on the percentage of teens in different age cohorts who reported having had sex by each year of age between ages 13 and 20 (Alan Guttmacher Institute, 1994). Comparisons were made between those who turned 20 between 1970 and 1972, versus those who turned 20 between 1985 and 1987. Among males, there was little difference between the two cohorts in the proportion who were sexually experienced by ages 13 and 14, but an increase in sexual experience was apparent during the middle and later teen years. For example, 20% of the earlier cohort had had sex by age 15 compared to 27% of those in the more recent cohort. The respective cohort proportions of male sexual experience by age 18 were 55% and 64%, an increase of 9%. Among females in the same two cohorts there was a much larger increase in sexual experience at each year of age among the more recent cohort. Although the percentage who have intercourse in the early teen years is small, more than twice as many young females in the recent cohort had sex by ages 14, 15, and 16 than those in the earlier cohort. Among females who turned 20 between 1970 and 1972, 35% had sex by age 18 compared to 52% of the later birth cohort, an increase of 17 percentage points.

These demographic and trend data are significant for understanding the formation of intimate relationships in adolescence because they point to considerable variability in the timing of sexual intercourse. Although biological variables are important precursors of individual adolescent sexual behavior, changes in historical and social circumstances are related to cohort shifts in sexual experience. The relationship of adolescent sex and romance needs to be further investigated under conditions of different cultural norms so that their interrelatedness can be more clearly understood. Perhaps sexual activity is increasing independently of romance. This conclusion is supported by Bernstein (1995), who found that teens are engaging in sex more and earlier, and that they are using sex as a way to establish intimacy with peers.

Integration of Romance and Sex in Adolescent Relationships

Romantic gestures like hand holding, affectionate facial expressions, and gazing into the eyes of one's partner are often precursors to activities of greater sexual intensity, such as direct stimulation of the genitals and intercourse. Increased heart rate and skin flush are physiological responses commonly associated with both romance and sex, whereas arousal of reproductive organs is more clearly sexual. Motivations for sexual fulfillment might include pleasure, stimulation, increased intimacy, and conquest, whereas motivations for romance are more likely to include seeking intimacy, security, and attachment.

Romantic relationships are formed during adolescence for nonsexual as well as sexual reasons. These reasons include social desirability, coming of age where sexual interests are strong, seeking security, developing a liking for another, seeking and/or receiving needed validation, feeling physically or emotionally attracted to a partner, and experiencing pressure from friends to "score." Adolescents feel validated when prioritized by their partner with affection and commitment, and they can achieve status by maintaining steady dating relationships over time.

Gay, lesbian, and bisexual adolescents would not be expected to feel any differently about seeking validation and security in relationships. They probably also feel infatuated with potential romantic partners in the same way as heterosexual teens. An important difference, however, is that they are less free to acknowledge or express their romantic feelings openly.

Romantic conceptualizations involve schematics that define who is perceived as attractive. Sexual fantasies or *sexualizing* others is based on creating mental images of potential partners who fulfill a perceived need. These kinds of sexual images become linked with emotional qualities. Although romance has historically been an essential relationship component, sexuality seems to be relatively more emphasized among contemporary adolescents. Greater sexual experimentation and experience are expected now before making serious relationship commitments. More than half of young Americans are estimated to cohabit (Bumpass & Sweet, 1989), suggesting that romance and sex are attainable without the high level of commitment required by marriage. This conclusion is also borne out in contemporary media, where teens are often portrayed as engaging in sexual relationships, with less emphasis placed on long-term commitments.

Traditionally, it was more socially acceptable for males than females to pursue strictly sexual relationships, but this double standard has diminished (Michael, Gagnon, Laumann, & Kolata, 1994). Being unfaithful to a romantic partner also has been more common among males than females, but this difference also has been declining (Smith 1994). Apparently, no research has been conducted about cheating among adolescents in established relationships. Adolescents might cheat on their romantic partner or end the relationship for various reasons – for example, if they don't get the reinforcement they need to feel desirable or attractive; if there are emotional conflicts in the relationship; if there is a lack of emotional or sexual expressiveness; or if there is a perceived loss of status.

Many teens are conflicted about or have distorted conceptions of what to expect from romantic relationships, including how troublesome sexual involvements can be. One study found that although there was a high incidence of sexual experience among adolescents, for half of them this was limited to one partner, and many, especially females, wished they had waited to have sex (De Gaston, Jensen, & Weed, 1995). This is not an image portrayed in popular teen culture. Bernstein (1995) stressed the uncertainty adolescents face in making decisions about having sex. Teens often do not differentiate between sex and love, so sex may be viewed as a means to attain status and acceptance. Females also might experience a conflict between not wanting to be labeled either a "prude" or a "slut." Although most adolescents have sexual intercourse during their teens, about one-fifth remain virgins to age 20 (Alan Guttmacher Institute, 1994); the transition to sexual intercourse is sometimes a difficult and potentially high-risk decision (Miller, 1995).

Gallotti, Kozberg, and Appleman (1990) found that as teens age, they view potential romantic relationship partners in a more mature way. They tend to base their appraisals more on mutuality of feelings and less on physical appearance or personality. Also, older adolescents emphasize long-term aspects of a romantic relationship and define commitment in the relationship based on emotional and cognitive dimensions. These data imply that delaying dating long enough to develop a close friendship first could increase the chance of engaging in responsible sexual behavior. Among older adolescents, perceptions of the partner could be more accurate and realistic, and pair commitment might be higher.

Coercion in the Development of Romantic and Sexual Relationships

It should be recognized that adolescent romantic and sexual relationships sometimes have a darker side. Romantic relationships are usually mutual and consensual, but sexual relationships sometimes are not. Sexual pressure and coercion come in many forms. Some children are molested or sexually abused at young ages, even in infancy or preschool years. Many teens experience sexual pressures from a dating partner, ranging from subtle verbal and nonverbal messages to outright physical force and date rape. The dynamics of date rape situations vary; sometimes it is clear to both parties that rape has occurred, but sometimes there is uncertainty. A female might "give in" to the male's sexual advances, hoping to gain greater intimacy and emotional closeness while not necessarily wanting to have sex. Among the most dysfunctional couples, coercive sexual relationships can provide a sense of security for the perpetrator via domination and for the victim by allowing herself to be dominated. Typically, though, the perceptions of perpetrator and victim are quite different regarding date rape incidents. Male offenders often tend to assume sexual desire on the part of their female partner, often overinterpreting cues from the way she dresses and offers affection. Females tend to interpret the same incident as the male's being coercive, and disregarding her verbal and/or nonverbal resistance to having sex. In some studies, males (Gillen & Muncer, 1991), or both males and females (Willis & Wrightsman, 1995) are less likely to define a situation as date rape, or assign blame to the male, when couples were steady partners or had been sexually intimate before. Evidence suggests that coercive sexual experiences can have profound effects on adolescent development, including later romantic and sexual relationships.

Prevalence

Estimates of the prevalence of sexual pressure and coercion vary widely, partly because it is difficult to define how these incidents should be counted. In a national survey of adult sexual behavior conducted in 1992,

22% of all women (aged 18 to 59) and 25% of the youngest women (aged 18 to 24) said that they were forced into "unwanted sexual behaviors" at some time compared to just 2% of men (Michael et al., 1994). Among youth aged 18 to 22 in the 1987 National Survey of Children, about 7% reported that they had been forced to have sexual intercourse against their will (Moore, Nord, & Peterson, 1989). The percentages were higher among females than males, and the younger the age at first sexual intercourse, the greater the probability that pressure or coercion was involved. Almost three-quarters of women who had intercourse before age 14 and 60% of those who had sex before age 15 reported having had intercourse against their will (Alan Guttmacher Institute, 1994; Moore et al., 1989).

Several studies indicate that female adolescents who become pregnant and give birth are much more likely than other teens to have had coercive sexual experiences. Butler and Burton (1990) found that more than half of females aged 16 to 25 who were pregnant as teenagers had been sexually abused in some way (molestation, forced sex, rape). This finding of sexual abuse among more than half of pregnant teenagers is consistent with another study that found that over 60% of 445 teen mothers had been forced into unwanted sexual experiences (Ounce of Prevention Fund, 1987). A similar proportion of forced sexual experiences was reported for 535 females aged 17 to 21 who were pregnant as teenagers, recruited from 35 agencies in the state of Washington (Boyer & Fine, 1992). Two-thirds of this sample reported some type of nonvoluntary sexual activity (including molestation, rape, or attempted rape). After analyzing the data to ascertain the timing of these events relative to pregnancy, the investigators concluded that 62% of the total sample had been molested or raped prior to their first pregnancy.

Effects of Sexual Coercion on Intimate Relationships

The preceding studies provide substantial support for the hypothesis that childhood and early adolescent sexual abuse is linked to high-risk sexual activity and teenage pregnancy. Additional clues about the mechanisms of this hypothesized linkage can be gleaned from other research (Erickson & Rapkin, 1991; Miller, Monson, & Norton, 1995). First and most obviously, females who are forced to have sex at a young age are at higher risk for pregnancy and sexually transmitted infections because of their prolonged exposure to intercourse; by comparison, many of their peers are able to delay sexual involvement. Second, those who were forced to have sex subsequently engage in riskier behaviors than those who did not report unwanted sexual experiences. These higher-risk subsequent behaviors, which could be considered consequences of sexual abuse, include (1) a younger age of first voluntary sexual intercourse; (2) lower level of contraceptive use at first sexual intercourse; (3) higher frequency of subsequent sexual activity; (4) lower subsequent use of contraception; (5) greater number of sexual partners; (6) higher use of drugs or alcohol; and (7) presence of mental health problems. Sexually abused young females also were much more likely to report "survival sexual experiences" that included exchanging sex for money, a place to stay, or drugs and alcohol (Biglan, Noell, Ochs, Smolkowski, & Metzler, 1995). They also were more likely to have been expelled or to have dropped out of school and to have older sexual partners. Sexual victimization, much more than previously recognized, appears to be a key factor in adolescent high-risk sexual behavior and adolescent pregnancy.

Donaldson, Whalen, and Anastas (1989) pointed out that some frequently reported negative effects of sexual abuse, such as premature and exaggerated sexual interest and vulnerability to subsequent sexual exploitation, have direct relevance to the risk of teen pregnancy. Among pregnant or parenting females, those who reported sexual abuse had a significantly earlier age of first intercourse (13.2) than those who reported no abuse (14.5). Zweig, Barber, and Eccles (1997) found that the lowest scores on personal well-being were reported by females who were pressured into having sexual activity; the lowest male scores were linked to violently coerced sexual involvement. According to Boyer and Fine (1992, p. 11), "for a large number of pregnant adolescents, a history of physical maltreatment and sexual victimization may have disrupted their developmental processes and undermined their basic competence."

Even if coercion is not involved, initiating sexual intercourse at a young age appears to be related to later sexual relationship development. Analyses based on data from females aged 15 to 44 in the National Survey of Family Growth (NSFG) found that women who had an early onset of first sexual intercourse (defined as before age 17) were more likely to have had multiple recent sexual partners than women who first had sexual intercourse when they were aged 17 or older (Seidman, Mosher, & Aral, 1992, 1994). Early sexual behavior apparently has enduring effects related to having multiple partners and more frequent intercourse, potentially increasing the risk of contracting sexually transmitted infections and becoming pregnant.

The studies referred to previously suggest that early and sexually coercive experiences can seriously disrupt victims' subsequent romantic relationships. Psychological meanings attached to abusive experiences are carried over into future relationships. Clinicians observe that children forced to engage in sexual behavior respond in sexualized ways that are not characteristic of their developmental stage. Research also documents that female adolescents who have had forced or coercive sexual experiences tend to experience negative psychological and sexual consequences (Miller et al., 1995). The basic premise upon which coercive sexual relationships are based is the misuse of power, and it will almost certainly influence, if not destroy, the development of a romantic relationship. Some research (Roth, Wayland, & Woolsey, 1990) indicates that distress reported by victims of date rape is equal in severity to that reported by victims of chronic child sexual abuse. Both child sexual abuse and date rape appear to have several psychological consequences in common, including fear, anger, sadness, and a loss of trust. Like the studies of child sexual abuse, date rape research (Friedman, 1993) also finds that the effects of coercive sexual experiences tend to be even more devastating to the victim when she is well acquainted with the perpetrator.

The trauma inflicted on victims of sexual abuse can be interpreted through concepts of self psychology (Westen, 1994) and object relations theory. Representations of the self are at risk to the impact of the abusive experience in a uniquely individual way. According to object relations theory, an individual constructs a schema for relationships based on very early interactions (Bowlby, 1969). Thus, a strong cognitive component accounts for both the forming and the understanding of relationships. The way in which the victimization experience becomes incorporated into a cognitive schema will be influenced by the developmental stage when the abuse occurred. For example, identity formation may involve the incorporation of the self as bad or damaged. Complications can arise for victims of sexual abuse both in future sexual relationships and in the type of behavior manifested. For example, a sexual abuse victim may become hypersexualized and take on a promiscuous role, such as prostitute, or be exploited sexually in some other way. In future romantic relationships, the victims of sexual abuse often have their emotions and sensations mixed with abuse memories in such a way that open expression and interaction in the new relationship are compromised. The abuse victim might be overly inclined to respond to a partner in a sexual way due to having been reinforced for such behaviors in the past. Certainly, these experiences would distort one's conceptualization of romance. The importance of understanding these relationship dynamics is that early and coercive sexualization can be highly confusing and distorting to the development of self-identity and to romantic and intimate relationships.

Conclusions

We have discussed the complex nature of, and interplay between, romantic and sexual relationships during adolescence. Although a simple definition of romance is elusive, romantic thoughts before and during dating and sexual relationships appear to be near-universal experiences for adolescents in Western societies. The way sex and romance are experienced varies greatly, however, being shaped most clearly by biological development, socialization, and cultural beliefs, as well as by race, gender, and sometimes traumatic events (e.g., sexual abuse).

Increased interest in sexual interaction usually follows the biological course of pubertal maturation in normal development, and romance generally complements these interests in Western cultures. Social and historical conditions suggest explanations for earlier sexual activity among contemporary adolescents than has been observed in the past. However, early exposure to coercive sexual experiences appears to alter the timing and subsequent course of adolescent romantic and sexual relationships.

We conclude by restating several questions that have been addressed in this chapter. Refining and studying these issues could further advance our understanding of the links between romantic and sexual relationship development during adolescence. Most fundamentally, we would like to know about the biological bases for romantic ideation and attraction that might be similar to the biological substrate for sexual maturation and sexual arousal. Perhaps a clearer understanding of hormones and biochemistry could be helpful in understanding romantic as well as sexual attraction. Additional research is needed to explain how early coercive and traumatic sexual experiences alter later life relationships by confusing or interfering with the development of normative romantic and sexual feelings and behavior.

Although most of this chapter has focused on heterosexual relationships, it could be that gay, lesbian, and bisexual teens experience romanticism in sexual relationships similar to that of heterosexual youth. Sexual orientation could be an important addition to research about the development of romantic and sexual relationships. Similarly, additional research is needed to understand gender differences in perceptions of romantic–sexual interactions that could help explain and intervene in sexual coercion and date rape. To a great extent, male and female adolescents conceptualize romantic relationships differently, and changing gender roles might be related to changing sexual experiences among adolescents.

Additional research on these issues has the potential to advance our understanding of adolescent intimate relationship development and provide direction for treating troubled individuals and relationships. These are important goals because of the universal pleasure and danger of human sexuality and the fundamental need for close personal relationships.

References

Alan Guttmacher Institute. (1994). *Sex and America's teenagers.* New York: Author.

Aune, K. S., Aune, R. K., & Buller, D. B. (1994). The experience, expression, and perceived appropriateness of emotions across levels of relationship development. *Journal of Social Psychology, 134,* 141–150.

Baxter, L. A. (1992). Root metaphors in accounts of developing romantic relationships. *Journal of Social and Personal Relationships, 9,* 253–275.

Beall, A. E., & Sternberg, R. J. (1995). The social construction of love. *Journal of Social and Personal Relationships, 12,* 417–438.

Benda, B. B., & DiBlasio, F. A. (1991). Comparison of four theories of adolescent sexual exploration. *Deviant Behavior, 12,* 235–257.

Benda, B. B., & DiBlasio, F. A. (1994). An integration of theory: Adolescent sexual contacts. *Journal of Youth and Adolescence, 23,* 403–420.

Benda, B. B., & Kashner, T. M. (1994). Adolescent sexual behavior: A path analysis. *Journal of Social Service Research, 19,* 49–69.

Bernstein, N. (1995). What's love got to do with it? *Youth Outlook* [On-line], 46–54. Available: http://www. diablopubs.com/DM9602Feat.html

Biglan, A., Noell, J., Ochs, L., Smolkowski, K., & Metzler, C. (1995). Does sexual coercion play a role in high-risk sexual behavior of adolescent and adult women? *Journal of Behavioral Medicine, 18,* 549–568.

Bowlby, J. (1969). *Attachment and loss: Volume 1. Attachment.* New York: Basic Books.

Boyer, D., & Fine, D. (1992). Sexual abuse as a factor in adolescent pregnancy and child maltreatment. *Family Planning Perspectives, 24,* 619–620.

Brooks-Gunn, J. (1987). The impact of puberty and sexual activity upon the health and education of adolescent girls and boys. *Peabody Journal of Education, 64,* 88–112.

Bumpass, L. L., & Sweet, J. A. (1989). National estimates of cohabitation. *Demography, 26,* 615–625.

Burchinal, L. G. (1964). The premarital dyad and love involvement. In H. T. Christensen (Ed.), *Handbook of marriage and the family* (pp. 623–674). Chicago: Rand McNally.

Butler, J. R., & Burton, L. M. (1990). Rethinking teenage childbearing: Is sexual abuse a missing link? *Family Relations, 39,* 73–80.

Cimbalo, R. S., & Novell, D. O. (1993). Sex differences in romantic love attitudes among college students. *Psychological Reports, 73,* 15–18.

De Gaston, J. F., Jensen, L., & Weed, S. (1995). A closer look at adolescent sexual activity. *Journal of Youth and Adolescence, 24,* 465–479.

Dolcini, M. M., & Adler, N. E. (1994). Perceived competencies, peer group affiliation, and risk behavior among early adolescents. *Health Psychology, 13,* 496–506.

Donaldson, P. E., Whalen, M. H., & Anastas, J. W. (1989). Teen pregnancy and sexual abuse: Exploring the connection. *Smith College Studies in Social Work, 59,* 288–300.

Dornbusch, S. M., Carlsmith J. M., Gross, R. T., Martin, J. A., Jennings, D., Rosenberg, A., & Duke, P. (1981). Sexual development, age, and dating: A comparison of biological and social influences upon one set of behaviors. *Child Development, 52,* 179–185.

Dunphy, D. C. (1963). The social structure of urban adolescent peer groups. *Sociometry, 26,* 230–246.

Ehrman, W. (1959). *Premarital dating behavior.* New York: Holt.

Erickson, P. I., & Rapkin, A. J. (1991). Unwanted sexual experiences among middle and high school youth. *Journal of Adolescent Health, 12,* 319–325.

Feingold, A. (1990). Gender differences in effects of physical attractiveness on romantic attraction: A comparison across five research paradigms. *Journal of Personality and Social Psychology, 59,* 981–993.

Freud, S. (1920). Beyond the pleasure principle. In J. Rickman (Ed.), *A general selection from the works of Sigmund Freud* (pp. 141–168). New York: Liveright, 1957.

Freud, S. (1933). *New introductory lectures on psychoanalysis.* New York: Norton.

Friedman, J. (1993). *Date rape: Secret epidemic: What it is, what it isn't, what it does to you, what you can do about it.* Deerfield Beach, FL: Health Communications.

Furman, W., & Wehner, E. A. (1994). Romantic views: Toward a theory of adolescent romantic relationships. In R. Montemayor, G. R. Adams, & T. P. Gullotta (Eds.), *Personal relationships during adolescence. Advances in adolescent development: An annual book series, Vol. 6* (pp. 168–195). Thousand Oaks, CA: Sage.

Furstenberg, F. F., Morgan, S. P., Moore, K. A., & Petersen, J. L. (1987). Race differences in the timing of adolescent intercourse. *American Sociological Review, 52,* 511–518.

Gagnon, J. H., & Simon, W. (1973). *Sexual conduct: The social sources of human sexuality.* Chicago: Aldine.

Galotti, K. M., Kozberg, S. F., & Appleman, D. (1990). Younger and older adolescents thinking about commitments. *Journal of Experimental Child Psychology, 50,* 324–339.

Gillen, K., & Muncer, S. J. (1991). Sex differences in the perceived causal structure of date rape: A preliminary report. *Aggressive Behavior, 21,* 101–112.

Halpern, C. T., Udry, J. R., Campbell, B., & Suchindran, C. (1993). Testosterone and religiosity as predictors of sexual activity. A panel analysis of adolescent males. *Psychosomatic Medicine, 55,* 436–447.

Hatfield, E., Schmitz, E., Cornelius, J., & Rapson, R. L. (1988). Passionate love: How early does it begin? *Journal of Psychology and Human Sexuality, 1,* 35–41.

Honeycutt, J. M., Cantrill, J. G., & Greene, R. W. (1989). Memory structures for relational escalation: A cognitive test of the sequencing of relational actions and stages. *Human Communications Research, 16,* 62–90.

Hong, S. M., & Faedda, S. (1994). Ranking of romantic acts by an Australian sample. *Psychological Reports, 74,* 471–474.

Inman-Amos, J., Hendrick, S. S., & Hendrick, C. H. (1994). Love attitudes: Similarities between parents and between parents and children. *Family Relations, 43,* 456–461.

Jankowiak, W. R., & Fischer, E. F. (1994). A cross-cultural perspective on romantic love. *Ethnology, 31,* 149–155.

Jessor, R., & Jessor, L. (1977). *Problem behavior and psychosocial development: A longitudinal study of youth.* New York: Academic Press.

Landolet, M. A., Lalumiere, M. L., & Quinsey, V. L. (1995). Sex differences in intra-sex variations in human mating tactics: An evolutionary approach. *Ethology and Sociobiology, 16,* 3–23.

Levesque, R. J. R. (1993). The romantic experience of adolescents in satisfying love relationships. *Journal of Youth and Adolescence, 22,* 219–251.

Liebowitz, M. R. (1983). *The chemistry of love.* Boston: Little, Brown.

McCabe, M. P. (1984). Toward a theory of adolescent dating. *Adolescence, 19,* 159–170.

McCabe, M. P., & Collins, J. K. (1984). Measurement of depth of desired and experienced sexual involvement at different stages of dating. *Journal of Sex Research, 20,* 377–390.

Medora, N. P., Goldstein, A., & Von der Hellen, C. (1994). Variables related to romanticism and self-esteem in pregnant teenagers. *Adolescence, 28,* 159–170.

Michael, R. T., Gagnon, J. H., Laumann, E. O., & Kolata, G. (1994). *Sex in America.* Boston: Little, Brown.

Miller, B. C. (1995). Risk factors for adolescent nonmarital childbearing. In *Report to Congress on out-of-wedlock childbearing* (pp. 217–227). DHHS Pub. No. (PHS) 95–1257. Washington, DC: Department of Health and Human Services.

Miller, B. C., Christopherson, C. R., & King, P. K. (1993). Sexual behavior in adolescence. In T. P. Gulotta, G. R. Adams, & R. Montemayor (Eds.), *Adolescent sexuality* (pp. 57–76). Newbury Park, CA: Sage.

Miller, B. C., & Fox, G. L. (1987). Theories of adolescent heterosexual behavior. *Journal of Adolescent Research, 2,* 269–282.

Miller, B. C., McCoy, J. K., & Olson, T. D. (1986). Dating age and stage as correlates of adolescent sexual attitudes and behavior. *Journal of Adolescent Research, 1,* 361–371.

Miller, B. C., Monson, B. H., & Norton, M. C. (1995). The effects of forced sexual intercourse on white female adolescents. *Child Abuse and Neglect, 19,* 1289–1301.

Moore, K. A., Miller, B. C., Glei, D., & Morrison, D. R. (1995). *Adolescent sex, contraception, and childbearing: A review of recent research.* Washington, DC: Child Trends.

Moore, K. A., Nord, C. W., & Peterson, J. L. (1989). Nonvoluntary sexual activity among adolescents. *Family Planning Perspectives, 21,* 110–114.

Morris, N. M. (1992). Determinants of adolescent initiation of coitus. *Adolescent Medicine: State of the Art Reviews, 3,* 165–180.

Ounce of Prevention Fund. (1987). *Child sexual abuse: A hidden factor in adolescent sexual behavior: Findings from a statewide survey of teenage mothers in Illinois.* Chicago: Department of Children and Family Services.

Patterson, J., Pryor, J., & Shields, J. (1995). Adolescent attachment to parents and friends in relation to aspects of self-esteem. *Journal of Youth and Adolescence, 24,* 365–376.

Phinney, V. G., Jensen, L. C., Olsen, J. A., & Cundick, B. (1990). The relationship between early development and psychosexual behaviors in adolescent females. *Adolescence, 25,* 321–332.

Reiss, I. L. (1986). A sociological journey into sexuality. *Journal of Marriage and the Family, 48,* 233–242.

Richards, M. H., & Larson, R. (1993). Pubertal development and the daily subjective states of young adolescents. *Journal of Research on Adolescence, 3,* 145–169.

Roth, S., Wayland, K., & Woolsey, M. (1990). Victimization history and victim–assailant relationship as factors in recovery from sexual assault. *Journal of Traumatic Stress, 3,* 169–180.

Rowe, D. C., & Rodgers, J. L. (1994). A social contagion model of adolescent sexual behavior: Explaining race differences. *Social Biology, 41,* 1–18.

Savin-Williams, R. C. (1995). An exploratory study of pubertal maturation timing and self-esteem among gay and bisexual male youths. *Developmental Psychology, 31,* 56–64.

Savin-Williams, R. C., & Berndt, T. J. (1990). Friendship and peer relations. In S. Feldman, & G. R. Elliott (Eds.), *At the threshold: The developing adolescent* (pp. 277–307). Cambridge, MA: Harvard University Press.

Seidman, S. N., Mosher, W. D., & Aral, S. O. (1992). Women with multiple sexual partners: United States, 1988. *American Journal of Public Health, 82,* 1388–1394.

Seidman, S. N., Mosher, W. D., & Aral, S. O. (1994). Predictors of high-risk behavior in unmarried American women: Adolescent environment as risk factor. *Journal of Adolescent Health, 15,* 126–132.

Shulman, S., Elicker, J., & Sroufe, L. A. (1994). Stages of friendship growth in preadolescence as related to attachment history. *Journal of Social and Personal Relationships, 11,* 341–361.

Smith, E. A. (1989). A biological model of adolescent sexual behavior. In F. R. Adams, R. Montemayor, & T. P. Gullotta (Eds.), *Biology of adolescent behavior and development* (pp. 143–167). Newbury Park, CA: Sage.

Smith, E. A., & Udry, J. R. (1985). Coital and non-coital sexual behaviors of white and black adolescents. *American Journal of Public Health, 75,* 1200–1203.

Smith, T. W. (1994). Attitudes towards sexual permissiveness: Trends, correlates, and behavioral connections. In A. S. Rossi (Ed.), *Sexuality across the life course* (pp. 63–97). Chicago: University of Chicago Press.

Thornton, A. (1990). The courtship process and adolescent sexuality. Special issues: Adolescent sexuality, contraception, and childbearing. *Journal of Family Issues, 11,* 239–273.

Toufexis, A. (1993, February 15). The right chemistry. *Time,* 49–51.

Townsend, J. M., Kline, J., & Wasserman, T. H. (1995). Low-investment copulation: Sex differences in motivations and emotional reactions. *Ethology and Sociobiology, 16,* 25–51.

Udry, J. R. (1988). Biological predispositions and social control in adolescent sexual behavior. *American Sociological Review, 53,* 709–722.

Udry, J. R. (1990). Hormonal and social determinants of adolescent sexual initiation. In J. Bancroft & J. M. Reinisch (Eds.), *Adolescence and puberty* (pp. 70–87). Oxford: Oxford University Press.

Udry, J. R., Billy, J. O. G., Morris, N. M., Groff, T. R., & Raj, M. H. (1985). Serum androgenic hormones motivate sexual behavior in adolescent boys. *Fertility and Sterility, 43,* 90–94.

Udry, J. R., & Campbell, B. C. (1994). Getting started on sexual behavior. In A. S. Rossi (Ed.), *Sexuality across the life course.* Chicago: University of Chicago Press.

Van Wel, F. (1994). A culture gap between the generations? Social influences on youth cultural style. *International Journal of Adolescence and Youth, 4,* 211–228.

Walters, S., & Crawford, C. B. (1995). The importance of mate attraction for intrasexual competition in men and women. *Ethology and Sociobiology, 15,* 5–30.

Westen, D. (1994). The impact of sexual abuse on self structure. In D. Cicchetti & S. L. Toth (Vol. Eds.), *Rochester symposium on developmental psychopathology: Volume 5, Disorders and dysfunctions of the self* (pp. 251–266). Rochester, NY: University of Rochester Press.

Willis, C. E., & Wrightsman, L. S. (1995). Effects of victim gaze behavior and prior relationship on rape culpability attributions. *Journal of Interpersonal Violence, 10,* 367–377.

Zweig, J. M., Barber, B. L., & Eccles, J. S. (1997). Sexual coercion and well-being in young adulthood: Comparisons by gender and college status. *Journal of Interpersonal Violence, 12,* 291–308.

PART II

Individual Differences in Romantic Relationships

6 Capacity for Intimate Relationships
A Developmental Construction

W. Andrew Collins and L. Alan Sroufe

The advent of romantic relationships is a hallmark transition of adolescence. Images of the sudden onset of preoccupation with the other, shyness and self-consciousness, awkwardness in interactions, and sexual awakening suffuse popular treatments of the topic. In developmental perspective, however, romantic relationships are embedded in fundamental human motivations to form and maintain close relationships (Baumeister & Leary, 1995; MacDonald, 1992) and in a meaningful progression of relationships across the life course (Ainsworth, 1989; Feeney & Noller, 1990; Furman & Wehner, 1994). Early caregiver–child relationships, peer relationships in preschool and middle childhood, and close mutual friendships in adolescence all potentially contribute to the behavioral patterns and emotional orientations that mark a relationship as romantic.

Romantic relationships are distinct from these forerunners in many ways. In contrast to the kinship or legal bonds that commonly circumscribe caregiving relationships, romantic relationships are voluntary and symmetrical. Literary and popular portrayals frequently depict as tragic the attempts of parents, other authority figures, or social conventions to coerce, nullify, or otherwise render involuntary the selection of a romantic partner. In contrast to caregiving relationships, in romance each partner is dependent upon the other, whereas the dependency of child on caregiver is asymmetrical. In contrast to friendships, the reciprocal dependency of romantic partners is typically greater and more extensive. Unlike any of these other types of close relationships, romantic relationships are marked by an amalgam of love, passion, and actual or anticipated sexual activity. Friendship may be caring and passionate as well (see Diamond, Dubé, & Savin-Williams, this volume), but romantic partners are likely either to express their passion in sexual activity or at least to anticipate that shared feelings of love and passion will be expressed sexually at some future time.

125

The intimacy of romantic relationships, however, is woven from experiences that support the development of intimacy in nonromantic relationships. Reis and Shaver (1988) have defined intimacy as

> an interpersonal process within which two interaction partners experience and express feelings, communicate verbally and nonverbally, satisfy social motives, augment or reduce social fears, talk and learn about themselves and their unique characteristics, and become "close". . . . (pp. 387–388)

They further note that emotionally close interactions at all ages derive their significance not only from mutually self-disclosing behaviors, but also from the experiences of feeling understood, validated, and cared for as a result of these behaviors.

Normatively, the interactions that serve these functions change in response to the maturity level and changing needs of individuals (Collins, 1996). With parents, closeness, as expressed by cuddling and extensive joint interactions, declines as children mature, whereas conversations in which information is conveyed and feelings are expressed increase. With peers, close relationships are increasingly defined in terms of mutual caring and commitment rather than merely as the patterns of shared activities that suffice as markers of friendship at earlier ages (Hartup, 1992). Especially during preadolescence and adolescence, when forming close mutual relationships is a normative developmental task, intimacy becomes increasingly central to social competence.

In this chapter we consider common features of these various forms of relating and unique contributions of each to the development of capacities for intimate romantic relationships. Drawing on findings from a 19-year longitudinal study, we briefly examine precursors of intimacy in early caregiver–child relationships and in relationships with peers in childhood. We then speculate about how experiences during childhood and adolescence may serve as precursors to entry into, and growth-enhancing experiences in, romantic relationships.

A Developmental View of Intimacy

The capacity for intimacy emerges through a transactive process. Expectations concerning self and relationships and patterns of arousal modulation characteristic of early relationships lead to particular forms of engagement with persons and objects. Other persons, in turn, react in a complementary way, thus perpetuating the pattern, albeit in new forms and in new contexts, across developmental periods (e.g., Ainsworth, 1989; Bowlby, 1973; Sroufe, Carlson, & Shulman, 1993; Sroufe & Fleeson, 1986, 1988).

We regard the capacity for intimacy as a classic developmental phenomenon. Intimacy has "emergent properties" that are not fully specified by earlier capacities but that evolve from those precursors through a series of transformations, each of which builds on the previous ones. In each life phase, beginning in infancy, children, through their experiences with parents and peers, lay down foundations that support the capacity for intimacy with peers in adolescence. The self-disclosure and sexual intimacy of adolescence, however, are qualitative advances. Nothing one can see in infancy would directly forecast such capacities. Only a developmental perspective allows researchers to discern links between infant or early peer experience and adolescent intimacy.

A developmental view also captures the complex motivational, emotional, and behavioral aspects of intimacy. To achieve intimacy, one must first be oriented to value and seek closeness. Second, one must be able to tolerate, and even embrace, the intense emotions that are inextricably part of close relationships and be able to share emotional experiences freely. Finally, one must be capable of self-disclosure, mutual reciprocity, sensitivity to the feelings of the other, and concern for the other's well-being. Although this totality is a unique achievement of adolescence, each of these aspects of intimacy emerges from an integration of family and peer experiences in earlier development (e.g., Furman & Wehner, 1994; Shulman, Elicker, & Sroufe, 1994). Children must practice and master closeness, reciprocity, and conflict resolution between equals within the peer group, but individuals with supportive family experiences are more likely to have the positive experiences that contribute to the capacity for intimacy with peers. Although positive peer experiences may be rehabilitative for individuals with unsupportive parenting histories, such children are the very ones who are least likely to have positive relations with peers.

Researchers have found impressive correlations between early caregiver–child relationships and childhood peer relationships and between both these earlier and later patterns and intimacy with friends in adolescence (Elicker, Englund, & Sroufe, 1992; Shulman et al., 1994). In the following sections, we outline the evidence for these links.

Early Relationships and the Capacity for Closeness

Theoretically, relationships in infancy contribute to three components of closeness and, ultimately, of intimacy. First, relationships with caregivers, when based on a history of availability and responsiveness, should lead to positive expectancies about interactions with others. In Bowlby's (1973) terms, children develop internal working models of self and others that guide them toward similar interactions with others, Second, such relationships provide a context for learning reciprocity, even though only the more mature (parental) partners can purposefully fit their behavior to the child's actions. Further, participating in a relationship with an empathic, responsive caregiver affords learning the very nature of empathic relating (Sroufe & Fleeson, 1986). Third, through a history of responsive care and support for autonomy, children develop a sense of self-worth and efficacy. These characteristics probably underlie behaviors that are likely to be attractive to future partners (e.g., self-confidence, curiosity, enthusiasm, and positive affect) (Elicker et al., 1992). Such experiences also orient children to expect and accept certain kinds of reactions from others.

Empirical Evidence of Links between Attachment History and Closeness

Our view of developmental precursors to romantic relationships has been shaped by experiences in the Minnesota Parent–Child Project, in which 190 first-born individuals have been studied since the third trimester of the mother's pregnancy. (See Egeland & Brunnquell, 1979, for an early report.) The primary measure of early relationships was the Strange Situation procedure (Ainsworth, Blehar, Waters, & Wall, 1978). Based on observations of children in this procedure, Ainsworth identified behaviors characteristic of both secure attachment and two forms of anxious attachment. In the Minnesota study, children who manifested these three contrasting patterns during infancy also later showed striking differences in peer relationships, manifested in differing ways across ages. The contrasts are apparent in the following descriptions of links from infancy to preschool and to middle childhood, respectively.

Security of attachment in infancy strongly predicted preschool characteristics of self-reliance, effective peer relationships (including empathy and affective engagement), and positive relationships with teachers (e.g., Sroufe, 1983; Sroufe, Schork, Motti, Lawroski, & LaFreniere, 1984). Children with secure histories were more popular and demonstrated greater competence by participating more actively in the peer group, manifesting more positive affect and less negative affect in their encounters than insecurely attached children. By contrast, children with histories of anxious attachments not only were significantly less competent in all of these respects, but also showed distinctive patterns of maladaptation. Those who had shown anxious-avoidant tendencies in infancy were noticeably aggressive in the classroom, whereas those with anxious-resistant histories were easily frustrated and oriented toward their teachers, which interfered with engaging peers (Sroufe, 1983; Sroufe, Fox, & Pancake, 1983).

Early attachment history also forecasts differences in qualities of interpersonal relationships during preschool, at times with extraordinary specificity. Children with early histories of secure attachment displayed greater reciprocity and dealt more effectively with conflicts in interactions with preschool peers (Liberman, 1977; Suess, 1987). Among pairs of children who played together frequently, the relationships of pairs containing at least one avoidant member were less characterized by mutuality, responsiveness, and affective involvement and also were more hostile than the relationships of the other pairs (Pancake, 1985). In addition, of 19 dyadic relationships in the subsample, 5 involved victimization, a repetitive pattern of physical or verbal exploitation or abuse by one child of the other (Troy & Sroufe, 1987). In all cases, the exploiter was a child with an avoidant history, and the victim was another anxiously attached child (avoidant or resistant); by contrast, children with secure histories were never victimizers or victims. Interactions with preschool teachers also varied predictably with children's histories of attachment with caregivers (Sroufe & Fleeson, 1986).

Middle-childhood relationships were related to both quality of infant attachment and quality of preschool functioning. Ten- to 11-year-olds who had been secure in their attachments at 12 to 18 months of age were more likely to form a friendship than were those who had been insecurely attached. Moreover, children who had been securely attached in infancy tended to form friendships with children who also had secure histories (Elicker et al., 1992). Although this might be attributable to a natural attraction among competent children, these friendships also differed in qualities that were consistent with a history of secure attachment (Shulman et al., 1994). Secure-secure friendships clearly were apparent when the children were part of a larger group, but these children also interacted freely with others. In contrast, two avoidant children who were friends often were physically separate from the others, seldom participated in voluntary groups, rarely interchanged with other individuals, and showed jealousy regarding each other. When either child was absent, the remaining partner had difficulty participating socially. In resistant-resistant pairs, children had difficulty sustaining their relationships. One of the two often became absorbed in the group, thus separating from the other. The two children showed little loyalty to each other.

Securely attached children also showed greater social competence by adhering to middle-childhood norms that favor interaction with same-gender peers (Maccoby, 1990). Children who violated gender boundary rules also generally showed lower social competence. They were less likely than other children to have one or more friends in the group. Longitudinally, gender boundary violation was associated with a history of anxious attachment and with earlier observed interactions with parents in which the parent had shown peerlike behavior toward the child. Paradoxically, maintaining separateness from the other gender in one developmental period may well be a forerunner of adaptive relating in later periods (Sroufe, Egeland, & Carlson, in press).

Explanations of "Carry-Forward" Mechanisms

The impressive continuities in relationships just outlined may occur for a variety of reasons. Some explanations emphasize persistence of the initial cause, arguing either that an endogenous child trait continues to be manifest (Kagan, Reznick, & Gibbons, 1989) or that environmental influences remain constant and account for the appearance of stability in child behavior (Lamb, 1984). Others argue that continuity results from both prior adaptation and current environment (e.g., Bowlby, 1973; Lewis, 1989). This latter view implies an interactional model in which environmental changes have different influences, depending on previous adaptation.

Our own view of continuity (Collins, 1995; Sroufe, Egeland, & Kreutzer, 1990; Sroufe & Fleeson, 1988) embodies a transactional process whereby children with particular patterns of adaptation and expectations both assimilate and accommodate to new circumstances. This transactional view is supported by two key points from the Minnesota longitudinal findings. First, although quality of care is indeed stable (Pianta, Sroufe, & Egeland, 1989), early adaptation or experience predicts later behavior even after accounting for contemporary environmental influence both in childhood and in adolescence (Sroufe, 1995; Sroufe et al., 1990). Second, later environmental influences are not independent of prior adaptation. For example, patterns of adaptation in infancy and earlier family experiences are correlated with treatment of children by both preschool teachers and classmates (Sroufe, 1983; Sroufe & Fleeson, 1988; Troy & Sroufe, 1987). Thus, children partly create their own environments through differential engagement and different reactions from others, based upon each child's history of relationships. This partially created environment feeds back on adaptation in an ongoing process. However, early relationships continue to account for unique variance in later relationships and, by implication, are likely to contribute to differing qualities of romantic relationships in adolescence.

Bowlby's (1973) notion of working models explicitly includes the possibility that patterns of feelings, expectations, thoughts, and behaviors can change with experience. The longitudinal evidence strongly implies that links between early and later relationships are mediated by experience-based variations in acquiring specific component or constituent skills for effective relating. Securely attached infants, having experienced and therefore internalized a responsive relationship, later were more empathic (Elicker et al., 1992; Kestenbaum, Farber, & Sroufe, 1989; Sroufe, 1983). By contrast, children with histories of anxious attachments reacted to the distress of others less empathically, but in distinctive ways. Those with avoidant histories, who presumably experienced chronic rebuffs to their expressed needs, were significantly more likely than both other groups to show *antiempathy* (behavior that would make another person's distress worse, e.g., taunting a crying child), whereas those with resistant histories behaved as though the distress were their own, blurring the boundary between self and other.

Differing patterns of interpersonal cognitions or representations also may contribute to varying relationship qualities. Comparing children who had been securely or anxiously attached as infants, Rosenberg (1984) found that those in the anxious group were less likely to incorporate people into fantasy play and that their fantasized resolutions for misfortunes or interpersonal conflicts were less likely to be positive. Such children may be less interested in interpersonal relationships, may value them less highly, or may expect negative outcomes in relationships, whereas securely attached children may regard relationships more positively. Attachment history also appears to be related to distinctive cognitive biases with respect to peers. Suess (1987; Suess, Grossmann, & Sroufe, 1993) found that securely attached children usually made realistic attributions or displayed a bias toward attributing benevolent intentions, whereas children with anxious-avoidant attachment manifested more unrealistic or hostile/negative biases in their attributions of intention. Likewise, independent ratings of the children's "positive expectations regarding peers," based on responses to Thematic Apperception Test (TAT)-like card and sentence completions at age 11, significantly discriminated between attachment groups. Those with secure histories more frequently told stories in which peers cooperated and conflict was resolved, and concluded sentence items (e.g., "Most kids . . .") with positive responses (". . . like to play with me"). In short, key components of the internal working models described by Bowlby (1973) are linked to attachment history and are evinced in connection with peer interactions in childhood.

Peer Relationships During Adolescence

Adolescents experience a wider and more diverse network of social relationships than children do. Romantic relationships thus emerge as part of a complex balancing of loyal friendships, intimate pair bonds, same-gender group affiliations, and mixed-gender group associations.

Despite this complexity, the normative patterns and social structures of adolescence support continuity between closeness in the relationships of childhood and adolescence (Collins, 1996; Collins & Repinski, 1994). Popular stereotypes of parent–adolescent relationships notwithstanding, surveys in European and North American samples consistently reveal that parents and adolescents alike perceive their relationships with one another as warm and pleasant. Of the 20% or so of families that encounter serious difficulties in this period, most have had a history of earlier problems (Offer, 1969; Offer, Ostrov, & Howard, 1981). Transitory disruptions and changes in the relative balance of positive and negative emotional expressions in parent–adolescent relationships help to realign expectations while preserving affectional bonds as adolescents change developmentally (Collins, 1995, 1996; Holmbeck, 1996; Steinberg, 1990).

Normative patterns in peer relationships also support the development of intimate functioning. Although specific friendships are not typically stable throughout adolescence, relationships with a "best" friend are more often stable than unstable over the course of a school year (Berndt, Hawkins, & Hoyle, 1986; Berndt & Hoyle, 1985; Berndt & Keefe, 1995; for a review, see Savin-Williams & Berndt, 1990). As networks expand and diversify, additional opportunities for expressing and experiencing intimacy become available. Relationships with friends, romantic partners, and family members serve overlapping but distinctive functions, and typical exchanges within each differ accordingly (Furman & Buhrmester, 1992; Furman & Wehner, 1994; for reviews, see Collins & Repinski, 1994; Laursen & Collins, 1994; Savin-Williams & Berndt, 1990). Relationships with parents are reported to be primary sources of support for children in fourth grade, but parents are viewed as less important than same-sex friends as sources of social support in early and middle adolescence and less important than same-sex friends and romantic partners at college age (Furman & Buhrmester, 1992).

Peer relationships contribute to socialization for relations among equals and to satisfaction of affiliative needs. Romantic relationships may be equally or more important for mutual sharing and emotional gratification, especially in late adolescence and early adulthood (Collins, 1996). Perceptions of intimacy in cross-gender relationships increase with age during early and middle adolescence, with reported intimacy between close female–male pairs at age 16 matching the level of intimacy perceived in female–female friendships (but not that reported for male–male friendships) (Sharabany, Gershoni, & Hofman, 1981).

Data from our longitudinal study document the developmental underpinnings of adolescent peer competence in general and, in a preliminary way, the capacity for intimacy in particular. Both peer experiences and family experiences are strongly predictive of individual differences in adolescence. We have found significant continuity in peer competence based on teacher ratings from early elementary school (and, for a subsample of participants, from preschool) through age 16 (Sroufe et al., in press). Even stronger evidence has come from the subsample of individuals whom we have studied intensively in nursery school and in summer camps at age 10. When those children who had been assessed as competent at earlier ages were observed at a weekend reunion at age 15, counselors rated them as more competent and observed that they participated more actively in the group. The findings were most striking for assessments keyed to age-salient issues. For example, a scale of "capacity for relationship vulnerability" was created especially to tap teens' ability to participate in the range of reunion activities, including those in which ego-salient feelings would arise (such as engaging members of the other gender at the evening party). Scores on this scale were related to competence indices at earlier ages. Correlations were especially strong with an observationally based intensity of same-gender friendship score in middle childhood. Scores also were correlated with the gender boundary maintenance rating from that period. Finally, for girls, both preschool and middle-childhood assessments, especially the friendship score ($r = .64$), were related to an interview-based measure of "friendship intimacy" at age 16 (see Ostoja, 1996). (This interview format may not have been adequate for our male participants at this age.)

Quality of attachment in infancy and quality of caregiver–child interaction at age 13 (described in a later section) also were related to adolescent peer relationship measures. Infant and early adolescent measures together were especially strongly related to reunion assessments, with correlations in the .50s. Moreover, each of the 8 participants involved in a couple relationship during the reunion had a history of secure attachment, a highly significant finding given that only half of the 41 participants had been secure. Those with secure histories were also rated higher on "leadership" and overall level of competence in a revealed differences group discussion situation; they also were significantly more frequently elected as spokesperson for their group (Englund, Levy, & Hyson, 1997). These correlations thus link initial attachment assessments to indicators of relationships assessed 14 years later.

Attachment history also was related to cognitive measures of adolescent experience. Among reunion participants who were interviewed concerning their knowledge of the peer group relationship structure, those with secure histories demonstrated superior knowledge and perceptiveness (Weinfield, Ogawa, & Sroufe, in press). In interviews conducted with all participants at age 16, a friendship intimacy index, based on "closeness" and "coherence of discourse" scales, was significantly related to a history of secure attachment. (Interview information concerning dating will be discussed later.)

These findings illustrate the importance of assessing both parent and peer relationships in research on the development of romantic relationships. Assessing relationships with peers during adolescence requires methods that are different both from those appropriate for parents and adolescents and from those that are valuable in research with peers during childhood. Hartup's (1996) admonition that multiple aspects of friendship are needed to comprehend their developmental significance implies that subjective, as well as observable, qualities of these relationships should be considered. Interviews with children and adolescents about peer relationships are particularly valuable sources of information about representations. Although more difficult, especially among older children and adolescents, direct observations of peer interaction also yield information about potential characteristics of later romantic relationships. For example, in an observational study with preadolescents, Cooper and Ayers-Lopez (1985) detected patterns of control and autonomy in interactions with peers that were similar to those observed in interactions between the same children and their parents. Observational studies also have revealed meaningful behavioral differences during a dyadic task among pairs of children and preadolescents previously identified as friends or acquaintances. These differences appear to be related partly to contrasting degrees of intimacy and felt security between partners (e.g., Daiute, Hartup, Sholl, & Zajac, 1993; Nelson & Aboud, 1985; Newcomb, Brady, & Hartup, 1979). Finally, observations of adolescents in larger groups may provide valuable information about aspects of functioning in the social crowds in which dating relationships are embedded (e.g., Englund, Levy, & Hyson, 1997).

Implications of Relationship History for Adolescent Intimacy and Romantic Relationships

Despite the stereotype of adolescence as "the age of sexual attraction and emergent love" (Zani, 1993), research on the transition to romantic relationships during adolescence is in its infancy. Consequently, we can only speculate about how such experiences may be linked to relationship history.

In this section, we consider three phenomena that are commonly considered part of the development of romantic relationships: dating; committed relationships, or those that are perceived as romantic (i.e., going steady or believing that one is in a relationship with at least some long-term potential); and becoming sexually active. For each of these topics, we address three key questions: (1) What is known about normative patterns for this form of romantic or proto-romantic involvement? (2) To what degree and in what ways might variations in the capacity for intimacy be manifested within these normative patterns? (3) How might variations in relationship history be associated with variations in the phenomena of adolescent relationships?

Dating

Dating usually stems from involvement with social crowds and is frequently no more than transitory and/or opportunistic affiliation, with no anticipation of the longer-term involvement that marks romantic relationships. Dating typically begins in junior high school (for reviews, see Savin-Williams & Berndt, 1990; Zani, 1993). Although often attributed to hormonal changes at puberty, dating in early adolescence actually appears to be governed largely by age-graded social expectations (e.g., Dornbusch et al., 1981). Roscoe, Diana, and Brooks (1987) reported that early and middle adolescents (i.e., 6th to 11th graders) in the midwestern United States say that they date as a form of recreation, to establish a special relationship with another person, and to gain status with their peers. In contrast, college students gave greater emphasis to intimacy, companionship, and socialization to relationships as reasons for dating. Although little is known about dating among gay, lesbian, and bisexual adolescents, social benefits such as enhanced peer status are probably less powerful inducements for them, whereas a desire for intimacy may be a relatively greater motivation than in heterosexual dating couples.

Historically, dating was highly ritualized and governed by extensively prescribed social expectations, and that is still true in some cultures.

Among U.S. adolescents, however, dating increasingly is an informal activity that often is carried out in connection with group activities and is marked by relatively superficial interactions between the participants (Douvan & Adelson, 1966; Miller & Gordon, 1986). Whether or not an adolescent dates and when dating begins are probably more highly related to general social competence and acceptance by peers than to a capacity for intimacy.

Several contrasts among the peer relations of children with different attachment histories probably forecast their dating experiences. Children with secure attachment histories have consistently been found to be highest in popularity with peers, mastery of social skills, and positive engagement in peer-group activities. Attachment theory implies that these characteristics likely reflect relationships with caregivers that foster positive expectancies about interactions with others and a sense of self-worth and efficacy.

These characteristics of individuals with secure histories carry several implications for dating. One is that early adolescents with such histories are relatively likely to be affiliated with crowds and thus have ready support and social "cover" for dating (Brown, Eicher, & Petrie, 1986; Dunphy, 1963). As extensive involvement with crowds diminishes normatively in middle and later adolescence, the stage is set for securely attached individuals to move smoothly toward increasingly intimate relationships with smaller groups of friends and romantic partners. A second implication is that securely attached individuals enter adolescence with relatively high self-esteem, which is generally correlated with involvement in dating (Long, 1983, 1989; Samet & Kelly, 1987). High self-esteem may support appropriate assertiveness and self-confidence with potential dating partners and also may protect against negative emotional effects of such common experiences as rejection and competition (Mathes, Adams, & Davis, 1985). Third, securely attached children's generally higher levels of general social skills, popularity, and perceived social competence probably portend smooth, on-time transitions to social groups that can facilitate dating (e.g., Coleman & Hendry, 1990; Miller, 1990). Finally, those with secure attachment histories will be more oriented toward the emotional depth that comes from ongoing, more durable relationships.

Preliminary data from the Minnesota longitudinal study support some of these theoretical links. In our camp reunions at age 15, crowdlike phenomena occurred; that is, a defined group emerged that included couples and other adolescents of both genders who consistently interacted across the days of the reunion. Each counselor independently completed sociograms, which showed remarkable concordance regarding membership in the crowd. In the camp where this phenomenon was most clear, all eight members of the crowd had secure histories, whereas none of the six with anxious attachment histories were part of the crowd (Sroufe et al., 1993).

In dating interviews with the total sample at age 16, participants with histories of anxious-resistant attachment were significantly less likely to have dated. This is consistent with the history of social immaturity of these children documented earlier. Those with secure and avoidant histories were similarly active in dating at age 16. Those with secure histories, however, were significantly more likely to have consistently dated the same person for 3 months, in accord with their theoretically predicted orientation toward depth and intimacy. Recent data analyses also reveal that aspects of peer competence in middle childhood forecast qualities of dating (Hennighausen, 1996). In particular, for girls, gender boundary maintenance in middle childhood (a measure of competence at that age) predicted more security and disclosure in dating relationships. Boundary maintenance also predicted later age of onset of sexual intercourse and more frequent use of contraception. For boys, a measure of boundary violation in middle childhood predicted a pattern of sexual promiscuity (i.e., a relatively large number of reported sexual partners but not closeness in dating relationships).

Relationship history also may provide clues to the likely selection of dating partners. Like the social context in which dating is embedded, selection follows in predictable ways from the salient social motives of different phases of adolescent development. Early adolescents, consistent with their emphasis on the social activity and status benefits of dating, place relatively greater emphasis than older adolescents on superficial features of potential partners (e.g., fashionable clothes) and approval by others (e.g., well liked by peers). In contrast, late adolescents give more weight to personality characteristics (Roscoe et al., 1987).

These normatively preferred attributes (e.g., Zani, 1993) may be especially influential in early adolescence, when social expectations govern much dating behavior. Findings from our studies of friendship pairings in childhood lead us to believe, however, that individual differences in preferences are likely, perhaps increasingly so in middle and late adolescence. Our observation of peer relationships in preschool and middle childhood showed that securely attached partners interact smoothly with others having both secure and anxious-resistant relationship histories. With anxious-avoidant partners, however, even secure children have difficulties. Pairs of securely attached children easily create a balance between connectedness and autonomy for each child, whereas pairs of either anxious-resistant or anxious-avoidant children differ in the salience of connectedness versus autonomy. Relationship history thus may affect what characteristics likely make a potential dating partner more or less salient among other eligible partners.

Finally, the relation of adolescent dating to social crowds is both an advantage and a source of controversy and tension in relationships. Pairing off can lead to increased isolation from the group and difficulty in balancing the demands of couplehood with those of group activities and relationships (Surra, 1990; Zani, 1993). Relationship history likely sets the stage for coping with these inevitable tensions. Even in middle childhood, anxiously attached pairs had notably greater difficulty in maintaining this balance than securely attached pairs (Shulman et al., 1994).

In short, attachment history is probably linked to dating experiences in ways that are similar to its association with other aspects of peer affiliation. For heterosexual adolescents, availability of same-gender associates decreases as more and more couples are formed, thus increasing pressure on the norms for selecting dating partners. A fruitful approach to supplementing the current paucity of research findings on selection of dating partners may be to examine similarities and differences between selecting dating partners and selecting friends during childhood and adolescence.

Committed Relationships

The designation *committed relationships* refers to pairings that are marked by greater expectation of sustained involvement by both partners than is the case with dating relationships (Diamond et al., this volume). According to contemporary norms in the United States, if romantic partners are not currently sexually active with each other, they are likely either to anticipate sexual relations in the future or to be actively delaying it until some later stage of the relationship (engagement or marriage) (Katchadourian, 1990).

Adolescents' self-reported experiences of love and related emotions are remarkably similar to the reported experiences of adults, according to recent findings from an ethnically and socioeconomically diverse sample of high-school students (Levesque, 1993). Just as with adults, adolescents' satisfaction with relationships was positively correlated with passion, giving and getting communication, commitment, emotional support, and togetherness. In Levesque's sample, adolescent relationships were also characterized by measures of extremity of positive emotion: feelings of exhilaration, growth, appreciation, and specialness. These adolescents' satisfactions were less related, however, to negative affect, perceived trouble, or conflict – variables that are inversely related in adults' reports of their romantic relationships (Surra, 1990). These findings await replication, but the initial patterns suggest that entry into romantic relationships may conform to the popular stereotype that "young love" is rosily optimistic.

For our purposes, the most important normative distinction between dating and romantic relationships is the relatively greater degree of intimacy between romantic partners (Reis & Shaver, 1988). Relationships can, by definition, be close (i.e., experience high levels of contact and causal interdependence) without being intimate (i.e., mutually perceiving understanding, validation, and caring from each other) (Reis & Patrick, 1996). Research findings with adults indicate that intimacy, in this sense, differentiates well-functioning romantic relationships from less well-functioning ones (for a review, see Berscheid & Reis, 1998).

Similarly, adolescent couples, like adult romantic partners, vary in the degree of intimacy attained. The data outlined earlier, although concluding in midadolescence and not focused on romantic relationships, lead us to predict that intimacy in adult relationships will be based on the foundation provided by earlier family and peer experiences. Those with secure attachment histories had deeper relationships with peers in preschool, more intense friendships in middle childhood (and commonly with other children similarly oriented), and more capacity for emotional vulnerability and sustained dating relationships in adolescence than those with histories of anxious attachment. Moreover, the quality of their peer relationships, when directly assessed in middle childhood, revealed a capacity for simultaneous autonomy and connectedness that we see as prerequisite for intimacy.

Forecasting from these findings, future research likely will reveal that intimacy with romantic partners is a joint function of contrasting caregiving histories and their functional sequelae in peer relationships in childhood and adolescence. One recent study, using the well-validated Adult Attachment Interview (Main & Goldwyn, in press) as a measure of the individual's attachment representations, is suggestive (Owens et al., 1996). These authors found that differences in security on the AAI were related to both descriptions of romantic relationships and behavior with romantic partners. Other cross-sectional research with adults shows that self-report measures of adult attachment styles are correlated with concurrent self-reported differences in characteristics of romantic relationships, including orientations to intimacy (Feeney & Noller, 1990). Secure subjects obtained low scores for avoidance of intimacy, whereas avoidant adults scored high on this measure. Investigators using other attachment-style instruments also report correlations between attachment representation and aspects of romantic relationships (Cohn, Silver, Cowan, Cowan, & Pearson, 1992; Collins & Read, 1990; Feeney & Noller, 1990; Hazan & Shaver, 1987; Pearson, Cohn, Cowan, & Cowan, 1994; Simpson, Rholes, & Nelligan, 1992). Although the measures of attachment style used in these studies cannot be equated either to early measures of attachment security such as the Strange Situation or to the Adult Attachment Interview, the results are consistent with what might be expected if appropriate measures were used in a longitudinal design. Even stronger relations across time might be expected with measures of closeness in childhood and adolescent peer relationships as additional predictors.

Becoming Sexually Active

Conceptually, sexual activity is distinguishable from both dating and committed relationships, but empirically, the differing types of relationships are significantly interrelated. Most researchers agree, based on somewhat dated evidence, that first heterosexual intercourse occurs on the average at about 16 and that it usually takes place in the context of a steady relationship (for a review, see Katchadourian, 1990). This generalization clearly does not capture the experiences of adolescents in all ethnic and cultural groups (Moore & Erickson, 1985) or those of acknowledged gay, lesbian, and bisexual youth (Savin-Williams, 1998).

Many adolescents, nevertheless, experience sexual activity as part of a dating relationship or as a transitory encounter with little connection to ongoing social relationships. Such experiences may involve relatively low levels of emotional intimacy and commitment (Diamond et al., this volume). Relationships in which sexual activity is the primary aspect nevertheless may arise for psychological reasons. Adolescents may hope that such relationships will cause them to feel, or to be perceived as, more mature, enhance their social prestige, or compensate for a lack of intimacy in their lives (Martin, 1982; Tripp, 1975). Some may use sexual relationships as a way of exploring or testing their sexual identity (Savin-Williams, 1994, 1998). Diamond et al. (this volume) suggest that such primarily sexual liaisons may be especially likely among gay, lesbian, and bisexual teenagers, who often fear the more public nature of dating and romantic relationships.

Relationship history, incorporating both caregiver and later peer relationships, may be associated both with the likelihood of a primarily sexual relationship and with the timing of beginning sexual intercourse.

Involvement in one or more sexual relationships, as opposed to romantic involvements, at any age is likely to be correlated with consistent patterns of insecure attachment. In individuals with anxious-avoidant histories, such a pattern would likely reflect avoidance of intimacy or an inadequate capacity for intimacy, even if desired. Such individuals demonstrate a tendency toward suspicion, jealousy, and unavailability that would likely impede true intimacy. In the case of anxious-resistant attachments, tendencies toward excessive dependency and anxiety, along with low self-confidence and poor regulation of affect, would interfere with the mutuality that supports intimate relationships.

Early transitions to sexual activity (i.e., becoming sexually active at age 15 or younger) are associated with broad-band assessments of personality similar to those that characterize differences among secure and insecure individuals. Jessor and his colleagues (Jessor, Costa, Jessor, & Donovan, 1983; Jessor, Donovan, & Costa, 1991) found that early-active adolescents, compared to later-active ones, placed higher value on noninterference by adults, professed less conventional values, and made earlier transitions to other behaviors that are tolerated in adults but not in early adolescents (e.g., alcohol use, smoking). Some adolescents who manifest these values undoubtedly have experienced secure, responsive relationships, but with socially unconventional parents; or they may have been reared in a community that is skeptical of conventional values. Conversely, many teenagers who show highly conventional behaviors may have experienced insecure relationships in their earlier lives. The pattern described by Jessor and colleagues is characteristic, however, of individuals identified in longitudinal research as having had insecure relationships with caregivers in infancy and poorly functioning relationships with peers in preschool and middle childhood. These links may be attributed to general patterns of social incompetence or pathology, or they may be seen as indications of continuity in the relationship patterns of individuals across time. Such coherence is consistent with relationship histories that have not supported the development of a capacity for intimacy.

The Minnesota longitudinal study will include data on dating, romantic relationships, and sexuality from our participants at age 19. Participants could respond with respect either to heterosexual or nonheterosexual partners. We expect that those who were securely attached more often will see intimacy as the foundation for sexuality and, moreover, will regard sexuality as having a role in deepening intimacy. Although these late adolescents certainly may explore their sexuality in less intimate relationships, they are unlikely to be promiscuous or casual regarding sexuality.

Conclusion

These speculative links between relationship history, the capacity for intimacy, and likely variations among aspects of romantic relationships could constitute a daunting research agenda. Yet they lie at the heart of widely held and compelling beliefs about the links between love in childhood and in adulthood.

Developmental research on romantic relationships must include multiple longitudinal assessments of parent–child relationships, peer relationships, and relationship representations. With such data, one can determine whether early attachment experiences predict adult relationship qualities beyond predictions from later family experiences, how predictions from attachment measures fare in comparison to peer data, and whether both family and peer data make independent contributions. Comprehensive information eventually also will permit us to address process issues such as whether attachment experiences are mediated through peer relationships and whether representations are indeed the carriers of relationship experiences across phases of development.

This framework for collecting data affords both the most comprehensive basis and the most promising prospect for establishing a link between early and intermediate close relationships and the emergence of romantic relationships during adolescence. Without intervening measures of experiences and representation, questions of how much of the relation between infant and adult measures is direct or how much is mediated cannot be addressed, nor can questions concerning change in internal working models or the relation between changing models and changing relationship experiences. These alternative explanations must be examined if we are to understand how learning to love permeates the course of human development.

References

Ainsworth, M. D. S. (1989). Attachments beyond infancy. *American Psychologist, 44,* 709–716.

Ainsworth, M. D. S., Blehar, M., Waters, E., & Wall, S. (1978). *Patterns of attachment.* Hillsdale, NJ: Erlbaum.

Baumeister, R. F., & Leary, M. R. (1995). The need to belong: Desire for interpersonal attachments as a fundamental human motive. *Psychological Bulletin, 117*(3), 497–529.

Berndt, T. J., Hawkins, J. A., & Hoyle, S. G. (1986). Changes in friendship during a school year: Effects on children's and adolescents' impressions of friendship and sharing with friends. *Child Development, 57,* 1284–1297.

Berndt, T. J., & Hoyle, S. G. (1985). Stability and change in childhood and adolescent friendships. *Developmental Psychology, 21,* 1007–1015.

Berndt, T. J., & Keefe, K. (1995). Friends' influence on adolescents' adjustment to school. *Child Development, 66*(5), 1312–1329.

Berscheid, E., & Reis, H. T. (1998). Attraction and close relationships. In S. Fiske (Ed.), *Handbook of social psychology* (4th ed., pp. 193–281). New York: Addison-Wesley.

Bowlby, J. (1973). *Separation.* New York: Basic Books.

Brown, B. B., Eicher, S. A., & Petrie, S. (1986). The importance of peer group affiliation in adolescence. *Journal of Adolescence, 9,* 73–96.

Cohn, D. A., Silver, D. H., Cowan, C. P., Cowan, P. A., & Pearson, J. (1992). Working models of childhood attachment and couple relationships. *Journal of Family Issues, 13,* 432–449.

Coleman, J. C., & Hendry, L. (1990). *The nature of adolescence* (2nd ed.). London: Routledge.

Collins, N. L., & Read, S. J. (1990). Adult attachment, working models, and relationship quality in dating couples. *Journal of Personality and Social Psychology, 58,* 644–663.

Collins, W. A. (1995). Relationships and development: Family adaptation to individual change. In S. Shulman (Ed.), *Close relationships and socioemotional development* (pp. 128–154). New York: Ablex.

Collins, W. A. (1996). Relationships and development during adolescence: Interpersonal adaptation to individual change. *Personal Relationships, 3,* 308–318.

Collins, W. A., & Repinski, D. J. (1994). Relationships during adolescence: Continuity and change in interpersonal perspective. In R. Montemayor, G. Adams, & T. Gullotta (Eds.), *Advances in adolescent development: Volume 5. Personal relationships during adolescence* (pp. 7–36). Thousand Oaks, CA: Sage.

Cooper, C., & Ayers-Lopez, S. (1985). Family and peer systems in early adolescence: New models of the role of relationships in development. *Journal of Early Adolescence, 5,* 9–22.

Daiute, C., Hartup, W. W., Sholl, W., & Zajac, R. (1993, March). *Peer collaboration and written language development: A study of friends and acquaintances.* Paper presented at the meeting of the Society for Research in Child Development, New Orleans, LA.

Dornbusch, S. M., Carlsmith, J. M., Gross, R. T., Martin, J. A., Jennings, D., Rosenberg, A., & Duke, P. (1981). Sexual development, age, and dating: A comparison of biological and social influences upon one set of behaviors. *Child Development, 52,* 179–185.

Douvan, E., & Adelson, J. (1966). *The adolescent experience.* New York: Wiley.

Dunphy, D. (1963). The social structure of urban adolescent peer groups. *Sociometry, 26,* 230–246.

Egeland, B., & Brunnquell, D. (1979). An at-risk approach to the study of child abuse: Some preliminary findings. *Journal of the American Academy of Child Psychiatry, 18,* 219–225.

Elicker, J., Englund, M., & Sroufe, L. A. (1992). Predicting peer competence and peer relationships in childhood from early parent–child relationships. In R. Parke & G. Ladd (Eds.), *Family–peer relationships: Modes of linkage* (pp. 77–106). Hillsdale, NJ: Erlbaum.

Englund, M., Levy, A., & Hyson, D. (1997, April). *Development of adolescent social competence: A prospective study of family and peer contributions.* Poster presented at the biennial meeting of the Society for Research on Child Development, Washington, DC.

Feeney, J. A., & Noller, P. (1990). Attachment style as a predictor of adult romantic relationships. *Journal of Personality and Social Psychology, 58,* 281–291.

Furman, W., & Buhrmester, D. (1992). Age and sex differences in perceptions of networks of personal relationships. *Child Development, 63,* 103–115.

Furman, W., & Wehner, E. (1994). Romantic views: Toward a theory of adolescent romantic relationships. In R. Montemayor, G. R. Adams, & T. P. Gullotta (Eds.), *Advances in adolescent development: Volume 6, Personal relationships during adolescence* (pp. 168–195). Thousand Oaks, CA: Sage.

Hartup, W. W. (1992). Friendships and their developmental significance. In H. McGurk (Ed.), *Contemporary issues in childhood social development* (pp. 175–205). London: Routledge.

Hartup, W. W. (1996). The company they keep: Friendships and their developmental significance. *Child Development, 67,* 1–13.

Hazan, C., & Shaver, P. (1987). Romantic love conceptualized as an attachment process. *Journal of Personality and Social Psychology, 52,* 511–524.

Henninghausen, K. C. (1996). *Connecting preadolescent gender boundary behavior to adolescent dating and sexual activity.* Predoctoral research paper, Institute of Child Development, University of Minnesota–Twin Cities.

Holmbeck, G. N. (1996). A model of family relational transformations during the transition to adolescence: Parent–adolescent conflict and adaptation. In J. A. Graber, J. Brooks-Gunn, & A. C. Petersen (Eds.), *Transitions through adolescence: Interpersonal domains and contexts* (167–200). Mahwah, NJ: Erlbaum.

Jessor, R., Costa, F., Jessor, L., & Donovan, J. E. (1983). The time of first intercourse: A prospective study. *Journal of Personality and Social Psychology, 44,* 608–626.

Jessor, R., Donovan, J., & Costa, F. (1991). *Beyond adolescence: Problem behavior and young adult development.* New York: Cambridge University Press.

Kagan, J., Reznick, J., & Gibbons, J. (1989). Inhibited and uninhibited types of children. *Child Development, 60,* 838–845.

Katchadourian, H. (1990). Sexuality. In S. S. Feldman & G. R. Elliott (Eds.), *At the threshold: The developing adolescent* (pp. 330–351). Cambridge, MA: Harvard University Press.

Kestenbaum, R., Farber, E., & Sroufe, L. A. (1989). Individual differences in empathy among preschoolers: Relation to attachment history. In N. Eisenberg (Ed.), *Empathy and related emotional responses* (pp. 51–56). San Francisco: Jossey-Bass.

Lamb, M. (1984). Fathers, mothers and childcare in the 1980s: Family influences on child development. In K. Borman, D. Quarm, & S. Gideonese (Eds.), *Women in the workplace* (pp. 61–88). Norwood, NJ: Ablex.

Laursen, B., & Collins, W. A. (1994). Interpersonal conflict during adolescence. *Psychological Bulletin, 115*(2), 197–209.

Levesque, R. J. R. (1993). The romantic experience of adolescents in satisfying love relationships. *Journal of Youth and Adolescence, 22,* 219–251.

Lewis, M. (1989). Commentary. *Human Development, 32,* 216–222.

Liberman, A. F. (1977). Preschoolers' competence with a peer: Relations with attachment and peer experience. *Child Development, 48,* 1277–1287.

Long, B. H. (1983). A steady boyfriend: A step toward resolution of the intimacy crisis for American college women. *Journal of Psychology, 115,* 275–280.

Long, B. H. (1989). Heterosexual involvement of unmarried undergraduate females in relation to self-evaluations. *Journal of Youth and Adolescence, 18,* 489–500.

Maccoby, E. E. (1990). Gender and relationships. *American Psychologist, 45,* 513–520.

MacDonald, K. (1992). Warmth as a developmental construct. *Child Development, 63,* 753–773.

Main, M., & Goldwyn, R. (in press). Adult Attachment Scoring and Classification System. In M. Main (Ed.), *Assessing attachment through discourse, drawings and reunion situations.* New York: Cambridge University Press.

Martin, A. D. (1982). Learning to hide: The socialization of the gay adolescent. *Adolescent Psychiatry, 10,* 52–65.

Mathes, E. W., Adams, H. E., & Davis, R. M. (1985). Jealousy: Loss of relationship rewards, loss of self-esteem, depression, anxiety and anger. *Journal of Personality and Social Psychology, 48,* 1552–1561.

Miller, K. E. (1990). Adolescents' same-sex and opposite-sex peer relations: Sex differences in popularity, perceived social competence and social cognitive skills. *Journal of Adolescent Research, 5,* 222–241.

Miller, R., & Gordon, M. (1986). The decline in formal dating: A study in six Connecticut high schools. *Marriage and Family Review, 10,* 139–156.

Moore, D. S., & Erickson, P. I. (1985). Age, gender, and ethnic differences in sexual and contraceptive knowledge, attitudes, and behavior. *Family and Community Health, 8,* 38–51.

Nelson, J., & Aboud, F. E. (1985). The resolution of social conflict between friends. *Child Development, 56,* 1009–1017.

Newcomb, A. F., Brady, J., & Hartup, W. W. (1979). Friendship and incentive condition as determinants of children's task-oriented social behavior. *Child Development, 50,* 878–881.

Offer, D. (1969). *The psychological world of the teenager.* New York: Basic Books.

Offer, D., Ostrov, E., & Howard, K. (1981). *The adolescent: A psychological self-portrait.* New York: Basic Books.

Ostoja, E. (1996). *Developmental antecedents of friendship competence in adolescence: The roles of early adaptational history and middle childhood peer competence.* Doctoral dissertation, University of Minnesota, Minneapolis.

Owens, G., Crowell, J., Pan, H., Treboux, D., O'Connor, E., & Waters, E. (1996). *The prototype hypothesis and the origins of attachment working models: Adult relationships with parents and romantic relationships.* In E. Waters, B. Vaughn, G. Posada, & K. Kondo-Ikemura (Eds.), *New growing points of attachment. Monographs of the Society for Research in Child Development.* Serial No. 244 (Vol. 60, pp. 216–233).

Pancake, V. R. (1985, April). *Continuity between mother–infant attachment and ongoing dyadic peer relationships in preschool.* Paper presented at the biennial meeting of the Society for Research in Child Development, Toronto.

Pearson, J. L., Cohn, D. A., Cowan, P. A., & Cowan, C. P. (1994). Earned- and continuous-security in adult attachment: Relation to depressive symptomatology and parenting style. *Development and Psychopathology, 6,* 359–373.

Pianta, R., Sroufe, L. A., & Egeland, B. (1989). Continuity and discontinuity in maternal sensitivity at 6, 24, and 42 months in a high risk sample. *Child Development, 60*(2), 481–487.

Reis, H. T., & Patrick, B. C. (1996). Attachment and intimacy: Component processes. In A. Kruglanski & E. T. Higgins (Eds.), *Social psychology: Handbook of basic principles* (pp. 523–526). New York: Guilford Press.

Reis, H. T., & Shaver, P. (1988). Intimacy as an interpersonal process. In S. W. Duck (Ed.), *Handbook of personal relationships* (pp. 367–389). New York: Wiley.

Roscoe, B., Diana, M. S., & Brooks, R. H. (1987). Early, middle and late adolescents' views on dating and factors influencing partner selection. *Adolescence, 22,* 59–68.

Rosenberg, D. M. (1984). *The quality and content of preschool fantasy play: Correlates in concurrent social-personality function and early mother–child attachment relationships.* Unpublished doctoral dissertation, University of Minnesota.

Samet, N., & Kelly, E. W. (1987). The relationship of steady dating to self-esteem and sex role identity among adolescents. *Adolescence, 22,* 231–245.

Savin-Williams, R. C. (1994). Verbal and physical abuse as stressors in the lives of lesbian, gay male, and bisexual youths: Associations with school problems, running away, substance abuse, prostitution, and suicide. *Journal of Consulting and Clinical Psychology, 62,* 261–269.

Savin-Williams, R. C. (1998). *And then I became gay: Stories from the lives of gay and bisexual youths.* New York: Routledge.

Savin-Williams, R. C., & Berndt, T. J. (1990). Friendship and peer relations. In S. S. Feldman & G. R. Elliott (Eds.), *At the threshold: The developing adolescent* (pp. 277–307). Cambridge, MA: Harvard University Press.

Sharabany, R., Gershoni, R., & Hofman, J. (1981). Girlfriend, boyfriend: Age and sex differences in intimate friendship. *Developmental Psychology, 27,* 800–808.

Shulman, S., Elicker, J., & Sroufe, L. A. (1994). Stages of friendship growth in preadolescence as related to attachment history. *Journal of Social and Personal Relationships, 11,* 341–361.

Simpson, J. A., Rholes, W. S., & Nelligan, J. S. (1992). Support seeking and support giving within couples in an anxiety-provoking situation: The role of attachment styles. *Journal of Personality and Social Psychology, 62,* 434–446.

Sroufe, L. A. (1983) Infant–caregiver attachment and patterns of adaptation in preschool: The roots of maladaptation and competence. In M. Perlmutter (Ed.), *Minnesota symposium in child psychology* (Vol. 16, pp. 41–83). Hillsdale, NJ: Erlbaum.

Sroufe, L. A. (1995, March). *Evaluating the role of early experience in adult love relationships.* Discussant paper presented at the biennial meeting of the Society for Research in Child Development, Indianapolis.

Sroufe, L. A., Carlson, E., & Shulman, S. (1993). The development of individuals in relationships: From infancy through adolescence. In D. C. Funder, R. Parke, C. Tomlinson-Keasey, & K. Widaman (Eds.), *Studying lives through time: Approaches to personality and development* (pp. 315–342). Washington, DC: American Psychological Association.

Sroufe, L. A., Egeland, B., & Carlson, E. (in press). One social world. In W. A. Collins & B. Laursen (Eds.), *Relationships as developmental contexts: The Minnesota Symposia on Child Psychology* (Vol. 29). Mahwah, NJ: Erlbaum.

Sroufe, L. A., Egeland, B., & Kreutzer, T. (1990). The fate of early experience following developmental change: Longitudinal approaches to individual adaptation in childhood. *Child Development, 61,* 1363–1373.

Sroufe, L. A., & Fleeson, J. (1986). Attachment and the construction of relationships. In W. Hartup & Z. Rubin (Eds.), *Relationships and development* (pp. 51–71). Hillsdale, NJ: Erlbaum.

Sroufe, L. A., & Fleeson, J. (1988). The coherence of family relationships. In R. A. Hinde & J. Stevenson-Hinde (Eds.), *Relationships within families: Mutual influences* (pp. 27–47). Oxford: Oxford University Press.

Sroufe, L. A., Fox, N., & Pancake, V. (1983). Attachment and dependency in developmental perspective. *Child Development, 54,* 1614–1627.

Sroufe, L. A., Schork, E., Motti, E., Lawroski, N., & LaFreniere, P. (1984). The role of affect in social competence. In C. Izard, J. Kagan, & R. Zajonc (Eds.), *Emotional cognition and behavior* (pp. 289–319). New York: Plenum.

Steinberg, L. (1990). Interdependency in the family: Autonomy, conflict, and harmony in the parent–adolescent relationship. In S. Feldman & G. Elliot (Eds.), *At the threshold: The developing adolescent* (pp. 225–276). Cambridge, MA: Harvard University Press.

Suess, G. J. (1987). *Auswirkungen frukindlicher Bindungserfabrungen auf die Kompetenz im Kindergarten* [Consequences of early attachment experiences on competence in preschool]. Unpublished doctoral dissertation, Universitat Regensburg, Regensburg, Germany.

Suess, G. J., Grossman, K. E., & Sroufe, L. A. (1993). Effects of infant attachment to mother and father on quality of adaptation in preschool: From dyadic to individual organization of self. *International Journal of Behavioral Development, 15*(1), 43–66.

Surra, C. A. (1990). Research and theory on mate selection and premarital relationships in the 1980s. *Journal of Marriage and the Family, 52,* 844–865.

Tripp, C. A. (1975). *The homosexual matrix.* New York: McGraw-Hill.

Troy, M., & Sroufe, L. A. (1987). Victimization among preschoolers: The role of attachment relationship history. *Journal of the American Academy of Child and Adolescent Psychiatry, 26*(2), 166–172.

Weinfield, N., Ogawa, J., & Sroufe, L. A. (in press). Early attachment as a pathway to adolescent peer competence. *Journal of Research on Adolescence.*

Zani, B. (1993). Dating and interpersonal relationship in adolescence. In S. Jackson & H. Rodriguez-Tome (Eds.), *Adolescence and its social worlds* (pp. 95–119). Hillsdale, NJ: Erlbaum.

7 Rejection Sensitivity and Adolescent Romantic Relationships

Geraldine Downey, Cheryl Bonica, and Claudia Rincón

A key function of romantic relationships is to make people feel accepted and loved, thus promoting well-being. Yet, many relationships do not serve this function. Adults give relationship difficulties as the most common reason for seeking therapy (Veroff, Kulka, & Douvan, 1981). People in conflicted marriages are often depressed (Coyne, Downey, & Boergers, 1994), and intimate violence is a leading cause of injuries to both adult and adolescent women (Browne, 1993; Centers for Disease Control, 1990). Because troubled romantic relationships are both pervasive and costly, there is considerable interest in understanding how relationships are undermined.

Initially, research on the causes of troubled intimate relationships focused on married couples. It is now clear that the destructive interactional patterns that undermine marriages are evident in adult dating relationships and may be present in adolescent relationships. Intimate violence is a case in point. Minor dating violence precedes serious marital violence in 25% to 50% of cases (Gayford, 1975; O'Leary & Arias, 1988; Roscoe & Benaske, 1985). The level of violence in adult dating relationships is similar to that found in marital relationships (Sugarman & Hotaling, 1989). Reported rates of dating violence in high school students range from 9% to 45% (Bergman, 1992; Downey, Lebolt, & O'Shea-Lauber, 1995; Henton, Cate, Koval, Lloyd, & Christopher, 1983; Molidor, 1993; O'Keefe, Brockopp, & Chew, 1986; Roscoe & Callahan, 1985; Roscoe, & Kelsey, 1986). In research with middle school children, we have found that 9% reported the use of physical aggression in their romantic relationships (Purdie, Downey & Bonica 1999).

This research was supported by grants from the National Institute of Mental Health (R29-MH51113), the Harry Frank Guggenheim Foundation, and a W.T. Grant Faculty Scholar Award.

148

The recognition that violence occurs in adolescent romantic relationships has helped prompt research on these relationships. Because adolescence is the time when romantic relationships typically begin, this is when the legacy of troubled family and peer relationships for romantic relationships may be first evident. Yet, although destructive relationship processes may emerge in adolescents, these processes are likely to be less ingrained than in adulthood. This means that adolescence may be a particularly opportune time for targeting interventions designed to promote healthy relationship skills in individuals at risk for troubled romantic relationships. A requisite preliminary step in the development of effective interventions involves answering the following questions: (a) What do adolescents bring with them from prior relationships that might undermine their romantic relationships? (b) What experiences in adolescent relationships can challenge the malevolent psychological legacy of past troubled relationships? The goal of this chapter is to describe our approach to answering these questions.

Rejection Sensitivity and Adolescent Romantic Relationships

Influenced by classical interpersonal theories (Bowlby, 1969, 1973, 1980; Erikson, 1950; Horney, 1937; Sullivan, 1953), we propose that a key way in which past relationships can influence adolescent romantic relationships is through their impact on expectations of attaining acceptance and avoiding rejection (Downey & Feldman, 1996; Downey, Feldman, Khuri, & Friedman, 1994; Feldman & Downey, 1994). An adolescent who has developed defensive (anxious or angry) expectations of rejection as a result of having experienced rejection, initially from parents and subsequently from peers, will be more sensitive to rejection from a romantic partner. We have termed individuals who anxiously or angrily expect, readily perceive, and react intensely to rejection as being *rejection sensitive*. We view rejection sensitivity as a cognitive-affective processing system (Mischel & Shoda, 1995) that originates in rejecting experiences and becomes activated in social situations where rejection is possible, influencing the course of the interaction in ways that may confirm and thus maintain rejection expectations. Our basic model is presented in Figure 7.1.

How does the rejection-sensitive adolescent approach the task of forming and managing romantic relationships? To shield the self from the rejection that is expected and feared, the youth may avoid or limit involvement and investment in romantic relationships. However, this strategy entails lost opportunities for attaining the sense of being accepted that has been miss-

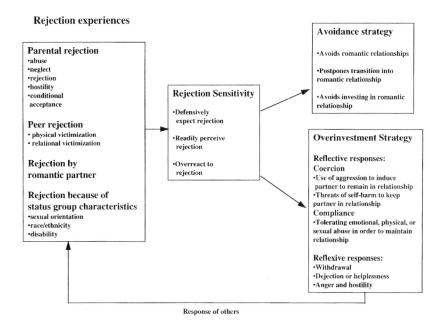

Figure 7.1. Implications of rejection sensitivity for adolescent romantic relationships.

ing from the adolescent's life. Also lost are opportunities for developing and refining important relationship skills, such as those involved in intimacy, sharing, autonomy, and self-disclosure.

Alternatively, the adolescent can enter into a romantic relationship hopeful that it will provide the acceptance absent from previous relationships. However, defensive expectations of rejection will make the adolescent hypervigilant for signs of rejection, such as the partner's being inattentive or being friendly to a potential rival. When even minimal or ambiguous rejection cues are detected, the adolescent will readily perceive intentional rejection and feel rejected. The perceived rejection can prompt intense affective and behavioral reactions, including hostility, despondence, withdrawal, or inappropriate efforts to regain acceptance. These types of responses to perceived rejection are likely to undermine relationships, thus fulfilling expectations of rejection.

Because no one is immune to rejection experiences, everyone will develop to some extent the cognitive-affective processing disposition that we have outlined. We consider rejection sensitivity to be on a continuum, and this assumption is reflected in the way we measure it (for details, see Downey & Feldman, 1996; Downey, Lebolt, Rincón, & Freitas, 1998). The people we characterize as rejection sensitive differ from the more typical person in the level of their defensive expectations of rejection, in their readiness to perceive rejection and in the intensity of their reaction to rejection.

We view defensive expectations of rejection as being at the core of rejection sensitivity and assume that these expectations are particularly likely to be activated in situations where the person is dependent on a significant/important other for something. These assumptions are reflected in our operationalization of the construct in the form of the Rejection Sensitivity Questionnaire (RSQ) (Downey & Feldman, 1996). The following is a sample situation from our late adolescent questionnaire: "Your boy/girlfriend has plans to go out with friends tonight, but you really want to spend the evening with him/her, and you tell him/her so." Individuals are asked (a) whether a significant other would be likely to agree to this request and (b) how concerned or anxious (or angry) they would be about the answer to their request. In keeping with an expectancy-value formulation, people's expectancies of rejection are weighted by their concerns about the outcome of the situation.

We have evidence that this processing system influences the peer relations of early adolescents (Downey et al., 1998) and the romantic relationships of late adolescents (Ayduk, Downey, Testa, Yen, & Shoda, in press; Downey & Feldman, 1996; Downey, Freitas, Michaelis, & Khouri, 1998; Feldman & Downey, 1994). We also have evidence that rejection from both parents and peers is associated with heightened levels of rejection sensitivity (Bonica & Downey, 1997; Downey et al., 1997). Our late adolescent studies are based mainly on first- and second-year Columbia University undergraduates. About half of the participants were Caucasian; a quarter were Asian American; the remaining participants were, in about equal proportions, Hispanic, African American, and mixed or other race. Our early adolescent studies are based primarily on children attending a public middle school that serves an economically disadvantaged, inner-city neighborhood with a large immigrant population. About 75% of the participants were Hispanic, 20% were African American, and the remainder were primarily Asian American.

After briefly outlining the theoretical background to the rejection sensitivity processing system, we describe the expectations, biases, and coping strategies that the rejection-sensitive adolescent brings to the task of forming and maintaining adolescent romantic relationships. We then consider how rejection sensitivity might influence and be influenced by adolescent romantic relationships.

Theoretical Background

The cognitive-affective processing system that we have proposed draws selectively on attachment (Bowlby, 1969, 1973, 1980; Hazan & Shaver, 1987), social-cognitive (e.g., Andersen, 1990; Baldwin, 1992; Bradbury & Fincham, 1988; Crick & Dodge, 1994), and interpersonal perspectives (e.g., Coyne, 1976; Gottman, 1979; Wachtel, 1977) on relationships.

Attachment Approach. Our emphasis on the expectations that people bring from one relationship to the next reflects the influence of attachment theory (Bowlby, 1969, 1973, 1980; Sroufe, 1990). The expectations that people have about whether others will satisfy their needs or reject them is a key component of the internal working models of relationships that Bowlby proposed to account for continuity between early and subsequent relationships. These expectations were seen as deriving initially from the reliability with which children's needs are met in early childhood (Bowlby, 1973; Sroufe, 1990). When their needs are met sensitively and consistently, children develop secure working models that incorporate the expectation that others will accept and support them. When children's needs are met with covert or overt rejection, they develop insecure working models that incorporate fears and doubts about whether others will accept and support them. Bowlby proposed that this defensive response can emerge as anxiety or anger. This view is consistent with theories of emotion that view both anxiety and anger as high-arousal, negative-valence, defensive reactions to a perceived threat (Lang, 1995).

Bowlby identified two alternative strategies that children can adopt to cope with anxiety about the supportiveness of a consistently or intermittently rejecting primary caretaker (Ainsworth, Blehar, Waters, & Wall, 1978; Bowlby, 1969, 1973, 1980). The anxious-avoidant strategy is characterized by an active avoidance of contact with the caretaker, whereas the anxious-ambivalent strategy is characterized by frequent demands for reassurance from the caretaker interspersed with displays of hostility (Ainsworth et al., 1978). Similar coping styles have been identified in several distinct literatures, including psychodynamic theories of personality (e.g., Horney, 1937), biological psychiatry (American Psychiatric Association, 1994; Davidson, Miller, Turnbull, & Sullivan, 1982; Heimberg, Holt, Schneider, Spitzer, & Leibowitz, 1993), and cognitive theories of depression (Beck, 1983). When used in subsequent relationships, these coping styles are likely to have negative consequences. We have already outlined some of the possible negative consequences that these styles may have for adolescent romantic relationships. We will return to this issue later.

Social-Cognitive Approach. Although theoretical analyses within the attachment framework have drawn attention to the operation of internal working models in social interaction (e.g., Sroufe, 1990), this attention is just beginning to translate into empirical studies (see Reis & Downey, in press; Reis & Patrick, 1996, for reviews). We have sought to contribute to this effort in conceptualizing the psychological legacy of rejection in terms of the immediate, moment-to-moment cognitive-affective antecedents of behavior (Bandura, 1986; Dweck & Leggett, 1988; Higgins & Bargh, 1987; Mischel, 1973; Mischel & Shoda, 1995). Thus, we view early rejection experiences and associated coping efforts as setting up relationship schemas that encompass relationship goals, expectations, values and concerns, interpretive biases, and self-regulatory scripts. Subsequent experiences of acceptance-rejection are interpreted from the standpoint of existing cognitive-affective schemas. However, people's working models or schemas of relationships are also continuously modified by experience, although the extent of their malleability probably decreases as relationship experiences cumulate.

Interpersonal Approach. Consistent with the view that internal working models or relational schemas reflect experience, we see the cognitive-affective processing system that we have outlined as maintained and modified within important peer, romantic, and parental relationships through social interactional processes that operate similarly across developmental periods. This assumption recognizes that relationships are at least dyadic, with each person bringing to the relationship distinctive cognitive-affective processing systems (Bradbury & Fincham, 1988; Reis & Downey, in press). Thus, in adolescent romantic relationships, if one person behaves in a hostile way when feeling rejected, his or her partner may respond by withdrawing. Alternatively, the partner may initiate a calm discussion focused on understanding what prompted the hostility. Whereas the former approach will maintain and perhaps intensify rejection expectations, the latter approach may help diminish rejection expectations. Thus, healthy romantic relationships may enable some adolescents to break cycles of troubled relationships by reducing their sensitivity to rejection.

Our efforts to identify the implications of rejection sensitivity for adolescent romantic relationships begin with a description of what rejection-sensitive adolescents bring to a romantic relationship that might influence the relationship's course and nature. We then describe the impact of rejection sensitivity on specific relationship processes. Our discussion draws on our research on early and late adolescents.

What Does the Rejection-Sensitive Individual Bring to Adolescent Romantic Relationships?

Rejection Sensitivity

Rejection-sensitive adolescents bring defensive expectations of rejection, a readiness to perceive rejection, and a tendency to react intensely to rejection to their romantic relationships. They also bring beliefs about the situations that are diagnostic for them of acceptance and rejection, as well as beliefs about the cues within such situations that signify acceptance or rejection. Although we expect a general similarity across individuals in the rejection sensitivity processing disposition and its behavioral consequences, we also expect that rejection-sensitive adolescents will differ in ways that reflect their individual developmental history, gender, age, and culture.

Situations that Activate Rejection Sensitivity. The specific situations in each individual's romantic relationship that activate defensive expectations of rejection will reflect how parents and peers communicated a rejecting intent. Parents can communicate rejection to their children through physical or verbal abuse, physical and emotional neglect, and acceptance that is conditional on the child's acceding to the parent's wishes (Downey et al., 1997). Peers can communicate rejection through overt physical or verbal victimization, exclusion, rumor spreading, and ignoring (Asher & Coie, 1990; Crick & Grotpeter, 1995).

Certain interpersonal situations are probably more likely to trigger concerns about rejection in boys than in girls, and vice versa, reflecting gender differences in socialization. One stereotyped expectancy for males is that they are dominant in their relationships. Expectancies for females emphasize the centrality of relationships and the importance of their preservation (Gilligan, 1982). These normative sex-role expectations permeate the typical socialization experiences of boys and girls both within families and within sex-segregated peer groups. Gender differences in situations that trigger rejection expectations may be even more pronounced in early adolescence, when the socialization effects of sex-segregated peer groups on romantic relationships may be strongest. For girls, situations that reflect threats to their relationship may be particularly likely to activate expectations of rejection. We therefore propose that for rejection-sensitive girls, conflict and partner inattentiveness are particularly threatening and trigger rejection sensitivity. Alternatively, for boys, situations that reflect threats to their status in the relationship may be more likely to elicit rejection concerns. Thus, situations that rejection-sensitive boys may view as threatening include occasions when their partner is showing interest in a potential alternative romantic partner or where their competence in valued domains is called into question.

Although this discussion has emphasized family and gender as determinants of situations that activate rejection concerns, cultural differences and differences in sexual orientation may also be important factors.

Defensive Expectations of Rejection. The primary way in which rejection expectations may differ among rejection-sensitive individuals is in the interpretation of the anticipatory distress experienced in situations that trigger rejection concerns. We propose that the distress will be interpreted as either angry or anxious expectations of rejection. Whether this distress is interpreted as anger or anxiety will reflect familial, gender, age, and cultural differences in the acceptability of expressing anger versus anxiety.

Family and peers may socialize girls to interpret anticipatory distress as anxiety. Boys may be socialized to interpret the same feelings as anger. Anxiety may promote vulnerability to feeling helpless and depressed when rejection is perceived. By contrast, anticipatory anger may set in motion a readiness to perceive rejection as intentional and unjustified, thus entitling retaliation. In this way, anticipatory anger may activate the hostile attributional bias and its aggressive consequences that have been identified by Dodge (Crick & Dodge, 1994; Dodge, 1980; Dodge, Pettit, McClaskey, & Brown, 1986). These observations suggest that rejection-sensitive women may show heightened vulnerability to depression, whereas rejection-sensitive men may be at risk for aggression.

Cultures may differ in the acceptability and functionality of anger and anxiety. The acceptability and functionality of anger and anxiety may also differ by the adolescent's level of development. Our research shows that among predominantly middle-class college students, anxiety appears to be the salient anticipatory affect in situations of possible rejection (Downey & Feldman, 1996). Among inner-city minority early adolescents, however, anticipatory anger is also salient. One environmental difference underlying this divergence could be the increased risk of violence faced by inner-city children relative to middle-class college students. In the relatively more physically dangerous inner-city context, the expression of anxiety could make a youngster appear vulnerable and a potential target of victimization. Thus, experiencing anger rather than anxiety may be a protective strategy that some inner-city children learn through reinforcement and modeling. In contrast, the majority of college students participating in our research were raised in environments in which the expression of fear and anxiety may have been less dangerous and in which the expression of anger and aggression may have been less acceptable.

Perceptions of Rejection. When defensive expectations of rejection are activated, individuals begin to scan for cues of rejection and their threshold for perceiving rejection is lowered. Thus, rejection-sensitive people readily perceive rejection in the ambiguously intentioned negative behavior of others. For this reason, they are vulnerable to perceiving rejection even when none was intended. However, they are not more likely than others to perceive rejection in negative behaviors for which there is an unambiguous situational explanation (Downey & Feldman, 1996; Downey et al., 1998). The specific cues that are interpreted as signifying acceptance or rejection will reflect the person's developmental history, gender, and culture, as well as the history of the relationship.

Reactions to Perceived Rejection. We expect that when rejection-sensitive individuals perceive rejection, they will overreact in characteristic ways that will undoubtedly reflect the influence of their family, peer group, gender, and culture. We distinguish two primary patterns of overreaction directed toward the romantic partner.

Reflective Responses. These strategic responses are enacted to control the situation in the belief that actions can be taken to prevent imminent rejection or to regain acceptance. These responses can be divided into those that seek to control the situation through (a) coercion or (b) compliance.

Coercion involves forcing the partner to accede to one's wishes through threats or guilt induction (Patterson, 1982). *Coercive processes* include:

1. Use of aggression or threats of aggression to induce partners to remain in the relationship for fear of the consequences of leaving.
2. Regulating partners' social contacts to keep them dependent on the relationship and to minimize their access to alternatives to the relationship. These strategies include wanting to know where the partner is all the time and with whom the partner is in contact.

3. Threats of self-harm to keep the partner in the relationship.

The use of compliance as a control strategy is based on the belief that changing oneself to comply with a partner's expressed or imagined wishes will prevent rejection. Such compliance becomes potentially harmful when it compromises personal safety and well-being. Examples of *compliance* in the service of avoiding rejection include the following:

1. Acquiescing to the partner's pressure to engage in forms of sexual intimacy for which the adolescent does not yet feel ready.
2. Initiating and maintaining sexual intimacy in the belief that it will strengthen a partner's commitment to the relationship and make rejection less likely.
3. Tolerating behavior that may compromise one's personal safety in order to maintain the relationship. For example, rejection-sensitive adolescents may tolerate emotionally, physically, or sexually abusive partner behavior to avoid rejection.
4. Acceding to the partner's pressure to engage in deviant behavior such as skipping school, using drugs or alcohol, or shoplifting.
5. Engaging in harmful behaviors to achieve ideal standards of physical attractiveness. Rejection-sensitive girls may be particularly vulnerable to engaging in unhealthy behaviors, such as excessive dieting or exercising, to approximate more closely ideal standards of physical beauty with the goal of attracting or maintaining a partner's interest.

Reflexive Responses. These disregulated emotional responses are an expression of one's immediate, affective reaction to the perceived rejection. These responses include withdrawal, dejection and helplessness, anger and hostility, and aggression. Implied in these types of responses is the belief that rejection is inevitable or has already occurred.

The negative emotions experienced in response to perceived rejection may disrupt the daily routines that serve long-term valued goals. Thus, an adolescent who has been rejected by a romantic partner may be so distressed that he or she is unable to function academically or socially at the same level as before. The intense pain of rejection may also prompt rejection-sensitive adolescents to engage in behaviors that are immediately gratifying but that may have negative long-term consequences. These behaviors include binge eating, substance abuse, and engaging in unprotected sex with numerous partners. It is also possible that some rejection-sensitive adolescent girls become pregnant in the misguided belief that a child will provide the unconditional acceptance that has been absent from their other relationships.

Normative Developmental Concerns

Although there are individual differences in the level of rejection sensitivity that adolescents bring to their relationships, adolescents as a group are likely to experience heightened sensitivity about acceptance and rejection by romantic partners. Adolescence is a period when issues of acceptance by peers and romantic partners are particularly salient as individuals work on the developmental tasks of autonomy and identity. Success in romantic relationships is normatively valued. Although all individuals face the possibility of rejection from a potential romantic partner, adolescents involved in their first romantic relationship have no prior experience of this type and thus may be especially sensitive to romantic rejection.

These conditions will generate defensive expectations of rejection in typical adolescents. The behavior of romantic partners or prospective partners may be carefully scanned for evidence of rejection or acceptance. Minimal cues will be interpreted as clear evidence of acceptance and rejection and will have a powerful effect on mood and behavior that are already labile. There may be a normative reduction in rejection sensitivity from early to late adolescence as more experience is acquired in selecting romantic partners and in entering and managing romantic relationships.

These normatively heightened rejection concerns are expected to be exaggerated in adolescents who have developed a generalized sensitivity to rejection based on experiences with peers and parents in the preadolescent years.

Relationship Skills and Peer Influences

In addition to providing opportunities for acceptance and rejection, peer relationships provide opportunities for adolescents to develop relationship skills, such as those involved in negotiating closeness, intimacy, and sharing. These skills carry over into their romantic relationships and are likely to influence whether these relationships become a source of acceptance or rejection (Connolly, this volume; Furman & Wehner, 1994; Neeman, Hubbard, & Masten, 1995). When rejection sensitivity prompts adolescents to avoid relationships or to react aggressively to ambiguous peer behavior, they forfeit opportunities for developing these relationships skills. These adolescents may also develop a negative social reputation among peers that may restrict their range of dating partners. The dating prospects of adolescents with a reputation for overreacting with aggression to real or imagined slights may be limited to individuals who are also deviant in their interpersonal behavior. The rejection-sensitive girl who withdraws from peers may be overlooked as a potential dating partner and, consequently, may lack opportunities for finding acceptance in romantic relationships.

Status Characteristics as New Sources of Rejection

Thus far, we have focused on the consequences of rejection directed at the individual's personal qualities or behaviors. Rejection because of status group characteristics will also sensitize individuals to expect and perceive rejection during interactions with nongroup members and in this way will influence decisions about whether and how to interact with nongroup members. Status characteristics that may elicit rejection include religion, race, ethnicity, disability, and sexual orientation. Rejection because of one's status may also contribute to a generalized sensitivity to rejection, especially when it is interpreted as personal. The dating context will undoubtedly create new sources of rejection for adolescents because of status characteristics.

Parents who have previously encouraged their children to be ecumenical in their choice of friends may attempt to constrain their children's choice of romantic partners to in-group members because of fear of marriages that are mixed in religion, race, ethnicity, or social class. This phenomenon is illustrated in Field's (1992) research on biracial (Black/White) adolescents girls who grew up white-identified in predominantly white neighborhoods where they were readily accepted by peer groups. These girls often faced difficulties in getting white dating partners, something they found hard to comprehend and very distressing.

A potential new source of acceptance and rejection that some adolescents confront is being gay or bisexual. For the first time, individuals are expected to enter into relationships that have an inherently sexual component. The sex of one's dating partner is a public statement of one's sexual orientation. Because of society's negativity about homosexuality, the mere suspicion of homosexuality can elicit peer and sometimes parental rejection. Mirroring societal fear and rejection of homosexuality, homosexual taunts are the most prominent type of sexual harassment that occurs in junior high and high school. Knowledge of how society in general and peers and families in particular treat gay or lesbian adolescents is likely to sensitize adolescents who develop same-sex sexual attractions to readily expect and perceive rejection. To avoid such rejection, they may keep their romantic relationships hidden; they may become involved in unsatisfying heterosexual romantic relationships; or they may decide to eschew romantic relationships. The efforts of gay and lesbian adolescents to negotiate romantic relationships may have a devastating toll on their mental health (Hammelman, 1993; Hetrick & Martin, 1987).

Summary

We have outlined a cognitive-affective processing system that, we argue, has important implications for adolescent romantic relationships. We have also delineated some sources of individual differences in the content of this system that might account for variability in the situations in which the system is activated and in its behavioral consequences. Finally, we have considered how people's sensitivity to rejection may be transformed by their experiences with adolescent romantic relationships, such as when adolescents who are attracted to same-sex rather than opposite-sex romantic partners become sensitized to expect rejection because of their sexual orientation.

Impact of Rejection Sensitivity on Relationship Processes

We now turn our attention to how rejection sensitivity affects specific relationship processes, potentially contributing to relationship difficulties. The question that we address is: How might rejection sensitivity influence the course of a relationship from start to finish?

Before addressing this question, we note three observations that help orient our discussion. First, it is necessary to distinguish *involvement* from *investment* in relationships. Particularly in early adolescence, individuals may become involved in relationships in which they are not invested. These relationships may serve as status symbols rather than provide a sense of closeness and commitment. However, as noted previously, some rejection-sensitive individuals never move on from this pattern. Most of our discussion is focused on relationships in which the adolescent is invested.

Second, by adolescence, people will have accumulated multiple sources of acceptance and rejection. Thus, understanding adolescents' decisions concerning romantic relationships requires identifying (a) which source of rejection or acceptance is most salient and (b) how the adolescent balances the demands of sometimes conflicting sources of acceptance and rejection. For example, adolescents may be in situations where avoiding rejection by their family or peer group is incompatible with gaining acceptance by a romantic partner. Whether adolescents are most concerned with approval from peers, parents, or romantic partners will undoubtedly influence their relationship decisions.

Third, information on the distinctions between the dating relationships of early and late adolescents will be used to qualify general considerations about the impact of rejection sensitivity on adolescent relationships. Our research shows that although early adolescents' understanding of what constitutes dating relationships resembles that of late adolescents, their relationships are less committed, less intimate, and of shorter duration than those of late adolescents (Purdie et al., 1999). Our research also shows that early adolescents' romantic conflicts are distinct from their peer conflicts in terms of both topics and tactics. Jealousy is the most common topic of conflict in romantic relationships. Peer conflicts center on games for boys and rumors for girls. The use of both physical and relational (i.e., behavior intended to damage the target's relationships; Crick & Grotpeter, 1995) aggression is less common in romantic than in peer conflicts. Behavior intended to induce jealousy emerges as a new tactic in romantic conflicts.

Entering Romantic Relationships

Earlier, we described two broad strategies that rejection-sensitive adolescents may adopt to regulate their concerns about rejection. One strategy is to avoid or postpone the transition to romantic relationships, losing opportunities for gaining acceptance. The adolescent who avoids age-appropriate romantic relationships will also miss opportunities to increase competencies in conflict resolution, establishing intimacy, and negotiating the boundaries between autonomy and connectedness in intimate relationships (Erikson, 1968; Havighurst, 1976; Sullivan, 1953). A similar loss of opportunities to develop relationship skills may accrue to adolescents who avoid rejection by not investing in the relationships in which they get involved. These adolescents may show a pattern of brief, superficial relationships because of their tendency to withdraw when they fear that they or their partner are becoming invested. Although this behavior pattern may be normal in early adolescence, its persistence through late adolescence and into young adulthood may prevent the person from developing the skills necessary to maintain a romantic relationship. The identification of these two avoidant strategies highlights the need to distinguish concern about first impressions from anxiety about being rejected as more of oneself is revealed (Downey & Feldman, 1996).

The second strategy that rejection-sensitive adolescents may adopt to avoid rejection is to overinvest in securing intimacy and unconditional love.

Thus, rejection sensitivity may affect adolescent romantic relationships by prompting adolescents to make the transition to exclusive dating relationships in which they are highly invested earlier than their peers. They may not yet be ready developmentally for such relationships in that they may not yet have sufficient practice in such relationship tasks as negotiating conflict or boundary management.

Moreover, they may not yet have developed sources of well-being that are independent of romantic partners, given that rejection-sensitive individuals often have a history of troubled relationships with parents and peers. As a consequence, their emotional well-being may be entirely dependent on how well their romantic relationship is going, and they may begin to perceive themselves solely in terms of this relationship. In such circumstances, concern about maintaining the relationship may constrain their decision making in important respects. For example, they may decide to engage in activities that they find uncomfortable or distressing in order to maintain the relationship. Some of the compliance strategies that they may engage in have already been outlined.

Why some rejection-sensitive adolescents specialize in one approach to their romantic relationship over another remains unclear in our investigations. Perhaps individuals differ in their relative valuation of attaining acceptance versus avoiding rejection. In his work on the development of promotion-focused (e.g., gaining acceptance) and prevention-focused (e.g., preventing rejection) motivational systems, Higgins (1991) has suggested some parenting antecedents of these distinct motivational systems.

Parental Influence. In addition to concern about rejection in romantic relationships, sensitivity to parental rejection is expected to influence the timing of adolescents' entry into romantic relationships. The precise way in which parents convey rejection may determine the nature of their influence on their adolescent child's entry into romantic relationships.

Children with parents whose acceptance is conditional on their fulfilling parental expectations may postpone or speed up involvement in romantic relationships simply to maintain parental approval. More generally, to maintain approval, the children of such parents may tolerate a high degree of parental intrusion into their decisions about romantic relationships. However, in evaluating the role of parents in their adolescent's romantic relationships, it is important to distinguish inappropriate intrusions from appropriate parental guidance within the context of a respectful, accepting relationship.

The decisions of adolescents with neglectful or overtly rejecting parents may be uninfluenced by their parents' views on romantic relationships.

These adolescents may have given up the hope of attaining parental acceptance and approval. Instead, they may seek acceptance by romantic partners as a substitute for parental acceptance. This reaction may accelerate adolescents' involvement in committed, exclusive romantic relationships, which, in turn, may have positive or negative consequences for them, depending on whether they become overly involved in a healthy or troubled relationship.

Peer Influence. Research has found that close friends and peer norms contribute to an adolescent's concepts of and expectations about romantic partners. Among adolescents who are especially sensitive to peer acceptance and rejection, the opinion of close friends and, more broadly, peer norms may be the key influence on the adolescent's decisions about romantic relationships. This may be especially true in early adolescence, when experimentation with romantic relationships often begins. At that time, many adolescents have little investment in their romantic partners. Instead, their motivation for romantic involvement may be to gain or maintain the acceptance of their peer group. In such cases, the peer group rather than the romantic partner is the salient source of acceptance or rejection.

Alternatively, rejection-sensitive adolescents who have experienced peer rejection may give up on peers as a source of acceptance and seek instead acceptance from romantic partners. As with parents, a history of conditional peer acceptance may characterize adolescents who are overly influenced by peers, whereas fairly consistent overt rejection or neglect may characterize adolescents who give up completely on peer acceptance.

Partner Selection

Rejection sensitivity may also affect the risk of becoming involved in an unhealthy or even abusive relationship through its impact on partner selection. Preoccupation with issues of acceptance and rejection may lead rejection-sensitive adolescents to overvalue partners who are attentive, who need them, and who seek a rapid intensification of commitment early in the relationship. Although these partner attributes may initially help allay rejection concerns, they may be harbingers of later difficulties. The clinical literature on battered women (e.g., Browne, 1987; Walker, 1984) suggests that excessively high levels of dependency early in the relationship may presage jealous and controlling behavior, with emotional and physical abuse as a potential outcome.

In addition to being at risk for selecting on the basis of valued characteristics that may predict the emergence of later difficulties, intimacy-seeking, rejection-sensitive adolescents may be insufficiently selective in choosing a romantic partner. For example, they may be more willing than others to overlook a prospective partner's history of being abusive, dishonest, or unfaithful, or of abusing drugs or alcohol. In sum, the need for acceptance may compromise rejection-sensitive adolescents' judgment in selecting a romantic partner.

Influence of Peers and Parents. The choice of romantic partners is also a potential cause of peer and/or parental rejection. Some parents may reject children who select partners who are dissimilar in ethnicity, class, and religion. Peers may expect peer group members to select as partners members of a particular social clique, rejecting and ostracizing transgressors. The dilemma of resolving a mismatch between their desired romantic partner and the type of partner acceptable to peers and/or parents may be especially upsetting for adolescents who are highly sensitive to peer or parental rejection. As a group, gay adolescents may be particularly vulnerable to rejection from peers and parents and its distressing consequences because of their choice of a romantic partner.

Thoughts, Feelings, and Behavior in Relationships

How do rejection-sensitive adolescents think, feel, and behave in romantic relationships in which they are invested? We first describe our findings on late adolescents. We then describe some recent findings on early adolescents.

Late Adolescents. Late adolescents who enter a romantic relationship disposed to expect rejection from significant others tend to (a) perceive intentional rejection in their partner's insensitive behaviors, (b) feel insecure and unhappy about their relationship, and (c) behave in ways that erode their partner's relationship satisfaction (Downey & Feldman, 1996). We found that the behaviors that eroded partner satisfaction differed in males and females. Rejection-sensitive men's jealous, controlling behavior helped explain their partner's dissatisfaction. Rejection-sensitive women's hostile, unsupportive behavior contributed to their partner's dissatisfaction.

To better understand the processes through which the romantic relationships of rejection-sensitive women begin to unravel, we examined their behavior in conflicts, which we expected to trigger their rejection concerns (Ayduk et al., in press; Downey et al., 1998). A daily diary study of naturally occurring conflict in dating couples revealed that when rejection-sensitive women felt rejected, they tended to report having a conflict with their partner the next day. During the conflict they behaved in a hostile way (e.g., lost their temper, said spiteful things). The next day, the relationship satisfaction and commitment of high-rejection-sensitive women's partners declined, whereas those of low-rejection-sensitive women's partners increased. The high-rejection-sensitive women were aware of their partners' reduced satisfaction and commitment, which emerged in diminished attentiveness and affection. Consistent with the view that the conflicts of rejection-sensitive women affect their partners in ways that matter for the relationship, the partner's level of commitment and dissatisfaction during the diary period predicted subsequent breakup.

To test more rigorously the impact of rejection-sensitive women's conflict behavior on their partners, we conducted an observational investigation of couples discussing an unresolved relationship issue. Consistent with self-reports, high-rejection-sensitive women behaved in a hostile manner, and this behavior helped maintain their partner's initial level of anger and resentment. The discussion led to a reduction in anger and resentment in the partners of women who were low in rejection sensitivity. Men's post-conflict anger helped distinguish couples who had broken up a year later.

These findings suggest that, whatever its origins, rejection sensitivity has a self-perpetuating quality: Expectations of rejection facilitate subjective perceptions of rejection, which cause behaviors that evoke objective rejection, reinforcing expectations of rejection (Jussim, 1986, 1991; Merton, 1948). So far, our research on late adolescents has addressed only one of the many hypothesized processes, outlined in the previous section, through which rejection sensitivity may undermine relationships and compromise well-being.

Early Adolescents. Our research suggests that rejection sensitivity can have profound consequences for late adolescents dating relationships. Does this characteristic have a similar impact on early adolescents' dating relationships? Our findings suggest an affirmative answer for girls but not boys (Purdie et al., 1998). In seventh- to ninth-grade girls, sensitivity to peer and teacher rejection measured 2 years earlier predicted heightened concern about their current romantic partner's commitment to the relationship. These girls worried about whether their partner was thinking of leaving the relationship, was interested in someone else, and might cheat on them. They felt uncomfortable when their boyfriend was doing something that did not involve them. They reported that they would do things with which they did not feel comfortable to maintain the relationship, suggesting that they are at heightened risk for using some of the potentially harmful compliance strategies that we have identified. They were the targets of more verbal aggression from partners than were girls low in rejection sensitivity. Rejection sensitivity was less predictive of early adolescent boys' relationship concerns, perhaps because their dating relationships are less serious and committed than those of their female peers. Early adolescent boys' relationships are shorter, and they are more likely to be involved with multiple partners.

Gender Differences in Vulnerability to Depression and Aggression

Our research with late adolescents suggests that rejection-sensitive individuals may be differentially vulnerable for depression and aggression. Rejection-sensitive young women, but not young men, show heightened vulnerability to depressive symptoms following rejection (i.e., having the relationship terminated) by their romantic partners (Kim, Ayduk, & Downey, 1998). These findings converge with Hammen and colleagues' finding that relationship disruptions prompted clinical levels of distress in young women concerned about rejection and abandonment (Hammen, Burge, Daley, Davila, Paley, & Rudolph, 1995). The results of these two longitudinal studies suggest the importance of considering whether disruptions in romantic relationships help contribute to the sharp increase in female depression during adolescence (Nolen-Hoeksema, 1994).

We have found evidence that rejection sensitivity may be a risk factor for physical abusiveness toward a romantic partner in college men (Downey, Feldman, & Ayduk, in press). Although relatively rare, aggression by rejection-sensitive men may be an outgrowth of their more general tendency to behave in a jealous, controlling way toward their partners (Downey & Feldman, 1996). Jealous, controlling behavior has been consistently identified as characterizing male batterers (Goldner, Penn, Sheinberg, & Walker, 1990; Walker, 1984).

Ending Relationships

During adolescence, romantic relationships begin and end with greater frequency than in adulthood. This is especially true in early adolescence. Nonetheless, rejection sensitivity may help account for individual differences in the length of relationships. In support of this prediction, we found that rejection sensitivity prospectively predicted the breakup of late adolescents' dating relationships.

We have suggested a process whereby rejection sensitivity may unintentionally lead to the termination of relationships by eroding the commitment and satisfaction of the rejection-sensitive individual's partner. It is also possible that belief in the imminence of rejection may prompt some rejection-sensitive adolescents to end the relationship themselves. They may prefer to reject a partner preemptively rather than to be rejected. Rejection-sensitive adolescents who continually reject romantic partners may never get beyond the casual stage of their romantic relationships.

Alternatively, a desire to maintain some degree of acceptance may help explain why some adolescents maintain unhealthy relationships. For example, battered women's commitment to their partners (Herbert, Silver, & Ellard, 1991) may sometimes reflect a motivation to avoid rejection and being alone. A similar motivation may underlie the solicitous overtures of 4-year-old victims of peer aggression studied by Troy and Sroufe (1987). These children's persistence in making positive overtures toward an abusive playmate may indicate a preference for abusive attention over no attention, as the following request by a victimized child ignored by his aggressor suggests: "Why don't you tease me? I won't get mad" (Troy & Sroufe, 1987, p. 169).

The decision to remain in or end a relationship may also be influenced by concern about peer and parental acceptance. Thus, when peers disparage a romantic partner's appearance or parents deem the partner's background to be unacceptable, adolescents who are sensitive to peer or parental rejection may break up with a partner they like.

Impact of Rejection by a Romantic Partner

Negative relationship experiences such as rejection by a prospective romantic partner, being belittled or demeaned by a partner, or being "dumped" may undermine an adolescent's confidence in romantic relationships. Such rejections may have a sensitizing effect even on adolescents who were not previously rejection sensitive. As a consequence, adolescents may decide to avoid future relationships. If they do get involved in relationships, they may be overly cautious and their defensive expectation of rejection may prompt a self-protective readiness to perceive rejection. However, rejection sensitivity that results from a bad experience in a single romantic relationship is probably more easily undone and less likely to generalize beyond romantic relationships than rejection sensitivity that results from parental rejection. Nonetheless, the corrosive effect of an abusive relationship on an adolescent's confidence in self and others should not be underestimated.

Breaking the Cycle of Rejection

Besides providing a context for the maintenance and intensification of rejection sensitivity, romantic relationships may provide adolescents with opportunities for change. Research on people who transcend severe childhood rejection suggests that relationships that are mutually satisfying and healthy may help rejection-sensitive adolescents change their tendency to expect, perceive, and react intensely to rejection. Having a supportive partner distinguishes women who break the intergenerational cycle of child abuse from those who continue the cycle (Egeland, Jacobvitz, & Sroufe, 1988; Quinton, Rutter, & Liddle, 1984).

What are the mechanisms through which supportive relationships can help adolescents transcend a legacy of rejection? By violating the expectation of rejection, partners can potentially alter rejection-sensitive adolescents' expectations and anxieties about rejection. Healthy, supportive partners can also act as models for generating less malevolent explanations for others' behavior and for developing more adaptive conflict resolution skills. Yet, rejection sensitivity is deeply ingrained. Thus, change is probably unlikely to occur unless the rejection-sensitive adolescent is highly motivated, and the partner is deeply committed and can provide effective guidance and encouragement.

What characteristics of the rejection-sensitive adolescent facilitate change? By adolescence, people have developed the cognitive competencies (i.e., formal operations) that permit them to think hypothetically, a skill that should help them to think through the implications of alternative ways of perceiving and reacting to other people's actions. They can also think reflectively about themselves and consider and map out alternative futures. These cognitive skills should provide an important tool for change. However, belief in the possibility of personal change may be a prerequisite for change to begin (Dweck & Leggett, 1988).

General self-regulatory competencies, such as the ability to delay immediate gratification in the pursuit of a long-term goal (Mischel, Cantor, & Feldman, 1996), can also help adolescents stop themselves from acting on their immediate feelings following perceived rejection. In most individuals, these competencies improve with age. However, even when people have the ability to delay gratification, they probably will not do so in the absence of a long-term goal. The desire to maintain an important romantic relationship may motivate some rejection-sensitive adolescents to work on inhibiting their tendency to respond reflexively to perceived rejection with aggression and to replace this tendency with responses that serve long-term goals.

What partner characteristics facilitate change? Effective change is probably possible only when the partner is able to convey a sense of acceptance, does not reciprocate the negativity that rejection-sensitive people often show when they fear or perceive rejection, knows how to initiate constructive discussion of relationship problems, and can negotiate boundaries between autonomy and connectedness. These are difficult requirements for any person, let alone an adolescent without much experience in romantic relationships. What kind of relationship history instills these capacities? One possibility is that a developmental history in which relationships have gone relatively smoothly allows such skills to develop. Alternatively, someone who has successfully negotiated challenging relationships with parents or peers may be more capable of helping the rejection-sensitive person change than someone who has not confronted such challenges.

Conclusion

In this chapter we have drawn selectively on attachment, social-cognitive, and interpersonal approaches to relationships to outline a model of adaptive and maladaptive approaches to adolescent romantic relationships. Our model proposes that rejection sensitivity, a legacy of rejecting experiences, influences whether and when adolescents enter romantic relationships; who they select as partners; how they think, feel, and behave in their relationships; and whether they remain in or end relationships. In particular, we have outlined some ways in which rejection sensitivity may lead adolescents to engage in behaviors that are potentially harmful to their relationship and to themselves. For example, we have argued that rejection sensitivity may contribute to heightened levels of depression in adolescent women and to partner aggression in adolescent men.

The framework allows for cultural, gender, and developmental differences in rejection sensitivity. It also draws attention to rejection directed at individuals because of status characteristics (e.g., sexual orientation), as well as personal characteristics or actions (e.g., being victimized by peers because of a tendency to overreact, being rejected by parents because of trivial misbehavior or noncompliance).

While accounting for continuity from parental and peer relationships to adolescent romantic relationships, the framework also allows for change. Our assumption that rejection sensitivity is maintained by experiences in relationships means that it can also be modified by disconfirmatory experiences. Thus, interventions can be designed to facilitate change toward more healthy ways of feeling, thinking, and behaving in relationships.

In closing, we caution that identifying maladaptive relationship patterns is not possible in the absence of knowledge of normative developmental change in adolescent dating relationships. Thus, although we have proposed an agenda for research on individual differences in adolescent dating relationships, we also emphasize the need for normative developmental studies.

References

Ainsworth, M., Blehar, M., Waters, E., & Wall, S. (1978). *Patterns of attachment: A psychological study of the strange situation.* Hillsdale, NJ: Erlbaum.

American Psychiatric Association. (1994). *Diagnostic and statistical manual of mental disorders* (4th ed.). Washington, DC: American Psychiatric Association.

Anderson, S. (1990). The inevitability of future suffering: The role of depressive predictive certainty in depression. *Social Cognition, 8,* 203–228.

Asher, S. R., & Coie, J. D. (1990). *Peer rejection in childhood.* New York: Cambridge University Press.

Ayduk, O., Downey, G., Testa, A., Yen, Y., & Shoda, Y. (in press). Does rejection elicit hostility in rejection sensitive women? *Social Cognition: Special Issue on Social Cognition and Close Relationships.*

Baldwin, M. W. (1992). Relational schemes and the processing of social information. *Psychological Bulletin, 112,* 461–484.

Bandura, A. (1986). *Social foundations of thought and action.* Englewood Cliffs, NJ: Prentice-Hall.

Beck, A. T. (1983). Cognitive therapy of depression: New perspectives. In P. J. Clayton & J. E. Barrett (Eds.), *Treatment of depression: Old controversies and new approaches* (pp. 265–290) New York: Raven Press.

Bergman, L. (1992). Dating violence among high school students. *Social Work, 37,* 21–27.

Bonica, C., & Downey, G. (1997). *Overt victimization by peers sensitizes children to rejection.* Unpublished data, Columbia University.

Bowlby, J. (1969). *Attachment and loss, Volume 1: Attachment.* New York: Basic Books.

Bowlby, J. (1973). *Attachment and loss, Volume 2: Separation.* New York: Basic Books.

Bowlby, J. (1980). *Attachment and loss, Volume 3: Loss, sadness, and depression.* New York: Basic Books.

Bradbury, T. N., & Fincham, F. D. (1988). Individual difference variables in close relationships: A contextual model of marriage as an integrative framework. *Journal of Personality and Social Psychology, 54,* 713–721.

Browne, A. (1987). *When battered women kill.* New York: Free Press.

Browne, A. (1993). Violence against women by male partners: Prevalence, outcomes and policy implications. *American Psychologist, 48,* 1077–1087.

Centers for Disease Control (1990). Violence against women. *Morbidity and Mortality Weekly Reports 39,* 525–529.

Coyne, J. C. (1976). Depression and the response of others. *Journal of Abnormal Psychology, 85,* 186–193.

Coyne, J. C., Downey, G., & Boergers, J. (1994). Depression in families: A systems perspective. In D. Cicchetti & S. Toth (Eds.), *Developmental approaches to the affective disorders: Rochester symposium on developmental psychopathology* (Vol. 4, pp. 211–249). Rochester, NY: University of Rochester Press.

Crick, N. R., & Dodge, K. (1994). A review and reformulation of social information-processing mechanisms in children's social adjustment. *Psychological Bulletin, 115,* 74–101.

Crick, N. R., & Grotpeter, J. K. (1995). Relational aggression, gender, and social-psychological adjustment. *Child Development, 66,* 710–722.

Davidson, J., Miller, R., Turnbull, C., & Sullivan, J. (1982). Atypical depression. *Archives of General Psychiatry, 39,* 527–534.

Dodge, K. (1980). Social cognition and children's aggressive behavior. *Child Development, 51,* 162–170.

Dodge, K., Pettit, G., McClaskey, C., & Brown, M. (1986). Social competence in children. *Monographs of the Society for Research in Child Development, 51*(2, Serial No. 213).

Downey, G., & Feldman, S. (1996). Implications of rejection sensitivity for intimate relationships. *Journal of Personality and Social Psychology, 70,* 1327–1343.

Downey, G., Feldman, S., & Ayduk, O. (in press). Rejection sensitivity and male violence in romantic relationships. *Personal Relationships.*

Downey, G., Feldman, S., Khuri, J., & Friedman, S. (1994). Maltreatment and child depression. In W. M. Reynolds & H. F. Johnson (Eds.), *Handbook of depression in childhood and adolescence* (pp. 481–508). New York: Plenum.

Downey, G., Freitas, A., Michaelis, B., & Khouri, H. (1998). The self-fulfilling prophecy in close relationships: Do rejection sensitive women get rejected by their partners? *Journal of Personality and Social Psychology, 75,* 545–560.

Downey, G., Khouri, H., & Feldman, S. (1997). Early interpersonal trauma and later adjustment: The mediational role of rejection sensitivity. In D. Cicchetti & S. Toth (Eds.), *Rochester symposium on developmental psychopathology: Volume 8, The effects of trauma on the developmental process* (pp. 85–114). Rochester, NY: University of Rochester Press.

Downey, G, Lebolt, A., & O'Shea-Lauber, K. (1995). *Rejection sensitivity and blaming as mediators of violence in adolescent peer and dating relationships.* Paper presented at the biennial meeting of the Society for Research in Child Development, April, Indianapolis, IN.

Downey, G., Lebolt, A., Rincón, C., & Freitas, A. (1998). Rejection sensitivity and children's interpersonal difficulties. *Child Development, 69,* 1072–1089.

Dweck, C. S., & Leggett, E. L. (1988). A social-cognitive approach to personality and motivation. *Psychological Review, 95,* 25–273.

Egeland, B., Jacobvitz, D., & Sroufe, L. A. (1988). Breaking the cycle of abuse. *Child Development, 59,* 1080–1088.

Erikson, E. H. (1950). *Childhood and society.* New York: Norton.

Erikson, E. H. (1968). *Identity: Youth and crisis.* New York: Norton.

Feldman, S., & Downey, G. (1994). Rejection sensitivity as a mediator of the impact of childhood exposure to family violence on adult attachment behavior. *Development and Psychopathology, 6,* 231–247.

Field, L. (1992). *Self-esteem and identity in biracial adolescents.* Unpublished doctoral dissertation, University of Denver.

Furman, W., & Wehner, E. A. (1994). Romantic views: Toward a theory of adolescent relationships. In R. Montemayor, G. R. Adams, & T. P. Gullotta (Eds.), *Advances in adolescent development: Volume 3, Relationships in adolescence* (pp. 168–195). Beverly Hills, CA: Sage.

Gayford, J. J. (1975). Wife battering: A preliminary survey of 100 cases. *British Medical Journal, 1,* 194–197.

Gilligan, C. (1982). New maps of development: New visions of maturity. *American Journal of Orthopsychiatry, 52,* 199–212.

Goldner, V., Penn, P., Sheinberg, M., & Walker, G. (1990). Love and violence: Gender paradoxes in volatile attachments. *Family Process, 29,* 343–364.

Gottman, J. M. (1979). *Marital interaction: Experimental investigations.* New York: Academic Press.

Hammelman, T. L. (1993). Gay and lesbian youth: Contributing factors to serious attempts or considerations of suicide. *Journal of Gay and Lesbian Psychotherapy, 2,* 77–89.

Hammen, C. L., Burge, D., Daley, S. E., Davila, J., Paley, B., & Rudolph, K. D. (1995). Interpersonal attachment cognitions and prediction of symptomatic responses to interpersonal stress. *Journal of Abnormal Psychology, 104,* 436–443.

Havighurst, R. J. (1976). A cross-cultural view of adolescence. In J. F. Adams (Ed.), *Understanding adolescence: Current developments in adolescent psychology* (3rd ed., pp. 52–83). Boston: Allyn & Bacon.

Hazan, C., & Shaver, P. (1987). Romantic love conceptualized as an attachment process. *Journal of Personality and Social Psychology, 52,* 511–524.

Heimberg, R., Holt, C., Schneider, F., Spitzer, R., & Liebowitz, M. (1993). The issue of subtypes in the diagnosis of social phobia. *Journal of Anxiety Disorders, 7,* 249–269.

Henton, J., Cate, R., Koval, J., Lloyd, S., & Christopher, S. (1983). Romance and violence in dating relationships. *Journal of Family Issues, 4,* 467–482.

Herbert, B. T., Silver, R. C., & Ellard, J. H. (1997). Coping with an abusive relationship: How and why do women stay? *Journal of Marriage and the Family, 53,* 311–325.

Hetrick, E., & Martin, D. (1987). Developmental issues and their resolution for gay and lesbian adolescents. *Journal of Homosexuality, 14,* 25–43.

Higgins, E. T. (1991). Development of self-regulatory and self-evaluative processes: Costs, benefits, and tradeoffs. In M. R. Gunnar & L. A. Sroufe (Eds.), *Self processes and development. Minnesota symposia on child psychology* (Vol. 23, pp. 125–165). Hillsdale, NJ: Erlbaum.

Higgins, E. T., & Bargh, J. (1987). Social cognition and social perception. *Annual Review of Psychology, 38,* 369–425.

Horney, K. (1937). *The neurotic personality of our time.* New York: Norton.

Jussim, L. (1986). Self-fulfilling prophecies: A theoretical and integrative review. *Psychological Review, 93,* 429–445.

Jussim, L. (1991). Social perception and social reality: A reflection-construction model. *Psychological Review, 98,* 54–73.

Kim, M., Ayduk, O., & Downey, G. (1998). *Rejection sensitivity, rejection, and depression in women.* Unpublished data, Columbia University.

Lang, P. J. (1995). The emotion probe. *American Psychologist, 50,* 372–385.

Merton, R. K. (1948). The self-fulfilling prophecy. *Antioch Review, 8,* 193–210.

Mischel, W. (1973). Toward a cognitive social learning reconceptualization of personality. *Psychological Review, 80,* 252–283.

Mischel, W., Cantor, N., & Feldman, S. (1996). Principles of self-regulation: The nature of willpower and self-control. In E. T. Higgins, & A. W. Kruglanski (Eds.), *Social psychology: Handbook of basic principles* (pp. 329–360). New York: Guilford Press.

Mischel, W., & Shoda, Y. (1995). A cognitive-affective system theory of personality: Reconceptualizing situations, dispositions, dynamics, and invariance in personality structures. *Psychological Review, 102,* 246–268.

Molidor, C. E. (1993, October). Adolescent dating violence: Prevalence rates and contextual issues. *Dissertation Abstracts International, 54*(4), 146.

Neeman, J., Hubbard, J., & Masten, A. (1995). The changing importance of romantic relationship involvement to competence from late childhood to late adolescence. *Development and Psychopathology, 7,* 727–750.

Nolen-Hoeksema, S. (1994). An interactive model for the emergence of gender differences in depression in adolescence. Special issue: Affective processes in adolescence. *Journal of Research on Adolescence, 4,* 519–534.

O'Keefe, N., Brockopp, K., & Chew, E. (1986). Teen dating violence. *Social Work, 31,* 465–468.

O'Leary, K. D., & Arias, I. (1988). Assessing agreement of reports of spouse abuse. In G. T. Hotaling, D. Finkelhor, J. T. Kilpatrick, & M. A. Straus (Eds.), *New directions in family violence research* (pp. 218–227). Newbury Park, CA: Sage.

Patterson, G. R. (1982). *Coercive family process.* Eugene, OR: Castalia.

Purdie, V., Downey, G., & Bonica, C. (1999). *Conflicts in early adolescent peer and romantic relationships.* Unpublished data, Columbia University.

Quinton, D., Rutter, M., & Liddle, C. (1984). Institutional rearing, parenting difficulties, and marital support. *Psychological Medicine, 14,* 107–124.

Reis, H. T., & Downey, G. (in press). Social cognition in relationships: Building essential bridges between two literatures. *Social Cognition.*

Reis, H. T., & Patrick, B. (1996). Attachment and intimacy: Component processes. In E. T. Higgins & A. W. Kruglanski (Eds.), *Social psychology: Handbook of basic principles* (pp. 523–563). New York: Guilford Press.

Roscoe, B., & Benaske, N. (1985). Courtship violence experienced by abused wives: Similarities in patterns of abuse. *Family Relations, 43,* 419–424.

Roscoe, B., & Callahan, J. E. (1985). Adolescents' self-report of violence in families and dating relationships. *Adolescence, 20,* 545–553.

Roscoe, B., & Kelsey, T. (1986). Dating violence among high school students. *Psychology, 23,* 53–59.

Sroufe, L. A. (1990). An organizational perspective on the self. In D. Cicchetti & M. Beeghly (Eds.), *The self in transition: Infancy to childhood. The John D. and Catherine T. MacArthur foundation series on mental health and development* (pp. 281–307). Chicago: University of Chicago Press.

Sugarman, D., & Hotaling, G. (1989). Dating violence: Prevalence, context, and risk markers. In M. A. Pirog-Good and J. A. Stets (Eds.), *Violence in dating relationships: Emerging social issues* (pp. 3–32). New York: Praeger.

Sullivan, H. S. (1953). *The interpersonal theory of psychiatry.* New York: Norton.

Troy, M., & Sroufe, L. A. (1987). Victimization among preschoolers: The role of attachment relationship history. *Journal of the American Academy of Child Psychiatry, 26,* 166–172.

Veroff, J., Kulka, R., & Douvan, E. (1981). *Mental health in America: Patterns of help-seeking from 1957 to 1976.* New York: Basic Books.

Wachtel, P. (1977). *Psychoanalysis and behavior therapy: Toward an integration.* New York: Basic Books.

Walker, L. E. (1984). *The battered woman syndrome.* New York: Springer.

8 Sex, Dating, Passionate Friendships, and Romance

Intimate Peer Relations Among Lesbian, Gay, and Bisexual Adolescents

Lisa M. Diamond, Ritch C. Savin-Williams, and Eric M. Dubé

Although the raw number of adolescent romantic and sexual involvements is well documented, the actual experience and meaning of these relationships for adolescents receives little attention. As a result, these relationships are frequently classed together on the basis of surface similarities, despite important structural and functional differences. Attention to these differences, however, reveals how young men and women craft adaptive constellations of peer relationships to meet changing needs for intimacy and social support during the multiple transitions of adolescence. In this chapter we put forth a typology of intimate peer relationships based on the *motives* prompting adolescents to pursue them, their specific *characteristics,* and the *functions* they serve. We specify four varieties of adolescent relationships – sexual relationships, dating relationships, passionate friendships, and romantic relationships – representing prototypical combinations of some of the most salient motives, characteristics, and functions.

Three qualifications are in order. First, our use of this typology is primarily heuristic. We do not suggest that all adolescent intimate relationships can or should be shoehorned into one of these categories or that such a task has any intrinsic value. Rather, we elaborate these relationship categories to demonstrate how an analysis of the motives, characteristics, and functions underlying adolescent intimate relationships elucidates their developmental significance better than an analysis of surface features alone. Second, our usage of otherwise general terms such as *romantic relationship* should be assumed to be specific to this chapter unless otherwise noted. *Romantic relationships, dating relationships, sexual relationships,* and *passionate friendships* will be defined with regard to the specific combination of motivations, characteristics, and functions we perceive to define archetypal examples of these relationships. Third, although certain relationships may prove more salient early in adolescence, whereas others take center stage later, our typology presumes no *inherent* developmental sequence. We hope, in fact, to provide an explicit counterpoint to the dominant developmental paradigm that specifies a normative progression from childhood infatuations to early adolescent dating to late adolescent and young adult romantic and sexual bonds. The most obvious drawback of any such normative model (implicit or explicit) is its failure to conceptualize adequately the development of individuals who deviate from its parameters. However, such a model has additional shortcomings when applied to adolescent intimate relationships. For example, because dating is considered the primary conduit through which adolescents make the transition to the mature intimacy, passion, and sexual relations of adulthood, it typically receives a disproportionately large share of attention.

Also, normative models often employ a reductionistic view of sexuality. For example, although the onset of sexual activity is typically considered an important developmental event, few investigate the meaning and personal relevance of sexual activity for the adolescent. The mountain of empirical data on the frequency of various sexual behaviors among adolescents, the number of sexual partners, and the negative outcomes associated with sexual activity (disease and pregnancy) tells us little about the role of sexuality in motivating different types of relationships and altering the course and experience of relationships already underway. Finally, atypical relationships – such as casual friendships involving regular sexual activity or intense romantic bonds *lacking* such activity – are undertheorized within such models, typically interpreted as temporary aberrations on the road to more "mature" relationships. Although this characterization may sometimes prove accurate, it is usually made on a presumptive rather than an empirical basis.

The distinctions set forth in our typology are pertinent to any analysis of adolescent peer relationships, but they are particularly critical for understanding the experiences of sexual-minority (i.e., lesbian, gay, or bisexual) youths, who have been historically neglected by researchers on this topic. Adolescents are almost always presumed to be heterosexual by the researchers who study them, and even firsthand reports of same-sex behavior are frequently dismissed as drive reduction or experimentation. When the existence of sexual-minority youths *is* acknowledged, it too often receives only a cursory examination. Researchers may disclaim that too little data exist to permit a substantive discussion (a characterization that is no longer accurate) or may argue that the relationship experiences of sexual-minority youths mirror those of heterosexuals save for the gender of their partners and the added stress of social stigma.

In actuality, sexual orientation exerts a far more significant and wide-ranging press on adolescent intimate relationships than these accounts imply. Consider a lesbian teenager who perpetually loses to boys the intimate female friends to whom she is powerfully drawn but to whom she is never permitted to reveal her true feelings. The emotional repercussions and threats to her sense of self-efficacy are direct and profound. So too for the gay male adolescent who imagines that his only prospect for establishing an intimate interpersonal connection with another male is through furtive sexual encounters, or who never enjoys the opportunity to date someone to whom he is *both* erotically and emotionally attracted until adulthood. The bisexual adolescent faces a particularly confusing set of hurdles. He or she may have no knowledge that bisexuality exists and may therefore lack an explanatory context in which to make sense of dual attractions and the conflicting paths, opportunities, and identities they represent.

Fortunately, the number of school and community support groups for sexual-minority youths has increased dramatically over the past 5 years, providing an unprecedented number of youths with the opportunity to meet supportive and similar peers. Formidable barriers remain, however, for those who wish to establish intimate peer relationships. The difficulty inherent in simply identifying other sexual-minority youths creates onerous risks. If an adolescent mistakenly attempts to initiate a same-sex relationship with a heterosexual acquaintance, he or she risks severe peer rejection and perhaps physical danger. In response to such risks, many sexual-minority adolescents may strike a tenuous balance between risk and reward, pursuing exclusively emotional or exclusively sexual relationships that allow them a measure of same-sex intimacy without placing them in social jeopardy. The particular compromise an adolescent makes may depend on his or her ethnic and racial identity, social class, religious identification, and geographic location.

By focusing attention on issues facing sexual-minority youth, we seek both to grant them a greater voice in adolescent research and to widen our discipline's perspective on the range of relationships that can be considered normative, adaptive, and developmentally appropriate for adolescents in different circumstances. The value of focusing on the motivations, characteristics, and functions underlying different relationships is perhaps most evident when considering adolescents whose relationship options are constrainted. If researchers were routinely to assume diversity in sexual orientation when formulating research questions and designing sampling strategies, we might find that current interpretations of adolescent peer relationships fail to do justice to the experiences of *either* heterosexual *or* sexual-minority adolescents.

Thus, it is within both an appreciative and a critical context concerning existing research that we offer our perspectives regarding adolescents' intimate peer relations. Although prior research has made great strides in parsing the landscape of the adolescent's social and emotional world, we argue that closer attention to the distinctions between sexual relationships, dating relationships, passionate friendships, and romantic relationships is critical to modeling their developmental significance for all youths. In discussing each type of relationship, special attention is devoted to describing the experiences of sexual-minority adolescents and outlining key areas for future research on this population. These suggestions will not only increase our understanding of sexual-minority social development, but will also help to clarify how diverse populations of both heterosexual and sexual-minority adolescents strategically weigh desires and opportunities against risks and social constraints in seeking and sustaining a differentiated network of peer relationships to meet their needs.

Sexual Relationships

Motivations, Characteristics, and Functions

Adolescents are participating in sexual activity in large numbers and at increasingly younger ages (see Hofferth, 1990, for a review). By age 18, the majority of adolescents – regardless of gender, ethnicity, geographic region, and sexual orientation – are sexually active, despite the proliferation of educational campaigns advocating abstinence. The risks of unplanned pregnancy and sexually transmitted diseases facing these youths make it imperative to investigate the antecedents of these behaviors. Although an excellent body of research has succeeded in identifying predictors and correlates of first coitus among male and female adolescents (Bingham & Crockett, 1996; Udry & Billy, 1987), this research continues a long tradition of studying sexual activity outside of the diverse relational contexts in which it may be embedded. When such contexts receive attention, they are usually presumed to be dating or romantic relationships.

We focus here on *sexual relationships,* defined as peer relationships extending for any period of time whose primary focus is sexual activity. Attraction between partners is a frequent but not necessary component; similarly, a high or even moderate degree of mutual emotional engagement is not integral to these relationships. Instead, sexual activity constitutes their defining characteristic. We define *sexual activity* to include a continuum of behaviors motivated by sexual desire and oriented toward sexual pleasure, even if these activities do not culminate in sexual release. It bears noting that the distinction between affectionate and sexual behavior is a vague one that baffles both adolescents and the researchers who study them. When, for example, might an intimate but nongenital caress be considered sexual rather than affectionate? Some might argue that such a determination is impossible and therefore meaningless. However, we maintain that as long as adolescents *themselves* perceive boundaries between sexual and affectionate behavior, researchers should honor the normative significance of these distinctions even when they are based on ambiguous or situationally variable criteria. Importantly, however, researchers must allow adolescents the final say in delimiting these categories. The interpretation of any instance of physical contact will vary according to an adolescent's personal and cultural standards concerning intimate touch. Thus, although we classify as sexual any physical contact motivated primarily by sexual pleasure and desire (rather than, for example, the provision of emotional support or the signaling of a certain degree of reciprocal intimacy), determination of which behaviors fit this description is left to the adolescent.

Sexual *relationships* may be easily conflated with the sexual *activity* that occurs within a dating or romantic relationship, but attention to their unique motivations, characteristics, and functions reveals important differences. Most notably, sexual activity that takes place within a dating or romantic relationship does not, according to our typology, constitute the *defining* characteristic of such a relationship. Alternatively, participants in a sexual relationship may rarely engage in the public activities typical of dating and romantic relationships, such as attending parties and events together. The entire relationship may take place out of public view. Also, sexual relationships typically lack the mutual emotional attachment characteristic of romantic relationships. Both partners may intentionally eschew emotional intimacy; in other cases, one participant may accept the terms of the relationship in the hope that over time, repeated sexual contact will inadvertently lead to an emotional bond. Finally, unlike either dating or romantic relationships, sexual relationships may entail little or no expectation of continued involvement from week to week or day to day. Termination of the relationship may require little more than the simple and unexplained withdrawal of one participant from the other.

Why might an adolescent pursue a sexual relationship instead of a dating or romantic relationship? Sexual relationships indisputably provide pleasure, an outlet for sexual gratification, and a means to explore one's sexuality, but researchers must additionally consider motivations revolving around the larger peer group. To the extent that adolescents associate sexual activity with maturity, sexual relationships may allow an adolescent to *feel* mature and to *convey* an impression of maturity to others, thereby achieving a measure of social status or prestige quite distinct from the status and maturity associated with dating and romantic relationships. Adolescent males may be particularly interested in telegraphing the fact that they engage in sex with a large number of women but refuse to be "tied down" by any particular partner.

Sexual relationships may also serve intimacy-related functions in spite of their disavowal of intimate engagement. In particular, adolescents whose peer and even familial relationships lack physical affection or emotional intimacy may turn to sexual relationships to compensate (Martin, 1982; Tripp, 1975). The physical contact inherent in these relationships may function to soothe and comfort these adolescents, allowing them to feel attractive and desired without requiring them to risk emotional vulnerability. For others, sexual relationships simply afford easy companionship outside the constraints of more established bonds. Finally, as discussed later, they can provide an important context for the negotiation of sexual identity. Because such relationships require no ongoing commitment, emotional attachment, or public acknowledgment, they may be viewed by sexual-minority youths as an ideal testing ground for confirming or disconfirming the strength and authenticity of same-sex attractions.

It must also be recognized that just as a significant number of adolescents forgo sexual *activity* (Miller & Moore, 1990), many adolescents never participate in sexual relationships as we have defined them. For some, moral and/or religious standards and fears of pregnancy and sexually transmitted diseases provide a motivation to abstain from sexual activity altogether; others may view such behavior as acceptable only within the context of an established and enduring relationship. Finally, some youths may forgo sexual relationships for reasons beyond their control. They may find few partners willing to accept the restricted parameters of such a relationship, or they may possess physical, personality, or social characteristics that reduce sexual involvement with peers.

Issues Regarding Sexual-Minority Youth

Participation in Other-Sex Sexual Activity. In order to discern the relevance of sexual *relationships* for sexual-minority youth, it is important to clarify that such youths typically engage in *both* same-sex and other-sex sexual activity (D'Augelli, 1991; Herdt & Boxer, 1993; Savin-Williams, 1990, 1998). In the majority of youth samples, approximately one-half of gay and bisexual men and three-quarters of lesbian and bisexual women report having engaged in heterosexual sex; the rates of same-sex sexual activity are approximately 90% for both groups (D'Augelli, 1991; Lever, 1994, 1995; Savin-Williams, 1990; Sears, 1991). Other-sex sexual activity may represent authentic heterosexual interest, an effort to stimulate such interest, an attempt to hide or deny same-sex attractions, or a means of confirming one's predisposition for the same sex. The existing data do not clarify the context in which sexual-minority youths typically engage in heterosexual sexual behavior, but it is plausible that such behavior is most likely to occur within established and publicly visible dating or romantic relationships (Savin-Williams, 1998).

The higher rates of heterosexual sex among young sexual-minority women have several possible explanations. Women report later onset of same-sex attractions and fantasies than men, later participation in same-sex sexual contact, and later identification as lesbian or bisexual (Bell & Weinberg, 1978; Chapman & Brannock, 1987; Herdt & Boxer, 1993; Sears, 1989), leaving women with a longer period of time during which they may experiment with or engage in sex with males. Additionally, Weinberg, Williams, and Pryor (1994) suggest that due to social and cultural influences, it may simply prove more difficult for a young lesbian than a young gay man to avoid heterosexual experiences. Finally, research suggests that a greater proportion of women than men experience attraction for both sexes (Laumann, Gagnon, Michael, & Michaels, 1994), and some lesbians with exclusive *current* same-sex attractions report having been attracted to men *in the past* (Diamond, 1998; Weinberg et al., 1994). These findings suggest that not all heterosexual sexual activity among sexual-minority women is wholly attributable to social pressure. Instead, the interplay between the female adolescent's social context and her emerging and fluctuating attractions must be assessed to understand her participation in heterosexual sex.

Same-Sex Sexual Activity and Relationships. Sexual activity with a member of the same sex may allow an adolescent to test homoerotic attractions and validate an emerging sexual-minority identity. Again, however, we rarely know the context in which this activity takes place. Although many assume that same-sex sexual activity occurs within developing same-sex romantic relationships, Herdt and Boxer (1993) found that less than 20% of sexual-minority adolescents had their first same-sex sexual experience in this context. In actuality, same-sex sexual activity frequently takes place within friendships, within sexual relationships, or outside of *any* relational context.

For some sexual-minority youths, sexual relationships with same-sex peers may provide the only avenue for same-sex intimacy. This is most true of young sexual-minority men, many of whom may lack opportunities to forge emotionally intimate bonds with other males. Additionally, youths may fear that establishment of such bonds will arouse suspicion among friends and family, possibly leading to rejection, harassment, or violence. Although homophobia is a concern for sexual-minority adults as well, it poses greater threats to the well-being of adolescents. A sexual-minority adolescent may already be privately plagued by the sense that he or she is profoundly different from other youths. To have this differentness acknowledged and perhaps ridiculed by peers may prove intolerable. Furthermore, adolescents' economic dependence on parents raises the stakes of familial rejection, and unlike adults, sexual-minority adolescents may have no knowledge of gay, lesbian, and bisexual support resources that could provide them a safety net. A gay male adolescent under these circumstances may find clandestine sex with other men considerably easier and safer to pursue than a dating or romantic relationship. Finally, youths who find themselves ejected from their homes and forced to live on the streets may rely on "survival" sexual relationships in order to acquire shelter, money, food, and emotional support (see the review in Savin-Williams, 1994).

For a variety of reasons, young sexual-minority women are less likely to pursue exclusively sexual relationships. Most notably, women place less emphasis than men on the sexual component of their lesbian or bisexual orientation, both during and after the process of sexual identity questioning (Blumstein & Schwartz, 1990; Cass, 1990; Esterberg, 1994; Sears, 1989). Instead, emotional attachments to other women often take precedence. Because expressions of physical affection are more culturally normative among women than among men, a young sexual-minority woman may manage to obtain both physical and emotional intimacy within same-sex friendships without disclosing her sexual identity. This may be particularly true within certain ethnic communities, many of which allow expressions of physical affection between women friends, such as prolonged hand holding and the sharing of sleeping quarters, that would arouse suspicion in mainstream culture.

Ethnicity can exert a critical influence on the pursuit of sexual relationships among sexual-minority youth. Many traditional cultures strongly condemn same-sex sexuality, and sexual-minority youths from these cultures may feel that their same-sex attractions deeply violate their cultural identity and familial loyalty. These youths may fear that disclosure of their sexual orientation would lead to rejection from their entire ethnic community, not just their immediate family. These factors often operate to prevent many youths of color from identifying themselves as lesbian, gay, or bisexual (see Manalansan, 1996, and Savin-Williams, 1996a, for reviews). Although young women may safely pursue same-sex intimacy in the context of emotionally intimate and physically affectionate friendships, young gay or bisexual men seldom have this option. Thus, secretive sexual relationships may constitute a male youth's sole outlet for same-sex intimacy. He may reason (to self or to others) that sex, pursued for its own sake and divorced from any emotional and/or relational context, serves simply as a physical release and has no relevance to sexual identity.

Directions for Future Research. Future research should attempt to document the frequency of sexual relationships among all adolescents, clarify the diverse motives propelling them into these relationships, and explore their developmental implications. For example, how might they affect a youth's emerging sense of self, emotional well-being, and overall perspective on the role of sexual intimacy within close interpersonal relationships? Investigation into the role of self-regard in influencing the timing of a sexual-minority adolescent's participation in same-sex sexual activity holds particular promise. It is possible that adolescents with high self-regard and a high level of comfort with their sexuality may be more likely to engage in sex with same-sex peers and to do so at an earlier age. Sexual relationships may or may not provide the primary context for this activity.

It should be noted that participation in *same-sex* sexual activity and relationships by sexual-minority youths and participation in *other-sex* sexual activity and relationships by heterosexual youths should not be presumed analogous. The social and psychological contexts in which sexual-minority adolescents pursue sexual activity and sexual relationships with *both* same-sex and other-sex partners render these activities distinctive phenomena worthy of substantive exploration. Attention to the motives propelling youths to pursue sexual activity across different contexts, the associated mental health benefits and drawbacks, and the developmental implications of adolescents' choices is clearly needed.

Dating Relationships Among Adolescents

Motivations, Characteristics, and Functions

Of all relationships under discussion, dating is the most public, the most culturally condoned, and the most socially scripted. For these reasons, both participation in and eschewal of dating relationships carry unique meanings and consequences for adolescents. As we define them, dating relationships entail a mutual expression of romantic interest between partners that is publicly expressed via participation in shared activities usually visible to the adolescents' peers and parents. Unlike romantic relationships, participants have not yet committed themselves to, and may not even be seeking, a sexual or romantic relationship. Thus, dating relationships may be easy to terminate. It is important to note that the public acknowledgment of a dating relationship is quite distinct from the public acknowledgment of the "couplehood" that accompanies romantic relationships. In the former case, there may be little expectation (among participants or their peers) that the pair will continue their association over time. A dating relationship may, in fact, last only as long as one or two dates. Although one may question whether such a brief association constitutes a dating relationship, we argue that this determination must be based on the specific motivations and functions underlying the dating relationship rather than its absolute duration.

For example, dating symbolizes an adolescent's entry into the adult arena of heterosexual relationships, and adolescents who date are generally considered attractive, popular, and mature by others (Samet & Kelly, 1987). Thus, adolescents may be motivated to date in order to convey precisely this impression to the imagined audience of their peers (Elkind, 1980) or to privately confirm that they are "mature" and "normal." These aims may be served in the course of only one or two sufficiently visible dates. Similarly, adolescents who seek dating relationships with particular peers in order to gain access to a socially desirable group may also find that a limited number of dates successfully accomplishes this goal.

Adolescents who seek dating relationships for the sheer excitement of pursuing someone and the feeling of achievement or conquest that ensues from dating a variety of people may participate in a series of brief dating relationships. In such cases, the significance and relevance of each relationship may prove less meaningful than the overall pattern of peer associations over time. Such patterns are similarly important in assessing the role of dating relationships in promoting familiarity with the other sex and fostering social competence (Paul & White, 1990). Because adolescents who are particularly shy or unfamiliar with the other sex may forgo dating altogether, they may prove less socially competent by the close of adolescence than their peers. Although it has been noted that adolescents who do not date exhibit depression as well as personality and emotional disorders (Bornstein & Bruner, 1993; Weiner, 1992), the extent to which an adolescent's lack of dating exacerbates or is itself a by-product of such problems is often unclear.

Of course, adolescents often date for the simplest and most obvious of reasons – the prospect of developing a romantic or sexual relationship with an attractive and riveting peer. Consequently, it is often difficult to disentangle motivations underlying dating relationships from motivations underlying romantic relationships. The functions served by each type of relationship, however, remain distinct. For example, dating interactions frequently take place in group contexts and are often characterized as superficial (Douvan & Adelson, 1966). Thus, regardless of what an adolescent hopes eventually to glean from a dating relationship, it will not typically provide substantive reciprocal intimacy and mutual validation until it develops into a romantic relationship.

It is difficult to identify the precise moment at which this transition occurs. Commitment is not the sole criterion, for even romantic relationships with low levels of commitment may entail the strong feelings of mutual emotional attachment that characterize romantic relationships. By the same token, some adolescents may pursue long-standing, committed romantic relationships that remain as emotionally guarded as casual dating relationships. Sexual behavior, of course, may take place in either type of relationship. Perhaps because researchers have not taken adolescents' love relationships as seriously as adult relationships, little is understood about the process by which an adolescent moves from the awkwardness and hesitancy of a dating relationship to the exhilaration of a budding romance to the comfort and security of a committed romantic relationship. Attention to the role of underlying motivations and functions in this process, rather than to shifts in the surface structure of a relationship, will yield the greatest insight into the developmental implications of these transitions.

Issues Regarding Sexual-Minority Youth

Participation in and Functions of Dating. Because dating relationships provide a common route to romantic relationships, many of the special considerations constraining sexual-minority youths' pursuit of same-sex dating relationships constitute de facto constraints on romantic relationships and should be interpreted as such. Most often, sexual-minority adolescents face two options: They can date members of the other sex or they can choose not to date at all. Only rarely can they glimpse the possibility of asking out a peer of the same sex (Sears, 1991). For this reason, dating is not a well-developed institution among sexual-minority youths, particularly in rural areas where such youths are likely to be few in number and less openly identified. When same-sex dating relationships *are* available, they may provide youths with a crucial sense of being normal, demonstrating that a lesbian, gay, or bisexual orientation does not prevent them from enjoying many of the activities and pleasures of a typical adolescence.

Dating relationships also provide a template for relationship norms within sexual-minority communities. Prior to the first dating relationship with a same-sex peer, a sexual-minority adolescent may wonder how same-sex dating differs from opposite-sex dating: Which person does the asking? Who pays? Whereas examples of heterosexual dating scripts abound in movies, television, and advice-giving tracts, few comparable cultural models exist for same-sex dating. Participation in same-sex dating may provide a youth's only practical, firsthand knowledge of how such relationships are conducted.

When a newly identified sexual-minority adolescent dates a more experienced same-sex peer, these relationships may serve to socialize the adolescent into larger sexual-minority communities. By attending community functions and activities with a seasoned peer, sexual-minority adolescents gain exposure to facets of the community that they might have been too intimidated to explore on their own. These experiences provide the adolescent an important sense of belonging within his or her local lesbian, gay, or bisexual community that may well outlast the initial dating relationship.

Of course, a sexual-minority adolescent need not *date* an experienced sexual-minority peer in order to experience this informal socialization. Friendships with peers and friendly contact with older mentors can serve this function equally well. Adolescents with access to youth-focused community resources may find it easy to meet and make friends with sexual-minority peers. However, adolescents without access to these resources may find it far more difficult to gain entry into the existing social circles of their local lesbian, gay, or bisexual community. Participation in a dating relationship with an experienced companion often provides easy access to social networks and community resources.

Finally, dating may serve as a "trial balloon" for the sexual-minority youth's emerging sexual identity, allowing him or her to decide whether the benefits of publicly acknowledging same-sex attractions are greater than the risks of peer and parental rejection that this acknowledgment all too frequently entails. On the basis of several dating experiences, some youths may decide not to pursue same-sex relationships until they finish high school, leave town, secure a job, or reach college. These and other life-course transitions often provide a buffer of distance between the youth and his or her family and community. In addition, they frequently put youths in contact with a larger array of lesbian, gay, and bisexual support resources and a larger pool of potential partners than are available in their high schools or home communities.

Although heterosexual dating is often viewed as a critical transition to adult heterosexual *relationships,* same-sex dating among sexual-minority adolescents may clearly function as a critical transition to a gay, lesbian, or bisexual *identity.* The casual and uncommitted nature of dating relationships allows recently identified lesbian, gay, and bisexual adolescents to experiment with their newfound sense of self without making daunting and premature commitments. For these reasons, such youth may be more eager to date than more experienced sexual-minority adolescents, who may often prefer sexual or romantic relationships.

Places of Contact. Perhaps the biggest obstacle to same-sex dating among sexual-minority youths is the identification of potential partners. Whereas heterosexual adolescents routinely assume that a peer of the other sex is available for a dating relationship, sexual-minority youths must first determine the sexual orientation of a desired peer. Mistakes can be costly. The repercussions for an adolescent who expresses romantic or sexual interest in a heterosexual peer of the same sex might involve inadvertent disclosure of his or her sexual orientation to parents, peers, and school officials, as well as pervasive stigmatization. Because of these risks, few sexual-minority adolescents attempt to meet potential dating partners in traditional school or extracurricular settings.

Instead, a youth may seek same-sex dates through lesbian, gay, and bisexual community resources. As such resources have become more widely available in recent years, they have vastly expanded adolescents' opportunities to meet similar youths. Because the first hurdle of same-sex dating – identifying sexual-minority peers – is eliminated in these contexts, these youths are free to engage in the same awkward, exciting, and public process of dating as heterosexual adolescents.

Many adolescents' first contact with other sexual-minority adolescents takes place in the context of a youth support group. Within the last 5 years, hundreds of such groups, often under the auspices of gay–straight alliances, have formed in local high schools throughout the United States. They are most common on the East and West coasts, in urban areas, and in liberal academic communities. These groups, which may meet as often as once a week, provide an informal setting in which to discuss concerns about coming out, parents, relationships, and any other topics of interest (for a detailed description of the workings of one such group, see Herdt and Boxer's 1993 ethnography of the Horizons youth group in Chicago). Because many sexual-minority youths have no other contact with sexual-minority peers, the simple opportunity to meet and share experiences with a group of sexual-minority age-mates is perhaps the most important service these groups provide. Adolescents often socialize after regular meetings at a local cafe or restaurant, engendering opportunities for all sorts of relationships.

Unfortunately, youth groups are often completely inaccessible to sexual-minority adolescents living in rural, isolated, small, or conservative communities. Although some may travel several hours by car or bus to attend meetings of groups in nearby cities, many do not have ready access to transportation. If an adolescent's hometown is large enough to support lesbian, gay, or bisexual community establishments or activities (such as bars, coffeehouses, Pride parades, picnics, or political organizations), he or she may meet friends and/or potential partners in these settings. Unfortunately, a bar may be the only establishment that a small community can support, and one can speculate that adolescents (as well as adults) who rely on bars for social interaction with other sexual minorities might face an increased risk of alcohol abuse.

Some urban areas have been increasingly successful in providing alcohol-free outlets for sexual-minority adolescent social contact, such as coffeehouses or juice bars. In large cities with dense sexual-minority populations, proms for sexual-minority youth have been organized to provide all the trappings of this classic adolescent rite of passage – live music, adult chaperones, slow dancing, crepe paper streamers, and the crowning of a king and queen – in a safe, affirmative setting. Such events have become increasingly popular. The *San Francisco Chronicle* reported that 800 youths between the ages of 14 and 25 were expected for the Second Annual Northern California Gay Prom. On balance, however, these options are few and far between, and most youth who venture into sexual-minority community settings will find themselves consistently outnumbered by adults.

The Internet has greatly expanded the range of available options for sexual-minority youths who want to meet same-age peers. Chat rooms, bulletin boards, list servers, and Web pages geared to sexual minorities in general and youths in particular have become increasingly common. Adolescents with access to networked computer systems have seized the opportunities presented by these forums to develop "pen-pal" friendships or engage in electronic courtships that may or may not culminate in actual relationships. These modes of interaction with other sexual-minority adults and adolescents provide an unprecedented degree of privacy, anonymity, and safety for sexual-minority youths who have no access to sexual-minority community resources or who cannot risk disclosing their sexual orientation by attending a lesbian, gay, or bisexual event. Of course, few youths from lower- or working-class backgrounds have the access to networked computer systems that wealthier adolescents enjoy. Until more public high schools are able to install the appropriate hardware and software, Internet sexual-minority resources will remain segregated by class and computer literacy.

Although the upsurge in community resources geared to sexual-minority youth has made it easier for such youths to meet and date same-sex partners, the majority of sexual-minority adolescents continue to face difficulty finding such partners. Women, in particular, tend to be less well represented in youth support groups than their male counterparts, largely because women tend to self-identify as lesbian or bisexual at later ages than men (Bell & Weinberg, 1978; Califia, 1979; Chapman & Brannock, 1987; Troiden, 1988). Thus, a young lesbian attending a support group might meet only two other women in the group, neither of whom she may find attractive (a point that is all too often overlooked). Because of the restricted pool of potential dating partners, their characterization of desirable partners, and their level of self-disclosure and self-identification, even sexual-minority youths with access to other such youths may rarely date these peers. Some may choose not to date, and others may expand their pool of potential partners to include sexual-minority adults.

Dating Adults. A sexual-minority adolescent is far more likely to meet sexual-minority adults than same-age peers in his or her local community, and these adults may be more willing to pursue a dating relationship openly than adolescents. Although dating relationships between adolescents and adults need not be considered inherently harmful (Savin-Williams, 1998), they introduce a number of special concerns. For example, an adolescent's expectations for a dating relationship may be starkly different from those of his or her adult companion, particularly in light of robust cohort differences regarding the definitions and meanings of dating. Furthermore, the age gap between adolescents and adults could introduce a sizable power differential that compromises an adolescent's ability to direct the course of the relationship or his or her confidence to do so; a youth's relative inexperience with same-sex relationships can have the same effect.

It bears noting that some adolescents may consciously seek dating relationships with adults for the security and experience that they represent or because they simply find older peers more desirable and attractive than same-age peers. Adults who are extremely familiar with the lesbian, gay, or bisexual community may serve as consummate socialization agents for adolescents, introducing them to local community norms and expectations regarding dress, relationship behavior, and even political ideology. An older peer who is more secure in his or her sexual identity may be (or, importantly, *seem*) better able to support the adolescent's process of self-identification and self-affirmation than another adolescent. Alternatively, some youths may wish to speed through this process, dating older peers in order to feel and/or appear more established in their lesbian, gay, or bisexual identity. Finally, an adolescent who has successfully traversed the process of identity development may not want to date peers who are still negotiating a nascent sexual-minority identity.

Thus, an adolescent who can choose to date either same-age or adult partners may prefer to form friendships with the former while dating the latter. It should not be forgotten that among heterosexuals and sexual minorities alike, older dating partners confer a coveted sense of status or maturity on adolescents. Thus, researchers should not assume that sexual-minority adolescents who have opportunities to meet sexual-minority age-mates will prefer to date these peers over adults. Nor should researchers assume that adult–adolescent relationships constitute a de facto danger for the adolescent. As noted earlier, such relationships offer both benefits and drawbacks, and the resulting balance depends largely on the individual adult an adolescent meets. Overall, however, opportunities for dating age-mates should be supported by the provision of greater resources for sexual-minority youth.

Interracial Dating. Just as youths are proportionately outnumbered by adults in sexual-minority community settings, lesbian, gay, and bisexual ethnic minorities of all ages are outnumbered by whites. Although large urban centers often have diverse sexual-minority communities and may even boast distinct and sizable sexual-minority communities of color, sexual and ethnic minority youths in all but the largest cities will likely find that their limited dating pool of same-sex peers is predominantly white. Although some may not object to dating white youths, others may strongly prefer to date peers with whom they share an ethnic culture, history, and community. These youths must therefore face a difficult choice: Either they can sacrifice this preference and date white youths or they can forgo same-sex dating altogether.

The pitting of sexual identity against ethnic identity may be all too familiar to these adolescents, as noted previously. The threat of stigma and ostracization from one's community may altogether crush an ethnic-minority adolescent's interest in dating same-sex youths, causing him or her to postpone same-sex dating until after leaving the community of origin. Sadly, the provision of physical distance between family life and sexual-minority community life may seem the only solution to incompatible identities. Again, the provision of greater services for ethnic-minority youth, through which they may access peers and mentors who have managed similar negotiations between sexual and ethnic identity, is the most effective means to increase the level of support and the range of relationship options available to these adolescents.

Other-Sex Dating. It must not be overlooked that, for a number of reasons, the majority of sexual-minority youths date heterosexually throughout adolescence (see Savin-Williams, 1996b, for a review). Heterosexual dating may provide an effective "cover" for a youth's true sexual orientation. Because dating relationships need not develop into romantic or sexual relationships, they might also allow sexual-minority adolescents to present a public façade of heterosexuality without requiring extensive involvement in heterosexual relationships.

Of course, many sexual-minority youths participate in dating relationships before they come to a realization of their nonheterosexual orientation. These youths may simply be performing a normative role, not understanding why their experiences seem less satisfying than those of their friends. Some may question and begin to recognize their sexual identity as a result of unsatisfactory heterosexual dating. Others may date repeatedly, hoping that finding the "right person" will eliminate their same-sex attractions or seeking to test the strength of their same-sex attractions against their heterosexual experiences (Herdt & Boxer, 1993). Bisexual youths, on the other hand, may be confused by their enjoyment of heterosexual dating. A bisexual youth may think, "If I like the person I'm dating so much, then I must not be gay. But I know that I'm still attracted to the same sex, so I must not be straight." Because many youths are unaware of the existence of bisexuality or do not understand its complex meaning and multiple permutations, they may see no explanation for their feelings.

Gay and lesbian adolescents, too, may face this confusion, especially those who recall their dating and relationship experiences with the other sex as highly pleasurable and enjoyable (Diamond, 1998; Savin-Williams, 1998). In some cases, sexual-minority adolescents may find their *same-sex* dating experiences less satisfying than their *other-sex* relationships, simply because their limited pool of eligible same-sex peers makes it harder to find a compatible partner. Thus, researchers should not presume on the basis of a youth's current sexual identity that his or her prior heterosexual involvements were universally devoid of meaning and pleasure. Traditional dating, as we have shown, serves a number of different purposes, and adolescents may derive pleasure from these experiences for a number of reasons. The nature, quality, and import of *both* same-sex and other-sex dating experiences should be considered open empirical questions.

Directions for Future Research. Although prior research has focused on the dating *activities* of heterosexual and sexual-minority adolescents, few investigations have examined the *meanings* of both same-sex and other-sex dating among sexual-minority youths. Rapid cultural changes in mainstream perceptions of sexual orientation and in the availability of opportunities for same-sex dating will have numerous and profound effects on these meanings. Future research should take advantage of the cultural changes underway by examining not only whether and how many sexual-minority adolescents date same-sex peers, but also how such dating affects sexual identity and self-concept at successive points along a youth's developmental trajectory. Furthermore, as the category *bisexual* becomes more widely known and appreciated, increasing numbers of bisexuals will likely identify as such during adolescence rather than after a temporary identification as lesbian or gay. The dating experiences of bisexuals have much to tell us about the ways in which sexual-minority adolescents evaluate the evidence of their own behavior, feelings, and attractions in coming to understand their sexual identity.

Finally, to the extent that heterosexual adolescents who do not engage in dating or romantic relationships have fewer opportunities to master the social skills relevant to those interactions, one might question whether the constraints on sexual-minority adolescents' dating and relationship opportunities systematically alter their social developmental trajectories. Sexual-minority adolescents who feel awkward in social situations may attribute the discomfort to their sexual orientation, perhaps supposing that they will never experience the social ease and self-confidence of heterosexual peers. Given the opportunity to engage in the range of dating and relationship interactions readily available to heterosexual youth, however, a sexual-minority adolescent may discover a pleasure and comfort in social discourse previously thought unattainable.

Passionate Friendships Among Adolescents

Motivations, Characteristics, and Functions

The propensity for young women to develop more emotionally intimate same-sex friendships than men has been widely noted (Buhrmester & Furman, 1987). Largely neglected, however, is the small but notable number of dyadic friendships that become infused with an intensity resembling that of romantic relationships, though lacking a sexual component. These relationships can be conceptualized as *passionate friendships,* a term borrowed from Faderman's (1981) discussion of 18th- and 19-century *romantic friendships* but intended to denote contemporary rather than historical instances. Both Faderman (1981, 1991) and Smith-Rosenberg (1975) demonstrated that emotionally primary relationships between women have a rich cultural history dating back to the 16th century. Faderman argued that by the mid 19th and early 20th centuries, passionate attachments between women were not only acknowledged but considered normative, especially at the women's colleges that were springing up in New England during this time. These relationships were called *smashes,* described in 1882 as "an extraordinary habit which they have of falling violently in love with each other . . . with as much energy as if one of them were a man. . . . They monopolize each other & 'spoon' continually, & sleep together & lie awake all night talking instead of going to sleep" (Sahli, 1979, p. 22).

The cultural categories of romantic friendship and smashing dissolved around 1920, when intense same-sex bonds between women became subject to attributions of lesbianism. These intense, nonsexual bonds between young women continued, however. Crumpacker and Vander Haegen (1993) described young women whose conflicts with best friends were recalled with the heartbreak, grief, and intensity more typical of love relationships than our usual portrait of peer friendships. Indeed, in a recent study of young women's sexuality, Diamond (1997) reported that many heterosexual women listed their best friend as the object of one of the most intense, yet nonsexual, attractions they had ever experienced. Cole (1993) noted that a number of heterosexual college students, after reading accounts of primary, asexual bonds among women, reported similar bonds:

> My primary relationships have always been with women, even when I'm involved with and committed to a particular man. Rather than sexual desire, I think I have soulful desire for women. My two closest

friends and I are talking about a lifelong commitment to each other and are trying to figure out how to actualize it. (p. 190)

Over and over, I develop highly intimate, very sensual relationships with women. Many people have asked if we're "involved" and I haven't known what to say. (p. 190)

Unlike other types of relationships under discussion, passionate friendships are not sought out by adolescents. They evolve over time, and the depth and intensity of the eventual relationship often take both participants by surprise. However, it is still meaningful to discuss an adolescent's motivation to form strong best friendships, out of which passionate friendships most commonly develop. These motivations include the desire for a trusted and reliable confidante, dependable companionship, intimacy, and a sense of being understood and accepted (Buhrmester & Furman, 1986; Sullivan, 1953). Although many of these qualities are sought in romantic relationships as well, best friendships provide a source of intimacy and support that is not dependent on enduring sexual/romantic interest. They may also be less fervently discouraged by parents. Some parents, however, may view the unusual level of intimacy between girls as indicative of lesbianism and may thus discourage the friendship. Clearly, although passionate friendships share certain motivations, functions, and characteristics with both best friendships and same-sex romantic relationships, their unique course and content necessitate that they remain conceptually distinct from either of these relationship types.

Although characteristics of passionate friendships may vary widely from case to case, common features can be discerned. As the preceding discussion suggests, both participants are usually women. Although passionate friendships need not be considered an *exclusively* female phenomenon, the high levels of reciprocal intimacy characterizing women's same-sex friendships (Caldwell & Peplau, 1982) make them more likely to develop in this context than between two young men or within a cross-sex friendship. One possible exception concerns two sexual-minority male adolescents who become emotionally enamored of each other but who do not yet experience their mutual interest as explicitly sexual in nature. Additionally, a sexual-minority male youth may become strongly, but nonsexually, attached to a close female confidante. Their passionate attachment might be mistaken for a traditional romantic relationship, providing cover (to self as well as others) for the youth's sexual orientation. Passionate friendships between young heterosexual men and women would probably spill over into explicit sexual interest and might therefore prove uncommon. Because of the apparent asymmetry in the prevalence of passionate friendships between men and women, the following discussion focuses on women's experiences.

Participants in a passionate friendship are unusually preoccupied with each other and often commit quite seriously to the relationship, sometimes even making joint plans for the future. Similar to lovers, they may affectionately stroke, hold, or cuddle each other and experience feelings of jealousy, possessiveness, and intense separation anxiety. Although a small number of passionate friendships eventually evolve into full-fledged romantic or sexual relationships, they are always initially asexual. Although some might argue for an expanded definition of sexual contact that includes the affectionate touching characteristic of passionate friendships, it is useful to maintain a distinction between the latter (which may be highly sensual and which may *border* on the sexual) and forms of touch that are clearly generated by sexual interest and build for the purpose of sexual release. Additionally, the forms of touch common to passionate friendships are often more similar to the caregiving interactions of parents and children than the sexually intimate interactions of lovers (Diamond, 1997).

The ego-related functions of passionate friendships are numerous and overlap considerably with the functions of traditional romantic relationships. For example, each participant in a passionate friendship feels highly valued and needed by the other. The adolescent gains a high level of intimacy, companionship, and affectionate physical contact, as well as a sense of stability and trust. Social learning takes place regarding the daily practice of building and maintaining a loving, committed relationship with another person. In fact, during the 19th century, some considered such relationships a form of rehearsal for adult marriage (Faderman, 1991). Passionate friendships are unique in that they serve these functions outside the context of a sexual bond and therefore without the special pressures, risks, and concerns that accompany sexual involvement.

To the extent that passionate friendships resemble asexual romantic relationships, it is fruitful to consider their developmental implications from the perspective of attachment theory (Ainsworth, Blehar, Waters, & Wall, 1978; Bowlby, 1982), conceptualizing them as primary attachment bonds in the same way that researchers have viewed adult love relationships as primary attachment bonds (Hazan & Shaver, 1994; Shaver, Hazan, & Bradshaw, 1988). Recent attention has turned to the process by which young men and women transfer the fundamental components of attachment – proximity seeking, separation distress, utilization of the caregiver as a safe haven, and utilization of the caregiver as a secure base from which to explore – from parents to peers during the course of adolescence. Romantic relationships are generally considered crucial for this process (Furman & Wehner, 1994). Hazan and Zeifman (1994) found that among the 41% of adolescents in their sample who considered a peer to be their primary attachment figure, 83% were involved in romantic relationships with this peer.

The key question, then, concerns the remaining 17%. Considering that adolescent women's same-sex friendships are highly emotionally intimate, some young women may form their first nonparental attachment to a female friend rather than to a male romantic partner. Perhaps it is the status of these relationships as full-blown attachments that renders them more intense than normative best friendships.

The physical affection that is common to passionate friendships may play an important role in this distinction. Hazan and Zeifman (1994) argued that because intimate physical contact fosters a feeling of security, such contact is a prerequisite for both the mother–infant attachment bond and adult attachment bonds. They noted that the forms of physical intimacy that characterize the infant's relationship to his or her primary caregiver – kissing, suckling, belly-to-belly contact, and extended mutual gazing – reemerge only in sexually intimate relationships. Passionate friendships appear to involve an unusual degree of physical affection, even taking into account the considerable latitude granted women in exchanging platonic physical affection with same-sex friends. The unusual degree of physical affection in passionate friendships may promote their transformation from normative best friendships into full-blown attachments, in spite of the absence of sexual contact.

Because passionate friendships have not received systematic study, it is difficult to discern their overall role in adolescent social development. For example, one might speculate that adolescents who form passionate friendships eventually develop more intimate and satisfying romantic relationships because they come to expect a deeper degree of intimacy from their closest relationships. Alternatively, an adolescent may form *less* intimate bonds with subsequent romantic partners, preferring to meet primary emotional needs through a stable platonic friendship. Importantly, researchers should not presume that these relationships are substitutes for, or transitions to, traditional romantic relationships without thorough investigation into the meanings these relationships hold for those who participate in them.

Issues Regarding Sexual-Minority Youth

Involvement in a same-sex passionate friendship does not necessarily suggest that one or both of the young women is lesbian or bisexual. To the contrary, these relationships occur regardless of sexual orientation. Among sexual-minority youths, however, passionate friendships may hold a special status. For young lesbians, bisexuals, and those women who are questioning their sexuality, these bonds constitute an important context for the process of clarifying their sexual identity. Many sexual-minority women first begin to question their sexual identity in response to unusually close attachments to their best friends, even in the absence of explicit sexual feelings (Butler, 1990; Hall Carpenter Archives, 1989; National Lesbian and Gay Survey, 1992).

For a young lesbian or gay man who is unable to find other sexual-minority youths or is unwilling to assume the risk of revealing his or her sexual identity, a passionate friendship may satisfy needs traditionally met by romantic relationships without entailing heterosexual sexual activity. Thus, these relationships may constitute one of the most important routes by which sexual-minority youths obtain the nurturing, support, and intimate contact that alleviates some of the inevitable stress of growing up gay in a heterosexual world. This does not suggest, however, that passionate friendships simply represent substitutes for romantic relationships or way stations on the road to such relationships. This characterization mistakenly assumes that traditional romantic relationships represent the universal pinnacle of adult intimacy and the natural endpoint of an adolescent's relational development. This view is incompatible with the finding that some lesbians choose to sustain *both* romantic bonds and intense, platonic friendships during adulthood, often privileging the latter over the former (Weinstock & Rothblum, 1996).

It bears noting that the distinction between a passionate friendship and a same-sex romantic relationship may not be clear to an individual woman and her family, friends, or community. To the extent that Western culture presumes that the most emotionally intimate and physically affectionate nonkin relationships necessarily involve sexual intimacy (O'Connor, 1992), women involved in a passionate friendship may wonder whether they are "actually" sexually attracted to their friend without having realized it. These concerns may prompt sexual questioning among women who might otherwise never consider themselves lesbian or bisexual. In some cases, women may sexually consummate their passionate friendships, yet may never again desire or engage in same-sex sexual activity. This activity does not resemble traditional sexual experimentation, yet neither does it necessarily signal a same-sex sexual orientation. Investigation of such cases might significantly enrich understanding of the role of sexual behavior, emotional intimacy, and sexual orientation in prefiguring an adolescent woman's trajectory of intimate relationships and the meaning she ascribes to them.

Directions for Future Research. Because passionate friendships are easily misperceived as either normative best friendships or unconsummated love relationships, researchers have consistently overlooked them in charting the role of intimate relationships in adolescent development. Little is therefore known about their prevalence among youth in general and among demographic subpopulations in particular. Just as it remains unknown whether passionate friendships have unique developmental implications, it remains unknown whether sexual-minority youths, particularly lesbian and bisexual women, are substantially more likely to engage in passionate friendships than their heterosexual counterparts. Similarly, it is unclear whether heterosexual women who have had a passionate friendship are more likely than other heterosexual women to consider experimenting with same-sex sexual activity later in life. The role of passionate friendships in different ethnic communities is also a fruitful area of study. Because many such communities permit greater expression of platonic affection among women than does mainstream culture, it is possible that passionate friendships are more common or more socially condoned. Finally, the conditions under which passionate friendships occur among *male* youths deserve systematic investigation.

Of particular interest are questions concerning the occurrence of such relationships in adulthood as opposed to adolescence. Adults engaged in romantic relationships are likely to sustain primary attachments *exclusively* to romantic partners. However, those without romantic partners may meet primary needs for intimacy and support through asexual relationships analogous to passionate friendships. Rothblum and Brehony (1993) found that a number of adult lesbians maintained such bonds to former lovers, often continuing to cohabit, raise children, and share expenses even after breaking up. Although sexual and/or romantic relationships with other women were sometimes pursued outside of this platonic bond, its primacy and centrality in each woman's life were never questioned. They called these relationships *Boston marriages,* a term originally referring to 19th-century American women living together in a romantic friendship.

The developmental tasks of adolescence, however, may render these relationships particularly likely. Because adolescents are engaged in transferring attachment functions from parents to peers, peer relationships may easily become infused with an unusual and perhaps unprecedented level of reciprocal intimacy. Clearly, linkages between adolescent and adult participation in intimate, primary, and yet asexual bonds provide a fascinating area for future developmental research. This research first requires, however, that developmental psychologists expand contemporary relationship categories and resist making hasty conclusions about the nature of unusually close bonds among adolescents. This may significantly enrich our understanding of heterosexual as well as sexual-minority adolescents.

Romantic Relationships

Motivations, Characteristics, and Functions

Romantic relationships are typically, though not universally, distinguished from dating relationships by a mutual agreement between partners to sustain the relationship and by public acknowledgment of the status of the participants as a couple. By declaring their relationship to family, friends, and the greater society, adolescents may receive validation and support for their mutual commitment. Public acknowledgment may also reinforce the strength of the relationship; a couple may sense that family and peers would be sorely disappointed if they were to dissolve the relationship. Of course, romantic relationships may take place in secret, in which case mutual commitment to the relationship is expressed privately between the partners.

Most adolescents desire romantic relationships and anticipate participating in them; the motivations underlying these relationships are numerous. For many adolescents, such a relationship represents the consummate mark of adulthood (U.S. Bureau of the Census, 1986), and participation in romantic relationships may most effectively communicate maturity to peers. Parents, too, may view these relationships as more mature than dating relationships and may extend privileges and freedoms to children actively sustaining a commitment to a single partner that they might withhold from children bringing home a different date each week.

Most important, however, adolescents may seek such relationships simply for the reciprocal intimacy, comfort, and security they provide. The degree of emotional intimacy achieved in romantic relationships is typically higher than that achieved in adolescents' other peer relationships, and these may be the first bonds in which adolescents experience full-blown attachment to someone other than a parent (Hazan & Zeifman, 1994). For this reason, feelings of love and passion typically shared by participants in a romantic relationship may be experienced as unusually intense and all-consuming. Although some adolescent romantic relationships are turbulent, others furnish stability, constancy, and a coherent picture of the future during a period otherwise marked by change and uncertainty (Ainsworth, 1989). This stability also derives from feelings of being loved, desired, and even prized that usually accompany participation in romantic relationships. Particularly for male adolescents, who less frequently engage in the intimate disclosure common to female friendships (Camarena, Sarigiani, & Petersen, 1990), romantic relationships may provide a critical context in which to confide previously unexpressed thoughts and feelings.

Although participants in romantic relationships almost always report sexual attraction to each other and usually engage in highly affectionate behavior, *sexual* behavior should not be assumed to be a necessary feature of these relationships. As indicated previously, a significant number of adolescents abstain from sex, despite their relationship status. However, the presence of mutual sexual attraction and interest distinguishes these relationships from passionate friendships, as does the fact that romantic relationships are *socially acknowledged* as primary bonds rather than "just friendships."

As noted earlier, commitment is a frequent but not universal feature of romantic relationships; in fact, some adolescents perceive it to be a *negative* attribute of such relationships (Feiring, 1996). Although the commitment between adolescents is certainly not equivalent to that between married adults, we maintain that adolescent romantic relationships involve a degree of mutual commitment frequently unappreciated by adults. Participants both think of and present themselves as a couple ("we") rather than as consistently individuated partners. They display a future orientation toward the relationship, including each other in plans for the short-term future and in decisions about the long-term future. Exclusivity on the part of both partners is a frequent component of participants' commitment to the relationship. Individuals typically avow to take part in only one romantic relationship, whereas they might pursue numerous dating relationships simultaneously. For these reasons, romantic relationships provide adolescents with the opportunity to master a number of relationship skills that are relevant for future romantic relationships: consistently taking another person's interests into account, successfully managing minor disagreements and major fights, and providing sustained comfort and security to another person.

However, romantic relationships also carry a number of drawbacks: The time and energy required to sustain these relationships may jeopardize competing interests such as friendship networks, the desire for multiple sexual partners, career goals, or extracurricular activities. Some parents may actively discourage romantic relationships until educational plans have been completed and the adolescent's career path is underway, viewing them as a hindrance to, rather than a mark of, full maturity. Parents who dislike their child's romantic partner may decree certain privileges conditional on the termination of the relationship. The willingness of many adolescents to pursue romantic relationships in spite of such obstacles testifies to their importance.

Issues Regarding Sexual-Minority Youth

Obstacles to Participation in Romantic Relationships. Like their heterosexual counterparts, most sexual-minority youth desire traditional romantic relationships (D'Augelli, 1991; Savin-Williams, 1990). Yet the larger society creates many barriers to the development of same-sex romantic relationships, such as the lack of positive role models of same-sex couples, failure to recognize these couples formally, and the constant threat of hate crimes against individuals who dare express common affection toward a same-sex partner. Just as many sexual-minority youths avoid dating in order to hide their same-sex orientation, many eschew sustained involvement with a same-sex partner for the same reason.

In addition, many sexual-minority youths are plagued by internalized homophobia, resulting in an aversion to same-sex romantic relationships. Some youths may view romantic relationships as definitive proof of their nonheterosexual orientation, whereas isolated dates or sexual encounters can be explained away as experimentation. Other youths may absorb social stereotypes of same-sex relationships as predominantly sexual, fleeting, and scarce. Because they may perceive that sexual-minority individuals are not expected to desire or participate in long-term relationships, they may come to share these low expectations and consequently forgo romantic relationships altogether. An added concern for young sexual-minority men in particular is the perception that romantic relationships are discouraged among certain factions within gay communities in favor of more casual pairings (Myer, 1989). This perceived lack of support, coupled with the dearth of positive models for same-sex relationships, may contribute to low rates of participation in romantic relationships among sexual-minority youth.

Finally, the social isolation encountered by many sexual-minority youths prevents them from encountering opportunities for initiating romantic relationships or gaining support for their continuance. As indicated earlier, simply finding a desirable, available, interested partner can be a significant hurdle for many sexual-minority adolescents seeking romantic relationships. As a result, some youths may choose to meet their needs for intimacy through friendships with sexual-minority peers or adult mentors, passionate friendships, and sexual relationships, postponing the pursuit of romantic relationships indefinitely or until they have found a large pool of potential partners and a more supportive community.

Unique Characteristics of Sexual-Minority Romantic Relationships. The limitations placed on sexual minorities create significant differences between sexual-minority and heterosexual youth regarding the motivations, characteristics, and functions of romantic relationships. For example, the public recognition of a same-sex romantic relationship may place a youth at risk for family and peer rejection. Thus, although typical romantic relationships are characterized by public acknowledgment, disclosure of such relationships among sexual-minority youths may be limited to the partners' closest social networks.

Furthermore, just as sexual-minority adolescents may date across age and ethnic lines due to the limited pool of potential partners (as well as for other, often idiosyncratic reasons), they may form romantic relationships across such lines as well. The complications of these relationships, discussed previously, are compounded when they become more serious. Romantic relationships between adolescents and adults may be beset by discrepancies in expectations, as well as capacities, for commitment. In addition, although some peers may admire an adolescent for having a "mature" relationship, others may strongly disapprove and withdraw needed support. Adolescents who are romantically involved with adults probably avoid disclosing these relationships to parents. Even parents who accept their child's sexual orientation may forbid him or her to date a sexual-minority adult, perhaps suspecting the adult of seducing the youth into homosexuality. Managing the difficulties of such relationships while keeping them secret places additional burdens on the sexual-minority adolescent.

Interracial relationships, too, present special challenges for sexual-minority youth. A traditional ethnic family that grudgingly permits a child to date a white peer may view romantic relationships as a more direct threat to family loyalty. Ethnic-minority youths caught in such a situation may conclude that their most intimate, satisfying, supportive relationship is incompatible with their ethnic or cultural identity. Obviously, the sacrifice of a full-fledged romantic relationship may devastate a youth more profoundly than the sacrifice of a casual dating relationship and may represent a more serious compromise at the level of sexual identity.

The very form of romantic relationships, and not only the choice of romantic partners, is frequently distinctive among sexual minorities. For example, although sexual exclusivity may be normative among and central to heterosexual couples, many gay and bisexual men are not involved in and do not desire sexually exclusive relationships (Kurdek & Schmitt, 1985–1986; Lever, 1994). Despite the stigmatization of nonmonogamous relationships as unhealthy and uncommitted, research has found no psychological differences between men in monogamous and nonmonogamous relationships (Kurdek & Schmitt, 1985–1986). Particularly noteworthy is the fact that gay and bisexual men displayed equally high levels of emotional commitment within sexually exclusive and nonexclusive relationships. It must not be assumed, therefore, that sexual and emotional commitments are equivalent, interchangeable, or uniformly linked within all relationships.

This does not suggest a norm of nonmonogamy among gay and bisexual men but rather a *plurality* of approaches to sexual and romantic relationships within this population. Types of relationships sought by a particular individual may be influenced not only by local community standards but also by the individual's sexual and relationship history. For example, Dubé (1997) identified two unique relationship trajectories among sexual minority men. Those who reported engaging in same-sex sexual contact *prior* to identifying as gay or bisexual eventually participated in a higher proportion of sexual than romantic relationships, whereas those who engaged in same-sex sexual contact *after* identifying as gay or bisexual participated in relatively fewer sexual relationships. The long-term developmental implications of these patterns clearly deserve systematic attention.

Unique Motivations and Functions of Sexual-Minority Romantic Relationships. Sexual-minority youth who have never had a same-sex romantic relationship may have long engaged in elaborate fantasies regarding such relationships and the satisfaction they are anticipated to bring. Consequently, adolescents in the early stages of identity development may be especially eager to enter into a romantic relationship with the first eligible partner they meet and may vastly accelerate the transition from a dating relationship to a romantic relationship. Alternatively, they may skip the dating phase altogether by initiating a romantic relationship within a preexisting friendship. These patterns may be especially likely among adolescents who are most isolated from established sexual-minority communities, such as those living in rural areas, and who face the most limited pool of available partners.

Romantic relationships often facilitate the process of coming to terms with same-sex attractions and provide, for many adolescents, a definitive confirmation of their sexual orientation. Romance may also hasten the disclosure of sexual identity to others, whether intentionally or unintentionally. To be frequently seen in the company of a particular same-sex peer may elicit suspicion from family and friends, perhaps compromising a youth's efforts to keep his or her sexual identity a secret. Among youths who *choose* to disclose their sexual identity, serious romantic relationships can create a critical safety net of support in the event of a negative or rejecting response. For this reason, many adolescents may decide to conceal their sexual orientation from their families of *origin* until they have managed to develop a nurturing family of *choice* composed of close friends, older mentors, and an intimate romantic partner. Sexual-minority youths who become isolated from their nuclear and extended families or religious and ethnic communities as a result of their sexual orientation may invest considerably more importance in romantic relationships than do their heterosexual counterparts.

This importance is reflected in the fact that the chosen families crafted by sexual minorities often incorporate *former* lovers as well as friends and current romantic partners. This is particularly true among lesbians, who frequently remain close friends with previous lovers (Becker, 1988; Hite, 1987; Nardi & Sherrod, 1994). Because many lesbian relationships are *initiated* in the context of an existing friendship (Gramick, 1984; Rose, Zand, & Cimi, 1993; Schafer, 1977; Vetere, 1983), the maintenance of a close platonic friendship after romance has ended is not entirely surprising. In some cases, this fluidity between friendship and romantic love creates confusion concerning the distinction between them (Rose et al., 1993). However, the maintenance of close ties with former lovers is certainly adaptive and beneficial for individuals who may not have access to traditional familial support. In some cases, these relationships may develop into the Boston marriages described earlier (Rothblum & Brehony, 1993).

Directions for Future Research. Research on romantic relationships among sexual-minority adolescents should examine the importance of these relationships for the well-being of the individual and the role they play in the overall process of coming out to self and others. Of equal importance are the ways in which sexual-minority youths define and regard romantic relationships. Researchers are often unaware of what these youths seek in romantic relationships and how their expectations fluctuate during adolescence and over the course of sexual identity development. Future investigators must also broaden the scope of their research to include adolescents of diverse ethnicities and social classes and must make concerted efforts to incorporate longitudinal observation. These improvements will clarify how expectations for and participation in romantic relationships change over time across different sexual-minority populations.

Additionally, researchers should not assume that a gay or lesbian adolescent's other-sex romantic relationships are meaningless, unsatisfying, fake, or devoid of authentic intimacy. Although sexual-minority youths often experience these relationships differently than do their heterosexual peers, they may still constitute a critical source of intimate friendship. Many lesbians recall their adolescent other-sex relationships as positive experiences characterized by warmth, affection, and even excitement; in a few cases, a particularly sensitive boyfriend was the first to delicately ask his girlfriend whether she might be happier with women than men (Diamond, 1997). Because adolescent males are less well versed in reciprocal intimacy than adolescent females, a sexual-minority male youth may derive more sustenance from a romantic relationship with a close female friend than from same-sex relationships. Again, researchers must explore the actual experiences and underlying motives and functions of an adolescent's entire constellation of peer relationships in order to assess their developmental significance.

Because of the increasing visibility of diverse sexual-minority populations and the growing number of sexual-minority youths who enjoy opportunities to meet and establish romantic relationships with other sexual-minority youths, this is an optimal time to ask these questions. Furthermore, considering recent discussions of the legal standing, moral value, and potential healthfulness of same-sex marriage, the answers to these questions are being sought with increasing urgency. Investigation of adolescents' participation in committed same-sex relationships has much to tell us about the role of relational intimacy in moderating both typical and atypical stressors during adolescence and the role of sexual identity in shaping adolescent intimacy development.

Conclusion

The importance of drawing careful distinctions among the motivations, characteristics, and functions of different types of adolescent relationships may not immediately strike researchers who have examined exclusively heterosexual relationships. After all, as long as adolescents themselves blur the boundaries among sex, dating, and romance, perhaps it is not a serious error for researchers to do the same. However, even a cursory examination of the experiences of sexual-minority adolescents provides a compelling argument for maintaining and investigating these boundaries. Each time a sexual-minority adolescent considers participating in a sexual, dating, or romantic relationship (whether with the same sex or the other sex), he or she must negotiate a distinct array of desires, risks, and benefits. Heterosexual youths must similarly balance these considerations, albeit less consciously and with lower stakes. For this reason, research on sexual-minority youths highlights competing concerns and criteria that are relevant to *all* youth.

At the same time, the most important insights to be gained from this research concern its target population. The contemporary cohort of self-identified sexual-minority adolescents is unprecedented in its size and visibility, and we have yet to discern how such visibility and openness will affect the types of relationships they seek and pursue throughout and after adolescence. For this reason, we have chosen to emphasize research questions that directly address the concerns of this population. How do differences in motivations affect participation in exclusively sexual *relationships* rather than simple sexual activity? How do sexual-minority adolescents use and experience other-sex dating relationships in the process of developing, questioning, or hiding a sexual-minority identity? How do these adolescents form enduring romantic relationships with same-sex peers, and how do these relationships shape identity? What outcomes are associated with disproportionate participation in one type of relationship?

As noted earlier, these questions are clearly relevant to heterosexual adolescents as well. Research that *assumes diversity* in sexual orientation and identity will most effectively discern the ways in which adolescent relationships shape and are shaped by other features of adolescent development. Passionate friendships provide an example of this point. These relationships remain invisible to both heterosexually oriented and sexual-minority oriented research programs; the former cannot distinguish them from normative best friendships, and the latter cannot distinguish them from unacknowledged and unconsummated same-sex romantic relationships. Only an approach that avoids blanket assumptions concerning sexuality and that provides room for unexpected variation will be able to account for the unique characteristics of these relationships.

Sociocultural changes are clearly leaving their mark on contemporary adolescent relationships. We may soon face a generation in which experimental same-sex dating and romantic involvement become common among *both* sexual-minority and heterosexual youths. To successfully investigate both the immediate and long-term effects of these changes on the development of intimate relationships over the life span, researchers must devote substantial attention to the understudied experiences of adolescents who have sought and experienced same-sex intimacy. The most important and successful research will integrate findings from both sexual-minority and heterosexual populations in order to construct dynamic working models of relationship formation, dissolution, and impact that apply across sexual orientations and over the life course.

References

Ainsworth, M. D. S. (1989). Attachments beyond infancy. *American Psychologist, 44,* 709–716.

Ainsworth, M. D. S., Blehar, M. C., Waters, E., & Wall, S. (1978). *Patterns of attachment: A psychological study of the strange situation.* Hillsdale, NJ: Erlbaum.

Becker, C. (1988). *Lesbian ex-lovers.* Boston: Alyson.

Bell, A. P., & Weinberg, M. S. (1978). *Homosexualities: A study of diversity among men and women.* Bloomington: Indiana University Press.

Bingham, C. R., & Crockett, L. J. (1996). Longitudinal adjustment patterns of boys and girls experiencing early, middle, and late sexual intercourse. *Developmental Psychology, 32,* 647–658.

Blumstein, P., & Schwartz, P. (1990). Intimate relationships and the creation of sexuality. In D. P. McWhirter, S. A. Sanders, & J. M. Reinisch (Eds.), *Homosexuality/heterosexuality: Concepts of sexual orientation* (pp. 307–320). New York: Oxford University Press.

Bornstein, M., & Bruner, J. (1993). *Interaction in cognitive development.* Hillsdale, NJ: Erlbaum.

Bowlby, J. (1982). *Attachment and loss: Volume 1, Attachment* (2nd ed.). New York: Basic Books.

Buhrmester, D., & Furman, W. (1986). The changing functions of friends in childhood. In V. J. Derlega & B. A. Winstead (Eds.), *Friendship and social interaction* (pp. 41–62). New York: Springer-Verlag.

Buhrmester, D., & Furman, W. (1987). The development of companionship and intimacy. *Child Development, 58,* 1101–1113.

Butler, B. (Ed.). (1990). *Ceremonies of the heart: Celebrating lesbian unions.* Seattle: Seal Press.

Caldwell, M. A., & Peplau, L. A. (1982). Sex differences in same-sex friendship. *Sex Roles, 8,* 721–732.

Califia, P. (1979). Lesbian sexuality. *Journal of Homosexuality, 4,* 255–266.

Camarena, P. M., Sarigiani, P. A., & Petersen, A. C. (1990). Gender-specific pathways to intimacy in early adolescence. *Journal of Youth and Adolescence, 19,* 19–32.

Cass, V. (1990). The implications of homosexual identity formation for the Kinsey model and scale of sexual preference. In D. P. McWhirter, S. A. Sanders, & J. M. Reinisch (Eds.), *Homosexuality/heterosexuality: Concepts of sexual orientation* (pp. 239–266). New York: Oxford University Press.

Chapman, B. E., & Brannock, J. C. (1987). Proposed models of lesbian identity development: An empirical examination. *Journal of Homosexuality, 14,* 69–80.

Cole, E. (1993). Is sex a natural function? Implications for sex therapy. In E. D. Rothblum & A. D. Brehony (Eds.), *Boston marriages* (pp. 187–193). Amherst: University of Massachusetts Press.

Crumpacker, L., & Vander Haegen, E. M. (1993). Pedagogy and prejudice: Strategies for confronting homophobia in the classroom. *Women's Studies Quarterly, 21,* 94–106.

D'Augelli, A. R. (1991). Gay men in college: Identity processes and adaptations. *Journal of College Student Development, 32,* 140–146.

Diamond, L. M. (1998). Development of sexual orientation among adolescent and young adult women. *Developmental Psychology, 34,* 1085–1095.

Diamond, L. M. (1997, March). *Passionate friendships among young lesbian, bisexual, and heterosexual women.* Paper presented at the annual meeting of the Association for Women in Psychology, Pittsburgh, PA.

Douvan, E., & Adelson, J. (1966). *The adolescent experience.* New York: Wiley.

Dubé, E. M. (1997). *Sexual identity and intimacy development among two cohorts of sexual-minority men.* Unpublished Master's thesis, Cornell University.

Elkind, D. (1980). Strategic interaction in early adolescence. In J. Adelson (Ed.), *Handbook of adolescent psychology* (pp. 432–444). New York: Wiley.

Esterberg, K. G. (1994). Being a lesbian and being in love: Constructing identities through relationships. *Journal of Gay and Lesbian Social Services, 1,* 57–82.

Faderman, L. (1981). *Surpassing the love of men.* New York: William Morrow.

Faderman, L. (1991). *Odd girls and twilight lovers.* New York: Penguin Books.

Feiring, C. (1996). Concepts of romance in 15-year-old adolescents. *Journal of Research on Adolescence, 6,* 181–200.

Furman, W., & Wehner, E. A. (1994). Romantic views: Toward a theory of adolescent romantic relationships. In R. Montemayor, G. R. Adams, & T. P. Gullotta (Eds.), *Personal relationships during adolescence* (pp. 168–195). Thousand Oaks, CA: Sage.

Gramick, J. (1984). Developing a lesbian identity. In T. Darty & S. Potter (Eds.), *Women-identified women* (pp. 31–44). Palo Alto, CA: Mayfield

Hall Carpenter Archives. (1989). *Inventing ourselves.* New York: Routledge.

Hazan, C., & Shaver, P. R. (1994). Attachment as an organizational framework for research on close relationships. *Psychological Inquiry, 5,* 1–22.

Hazan, C., & Zeifman, D. (1994). Sex and the psychological tether. In D. Perlman & K. Bartholemew (Eds.), *Advances in personal relationships: A research annual* (Vol. 5, pp. 151–177). London: Jessica Kingsley.

Herdt, G., & Boxer, A. M. (1993). *Children of Horizons: How gay and lesbian teens are leading a new way out of the closet.* Boston: Beacon Press.

Hite, S. (1987). *Women and love.* London: Penguin Books.

Hofferth, S. L. (1990). Trends in adolescent sexual activity, contraception, and pregnancy in the United States. In J. Bancroft & J. M. Reinisch (Eds.), *Adolescence and puberty* (pp. 217–233). New York: Oxford University Press.

Kurdek, L. A., & Schmitt, J. P. (1985–1986). Relationship quality of gay men in closed or open relationships. *Journal of Homosexuality, 12,* 85–99.

Laumann, E. O., Gagnon, J. H., Michael, R. T., & Michaels, F. (1994). *The social organization of sexuality: Sexual practices in the United States.* Chicago: University of Chicago Press.

Lever, J. (1994, August 23). Sexual revelations. *The Advocate,* pp. 17–24.

Lever, J. (1995, August 22). Lesbian sex survey. *The Advocate,* pp. 22–30.

Manalansan, M. F., IV. (1996). Double minorities: Latino, Black, and Asian men who have sex with men. In R. C. Savin-Williams & K. M. Cohen (Eds.), *The lives of lesbians, gays, and bisexuals: Children to adults* (pp. 393–415). Fort Worth, TX: Harcourt Brace.

Martin, A. D. (1982). Learning to hide: The socialization of the gay adolescent. *Adolescent Psychiatry, 10,* 52–65.

Miller, B., & Moore, K. (1990). Adolescent sexual behavior, pregnancy, and parenting: Research through the 1980's. *Journal of Marriage and the Family, 52,* 1025–1044.

Myer, J. (1989). Guess who's coming to dinner this time? A study of gay intimate relationships and the support for those relationships. *Marriage and Family Review, 14,* 59–82.

Nardi, P. M., & Sherrod, D. (1994). Friendship in the lives of gay men and lesbian. *Journal of Social and Personal Relationships, 11,* 185–199.

National Lesbian and Gay Survey. (1992). *What a lesbian looks like.* London: Routledge.

O'Connor, P. (1992). *Friendships between women: A critical review.* New York: Guilford Press.

Paul, E., & White, K. (1990). The development of intimate relationships in late adolescence. *Adolescence, 25,* 375–400.

Rose, S., Zand, D., & Cimi, M. A. (1993). Lesbian courtship scripts. In E. D. Rothblum & K. A. Brehony (Eds.), *Boston marriages* (pp. 70–85). Amherst: University of Massachusetts Press.

Rothblum, E. D., & Brehony, A. D. (Eds.). (1993). *Boston marriages.* Amherst: University of Massachusetts Press.

Sahli, N. (1979). Smashing: Women's relationships before the fall. *Chrysalis, 8,* 17–27.

Samet, N., & Kelly, E. W. (1987). The relationship of steady dating to self-esteem and sex role identity among adolescents. *Adolescence, 22,* 231–245.

Savin-Williams, R. C. (1990). *Gay and lesbian youth: Expressions of identity.* New York: Hemisphere.

Savin-Williams, R. C. (1994). Verbal and physical abuse as stressors in the lives of lesbian, gay male, and bisexual youths: Associations with school problems, running away, substance abuse, prostitution, and suicide. *Journal of Consulting and Clinical Psychology, 62,* 261–269.

Savin-Williams, R. C. (1996a). Ethnic- and sexual-minority youth. In R. C. Savin-Williams & K. M. Cohen (Eds.), *The lives of lesbians, gays, and bisexuals: Children to adults* (pp. 152–165). Fort Worth, TX: Harcourt Brace.

Savin-Williams, R. C. (1996b). Dating and romantic relationships among gay, lesbian, and bisexual youths. In R. C. Savin-Williams and K. M. Cohen (Eds.), *The lives of lesbians, gays, and bisexuals: Children to adults* (pp. 166–180). Fort Worth, TX: Harcourt Brace.

Savin-Williams, R. C. (1998). *. . . and then I became gay: Young men's stories.* New York: Routledge.

Schafer, S. (1977). Sociosexual behavior in male and female homosexuals. *Archives of Sexual Behavior, 6,* 355–364.

Sears, J. T. (1989). The impact of gender and race on growing up lesbian and gay in the South. *National Women's Studies Association Journal, 1,* 422–457.

Sears, J. T. (1991). *Growing up gay in the South: Race, gender, and journeys of the spirit.* New York: Harrington Park Press.

Shaver, P., Hazan, C., & Bradshaw, D. (1988). Love as attachment: The integration of three behavioral systems. In R. J. Sternberg & M. L. Barnes (Eds.), *The psychology of love* (pp. 193–219). New Haven, CT: Yale University Press.

Smith-Rosenberg, C. (1975). The female world of love and ritual: Relations between women in nineteenth century America. *Signs, 1,* 1–29.

Sullivan, H. S. (1953). *The interpersonal theory of psychiatry.* New York: Norton.

Tripp, C. A. (1975). *The homosexual matrix.* New York: McGraw-Hill.

Troiden, R. (1988). *Gay and lesbian identity: A sociological analysis.* Six Hills, NY: General Hall.

Udry, J. R., and Billy, J. O. G. (1987). Initiation of coitus in early adolescence. *American Sociological Review, 52,* 841–855.

U. S. Bureau of the Census. (1986). Marital status and living arrangements: March 1985. *Current Population Reports* (Vol. Pj-20). Washington, DC: U.S. Government Printing Office.

Vetere, V. A. (1983). The role of friendship in the development and maintenance of lesbian love relationships. *Journal of Homosexuality, 8,* 51–65.

Weinberg, M. S., Williams, C. J., & Pryor, D. W. (1994). *Dual attraction: Understanding bisexuality.* New York: Oxford University Press.

Weiner, J. (1992). *Psychological disturbance in adolescence.* New York: Wiley.

Weinstock, J. S., & Rothblum, E. D. (Eds.). (1996). *Lesbian friendships: For ourselves and each other.* New York: New York University Press.

9   Gender Identity and the Development of Romantic Relationships in Adolescence

Candice Feiring

Gender is obviously a key component for understanding romantic relationships in adolescence. If we listen to the narratives of high school seniors describing particular romantic relationships, our assumptions about expected sex-role-appropriate behavior or constructions may be violated or confirmed.

> Person 1: "Um, we're both very easygoing. Um, we like a lot of affection. Um, not like public affection, but um, just knowing that we, we care for each other. Um, uh, it doesn't even have to be physical affection, just any type. We like cuddling with each other. Um, we enjoy going out and doing things with each other and each other's friends. . . . We enjoy high action things together. Um, pretty much . . . we have a very open relationship, and we can talk about anything."

> Person 2: "I think after a while like, [person] following me around and wanting to be with me all the time, and maybe the fact that I had a lot to say and had the power . . . I'd, just like, I don't know, I still think like that. I don't know why but [person] . . . was getting too serious by following me around all the time and, you know, wanting to spend every minute of the day. . . . You know I'm like, 'I do have friends I need to talk to.' . . . I was just like, 'Aaah! Go away!'"

> Person 3: "It's like . . . you know . . . we love each other so much . . . it's great. We have so much fun. We get mad at each other sometimes, and, you know, we make up, and, you know, we hug. It's great. I mean

This work was made possible in part by support from the William T. Grant Foundation. I want to thank Richard Ashmore, B. Bradford Brown, Deborah Coates, Wyndol Furman, Michael Gara, and Ritch Savin-Williams for their helpful feedback on this chapter.

211

[person] is wonderful! . . . We, like, we just have a lot of fun, and we have a lot of heartache, but it's perfect because of that, you know. If it was all fun all the time, what's wrong? And if it's all bad all the time, something's wrong. It's right in the middle. It's right where it should be."

Person 4: "I'm not really a relationship person. If I meet someone, I want to be able to, you know, to uh, you know . . . not have any restraints or anything. Basically, I run into someone who I think is cool and all that about twice a month. . . . The friends before are friends after. Most of them are probably physical. Um, I don't have any regrets. . ."

Without knowing the sex of the speaker or the romantic partner, it is not immediately obvious from the style or content of these reports whether the narrator is female or male. The quotes were chosen because they show a range of responses that go beyond what conformity to sex roles might predict and illustrate the need to maintain a sense of the individual person in developing ideas about the importance of gender in understanding romantic relationships in adolescence.

In this chapter, I explore the concept of gender identity as a means of articulating gender-related issues in the development of intimacy and identity formation. More specifically, I consider the extent to which gender identity and the development of romantic relationships are related. This chapter begins by considering the characteristics and advantages of a gender identity approach. Next, gender identity and the development of romantic relationships in early and late adolescence are examined, followed by a discussion of some methodological considerations.

Gender in Adolescent Research

The majority of work in adolescence focuses on gender differences in behavior in domains other than romantic relationships. For example, researchers interested in development in early adolescence have noted that girls and boys during this period show increasing divergence in several important psychosocial domains, including self-esteem (Simmons, Blyth, VanCleave, & Bush, 1979), behavior problems (Nolen-Hoeksema, 1990), academic achievement (Linn & Petersen, 1986), and sex role attitudes (Galambos, Almeida, & Petersen, 1990). My own work has found gender differences in middle and late adolescents' reports of romantic relationships, with girls being more likely to mention self-disclosure, support, and jealousy than boys (Feiring, 1996; in press).

Since I wanted to explore the idea of the role of gender in romantic relationships, it was clear to me that although a gender difference approach provides a guide to areas of interest, it offered a conceptually limited framework for examining self-development. There are several problems with this body of work, including my own, when it comes to the level of understanding obtained about how gender comes to influence the attitudes, personality, and behavior of individuals. Gender differences apply to average group differences that do not necessarily characterize particular individuals. As illustrated in the vivid chapter-opening quotes, maintaining a focus on the individual should be an important goal. How gender is related to intraindividual configurations of activities and interests, personal-social attributes, and social relationships cannot be understood by summing over group differences.

For example, two early adolescent girls may each have a boyfriend, several same-sex close friends, and an interest in cooking, and may see themselves as friendly and understanding. These roles, interests, and personality traits are consistent with stereotypes of feminine characteristics. However, these girls may be quite different in other aspects of their self-definition of femininity. One girl believes having a boyfriend is very important for verifying her sense of femininity and views her relationship with her boyfriend as more important than her relationships with parents or close friends. She is more compliant with her boyfriend's demands and more vulnerable to feelings of low self-worth when he disagrees with her. The other girl places less emphasis on having a boyfriend in defining her sense of femininity and views her relationship with her boyfriend as less important than her relationships with parents or close friends. Conflicts with her boyfriend are not related to feelings of low self-worth. Examination of gender differences in personality, interests, or friendship patterns would not provide information on when these particular girls adhere to traditional views of gender or how their gender-based self-views are related to their perceptions of and behavior in romantic relationships.

The concept of gender identity has been used in a variety of ways and has often been employed interchangeably with gender/sex-role preferences or behavior, typing, schema, and attitudes. Here *gender identity* is defined as an individual's phenomenological sense of being masculine or feminine in roles, preferences, interests, attitudes, and behavior. A fundamental and earliest component of gender identity is the acquisition of gender constancy in which children come to understand that they are male or female and that there are physical and social attributes and behaviors associated with these categories. *Gender constancy* follows a developmental sequence such that children first understand that they can categorize themselves and others according to gender (identity), then understand that gender is stable over time (stability), and finally that gender remains consistent across situations, appearance, and behavior (Kohlberg, 1966; Slaby & Frey, 1975). As children come to identify themselves as male or female, they also develop characteristics, interests, attitudes, roles, and behaviors that they attribute to themselves or others as a function of gender.

One approach to considering gender at the individual level, which grows out of the concept of gender constancy and its centrality for self-definition, is that of gender schema. A *gender schema* is the organization of information about the self and behavior in terms of society's specification of what goes with the female–male distinction. Children are viewed as attempting to match their own behavior to the content of their gender schema, eschewing those behaviors, relationships, and attributes associated with the other gender and attending to and conforming to what is appropriate for their own gender (Martin & Halverson, 1981).

According to Bem (1981, 1985, 1987), the child's self-concept may be assimilated to the gender schema, and the schema can function to prescribe behavior and to describe the self. Society's expectations or the culture's gender schema is conceptualized as homogeneous, so that, for example, the possibility of variations by ethnicity, peer group, or family structure is ignored. Gender schema theory represents a form of the traditional bipolar model of masculinity–femininity in which sex-typed girls and boys develop a strong sex role identification that leads them to acquire and express the numerous traits, attitudes, and behaviors expected of their gender by society. Thus, a girl who views herself as highly feminine would be expected to show consistency across the different domains of sex-typed personality traits, interests, appearance, and behavior in romantic relationships. For example, the highly feminine girl should be sensitive and understanding (personality), wear short skirts and makeup (appearance), be compliant in decision making, date one boy (behavior in social relationships), and be attracted to football players (preferences).

An alternative to the unifactorial model of gender schema is a multifactorial approach. A wide variety of attributes and behaviors must be considered in order to understand gender influences. Huston (1983) suggested a matrix based on two criteria, content and construct. *Contents* include biological gender, activities and interests, personal-social attributes, gender-based social relationships, and stylistic-symbolic communication; *constructs* include beliefs, identity, attitudes, and behavior. In this approach, the various contents that differentiate between girls and boys, women and men in a given culture do not represent a given underlying masculinity or femininity trait or schema but instead reflect a number of more or less independent factors. Thus, for example, preferences for same-sex friendships or other sex-romantic partners do not mean that an individual will endorse only stereotypical personality traits (e.g., expressive for girls versus instrumental for boys) or be involved in traditional interests or activities (e.g., cooking versus competitive sports). Research indicates that lay concepts of masculinity and femininity are diverse (over 100 possible features) and broad and include interests, personality traits, and appearance. There is substantial variation across individuals in the frequency with which particular features are mentioned as describing masculinity or femininity, and consensus on defining features is far from unanimous (Helgeson, 1994).

Building on a multifactorial assumption, Spence (1984, 1985, 1993) has elaborated the construct of gender identity. She suggests that the fundamental sense of gender identity most people develop in early childhood remains a central part of their self-concept throughout life. The term adolescent boys and men use to label their gender identity or psychological sense of maleness is *masculinity,* and the comparable term for adolescent girls and women is *femininity.* However, even among people with a strong, unambiguous gender identity of masculinity or femininity, individuals do not possess all of the characteristics, attitudes, interests, abilities, roles, and behaviors expected of their sex according to the prescriptions of their culture. Individuals vary in the extent to which they accept as part of their self-concept attributes and behaviors traditionally associated with the other sex.

Each gender-differentiating content (attitudes, interests, etc.) has various degrees and types of relations to other contents, and this configuration of content shows considerable variation within each sex. These configurations vary with developmental period and interact in complex ways to influence behavior. Although there is substantial heterogeneity across individuals in these configurations, the majority of both sexes develop a clear sense of gender identity. This is because members of both sexes use the attributes, roles, and interests that are congruent with gender stereotypes to verify their gender identity. The role of boyfriend or girlfriend in the romantic and sexual sense is new in adolescence and becomes increasingly important for defining a person's gender identity. Although there are individual differences in timing, the majority of adolescents will acquire this role to verify their gender identity. Within individuals and particular couples, how this role is enacted can vary greatly and is related to the individual's view of what is gender-appropriate or acceptable behavior. The focus here is on how individuals' views of their own and their partner's behaviors are linked to gender. Gender-linked views of the self and the partner influence the quality of romantic relationships and, conversely, romantic relationships alter gender-linked views of the self and the partner.

Within both sexes, the configuration of gender-relevant attributes an individual possesses and the gender roles occupied at a given time operate primarily to define and to verify a personal sense of masculinity for boys and femininity for girls. What is viewed as gender relevant can include a wide variety of behaviors and attributes, some of which fit sex-role stereotypes and some of which do not. Take, for example, two adolescent boys who cry in front of their romantic partners. Each one has a large network of same-sex friends, plays competitive sports, and dates individuals of the other sex. Thus, in certain behaviors, interests, and gender-based social relationships/roles, each boy views himself as masculine and would probably receive validating feedback from peers about his masculinity. However, one believes that to be strong and masculine he should not show weakness, and therefore he refuses to tell his partner what is bothering him. His partner also shares his view of crying behavior in boys, and thus ignores his crying and does not encourage him to talk about what has upset him. The other boy believes that because he is sensitive, he is able to let down his guard, cry, and tell his partner what is bothering him. This behavior or view of himself as sensitive does not invalidate his sense of masculinity. His partner does not view his crying as a sign of weakness and encourages him to talk about what is upsetting him. The former boy has adopted the traditional view of masculinity, which eschews showing vulnerability, whereas the latter does not view his crying as a threat to his sense of masculinity. This example illustrates how a component of one's configured gender identity may influence behavior in romantic relationships and how experience in romantic relationships, in this case the partner's response to crying, may validate one's view of what is acceptable behavior.

It is also possible to use this example to show how the same individual might change his view of himself and his behavior, depending on development and experience in romantic relationships. In early adolescence, when traditional stereotypes might govern behavior in the new role of boyfriend, a boy may view crying as a sign of weakness and a violation of his view of acceptable behavior for boys in romantic relationships. However, after some experience with partners who do not belittle him for crying and instead encourage him to talk, he may redefine his sense of masculinity in romantic relationships such that crying does not result in negative self-evaluations.

Considering the role of gender in romantic relationships, two components of gender identity need to be addressed, as they may shape and be shaped by romantic experiences. The first I call *general gender identity* to indicate an overall sense of masculinity for boys and femininity for girls. General gender identity is defined as knowing that one is male or female and that this biological distinction has social meaning for behavior. It is an important component of one's social identity. The second I refer to as *configured gender identity,* defined as when the individual takes the social construction of gender and the biological facts of sex to create a set of gender-related characteristics, attitudes, and behaviors that are viewed as reflecting one's masculinity or femininity (Ashmore, 1990). This conceptualization emphasizes the heterogeneity of configured gender identity. The theoretical and empirical tasks then become identification of content-specific components of configured gender identity in regard to thinking about, experiencing, and expressing the self in the context of romantic relationships. I propose that for heterosexual adolescents, general gender identity does not undergo significant change in adolescence. Rather, it is the configured gender identity – that is, the constellation of gender-related contents that verify one's sense of general gender identity – that influences and is influenced by romantic relationships. Expectations and behavior that are viewed as appropriate for oneself and one's partner as a function of gender can be revised as a result of interpersonal interactions (Deaux & Major, 1987).

Gender Identity and Romantic Relationships in Early Adolescence

Literature on early adolescence emphasizes this period as a time of heightened differentiation of masculine and feminine personality characteristics and roles (e.g., Block, 1973; Galambos et al., 1990; Hill & Lynch, 1983; Huston & Alvarez, 1990; Richards, Gitelson, Petersen, & Hurtig, 1991). It has been argued that a pattern of increasing differentiation between boys and girls across adolescence occurs, with boys adhering more closely to the stereotype of masculinity that emphasizes instrumental behaviors and roles and girls adhering more closely to the stereotype of femininity that emphasizes expressive behaviors and roles (e.g., Hill & Lynch, 1983; Worell, 1981). Reviewing gender differences and explanations for them in adolescence, Hill and Lynch (1983) proposed that at around the time of the onset of puberty, girls and boys experience an intensification of gender-related expectations. Whereas gender intensification is seen as associated with puberty, the physical developments are seen as less central than the changes in social factors that coincide with them. The gender intensification hypothesis argues that in several domains, including social relationships, self-esteem, coping, and achievement, differences between girls and boys increase with age and are the consequence of increased socialization to conform to traditional feminine and masculine sex roles. *Role* refers to a group consensus about patterns of demands, values, or behaviors related to a given position in a given social system. Although parents, teachers, and peer groups have been considered as possible agents of sex typing and gender intensification, interactions with romantic partners have been overlooked.

Reframing the gender intensification hypothesis in terms of configured gender identity would involve examining the number of sex-typed characteristics and behaviors that are viewed as part of the configured gender identity within and across different domains of functioning and whether this number increases in early adolescence. More specifically in the context of romantic relationships, it would be necessary to examine the degree to which the configured gender identity and one's view of an acceptable partner are characterized by stereotypical behaviors and beliefs. As suggested by Brown's ideas on peer group influences (this volume), one might expect to find a greater number of adolescents with configured gender identities high on stereotypical characteristics during the prestige phase of romantic relationships. In this phase, the individual looks outward to the broader peer culture to help define what is acceptable romantic behavior for a girl or boy and acceptable views of the self and the partner. Depending on the nature of the crowd to which one belongs, the prescription to conform to stereotypical forms of romantic relationships may vary. Finding a crowd that is compatible with one's configured gender identity and one's ideas about the important gender-related qualities of potential partners is a critical activity for self and romantic relationship development.

One obvious source of stereotypes about maleness and femaleness, and models of what to expect and how to behave in romantic relationships, is the media – movies, TV, videos, music, books, and computer games. Adolescents make active choices about which media models are relevant for their own romantic relationships (McRobbie, 1994). Models of gender-related action should affect expectations and behavior in interactions with potential romantic partners, especially when there is little or limited previous experience.

There are multiple models depicting male and female romantic interactions that adolescents may use to construct their ideas about appropriate romantic behavior. For example, a study examining female–male conflict in the most popular movies in the United States from 1986 to 1990 (Hedley, 1994) found that women were portrayed as relatively powerless and passive. They were less successful than men in resisting power assertion to alter their wishes or behavior. In contrast, Alanis Morissette, who is popular with some teenage girls in North America, composes and sings music about conflicts with boyfriends in which a strong sense of self-assertion is clear. She writes about not wanting to be the feminine stereotype of the all-giving, compliant girlfriend; "I don't want to be your babysitter. . . . I don't want to be the glue that holds your pieces together" (from the song "Not the Doctor" by A. Morissette, 1995). We do not know the degree to which individual adolescents accept or reject stereotypes of dominance and submission as part of their configured gender identity and how experience with real partners confirms or contradicts such stereotypes.

At the onset of adolescence, the configured gender identity will in most cases not contain attitudes, behaviors, or experiences based on direct experience in romantic relationships. The self is a social construction that in large part represents the attitudes significant others hold about one's self (Harter, 1986). In early adolescence, romantic partners have usually not achieved the importance of significant other status. Experience of the self in interaction with another person who has the potential to be a romantic partner is limited or nonexistent. The configured gender identity in the context of romantic relationships is essentially a peripheral identity. However, it contains expectations and imagined experiences about the self in romantic encounters. It also contains characteristics, attitudes, and behaviors that will influence the choice of partners and the nature and course of the relationship.

One example of social behavior and preferences that can influence the nature of early romantic relationships is the consistent observation that children prefer to play with a member of their own sex (Maccoby & Jacklin, 1987). For some children, the limited experience with mixed-sex interactions may be related to their ability as an adolescent to be comfortable and form satisfying relationships with the other sex (Maccoby, 1990). However, some children may build better bridges to relationships with the other sex, as they have reciprocal other-sex friendships within a predominantly same-sex friendship network. Such children may develop the social skills for acceptance by peers of both sexes prior to and as they begin romantic relationships (Collins & Sroufe, this volume; Kovaks, Parker, & Hoffman, 1996). They also may have a less stereotypical view of what is acceptable behavior for themselves and their partners.

Physical appearance is another area in which gender-related characteristics and attitudes will have an impact on romantic relationships in early adolescence. Recent evidence suggests that pubertal maturation is related to increased feelings of being in love for both sexes (Richards & Larson, 1993). The meaning and consequences of such maturation vary by and within gender. The timing of pubertal changes appears to be related to differential self-evaluations. Early timing for girls has been associated with a poorer body image and lower self-esteem, whereas the reverse seems to be the case for boys (Richards, Boxer, Petersen, & Albrecht, 1990; Simmons & Blyth, 1987). One's physical appearance serves as a stimulus for both self-evaluation and social evaluation (Cash, Dawson, Davis, Brown, & Galumbek, 1988; Harter, 1990; Lerner, 1987). Perceived physical attractiveness is the best predictor of overall self-worth from childhood on. However, feelings of physical attractiveness in regard to imagined or real judgments of romantic partners should emerge as highly salient in early adolescence. Throughout adolescence, how an individual views and evaluates bodily changes and physical attractiveness is a central component of configured gender identity that should be related to expectations and interactions in romantic relationships. Gender intensification should be expected in the form of more prevalent feedback from friends and romantic partners about one's physical attractiveness. This should be related to the number and evaluation of one's physical attributes viewed as important for defining one's appeal to potential or real romantic partners. Although the tendency to judge one's physical appeal negatively against unattainable media models may be quite high in early adolescence, variability is expected in the extent and negative valence of such evaluations. Some adolescents are more likely to judge their physical appearance in a way that makes them feel at a disadvantage in attracting and keeping desirable partners. Others may be more likely to utilize alternative or self-derived standards to judge their appearance and their appeal to romantic partners. For example, I may not be as tall as I would like to be, but I am a great dancer; or I wish I were thinner, but I have pretty eyes.

Early adolescents are supposed to be keenly aware of the real and imagined evaluations of them made by others (Elkind, 1978). If they consider themselves to be unattractive, they expect negative social feedback from others and might be reluctant to initiate interactions with potential romantic partners or be less discriminating in partner choice. Generally, girls view physical appearance and heterosexual attractiveness as more important for their self-definition than do boys (Archer, 1992; Douvan & Adelson, 1966). Adolescent girls' bodies are targeted for sexual objectification more often than adolescent boys' bodies (Kaschak, 1992). With changes in observable secondary sex characteristics, girls' bodies are increasingly looked at, commented on, and publicly evaluated by others (Brownmiller, 1984; Dion, Dion, & Keelan, 1990). This may lead to girls being at risk for adopting an observer's perspective of their physical selves (Bartky, 1990; Beauvoir, 1961). Early adolescent girls are particularly vulnerable to the impact of appearance-contingent feedback from friends regarding their physical appeal to potential romantic partners and, of course, from potential and actual partners themselves. For those adolescents of either sex for whom physical appeal is a central component of their configured gender identity in romantic relationships, negative evaluation of their physical attributes they deem important for attractiveness could lead to greater self-consciousness and anxiety with romantic partners.

Gender Identity and Romantic Relationships in Late Adolescence

By late adolescence, at which time some experience with romantic encounters has likely occurred (Connolly & Johnson, 1996; Feiring, 1995; Furman & Buhrmester, 1992), the majority of individuals have components of their configured gender identity that are derived and shaped by experience in romantic relationships. For many adolescents, the self with a romantic partner will have become a more central identity and more elaborated in terms of representations of the self and of actual or potential romantic partners. Brown (this volume) suggests that during the affection phase of the development of romantic relationships, which may typically be expected to occur during middle to late adolescence, the relative salience of romantic relationships compared to friendships and parental relationships increases. The focus of the relationship becomes the interests and needs of the partner and the mutual construction of a relationship. As the salience of romantic relationships increases, the salience of the configured gender identity in romantic relationships should also increase and become more central for defining the individual's general gender identity. Furthermore, as the romantic partner becomes more central in terms of providing sexual, affiliative, caregiving, and attachment needs, the partner's positive and negative feedback about the nature of one's configured gender identity should become more important and more likely to change one's self-view.

Part of constructing a mutual relationship involves sharing personal feelings and thoughts. Such self-disclosure creates the opportunity for self-exploration and self-clarification involved in defining an individual's sense of the relationship, and the self in the relationship, thus making it an important process for the development of configured gender identity. Because individual differences in self-disclosure are typically found in relation to gender, this is an obvious area to examine for the development of gender identity and romantic relationships in adolescence.

Greater emphasis on self-disclosive intimacy and support in girls compared to boys would appear to be the case in middle and late adolescence (Connolly & Johnson, 1996; Feiring, 1996; in press). Whereas self-disclosure may be the primary means of establishing intimacy for girls, boys may rely more on shared activities (Buhrmester & Furman, 1987; Camarena, Sangiani, & Petersen, 1990). Consequently, emotional closeness for girls may be defined more in terms of self-disclosure, whereas for boys, shared experiences is the more defining feature (Camarena et al., 1990).

However, it is not clear whether such gender differences in intimacy expression are due to differential competence and/or preference, depending on the gender of one's interaction partner. Adolescent boys should differ in the extent to which they view the disclosure of feelings and thoughts as permissible in their concept of themselves as masculine, particularly in the context of interactions with romantic partners (for this view might be different in the context of male friendships). To the extent that an adolescent boy is concerned with power and dominance, he may be reluctant to express personal feelings and information with his romantic partner because he perceives such behavior as a sign of vulnerability and unmasculine behavior. Some adolescent boys may be more likely to link dominance with eschewing self-disclosure because such a pattern may be established with male friends (Aires, 1987; McAdams & Losoff, 1984) and there is limited experience with girlfriends. Variation in boys' acceptance of self-disclosure as part of their configured gender identity might be related to their capacity to form relationships that have open communication and greater likelihood of stability (Gottman & Mettetal, 1986). Some adult research suggests that men who view dependency and lack of self-sufficiency as unmasculine are less likely to disclose feelings to their romantic partners and more likely to be classified as having a pseudointimate romantic relationship (Orlofsky, 1993).

Shared interests and experiences are another important part of constructing a mutual relationship. In a review of gender differences in topics of conversation, women have been found to discuss people, appearances, and relationships more often, whereas men are more likely to talk about work, money, and sports (Bischoping, 1993). Early interactions with potential romantic partners may be particularly awkward for those romantic dyads in which the number of same-sex interests is high and important for self-definition compared to other-sex or neutral interests. Adolescents differ in the extent to which they cultivate interests that are considered same-sex or other-sex typical or gender neutral (Katz & Ksansnak, 1994). More flexibility in interests should be related to more comfortable initial interactions and greater satisfaction with the relationship.

An alternative position to gender intensification is that gender traditionality should decrease during adolescence. Theorists working within this framework focus on the development of gender role flexibility. Flexibility in gender-related preferences and perceptions of the self, as well as tolerance for others engaged in gender-atraditional behavior, increases throughout adolescence (Katz & Ksansnak, 1994). Perceptions of flexibility in family, same-sex siblings, and peers are related to flexibility in gender-related preferences and perceptions of the self, as well as tolerance for others engaged in gender-atraditional activities. Adolescents who are the most flexible with regard to their own preferences report being more influenced by other-sex peers. This work suggests that configured gender identity may become more flexible in adolescence in regard to the extent to which other-sex behaviors are viewed as acceptable. Such flexibility may be an important component in the establishment of satisfactory companionship, intimacy, and the ability to communicate and resolve conflicts with romantic partners. Adolescents with more atraditional configured gender identities in regard to romantic relationships may be more likely to seek out partners with a similar level of atraditionality. Such partners might be more open to mutual influences in terms of the variety of behaviors and characteristics acceptable as part of one's identity in regard to the romantic partner.

In considering factors that may influence the extent to which the components of configured gender identity in romantic relationships would be more or less traditional, the role of attachment to parents merits examination. It has been proposed that a secure attachment lays the foundation for children to comply with family socialization goals and expectations (Waters, Kondo-lkemura, Posada, & Richters, 1990). This would lead to the suggestion that adolescents who are secure in their relationship with their parents would be more likely to adopt their parents' view of how males and females should relate to one another in romantic relationships, regardless of whether the parents are traditional or atraditional. This would be expected to be more true in early adolescence. Because secure adolescents are supposed to be more free to evaluate their own and others' behavior (Kobak, Cole, Ferenz-Gillies, Fleming, & Gamble, 1993), one would predict that the configured gender identity of such individuals would change in response to experience with actual partners, although they might also be more likely to maintain relationships with partners who confirmed their own and their family's view of gender roles, characteristics, and behavior.

It is necessary to acknowledge that much of the discussion thus far applies to heterosexual rather than gay, lesbian, or bisexual adolescents. There is some indication that youth with a minority sexual orientation may feel the need to construct a configured gender identity that is quite traditional in all domains except with romantic partners in order to feel more confident in their general gender identity. This may be the case especially when contexts for safe peer interaction are unavailable and the exploration of the nature of one's configured gender identity through romantic relationships is dangerous (Diamond, Savin-Williams, & Dubé, this volume; Savin-Williams, 1994). In some such youths, biological sex and general gender identity may not be as closely tied as appears to be the case for heterosexual youths. It is also possible that some youths may question the validity of any type of general gender identity and reject the notion of masculinity or femininity altogether (Bailey & Zucker, 1995). For youths of heterosexual or minority sexual orientation, an important question is the extent to which the configured gender identity consists of stereotyped rather than nontraditional characteristics and behaviors in regard to romantic relationships, and whether the observed pattern for romantic relationships is similar to or different from that of other relationships (e.g., with parents and close friends). There is considerable support for the increasing differentiation of the self-concept during adolescence and for variation of self-descriptions across different social roles or contexts (Harter, 1986, 1990; Harter & Monsour, 1992; Rosenberg, 1988; Smollar & Youniss, 1985). The lack of traditionality in one's romantic identity does not mean that other identities might not be quite traditional.

Individual Voices and Gender Identity

The quotes from the teenagers at the beginning of this chapter illustrate the need for an individually centered, developmental, multidimensional perspective for examining the role of gender in romantic relationships. Persons 2 and 3, both adolescent girls, rate themselves high on the adjective femininity and low on the adjective masculinity using the Bem Sex Role Inventory (BSRI). They also rate themselves as possessing traits reflecting both expressivity (e.g., understanding, sympathetic) and instrumentality (e.g., athletic, independent). This is true at the beginning of adolescence before either have had much experience with romantic relationships (i.e., age 13) and in late adolescence, by which time they have each had one stable relationship. However, Person 2 reports behaviors perhaps more typically stereotyped as masculine reluctance to be tied down, whereas Person 3 talks effusively about the expressive nature of her relationship with her current boyfriend. I would argue that both of these adolescents have a strong, stable sense of general gender identity but that their configured gender identities differ in how they view themselves in relation to their romantic partners. Further evidence of this is seen in Person 2's emphasis on equality of power within romantic relationships and her past history of protesting when a boyfriend ignored or was obnoxious to her when among his male friends. Person 3 also is concerned with the issue of power in her current romantic relationship, but she sees herself as having to be indirect in the methods she uses to achieve equal influence and as having to give in so that her partner does not get too angry.

Persons 1 and 4, both adolescent boys, rate themselves as high on the adjective masculinity and low on the adjective femininity in early and late adolescence using the BSRI. They also view themselves as possessing traits reflecting expressivity (e.g., understanding, loves children) and instrumentality (e.g., athletic, takes risks) at both age points. Person 1 is involved in a stable relationship, whereas Person 4 has had a series of short-term relationships. I propose that both of these boys, like the girls, have a strong, stable sense of general gender identity. However, the configured gender identity of these boys in late adolescence in regard to romantic relationships appears quite different. Person 1 discusses the importance of trust, caring, sharing of feelings, and reliability in his partner, behaviors associated with expressivity and the traditional feminine stereotype. He does recall trying to be "macho" in early adolescence by not letting on that he wanted girls to pay attention to him and holding back his emotions because he "didn't trust girls." Person 1 illustrates how the contents of his configured gender identity – be macho, don't show feelings – may have affected his early romantic relationships but also how experience, especially with his current partner, has changed his view of acceptable behavior. Person 4's configured gender identity appears to emphasize the physical aspect of relationships and the desire to avoid being tied down, a set of behaviors more consistent with the "bachelor" stereotype. This person has several friends of the other sex and one with whom he is particularly close. He goes to her for advice on how to interpret the behavior of girls with whom he has a sexual relationship. Person 4's configured gender identity may not exclude self-disclosure to girls who are friends, but it seems to exclude confiding in girls to whom he is sexually attracted.

Methodological Considerations

Central to any study of gender identity and romantic relationships must be a focus on individual adolescents' descriptions of themselves, their romantic partners, and other important persons in their lives. One methodology that I believe has great potential for examining gender identity at the individual level is a multidimensional approach that maps out how individuals view themselves, other people, and their roles and relationships (Ashmore, 1990; Gara, 1990; Rosenberg, 1988). Adolescents are first asked to generate a list of people in their lives, including family, relatives, friends, and people known through school and other organizations. They can also be asked to generate a set of personal identities such as daughter, sister, friend, and/or girlfriend/boyfriend. Second, the self with each person is described one at a time by listing a set of personal features that comes to mind, which may include behaviors, traits, feelings, values, and other relevant attributes for how the adolescent sees the self in the relationship. A matrix is created that consists of persons as rows and all personal features (in the adolescent's own words and phrases) as columns, and the adolescent indicates whether a particular feature applies to what she or he is like with a particular person. The resulting data matrix can then be analyzed using a hierarchical clustering algorithm (HICLAS) that represents simultaneously both persons and features. Figure 9.1 illustrates the kind of information obtainable with this method. It shows the superset (boxes at the top of the figure) to subset (boxes at the middle and bottom of the figure) relations among the clusters of persons with features. Supersets contain all features unique to themselves (in their box) and all features in the subsets listed below them to which they are connected with arrows.

Figure 9.1a shows a hypothetical early adolescent girl's self with family members, best friend of 2 years, and boyfriend of 6 weeks. Self-with-mother is the most central identity and includes unique characteristics of the self-with-mother (obnoxious), as well as shared characteristics also applicable to best friend, older sister and self-with-my crowd (e.g., share secrets, loving, warm, confident, independent). The self-with-boyfriend is a peripheral identity with only unique features applicable to this relationship (awkward, giddy, yielding). Note that the identity with the boyfriend has two features that are viewed as sex role stereotyped, whereas the identities with mother, sister, and best friend are a mix of traditional (e.g., warm, caring) and atraditional (independent, goofy) qualities. Figure 9.1b shows the same girl in late adolescence. At this point, her identity with a boyfriend of 1 year has become more central; shares all the features of the self with best friend, sister, and my crowd; and contains the unique features of passionate and exciting. The self-with-boyfriend identity has both traditional (e.g., caring) and atraditional (e.g., independent) qualities. This multidimensional approach allows for the ideographic study of configured

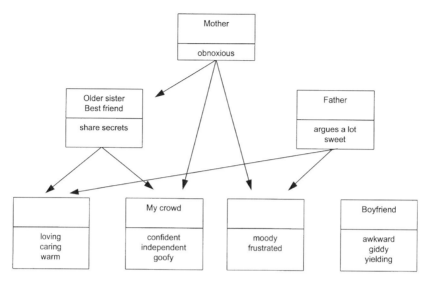

Figure 9.1a. A hypothesized adolescent girl's HICLAS representation of her self in relationships with family, friends, and boyfriends. *Above:* An early adolescent girl's self-with-other descriptors.

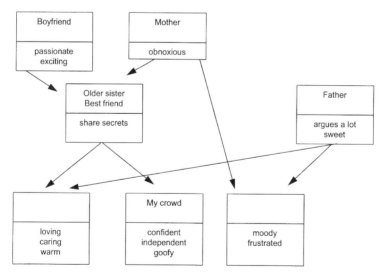

Figure 9.1b. A late adolescent girl's self-with-other descriptors.

gender identity. It can indicate how identities with family, friends, and romantic partners may be similar or different and the extent to which sex-stereotypic features are characteristic within particular identities and across identities. Nomothetic analysis also can be applied to the types of personal identity configurations illustrated in Figure 9.1. For example, it is possible to compare individuals, as well as individuals and their partners, on the centrality of identities; the number of shared and unique qualities, and the extent to which traditional and atraditional gender-linked features are present within and across identities.

Concluding Comments

In this chapter I have argued for a gender identity approach for understanding the role of gender in the development of adolescent romantic relationships. Recognition of the multifaceted nature of individuals' self-views and the variation of behavior, depending on the context or the particular relationship, points to the need to employ more ideographic methodology. In order to capture the complexity of the ways adolescents incorporate gender into their self-perceptions and their relationships with romantic partners, beginning at the individual level is imperative. By first understanding how adolescents define themselves in relation to their romantic partners and the extent to which such self and relationship views are linked to gender, it will then be possible to investigate more clearly the processes within the romantic and other relationships that are related to these self-views and relationship characteristics.

References

Aires, E. (1987). Gender and communication. In P. Shaver & C. Hendrick (Eds.), *Review of personality and social psychology* (Vol. 7, pp. 149–176). Beverly Hills, CA: Sage.

Archer, J. (1992). Childhood gender roles: Social content and organization. In H. McGurk (Ed.), *Childhood social development: Contemporary perspectives* (pp. 31–62). Hove, U.K.: Erlbaum.

Ashmore, R. (1990). Sex, gender, and the individual. In L. A. Pervin (Ed.), *Handbook of personality: Theory and research* (pp. 486–526). New York: Guilford Press.

Bailey, J. M., & Zucker, K. S. (1995). Childhood sex-type behavior and sexual orientation: A conceptual analysis and quantitative review. *Developmental Psychology, 31*(1), 43–55.

Bartky, S. L. (1990). *Femininity and abomination: Studies in the phenomenology of oppression.* New York: Routledge.

Bem, S. L. (1981). Gender schema theory: A cognitive account of sex typing. *Psychological Review, 88,* 354–364.

Bem, S. L. (1985). Androgyny and gender schema theory: A conceptual and empirical integration. In T. B. Sonderegger (Ed.), *Nebraska symposium on motivation* (Vol. 32, pp. 179–226). Lincoln: University of Nebraska Press.

Bem, S. L. (1987). Gender schema theory and the romantic tradition. In P. Shaver & C. Hendrick (Eds.), *Review of personality and social psychology: Sex and gender* (Vol. 7, pp. 251–271). Beverly Hills, CA: Sage.

Bischoping, K. (1993). Gender differences in conversation topics. *Sex Roles, 28*(1,2), 1–18.

Block, J. H. (1973). Conceptions of sex role: Some cross-cultural and longitudinal perspectives. *American Psychologist, 28,* 512–526.

Brownmiller, S. (1984). *Femininity.* New York: Linden Press.

Buhrmester, D., & Furman, W. (1987). The development of companionship and intimacy. *Child Development, 58,* 1101–1113.

Camarena, P. M., Sangiani, P. A., & Petersen, A. C. (1990). Gender-specific pathways to intimacy in early adolescence. *Journal of Youth and Adolescence, 19,* 19–32.

Cash, T. F., Dawson, K., Davis, P., Brown, M., & Galumbek, C. (1988). Effects of cosmetics use on the physical, attractiveness, and body images of American college women. *Journal of Social Psychology, 29,* 349–355.

Connolly, J. A., & Johnson, A. M. (1996). Adolescents' romantic relationships and the structure and quality of their close interpersonal ties. *Personal Relationships, 3,* 185–195.

Deaux, K., & Major, B. (1987). Putting gender into context: An interactive model of gender-related behavior. *Psychological Review, 94,* 369–389.

de Beauvoir, S. (1961). *The second sex.* New York: Knopf.

Dion, K. L., Dion, K. K., & Keelan, J. P. (1990). Appearance anxiety as a dimension of social-evaluation anxiety: Exploring the ugly duckling syndrome. *Contemporary Social Psychology, 14,* 220–224.

Douvan, E., & Adelson, J. (1966). *The adolescent experience.* New York: Wiley.

Elkind, D. (1978). Understanding the young adolescent. *Adolescence, 49,* 127–134.

Feiring, C. (1995, March). *The development of romance from 15 to 18 years.* Poster presented at meeting of the Society for Research in Child Development, Indianapolis, IN.

Feiring, C. (1996). Concepts of romance in 15-year-old adolescents. *Journal of Research on Adolescence, 6*(2), 181–200.

Feiring, C. (in press). Other-sex friendship networks and the development of romantic relationships in adolescence. *Journal of Youth and Adolescence.*

Furman, W., & Buhrmester, D. (1992). Age and sex differences in perceptions of networks of personal relationships. *Child Development, 63,* 103–115.

Galambos, N. L., Almeida, D., & Petersen, A. C. (1990). Masculinity, femininity, and sex role attitudes in early adolescence: Exploring gender intensifaction. *Child Development, 61,* 1905–1914.

Gara, M. A. (1990). A set-theoretical model of person perception. *Multivariate Behavioral Research, 25,* 275–293.

Gottman, J., & Mettetal, G. (1986). Speculations about social and affective development: Friendship and acquaintanceship through adolescence. In J. Gottman & J. Parker (Eds.), *Conversations of friends: Speculations on affective development* (pp. 192–237). New York: Cambridge University Press.

Harter, S. (1986). Processes underlying the construction, maintenance, and enhancement of the self-concept in children. In J. Suls & A. Greenwald (Eds.), *Psychological perspectives on the self* (Vol. 3, pp. 137–181). Hillsdale, NJ: Erlbaum.

Harter, S. (1990). Developmental differences in the nature of self-representations: Implications for the understanding, assessment, and treatment of maladaptive behavior. *Cognitive Therapy and Research, 14*(2), 113–142.

Harter, S., & Monsour, A. (1992). Developmental analysis of conflict caused by opposing attributes in adolescent self-portrait. *Developmental Psychology, 28,* 251–260.

Hedley, M. (1994). The presentation of gendered conflict in popular movies: Affective stereotypes, cultural sentiments, and men's motivation. *Sex Roles, 31* (11/12), 721–740.

Helgeson, V. S. (1994). Prototypes and dimensions of masculinity and femininity. *Sex Roles, 31*(11/12), 653–682.

Hill, J., & Lynch, M. T. (1983). The intensification of gender-related role expectations during early adolescence. In J. Brooks-Gunn & A. Petersen (Eds.), *Girls at puberty* (pp. 201–228). New York: Plenum.

Huston, A. C. (1983). Sex-typing. In E. M. Hetherington (Vol. Ed.), *Handbook of child Psychology: Socialization, personality, and social development, Volume 4* (4th ed., pp. 387–467). New York: Wiley.

Huston, A. C., & Alvarez, M. M. (1990). The socialization context of gender role development in early adolescence. In R. Montemayo, I. G. Adams, & T. Gullotta (Eds.), *From childhood to adolescence* (pp. 156–179). Newbury Park, CA: Sage.

Kaschak, E. (1992). *Engendered lives: A new psychology of women's experience.* New York: Basic Books.

Katz, P. A., & Ksansnak, K. R. (1994). Developmental aspects of gender role flexibility and traditionality in middle childhood and adolescence. *Developmental Psychology, 36*(2), 272–282.

Kobak, R. R., Cole, H. E., Ferenz-Gillies, R., Fleming, W. S., & Gamble, W. (1993). Attachment and emotion regulation during mother–teen problem-solving: A control theory analysis. *Child Development, 64*(1), 231–245.

Kohlberg, L. A. (1966). A cognitive-developmental analysis of children's sex-role concepts and attitudes. In E. E. Maccoby (Ed.), *The development of sex differences* (pp. 82–173). Stanford, CA: Stanford University Press.

Kovacs, D. M., Parker, J. G., & Hoffman, L. (1996). Behavioral, affective, and social correlates of involvement in cross-sex friendship in elementary school. *Child Development, 67,* 2269–2286.

Lerner, R. M. (1987). A life-span perspective for early adolescence. In R. M. Lerner & T. T. Foch (Eds.), *Biological–psychosocial interactions in early adolescence* (pp. 9–34). Hillsdale, NJ: Erlbaum.

Linn, M. C., & Petersen, A. C. (1986). A meta-analysis of gender differences in spatial ability: Implications for math and science achievement. In J. S. Hyde & M. L.

Linn (Eds.), *The psychology of gender: Advances through meta-analysis* (pp. 67–101). Baltimore: Johns Hopkins University Press.

Maccoby, E. E. (1990). Gender and relationships: A developmental account. *American Psychologist, 45,* 513–520.

Maccoby, E. E. & Jacklin, C. (1987). Gender segregation in childhood. In H. W. Reese (Ed.), *Advances in child development* (pp. 239–287). Orlando, FL: Academic Press.

Martin, C. L., & Halverson, C. F., Jr. (1981). A schematic processing model of sex-typing and stereotyping in young children. *Child Development, 52,* 1119–1134.

McAdams, D. P., & Losoff, M. (1984). Friendship motivation in fourth and sixth graders: A thematic analysis. *Journal of Social and Personal Relationships, 1,* 11–27.

McRobbie, A. (1994). *Postmodernism and popular culture.* New York: Routledge.

Nolen-Hoeksema, S. (1990). *Sex differences in depression.* Stanford, CA: Stanford University Press.

Orlofsky, J. L. (1993). Intimacy status: Theory and research. In J. E. Marcia, A. S. Waterman, D. R. Matteson, S. L. Archer, J. L. Orlofsky (Eds.), *Ego identity: A handbook for psychosocial research* (pp. 111–133). New York: Springer-Verlag.

Richards, M. H, Boxer, A. M., Petersen, A. C., & Albrecht, R. (1990). The significance of weight to feelings of attractiveness in pubertal boys and girls. *Developmental Psychology, 26,* 313–321.

Richards, M. H., Gitelson, I. B., Petersen, A. C., & Hurtig, A. L. (1991). Adolescent personality in girls and boys: The role of mothers and fathers. *Psychology of Women, 15,* 65–81.

Richards, M. H., & Larson, R. (1993). Pubertal development and the daily subjective states of young adolescents. *Journal of Research on Adolescence, 3*(2), 145–169.

Rosenberg, S. (1988). Self and others: Studies in social personality and autobiography. In L. Berkowitz (Ed.), *Advances in experimental social psychology* (Vol. 21, pp. 57–95). San Diego, CA: Academic Press.

Savin-Williams, R. C. (1994). Verbal and physical abuse as stressors in the lives of lesbian, gay male, and bisexual youths: Associations with school problems, running away, substance abuse, prostitution, and suicide. *Journal of Consulting and Clinical Psychology, 62*(2), 261–269.

Simmons, R. G., & Blyth, D. A. (1987). *Moving into adolescence: The impact of pubertal change and school context.* Hawthorne, NY: Aldine de Gruyter.

Simmons, R. G., Blyth, D. A., VanCleave, E. F., & Bush, D. M. (1979). Entry into early adolescence: The impact of school structure, puberty, and early dating on self-esteem. *American Sociological Review, 44,* 948–967.

Slaby, R. G., & Frey, K. S. (1975). Development of gender constancy and selective attention to same-sex models. *Child Development, 46,* 849–856.

Smollar, T., & Youniss, J. (1985). Adolescent self-concept development of self. In R. L. Leahy (Ed.), *The development of self* (pp. 247–266). San Diego, CA: Academic Press.

Spence, J. T. (1984). Masculinity, femininity, and gender-related traits: A conceptual analysis and critique of current research. In B. A. Maher & W. B. Maher (Eds.), *Progress in experimental personality research* (Vol. 13, pp. 1–97). Orlando, FL: Academic Press.

Spence, J. T. (1985). Gender identity and implications for concepts of masculinity and femininity. In T. B. Sonderegger (Ed.), *Nebraska symposium on motivation: Psychology and gender* (Vol. 32, pp. 59–96). Lincoln: University of Nebraska Press.

Spence, J. T. (1993). Gender-related traits and gender ideology: Evidence for a multi-factorial theory. *Journal of Personality, 64*(4), 624–635.

Waters, E., Kondo-Ikemura, K., Posada, G., & Richters, J. E., III. (1990). Learning to love mechanisms and milestones. In M. Gunnar & L. A. Sroufe (Eds.), *Minnesota symposia on child psychology* (Vol. 23, pp. 217–255). Hillsdale, NJ: Erlbaum.

Worrell, J. (1981). Life-span sex roles: Development, continuity, and change. In R. M. Lerner & N. A. Busch-Rossnagel (Eds.), *Individuals as producers of their development: A life-span perspective* (pp. 131–347). New York: Academic Press.

PART III

The Social Context of Romantic Relationships

10   Adolescent Romance and the Parent–Child Relationship

A Contextual Perspective

Marjory Roberts Gray and Laurence Steinberg

The emergence of romantic relationships in early adolescence seldom has been examined within a contextual framework. To date, most theoretical writing on romantic relationships in adolescence has focused on the intraindividual developments characteristic of the adolescent years presumed to affect youngsters' capacity for, and interest in, intimate relationships with age-mates. Much of this work has been informed by psychoanalytic (Freud, 1958), Eriksonian (Erikson, 1959), and Sullivanian views of adolescent development (Buhrmester & Furman, 1987; Furman, this volume; Furman & Wehner, 1994; Sullivan, 1953). Among the factors thought to influence the emergence and progression of romantic relationships are the biological changes of puberty (believed to stimulate interest in sexuality and, consequently, in romance), the onset of abstract thinking (believed to increase youngsters' social cognitive abilities and, accordingly, their capacity for engagement in more interpersonally sophisticated relationships), and changes in individuals' need for intimacy (believed to steer youngsters to relationships that integrate emotional intimacy and sexuality). Empirical research on the subject, sparse as it is, has focused mainly on the meaning and nature of intimate relationships to individual adolescents – how young people view romantic relationships, what takes place within romantic dyads, and what adolescents seek in their intimate partners (e.g., Feiring, 1996).

During the last decade, the study of adolescence has taken on a more ecological emphasis as researchers have begun to examine contextual, as well as intraindividual, influences on behavior and development (e.g., Steinberg, 1996). Not surprisingly, the primary focus of such contextual analyses of the development of romantic relationships in particular has been the setting in which romance most often plays out: the adolescent peer group. Drawing on studies of changes in peer group structure and function during adolescence, several writers have argued that romantic relationships emerge not solely because of intraindividual changes in the young person, but in part because of transformations in adolescent peer dynamics (e.g., Brown, this volume; Dunphy, 1963). As group activities become more oriented to mixed-sex socializing, adolescents internalize new norms and standards for appropriate patterns of social activity. To the extent that a young person's peers get involved in dating and related activities, he or she will be inclined to follow suit. Indeed, research suggests that adolescents' interest in dating and sex is more likely a function of their peers' behavior (and the normative standards that this behavior suggests) than of their own biological development (Dornbusch et al., 1981). In other words, although biological and psychological change may initially draw *some* adolescents (presumably, those high in popularity or status) into romantic activity, it is the interpersonal reorganization of the peer group, and not the intrapsychic reorganization of the individual, that accounts for much of the action.

Focusing on the contribution of changing peer dynamics to the emergence of romance in adolescence is essential to a full understanding of adolescent sexual and emotional intimacy. A contextual perspective, however, demands that we also look beyond the most obvious settings thought to influence particular patterns of development and turn our attention to the entire complex of settings that influence young persons' behavior. In this spirit, this chapter examines mainly uncharted territory in the study of adolescent romance: the links between adolescent involvement in romantic relationships and concomitant events within the parent–child relationship. Although most of our discussion implies heterosexual romance, the parameters that define romance among gay and lesbian youth (i.e., intimacy plus sexuality) are the same as those that define it among their straight counterparts (for a discussion of homosexual romance in adolescence, the reader is directed to Diamond, Savin-Williams, & Dube, this volume).

The notion that there are connections between the home environment and other contexts in which adolescents develop is not new, of course. Indeed, this tenet is an integral part of the ecological view of human development (e.g., Bronfenbrenner, 1979), which holds that examining the broader ecology of development permits the most comprehensive understanding of psychosocial development. This broader ecology includes the linkages among the adolescent's relational contexts (e.g., between the parent–child relationship and the child's peer relationships), the linkages between the adolescent's relational contexts and those that affect significant others in the young person's life (e.g., between the child's peer relationships and his or her parents' marriage), and between the child's relational contexts and the wider environment defined by the social and historical milieu. Although the ecological approach has been applied to the study of other aspects of adolescent development, to our knowledge it has not yet been applied to the study of adolescent romance.

In our discussion of the influence of the parent–adolescent relationship on adolescent romance, we look first at the emergence of romantic interest as a developmental phenomenon in early adolescence. What makes adolescence the developmental period during which individuals first express genuine and intense interest in romantic relationships? Although there are many possible, and mutually compatible, answers to this question – ranging from the neurochemical to the sociocultural – we choose to explore this issue within a family-oriented framework. More specifically, we consider early adolescent romance in light of the parents' role in the psychological, social, and biological tasks of this period of adolescence. We argue that young adolescent romantic relationships are best understood not as an intraindividual phenomenon, or even as a peer phenomenon, but rather as part of a developmental process that is intricately linked to changes in the parent–child relationship during this developmental era.

In the second half of this chapter, we turn our attention from the nomothetic to the idiographic. As we shift from the universal developmental tasks facilitated by early adolescent romance to individual differences in the emerging capacity for intimacy in late adolescence, we ask whether variations in adolescents' experiences in the family help explain variations in their late-adolescent romantic encounters. In exploring possible antecedent events in the family of origin, we review aspects of the marital relationship as well as of the parent–child relationship.

Adolescent Romance and the Parent–Child Relationship: A Functional Analysis

The emergence of romantic relationships at adolescence is virtually universal within industrialized societies, which raises the question of why and what function this developmental transition serves. Pointing the finger at the endocrinological changes of puberty gives only a partial, and ultimately unsatisfying, answer: Hormones may produce adolescent lust, but they probably do not produce very much in the way of love. Furthermore, hormonal shifts do not adequately explain the development of the longing for emotional intimacy, the desire to "go steady," love letters, or fantasies about long-term courtship – the hallmarks of teenage romance.

Hormonally instigated sexual desire undoubtedly plays some role in fueling the phenomenon, but in order to understand why romance is romance, and not simply sex, we need to look at the context, as well as the neurobiology, of biological maturation. A critical part of this context is the parent–child relationship and its role in the development of autonomy during adolescence.

In the following analysis, we consider three links between the emergence of romantic relationships and autonomy-related changes in family relationships during the early adolescent transition. First, the development of romantic interest is inherently linked to the tasks of separation and individuation (see also Connolly, this volume). More specifically, the emergence of romantic activity in adolescence can be seen as part of the more general process of the development of emotional autonomy in the family context (Brown, this volume). As the adolescent seeks to individuate from parental models, he or she redirects interpersonal energy to intimate and sexual relationships with age-mates (Buhrmester & Furman, 1987; Sullivan, 1953). We suggest that this process is bidirectional, with individuation stimulating, and being stimulated by, involvement in romantic relationships.

Second, adolescent involvement in romantic relationships is associated with changes in interpersonal status within the family. In earlier eras, a variety of options allowed adolescents to demonstrate their social maturity; they could leave home, enter the labor force, become an apprentice, or take steps toward marriage. As adolescents have become more economically dependent on their parents, however, they have had to find other means of establishing themselves as grown up in the eyes of others. Involvement in romantic relationships provides a status-enhancing mechanism that helps to mitigate against other forces in contemporary society that have prolonged adolescent dependence and social immaturity.

Finally, the sociobiology of adolescence connects romantic relationships and family life. Across all nonhuman primate species, juveniles' emancipation from their family of origin is closely linked to their involvement in sexual relationships with age-mates. Specifically, among other primate species, juveniles seldom live with their parents continuously once they have attained sexual maturity. From an evolutionary viewpoint, this physical separation may represent a mechanism to minimize the potential for inbreeding. The development of romance in adolescence may then provide a psychological vehicle through which humans maintain distance from parents during early puberty – an evolved behavior pattern with clear adaptive significance.

Across these three realms of interpretation, then, romantic activity in adolescence is not often what it appears. Rather, we suggest that a functional analysis of adolescent romance within the family context reveals that young people's interest and involvement in romantic relationships serves multiple purposes that on the surface have little to do with romance or intimacy per se.

Romance and Emotional Autonomy

Today, with orthodox psychoanalytic theory largely out of fashion among scholars of adolescent development, any suggestion that adolescents' interest in establishing romantic or sexual relationships with age-mates derives from young people's unconscious feelings toward their parents may be viewed as an amusing anachronism. Yet, in our view, the emergence of romantic relationships in adolescence in conjunction with the growth of emotional autonomy in the parent–child relationship suggest that the two processes may necessarily go hand in hand. As adolescents change their view of their parents and of their own relationship with them, they are increasingly likely to seek emotional support and companionship outside the family. And, as adolescents spend more and more time in intimate relationships with age-mates, their view of their parents, and of themselves in relation to their parents, is likely to be transformed (Laursen & Williams, 1997; Youniss, 1980).

Although this account helps explain why early adolescents make complementary movements away from emotional intimacy with parents and toward emotional intimacy with peers, it does not explain the emergence of *romantic* interests per se. Presumably, adolescents' desire to find emotional intimacy outside the parent–child relationship could be satisfied through nonsexual intimacy with same-sex peers. Wherefore romance, then, from the psychoanalytic perspective?

The answer to this question resides in early writings on emotional autonomy by Anna Freud (1958) and others. Freud argued that the physical changes of puberty cause substantial disruption and conflict inside the family system specifically because intrapsychic conflicts that young children repress are reawakened by the resurgence of *sexual* impulses in early adolescence. The resolution of these conflicts requires not just that the adolescent seek emotional intimacy with age-mates outside the family, but that he or she "do something" with the revivified sexual energy as well. Family members remain unaware, of course, of the sources of their intrapsychic discomfort, but the reawakened conflicts take the form of nattering, bickering, and a certain degree of free-floating tension between parents and teenagers. This tension, the theory goes, drives early adolescents to separate themselves emotionally from their parents. The formerly obedient and respectful young adolescent "regresses" to a more psychologically primitive state and turns spiteful, vengeful, oppositional, and unpredictable (Freud, 1958). Simultaneously, young adolescents turn their energies to relationships with peers – and in particular, peers of the opposite sex. This process is known as *detachment* in psychoanalytic theory.

Detachment, and the accompanying storm and stress inside the family, signified to Freud and her followers normal, healthy, and inevitable aspects of emotional development during adolescence. In fact, Freud believed that the absence of conflict between adolescent and parents suggested maturation problems in the young person and forecast difficulties in the formation of healthy sexual relationships with age-mates.

In the past two decades, orthodox psychoanalytic views of detachment have given way to more tempered, neoanalytic theories that emphasize the process of adolescent *individuation.* Blos, the most important proponent of this theoretical orientation, has written extensively about the *second individuation process* (1979). Individuation occurs as the young person develops a clearer sense of himself or herself as psychologically separate from parents. Neoanalytic perspectives generally downplay the behavioral turbulence of the adolescent's movement toward emotional and behavioral emancipation suggested in Freud's account, and emphasize instead the more pacific process through which the adolescent develops a new view of self and parental figures. For Blos, the individuation process is marked by the repudiation of parents, a largely cognitive rather than behavioral process that does not necessarily involve overt rebellion or oppositionalism. Nevertheless, even within this less melodramatic approach to the development of emotional autonomy, the adolescent's interest in romantic relationships stems from his or her underlying desire to separate from parents.

Placing teenage romance within the context of the development of emotional autonomy in the family implies something quite interesting, and perhaps unsettling, about the way in which we view the emergence of romantic interest in early adolescence. In contemporary culture, especially in the second half of the 20th century, we tend to define adolescent romances as ends in themselves. Teenage romance, is, for lack of a better word, *romanticized* – in books (e.g., *Endless Love),* films (e.g., *Sixteen Candles*), and television (e.g., *My So-Called Life)* as the pursuit of "that special someone." When cast as a part of the development of emotional autonomy, however, the pursuit of the romantic partner represents a secondary rather than a primary goal: Romantic relationships provide a solution to the problem of unconscious conflicts about, and sexual desires toward, parental figures. As such, if young adolescents seek romance in order to separate from their parents, and not to connect with a specific age-mate, then romance in adolescence may be more significant for what it symbolizes than for what it is.

The links between emotional autonomy and the adolescent's developing interest in romantic involvement have implications not only for the young person's sense of autonomy but for his or her parents' mental health as well. In one study of some 200 families negotiating the transition to adolescence (Steinberg & Steinberg, 1994), mothers' feelings of self-doubt, regret over past decisions, and reported desire to change their life circumstances significantly increased when their son or daughter began to date. Among fathers, comparable effects emerged most notably in households with sons. Fathers of sons who were dating reported an intriguing combination of more anxiety and depression but higher self-esteem, particularly if their sons began dating early. The son's dating may have triggered both feelings of envy (which led to the anxiety and depression) and vicarious pleasure over the son's enjoyment of the experience (which contributed to the high self-esteem). Interestingly, regardless of whether their child was a son or a daughter, fathers whose child was dating reported much lower marital satisfaction than did those whose children did not have an active social life.

Several reasons may explain the link between the adolescent's burgeoning interest in romance and the parent's mental health. Seeing a child date calls forth a mixture of anxiety (over the adolescent's sexuality), envy (over the adolescent's freedom), regret (over the romantic choices one didn't pursue), and longing (for one's youth). Indeed, research indicates that seeing one's child mature sexually presents one of the most difficult challenges of the adolescent passage for parents, especially in households with adolescent girls, who display more obvious signs of sexual maturation (Steinberg & Steinberg, 1994). For many parents, the adolescent's sexual maturation unleashes a torrent of emotions and conflicts about their *own* physical attractiveness, their *own* sexuality, and their *own* sexual experiences as teenagers, as well as their marriage. More often than not, the effects are negative, making parents feel unattractive, envious of their child's potential, longing for their own "lost" youth, and, if married, dissatisfied with their spouse. These feelings of dissatisfaction may spill over into the parent–child relationship, contributing to parent–adolescent bickering and squabbling. In turn, increased conflict between parent and adolescent may further impel the young person to seek emotional intimacy outside the family.

Romance and the Social Redefinition of the Adolescent

Romance not only contributes to the adolescent's personal sense of emotional independence but also redefines the adolescent socially, both inside the family and with peers. Although the status-enhancing impact of romantic involvement within the peer group has been the subject of a small amount of previous research and writing (see Brown, this volume), the role of romance in redefining relationships within the family has not, to our knowledge, received any attention. As in the case of emotional autonomy, the links between romantic involvement and social redefinition within the family are reciprocal. Before we examine the specifics of these links, we offer a few general words about social redefinition.

All societies distinguish between individuals defined as children and those who are ready to become adults. Some cultures mark the social redefinition of the adolescent by a formal rite of passage. In most contemporary societies, however, the transition from childhood to adulthood is primarily denoted not by ceremony, but by changes in the individual's rights, responsibilities, and privileges. Whether formally regulated (e.g., voting, driving, entering the formal labor force) or informally regulated (e.g., curfew, household responsibilities), transformations in what the adolescent is permitted or expected to do reflect and influence the definition of the individual as a child, adolescent, or adult.

Historically, industrialized societies have socially defined, and redefined, individuals in three main arenas: economic (the extent to which individuals support themselves), residential (the extent to which individuals live under adult supervision), and interpersonal (the extent to which individuals are involved in intimate sexual relationships outside the family). In recent years, some very interesting trends have emerged in each of these arenas (Steinberg, 1996). In the economic domain, the movement from childhood to adulthood has lengthened considerably due to the extension of formal schooling, with individuals remaining economically dependent on their parents for longer periods of time. In the residential domain, the transition to adulthood has been prolonged as well, again in part because of the extension of schooling (which theoretically places many young adults under the control of adults) but also because of a substantial rise in the cost of housing (which has forced greater numbers of adult children to reside with their parents).

Within the interpersonal domain, however, the trend has moved in the opposite direction: Individuals begin to date and have sex at an earlier age today than in the past. Our suspicion is that as adolescents find it increasingly difficult to establish themselves as adults in the economic and residential spheres, they seek other routes through which to demonstrate their social maturity. This is not to say that adolescents consciously choose to form romantic attachments in order to compensate for their economic or residential immaturity. It does suggest, however, that young people often turn to whatever avenues toward adulthood remain open to them, and that when some roads are closed, others appear more desirable. Romantic involvement – having a boyfriend or girlfriend – thus takes on additional symbolic significance within a sociocultural and familial context that in other ways keeps adolescents all too painfully aware of their prolonged transition to adulthood.

The notion that romantic experience has taken on increased importance for the social redefinition of the individual supports our argument about the functional significance of romantic involvement in adolescence. Once again, we come to the conclusion that in early adolescence, neither the choice of a specific partner nor what takes place within the romantic relationship matters as much as what the relationship signifies: movement toward adulthood in the eyes of parents and significant others.

A Sociobiological View of Adolescent Romance

The functional significance of adolescent romance is also apparent from a sociobiological perspective. Human adolescence has a great deal in common with adolescence in other mammalian species and, in particular, with adolescence among other primates, in that the period involves transition and transformation in the nature of the parent–child relationship. Most important, among most nonhuman primates living in the wild, pubertal maturation is generally accompanied by increased distance in the parent–child relationship, either in terms of increased physical distance or in terms of heightened aggression (Caine, 1986; Steinberg, 1989). This observation raises questions about the standard psychoanalytic interpretation of increased parent–adolescent bickering at puberty since monkeys and apes probably do not harbor unresolved Oedipal tension. Instead, the fact that parent–adolescent distance occurs routinely at puberty across primate species suggests that it probably played some role in primate evolution. In all likelihood, parent–adolescent conflict at puberty mainly serves to minimize the chances of inbreeding (Steinberg, 1989).

A number of important differences between parent–adolescent relations in humans versus nonhumans, however, inform our understanding of adolescent romance. In the wild, most other adolescent primates leave their natal group during or shortly after puberty, either willingly or in response to parental pressure. In some species, this pattern is limited to males; in others, it is females who leave; in still others, adolescent emigration is typical of both genders. Studies of primates and other mammals living in captivity show that disruptions of this migration stall the juvenile's reproductive development (Tardif, 1984). In contrast, contemporary human parents and their offspring continue to live together after the adolescent has reached full sexual maturation. (Note that prior to the mid-19th century, emancipation from home generally coincided with biological maturation.) Indeed, because of the odd contemporary combination of earlier human pubertal maturation (the average age of menarche in the industrialized world is now about 12 years) and prolonged economic dependence of the adolescent, it is not unusual for parents to live with sexually mature offspring for a full decade. From a sociobiological as well as a historical perspective, this arrangement is highly unusual.

The emergence of romantic interest in early adolescence could thus provide a socially invented device designed to protect against genetic inbreeding within the context of a family environment that necessitates prolonged contact between parents and their reproductively mature offspring. Romantic relationships, with all their trappings, permit the adolescent an expression of normally developing sexual desire outside the family context. In the absence of pathways in contemporary society through which the adolescent can establish genuine physical independence from parents, and in a world in which early marriage and childbearing are economically undesirable, romantic relationships with age-mates offer a relatively safe means of preparing the adolescent for adult sexuality while protecting him or her against incest.

Individual Differences in Patterns of Adolescent Romance: The Influence of the Parent–Child Relationship

Although the establishment of early adolescent romantic relationships may reflect a general developmental need for greater emotional autonomy from the family of origin, it is important to acknowledge that wide interindividual variation exists in the quality of the romantic relationships adolescents have with peers, particularly in late adolescence. Thus, we argue that although universal forces instigate the emergence of romance in adolescence, there are many sources of individual difference in the nature of these relationships as adolescence progresses.

Although few studies have directly investigated these sources, the indirect evidence on the evolution of interpersonal development is quite consistent: In general, a family environment characterized by a harmonious marriage as well as parental warmth, structure, and emotional availability promotes in the adolescent a healthy, lasting capacity for relatedness and intimacy (see also Collins & Sroufe, this volume). Accordingly, in the following synopsis of this work, we take our contextual analysis into the adolescent's family of origin, exploring the developmental antecedents of adolescent interpersonal competence by looking at the impact of the marital relationship, as well as the broad and complex realm of parent–child interaction. We begin by considering the notion of relational continuity within families.

The Evidence for Relational Continuity

Both clinical experience and intuitive observation suggest that childhood experience within the family of origin influences adult adjustment, including the quality of relationships one establishes and maintains. Specifically, relationship patterns appear to remain "all in the family," such that problematic ways of relating repeat themselves from one generation to the next. Putting this notion to empirical test, several longitudinal investigations have produced evidence that a child's earliest experiences in relationships – whether as observer or participant – appear to function like a template for the nature and quality of later relationships. Though a review of the literature on family dysfunction goes beyond the scope of this chapter, data from these studies support the contention that problematic patterns in one generation tend to carry forward into subsequent generations (see Belsky & Pensky, 1988, for a review). Although these studies generally have relied on retrospective reports of childhood events, this research suggests that a history of child abuse, spouse abuse, or marital instability in one's family of origin increases the likelihood that such problems will recur in one's family of procreation. Similarly, markers of healthy psychosocial development in one generation bode well for marital and parent–child relationships in members of the next generation (Belsky & Pensky, 1988). These conclusions hold when researchers follow families over time, across multiple generations (e.g., Elder, Caspi, & Downey, 1986; Vaillant, 1974; Vaillant & Vaillant, 1981). Vaillant and his colleagues (Vaillant, 1974; Vaillant & Milofsky, 1980), for example, tracked a sample of males from late adolescence to midlife and found a strong correlation between a warm home atmosphere reported in adolescence and the experience of close friendships, good relationships within one's family, and a stable marriage at age 47. In a similar vein, Vaillant and Vaillant (1981) found that inner-city male youths who reported a cohesive family environment and authoritative parenting during adolescence were more likely to score high on a measure of "adolescent industry," which tapped individuals' level of academic, work, and extracurricular involvement. Industriousness, in turn, strongly predicted the ability to establish and maintain warm relationships in adulthood.

Data from the Oakland and Berkeley Growth Studies substantiate the hypothesis that authoritative, happy parents raise socially and personally competent adolescents who develop a greater degree of social maturity in adulthood. Not surprisingly, social maturity predicts a happier marriage, as well as a better emotional climate in the family of procreation (Brooks, 1981). Troubled relationships, too, appear to run in families. In one investigation spanning four generations, hostile family environments provided the link between problem behavior among parents and their children (Elder et al., 1986). More specifically, the evidence supported an intergenerational model that began with the sort of conflicted marriage and hostile parenting typically associated with unstable psychological functioning. These parenting difficulties provoked quarrelsome, irritable, and generally negative behavior in children, who then re-created aversive family relationships in adulthood. In turn, this second-generation family dysfunction moderately predicted children's undercontrolled behavior. These same links were found in an investigation that compared girls who spent most of their childhood in institutional care with girls raised at home (Dowdney, Skuse, Rutter, Quinton, & Mrazek, 1985; Quinton, Rutter, & Liddle, 1984; Rutter & Quinton, 1984). Again, those who grew up in a relatively impoverished early environment experienced greater disturbances in personality development and, subsequently, more substantial problems in marital relationships and in the task of parenting.

Despite the strong story line of continuity, however, it is important to note that associations between intergenerational variables are typically quite small in magnitude. This suggests that under certain conditions, discontinuity in developmental trajectories occurs (Belsky & Pensky, 1988). Thus, some children overcome notable deficits in their upbringing to establish supportive marriages and, as a result, go on to become skilled parents – a finding that highlights the power of a corrective emotional experience in building one's capacity for intimacy. At the same time, many individuals who are raised in supportive interpersonal environments have difficulty establishing or maintaining satisfying romantic relationships for reasons outside the family of origin.

Links Between the Marital Relationship and the Adolescent's Relationships with Age-mates

As the data on relationship patterns suggest, the marital relationship constitutes one important realm of influence on socioemotional development in childhood and adolescence. This link has received the most extensive attention in the literature on marital discord and divorce. Exposure to a distressed marriage routinely has been associated with psychological disorder and distress in children (e.g., Hetherington, Cox, & Cox, 1976; Porter & O'Leary, 1980), despite the moderating influence of a child's age, cognitive level, and gender, among other factors. Children exposed to a troubled marriage, whether or not it ends in divorce, appear to have an unusually difficult time establishing or maintaining successful peer relations. For example, boys from divorced families display more negativity and aggression toward peers and are not as well liked (Hetherington, Cox, & Cox, 1979). Conversely, higher marital satisfaction predicts more positive play among children and less negative interaction with age-mates (Gottman & Katz, 1989).

Beyond interpersonal functioning in childhood, emotional and behavioral aspects of the marital relationship may exert a longer-range influence on romantic attitudes and behavior during late adolescence and adulthood. In addition to the well-established finding that marital violence in one generation increases its likelihood of occurrence in the next (e.g., Kalmuss, 1984; Steinmetz, 1977), recent evidence suggests that children exposed to marital violence are more likely to use physical aggression toward romantic partners in adolescence (Capaldi, Crosby, & Clark, 1996; Downey & Feldman, 1996). In the Oregon Youth Study, a longitudinal investigation of children at risk for delinquency, conflict and aggression between a boy's parents reported in early adolescence predicted his tendency in late adolescence to abuse an intimate partner physically, as well as to abuse her emotionally – to verbally offend or degrade her.

Even in the absence of violence, observing parental conflict may negatively affect a child's ability to operate harmoniously in intimate relationships later on. The conflict tactics parents use with each other – whether verbal aggression, physical aggression, or avoidance – appear to be significantly related to the way in which college-age children handle conflict with their parents and, later, with romantic partners (Martin, 1990). Exposure to parental conflict also has been linked to an impaired ability to listen to and consider a romantic partner's point of view in late adolescence, particularly among children who believe that the conflict involves them or who feel responsible for their parents' arguments (Reese, Creasey, Bergner, Criss, & Ottlinger, 1995). However, adolescents who experience the most intense and frequent conflict between their parents do not necessarily demonstrate the most ineffective conflict resolution skills, suggesting that other unidentified variables, such as coping skills, may moderate the detrimental effects of marital conflict on children's interpersonal functioning (Reese et al., 1995).

Positive perceptions of the marital relationship, on the other hand, appear to bode well for a child's subsequent expectations about and experiences with intimacy. Adults who recall their parents sharing a high-quality marriage, described by adjectives such as *loving, supportive, caring, playful, trusting, close,* and *passionate,* express greater optimism that they, too, will have a successful marriage (Carnelley & Janoff-Bulman, 1992). In an early investigation on the parallels between romantic love and parent–child attachment (Hazan & Shaver, 1987), those who classified themselves as secure – facile and comfortable with intimate relationships – reported an affectionate, caring relationship between their parents significantly more often than did those who described themselves as insecure – either avoidant of intimate relationships or ambivalent about them. Both forms of insecure attachment among college students (i.e., avoidant and ambivalent, as assessed by self-report) are related to the experience of frequent and severe family violence, whether as a witness to marital violence or as a victim of child abuse (Downey et al., this volume; Feldman & Downey, 1994). These researchers found that an internalized expectation of rejection in close relationships, which they labeled *rejection sensitivity,* explained approximately half of the variance in the association between the experience of family violence in childhood and adult attachment behavior.

Many questions remain about the specific impact of the marital relationship on adolescent behavior in romantic relationships. In particular, it would be useful to explore the effects of marital conflict on the timing, course, and intensity of adolescents' romantic relationships. By early adolescence, it appears that the marital relationship affects the adolescent's understanding of the way in which conflict and negative emotions should be handled in the ideal romantic relationship (Connolly, Ben-Knaz, Goldberg, & Craig, 1996). Like divorce, however, exposure to marital conflict does not always impair children's social competence and peer relations. The amount and type of damage it inflicts in these realms – and perhaps, by extrapolation, on the capacity for romantic intimacy – depends on various aspects of marital conflict, such as its content, frequency, and intensity (e.g., Grych & Fincham, 1990; Long, Forehand, Fauber, & Brody, 1987).

Although we know little about the way in which exposure to marital conflict may manifest itself in adolescents' romantic interactions, some work suggests that continual exposure to unresolved anger in one's home environment leads to antisocial and/or anxious behavior in general (Cummings & Cummings, 1988; Grych & Fincham, 1990). In at least one study (Capaldi et al., 1996), antisocial behavior provided the mediating link between parental aggression and youth aggression in romantic relationships. In the case of divorce, research suggests that girls from disrupted families are more likely to become pregnant prior to marriage as well as to marry at young ages, often choosing men with few psychological and financial resources (Hetherington, Cox, & Cox, 1978; Mueller & Pope, 1977).

Rather than observing a direct connection between marital relations and adolescent romance, we may ultimately learn that disruptions in the parent–child relationship mediate between the child's experience of marital conflict and the subsequent occurrence of problematic behavior in peer relationships (e.g., Grych & Fincham, 1990; Peterson & Zill, 1986). This model holds that when marital tension leads to cold, unresponsive, or hostile parenting, a child may begin to display behavior problems that ultimately impede his or her ability to form successful relationships with age-mates (Gottman & Katz, 1989) and, presumably, to negotiate the complexities of romantic relationships. Mitigating factors, however, could potentially steer interpersonal development onto a more fortuitous and fulfilling path, including positive experiences in other settings such as school (Quinton et al., 1984) or the establishment of a "corrective" relationship with an authority figure outside of the home (Belsky & Pensky, 1988).

Links Between the Parent–Child Relationship and the Adolescent's Relationships with Age-mates

The capacity to establish and maintain meaningful, close relationships stems not only from the first intimate relationship we observe, but also from the first intimate relationship in which most of us participate: the parent–child relationship. Whether we examine this connection from the quality of the emotional base it provides or from the affective tone and behavioral expectations communicated by parenting style, early parent–child dynamics are likely to set the stage for the individual's adjustment to, and functioning in, a variety of relationships over time.

Attachment. In the earliest stages of interpersonal experience, infants use behavioral cues from their primary caregiver to develop the attachment bond. Whereas responsive and available care facilitates a secure attachment, insensitive parenting leads to an insecure attachment (Bowlby, 1969). This most primitive dynamic teaches the child what to expect in social exchanges, a lesson about self and others that the child carries forward in the form of an *internal working model* (Bowlby, 1969). Among other relational capacities, this lesson appears to influence social competence throughout childhood and into early adolescence, giving securely attached children the ability to interact with peers more effectively and to make friends more easily. Studies of preschool and school-age children have consistently documented an association between the quality of infant–parent attachment and the quality of children's social interactions with peers (for reviews, see Elicker, Englund, & Sroufe, 1992; Putallaz & Heflin, 1990). Securely attached children demonstrate better social skills, such as the ability to engage in reciprocal, positive interactions with age-mates (e.g., Lieberman, 1977), especially when matched with another secure child (Park & Waters, 1989). Conversely, an insecure attachment in infancy is more predictive of peer rejection, an aggressive and disruptive reputation, problem behavior, and few friendships, particularly among boys (Cohn, 1990; Lewis & Feiring, 1989; Lewis, Feiring, McGuffog, & Jaskir, 1984).

As attachment representations evolve in adolescence and adulthood, they continue to influence interpersonal functioning beyond the realm of peer relations, further supporting the theoretical claim that internal working models perpetuate relational experiences outside the family of origin. In general, a secure attachment representation in adolescence is associated not only with broad indicators of psychological adjustment that contribute to social competence, but also with the beliefs and attitudes, emotional demeanor, and practical skills that promote success in intimate relationships.

The small but growing literature on attachment relationships in adolescence supports the contention that a secure attachment represents an organization of behavior that facilitates other adaptive behavioral organizations, concurrently and prospectively (Waters & Sroufe, 1983). A meta-analysis of these studies (Rice, 1990) revealed a modest correlation between healthy attachment in adolescence and general adolescent adjustment, with self-esteem or self-concept demonstrating the strongest association with attachment security, followed by consistent positive correlations between attachment security and measures of social competence, identity, and emotional adjustment. This analysis also revealed a developmental trend in which attachment was more strongly linked to social and emotional well-being among high school students than among any subsequent age group through young adulthood, suggesting that periods marked by significant transitions may activate the need for support and a secure base (Sroufe & Waters, 1977).

Adolescent attachment styles also predict patterns of emotional regulation (Kobak, Cole, Ferenz-Gillies, & Fleming, 1993; Kobak & Sceery, 1988), an important component of intimate relationships. College freshmen who describe their parents as loving, supportive, and available during distressing events – secure individuals – appear better able than insecure individuals to modulate affect in social situations, including dating interactions and scenarios that require assertiveness (Kobak & Sceery, 1988). Secure adolescents also demonstrate more effective emotional regulation than insecure adolescents while working on a problem-solving task with their mothers, expressing anger more appropriately, and maintaining a balance between assertion and cooperation (Kobak et al., 1993). These findings imply that a secure attachment allows adolescents to utilize affectional bonds judiciously during times of stress, as well as to negotiate successfully autonomy-related changes in the parent–child relationship discussed earlier.

A securely attached adult fares equally well in relationships. Adults who classify themselves as secure are likely to recall harmonious, positive early family experiences (Bringle & Bagby, 1992; Feeney & Noller, 1990; Hazan & Shaver, 1987). Secure adults tend to hold positive views of love and make optimistic predictions about their romantic potential (e.g., Carnelley & Janoff-Bulman, 1992; Feeney & Noller, 1990; Hazan & Shaver, 1987), which suggests that their cognitive maps for intimate relationships – their internal working models – portray the self as desirable and others as available. And as a rule, secure adults get what they expect: enduring, stable, and meaningful romantic relationships (Bartholomew & Horowitz, 1991; Carnelley, Pietromonaco, & Jaffe, 1994; Hazan & Shaver, 1987; Pistole, 1989; Simpson, 1990).

Parenting Style. The particular style a parent adopts in socializing children – that is, the levels of warmth and control a parent generally displays – constitutes another major base from which children build a social repertoire. Several decades of research have demonstrated that high levels of both affection and control, a style known as *authoritative parenting,* facilitate healthy psychosocial development in childhood and adolescence. Studies of the association between parenting style and peer relations indicate that children who come from authoritative homes generally meet with a warmer reception from the world of their peers, perhaps because these children tend to engage in the types of friendly, prosocial exchanges with age-mates that make them desirable companions (see Cohn, Patterson, & Christopoulos, 1991, for a review). For example, girls who view their mothers as appropriate models report more intimate, affectionate, and mutual relationships with their closest girlfriend (Gold & Yanof, 1985). In contrast, children from *authoritarian* homes – in which affection is relatively low and control is relatively high – may experience more difficulties in forging appropriate or gratifying connections with peers. Various negative parenting behaviors, such as inconsistency, hostility, overcontrol, or a punitive attitude, have consistently demonstrated an association with antisocial and aggressive behavior in children, as well as with social isolation and peer rejection (e.g., Dishion, 1990; Pettit, Harrist, Bates, & Dodge, 1991; Putallaz, 1987).

In adolescence, the correlates of authoritative parenting shift in a way that appears to reflect the increasing intensity and importance of peer relationships to one's evolving identity. Early adolescents, for example, report a greater sense of social acceptance when their mothers stay apprised of their expanding social involvement, particularly with opposite-sex friends (Feiring & Lewis, 1993). Attentive parental monitoring may not only give adolescents a feeling of support and acceptance as they begin to socialize with peers of the opposite sex, but may also indirectly promote more favorable social experiences through the sense of social competence it fosters. In contrast, early adolescents who experience hostile, rejecting treatment at home generally expect the same from peers, which may become a self-fulfilling prophecy (Downey, Lebolt, Rincon, & Lipani, 1995). Indeed, negative childhood interactions with parents, such as the experience of parental rejection, indifference, or hostility, may foster negative expectations for intimate relationships in general. Young adults who anxiously anticipate rejection in fact readily perceive it in romantic partners, even in ambiguous situations, and such rejection-sensitive people, along with their partners, are more dissatisfied with their relationships (Downey & Feldman, 1996).

Various dimensions of the parent–child relationship also influence broader aspects of peer dynamics. An adolescent's level of susceptibility to peer pressure, for instance, depends in part on the extent to which the adolescent feels his parents support and like him. The adolescent who reports positive relations with his parents is more vulnerable to peer pressure *only* if his peers concur with parental principles, goals, and aspirations (Mounts

& Steinberg, 1995; Savin-Williams & Berndt, 1990), a finding that supports the more general hypothesis that peer relations generally complement the parent–child bond (Brown, 1990; Youniss & Haynie, 1992). Adolescents who describe parents as authoritative are also more likely to affiliate with a well-rounded peer group that endorses both adult and peer values – such as the "brains" or the "populars" – whereas youths who view their parents as uninvolved tend to choose groups that reject adult norms – such as the "druggies" (Durbin, Darling, Steinberg, & Brown, 1993). Specific authoritative parenting practices, including the encouragement of achievement and joint decision making, as well as attentive monitoring, appear to influence crowd affiliation via the adolescent outcomes these practices cultivate: academic achievement, avoidance of drug use, and a feeling of self-reliance (Brown, Mounts, Lamborn, & Steinberg, 1993).

Although we would expect differences in parenting style to predict differences in nonfamilial adolescent relationships, we also anticipate that a reciprocal process occurs: Adolescent romantic involvement likely exerts a substantial effect on the way in which parents respond to their teenagers. As the adolescent explores this new domain of his or her life, parents must learn to face the various consequences of romantic activity, ranging from concerns about pregnancy, to the choice of an unappealing partner, to a decrease in the amount of time the adolescent spends with the family. In addition, romantic relationships symbolize a move away from childhood and toward adulthood, which changes the adolescent's expectations for parent–child interaction (Laursen & Williams, 1997; Youniss, 1980) and impels parents to face a gradual transformation in the power differential between themselves and their son or daughter.

We presume that this transition proceeds more smoothly for the authoritative parent, for several reasons. These parents generally treat the child's individuality and experience as legitimate and view parent–child interaction as a democratic process – in other words, they generously grant autonomy. This approach may help to facilitate difficult discussions about sensitive topics such as undesirable partners or homosexual romantic attractions in that it gives adolescents a say in these matters and parents an opportunity to hear their child's perspective. At the same time, authoritative parents firmly structure their adolescent's behavior, allowing sufficient freedom for the adolescent to experiment with dating while conveying an expectation that he or she must still comply with parental rules and limits. For the excessively enmeshed or restrictive parent, on the other hand, adolescent romantic involvement may trigger a family crisis by straining the status quo in the dynamic between parent and child. These parents may regard romantic relationships as a sign of either shifting loyalty or outright defiance on the part of the adolescent and, in both cases, may respond to such exploration as a threat (Steinberg & Steinberg, 1994). Although each of the preceding scenarios remains largely speculative, it seems likely that the challenges posed by adolescent romantic relationships would feel less daunting to parents who have all along adapted and adjusted to the ever-changing needs of a growing child.

From Parent to Child: Processes of Transmission

Despite diverse empirical support linking the capacity for intimacy with the parent–child relationship, the mechanisms of transmission involved remain largely theoretical. A fundamental question concerns the route by which features of dyadic functioning eventually become manifest in the individual (see Rutter, 1988, for a discussion). Because humans relate to each other on a behavioral as well as an emotional level, we propose that a number of mechanisms may be operating simultaneously in each of these realms. Specifically, we believe that socialization approaches derived mainly from social learning theory coupled with attachment theory provide a framework for understanding how parents transmit to their children a behavioral repertoire as well as an affective disposition toward opportunities for intimacy.

Clearly, parents influence the development of general social competencies and skills, which gain expression in the behaviors adolescents adopt in romantic relationships as well as in other interpersonal arenas. Consequently, we would expect these behaviors to vary at least in part as a function of parental socialization practices. As discussed earlier, the health of the marital relationship seems to provide a qualitative backdrop for parenting styles, the primary vehicle of socialization. Parents who support each other in the marital relationship appear to make the most effective parents (e.g., Quinton et al., 1984), whereas stressed parents engage in less optimal, inconsistent socialization (e.g., Easterbrooks & Emde, 1985; Hetherington, Cox, & Cox, 1982; Rutter & Quinton, 1984), including compromised disciplinary tactics (Easterbrooks & Emde, 1988).

The emotional unavailability of a distressed parent may impair the socialization of affect, a notion strengthened by empirical connections between inconsistent discipline and child behavior problems, especially impulse control (Becker, 1964; Patterson, 1977). Children of highly directive, controlling parents also tend to have more trouble encoding and decoding emotional expressions, which could in turn compromise social competence with peers (Parke et al., 1989). In addition, troubled parents have difficulty fostering the socially competent behavior that popular children display, such as the ability to integrate into the activity of an established group (Dodge, Schlundt, Schoken, & Delugach, 1983; Putallaz, 1983) and to maintain interactions with peers for longer periods of time (Dodge, 1983). Finally, marital dissatisfaction appears to promote gender-stereotypical socialization that encourages compliance in adolescent girls and assertiveness in adolescent boys (Feiring, this volume), traits that are likely to shape interactions with romantic partners.

As an interest in and a capacity for intimacy increase in adolescence, the "by-products" of socialization may begin to influence an adolescent's choice of environments and relationships in which to get involved, such that earlier behaviors are maintained in new settings. Indeed, findings from the Berkeley Guidance Study suggest that behavioral undercontrol in a sample of girls predicted their eventual choice of nonassertive men as mates. These women went on to display impulsive tendencies as wives and mothers, and were thus most likely to have conflicted marriages and to be viewed as ill-tempered mothers (Caspi & Elder, 1988).

In addition, adolescents' behavior in romantic relationships may derive in part from observations of their parents' intimate behavior. In particular, an adolescent may model characteristic features of parental interaction, such as displays of affection, patterns of communication, and conflict resolution styles. Findings cited previously on the intergenerational transmission of violent behavior within families suggest that modeling violence in romantic relationships begins as early as late adolescence (Capaldi et. al, 1996; Downey & Feldman, 1996). Conversely, when parents report greater marital satisfaction, young children have more positive exchanges (as well as fewer negative interactions) with best friends (Gottman & Katz, 1989), raising the possibility that children imitate what they know, whether for better or for worse.

Modeling may also occur in broader family dynamics if characteristics of parents' interactions with each other – as they negotiate difficult decisions, for example, or discuss areas of disagreement – take a similar form in exchanges with children. In turn, children may reproduce these relational patterns outside the family. Conflict resolution styles between parents and adolescents, for example, appear to resemble strategies used in the marital relationship, whether verbal aggression, physical aggression, or avoidance (Martin, 1990). There is also evidence for a general congruence between child–parent and child–romantic partner conflict styles, particularly among youth who tend to use avoidance when problems or disagreements occur (Martin, 1990). Children also imitate general aspects of family communication styles with friends; several studies have linked a collaborative approach to communication at home with the same kinds of egalitarian exchanges between peers (Cooper & Cooper, 1988).

The socialization of an interpersonal repertoire is an important mechanism that links adolescent romance with experiences in the family of origin, but an additional developmental process underlies the links between parent–child dynamics and adolescent romance, particularly in late adolescence, when emotional intimacy assumes a more prominent role in these relationships (Connolly, this volume; Sullivan, 1953). Romantic attachment theory conceptualizes love as a complex tendency to think and act in certain ways toward another person (Shaver & Hazan, 1988), governed by an internalized set of beliefs about whether one is lovable and others are responsive (Bowlby, 1969). According to some theorists, these internal working models, formed based on the nature of one's earliest affectional bond with parents, guide the negotiation of a host of intimacy issues in adolescent romantic relationships, such as the level of trust an adolescent places in a partner, how the adolescent sets emotional boundaries in the relationship, and to what degree he or she successfully establishes a mutually validating bond. General working models of relationships may also influence the way an adolescent handles a number of negative emotions these relationships tend to introduce, including jealousy and conflict (Connolly, this volume; Connolly et al., 1996; Feiring, 1996; Martin, 1990).

Securely attached children have positive models of themselves and others (Bartholomew & Horowitz, 1991), as well as greater flexibility to amend these models based on contemporary experiences in relationships (Kobak et al., 1993), which likely enables them to deal more comfortably and competently with the emotional vicissitudes of intimacy. For example, they might find it easier to offer care to and receive it from a romantic partner or to share trust. Models that reflect various patterns of insecurity, in contrast, may cause adolescents to remain aloof and suspicious in romantic relationships, or perhaps to immerse themselves inappropriately and thus invite an asymmetrical emotional exchange. Another related path by which mental representations of early relationships may influence the experience of later ones involves the process of interactional continuity (Caspi & Elder, 1988). This process occurs when individuals project characteristic ways of interacting onto new relationships, thereby generating a dynamic that confirms preexisting feelings about themselves and others.

Other mechanisms, as well, may mediate the link between adolescent patterns of relating within and outside the family of origin. One possibility is that patterns of attachment represent a set of internalized rules for responding to affectively charged situations (Kobak & Sceery, 1988). This model proposes that different types of emotional regulation provide the foundation for similarity between past and present relationships. Another potential process involves the concept of *views* (Furman & Wehner, 1994). This concept extends Bowlby's notion of internal working models by allowing for the possibility that adolescents have different perceptions of themselves and of their partners in *different* relationships. Thus, views are relatively malleable mental representations informed not only by past experience in a range of relationships – familial, companionate, and romantic – but also by one's present romantic involvement.

Finally, affective or social aspects of personality suggest an additional path by which early relationship functioning may be reproduced in adolescence and adulthood. One's disposition determines whether the individual attends to or avoids the moment-by-moment flow of affective-social information, as well as his or her reaction to it. As a consequence, the individual's personality likely shapes the responses of others in a way that serves to maintain a habitual interpersonal milieu (Belsky & Pensky, 1988). An individual who is characteristically interpersonally inattentive, for example, may provoke in others actions and emotions that undermine relationship quality, which, in turn, may lead to more avoidance of interpersonal information. Conversely, someone who is especially sensitive and responsive to others' interpersonal cues may behave in ways that facilitate interpersonal intimacy and disclosure and thereby enhance relationship quality.

Concluding Comments and Future Directions

In this chapter, we have explored the universal forces that likely instigate the emergence of romantic relationships in adolescence, as well as sources of individual differences in the form these relationships take. Using the parent–child relationship as an organizing framework for our discussion in each case, we examined romance as a phenomenon that originates in adolescence largely because it enables negotiation of the psychological, social, and biological tasks of this stage of development. In the first of these realms, we argued that the emergence of romantic activity in adolescence, which involves shifting interpersonal energy toward intimate and sexual relationships with peers, reflects a more general effort to individuate from parents. In the social domain, we noted that adolescents may find it increasingly difficult to establish themselves as adults in the economic and residential spheres because of the increasingly lengthy transition in our society from childhood to adulthood. As a result, adolescents are likely to seek other routes by which to demonstrate their social maturity. Finally, we argued that in the biological realm, adolescent romantic relationships may provide a socially invented form of protection against genetic inbreeding within the context of a family environment that greatly prolongs contact between parents and their reproductively mature offspring. Our argument is that romantic activity in adolescence serves multiple purposes that on the surface have little to do with romance or intimacy per se.

We then considered the developmental antecedents of adolescent interpersonal competence within the family of origin. Research on parents' relationships with spouses and children consistently suggests that families in which parents have a harmonious marriage and offer the adolescent warmth, structure, and emotional availability promote a healthy, lasting capacity for relatedness and intimacy in their children. We also speculated on the processes involved in the intergenerational transmission of relationship functioning. We suggested that socialization-based models of observational learning in the family, and attachment-based notions of internal working models, together provide a framework for understanding the way in which parents transmit a behavioral and emotional repertoire for intimacy.

We recognize that other sources of variation in adolescent life likely moderate the processes we have considered in this chapter. These variations in context provide the bases for a number of interesting research questions, and we would be remiss as "contextualists" if we did not acknowledge some of them. The systematic links we predicted between family processes and adolescent romance may well vary, depending on the gender, age, and sexual orientation of the adolescent; the socioeconomic status and ethnic background of the family; the presence of various stressors on one or more family members; and the broader sociocultural milieu in which the family lives. Perhaps most obvious, involvement in romantic relationships as a means of achieving individuation or expressing maturity depends to some degree on one's stage of adolescence – whether early, middle, or late – and on the cultural norms that shape patterns of interpersonal relationships within a particular ethnic group. Family economic status may also affect romantic experience in that adolescents who must join the adult workforce as soon as they are able – thereby reaching economic independence before many of their peers – might feel less compelled to seek romantic relationships as a "surrogate" demonstration of maturity. Significant sources of stress on the family, including major moves, divorce, or death, introduce other potential moderating variables, in part because these events can disrupt the individuation process, as well as the onset and quality of adolescent romantic experience. Adolescents who pursue romantic opportunities abnormally early or late, for example, may bring to these relationships a number of unresolved issues concerning dependency and intimacy that could affect the stability and satisfaction they experience with romantic partners (Connolly, this volume).

Gender is also likely to moderate the pattern of individual differences observed. Whatever the quality of their family relationships, adolescent girls generally place greater value than boys on interpersonal disclosure and intimacy in romantic relationships (as well as in same-sex friendships), and various aspects of intimate behavior such as self-disclosure and perspective-taking emerge earlier in girls (e.g., Berndt, 1992; Buhrmester & Furman, 1987; Feiring, 1996; Gilligan, 1982; Sharabany, Gershoni, & Hofman, 1981). In addition, adolescent boys may have difficulty with such intimate acts as disclosing their thoughts and feelings, particularly with a romantic partner, depending on how traditionally masculine their gender identity is (Feiring, this volume).

We suspect that the universal patterns and individual differences delineated in this chapter may interact in unique ways to shape adolescent romantic experience, a topic that provides another promising direction for future empirical investigations. One possibility, for instance, is that securely attached adolescents utilize romantic opportunities as a vehicle for individuation more comfortably and effectively than do insecure adolescents, who presumably experience more conflict in general over establishing intimate connections. Authoritative parents, too, may facilitate the process of individuation by taking an open but firm stance toward dating interests and activities while also granting the adolescent enough autonomy to explore this new realm of experience. In contrast, an excessively authoritarian parent could restrict participation in potential romantic relationships enough to delay substantially the tasks of separation and individuation. This scenario might involve overly strict limitations on opportunities to socialize with peers, as well as on the adolescent's freedom to negotiate a host of new feelings, reactions, and issues often stirred by romantic encounters. Alternatively, indulgent or neglectful parenting may communicate permissiveness or indifference to the adolescent, which could promote premature exploration of these issues and concomitant confusion about setting appropriate boundaries in intimate relationships. The timing of biological maturation in adolescence may also interact with either the quality of attachment between parent and child or the predominant parenting style in a given family to impel or impede movement toward achieving nonfamilial intimacy. We leave open the possibility for bidirectional influences in this relationship, as well as in any of those we have explored in this chapter, and we encourage future efforts aimed at improving our overall understanding of the complex links between parent–child dynamics and adolescent romance.

References

Bartholomew, K. & Horowitz, L. M. (1991). Attachment styles among young adults: A test of a four-category model. *Journal of Personality and Social Psychology, 61*(2), 226–244.

Becker, W. C. (1964). Consequences of different kinds of parental discipline. In M. Hoffman & L. W. Hoffman (Eds.), *Review of child development* (Vol. 1). New York: Russell Sage Foundation.

Belsky, J., & Pensky, E. (1988). Developmental history, personality, and family relationships: Toward an emergent family system. In R. A. Hinde & J. Stevenson-Hinde (Eds.), *Relationships within families: Mutual influences* (pp. 193–217). New York: Oxford University Press.

Berndt, T. J. (1992). Friendship and friends' influence in adolescence. *Current Directions in Psychological Science, 1,* 156–159.

Blos, P. (1979). *The adolescent passage.* New York: International Universities Press.

Bowlby, J. (1969). *Attachment and loss: Volume 1. Attachment.* New York: Basic Books.

Bringle, R. G., & Bagby, G. J. (1992). Self-esteem and perceived quality of romantic and family relationships in young adults. *Journal of Research in Personality, 26,* 340–356.

Bronfenbrenner, U. (1979). *The ecology of human development: Experiments by nature and design.* Cambridge, MA: Harvard University Press.

Brooks, J. (1981). Social maturity in middle-life and its developmental antecedents. In D. Eichorn, J. Clausen, N. Haan, M. Honzik, & P. Mussen (Eds.), *Present and past in middle life* (pp. 243–265). New York: Academic Press.

Brown, B. B. (1990). Peer groups and peer cultures. In S. S. Feldman & G. R. Elliott (Eds.), *At the threshold: The developing adolescent* (pp. 171–196). Cambridge, MA: Harvard University Press.

Brown, B.B., Mounts, N., Lamborn, S. D., & Steinberg, L. (1993). Parenting practices and peer group affiliation in adolescence. *Child Development, 64,* 467–482.

Buhrmester, D., & Furman, W. (1987). The development of companionship and intimacy. *Child Development, 58,* 1101–1113.

Caine, N. (1986). Behavior during puberty and adolescence. In G. Mitchell & J. Erwin (Eds.), *Comparative primate biology: Volume 2A; Behavior, conservation, and ecology* (pp. 327–361). New York: Alan R. Liss.

Capaldi, D. M., Crosby, L., & Clark, S. (1996). *Origins of domestic violence: Prediction of aggression in young couples' interactions.* Paper presented at the National Institute of Mental Health Conference on Prevention Research, McLean, VA.

Carnelley, K. B., & Janoff-Bulman, R. (1992). Optimism about love relationships: General vs. specific lessons from one's personal experiences. *Journal of Social and Personal Relationships, 9,* 5–20.

Carnelley, K. B., Pietromonaco, P. R., & Jaffe, K. (1994). Depression, working models of others, and relationship functioning. *Journal of Personality and Social Psychology, 66*(1), 127–140.

Caspi, A., & Elder, G. (1988). Emergent family patterns: The intergenerational construction of problem behavior and relationships. In R. A. Hinde & J. Stevenson-Hinde (Eds.), *Relationships within families: Mutual influences* (pp. 218–240). New York: Oxford University Press.

Cohn, D. A. (1990). Child–mother attachment in six-year-olds and social competence at school. *Child Development, 61,* 152–162.

Cohn, D. A., Patterson, C. J., & Christopoulos, C. (1991). The family and children's peer relations. *Journal of Social and Personal Relationships, 8,* 315–346.

Connolly, J., Ben-Knaz, R., Goldberg, A., & Craig, W. (1996, March). *Early adolescent's conceptions of romantic relationships.* Poster presented at the biennial meeting of the Society for Research on Adolescence, Boston.

Cooper, C. R., & Cooper, R. G., Jr. (1988). Links between adolescents' relationships with their parents and peers: Models, evidence, and mechanisms. In R. D. Parke & G. W. Ladd (Eds.), *Family–peer relationships: Modes of linkage* (pp. 135–158). Hillsdale, NJ: Erlbaum.

Cummings, E. M., & Cummings, J. L. (1988). A process-oriented approach to children's coping with adult's angry behavior. *Developmental Review, 8,* 296–321.

Dishion, T. J. (1990). The peer context of troublesome child and adolescent behavior. In P. E. Leone (Ed.), *Understanding troubled and troubling youth* (pp. 128–153). Newbury Park, CA: Sage.

Dodge, K. A. (1983). Behavioral antecedents of peer social status. *Child Development, 54,* 1383–1385.

Dodge, K. A., Schlundt, D., Schoken, I., & Delugach, J. D. (1983). Social competence and children's sociometric status: The role of peer group entry strategies. *Merrill-Palmer Quarterly, 29,* 283–307.

Dornbusch, S., Carlsmith, J., Gross, R., Martin, J., Jennings, D., Rosenberg, A., & Duke, P. (1981). Sexual development, age, and dating: A comparison of biological and social influences upon one set of behaviors. *Child Development, 52,* 179–185.

Dowdney, L., Skuse, D., Rutter, M., Quinton, D., & Mrazek, D. (1985). The nature and qualities of parenting provided by women raised in institutions. *Journal of Child Psychology and Psychiatry, 26,* 599–625.

Downey, G., & Feldman, S. (1996). The implications of rejection sensitivity for intimate relationships. *Journal of Personality and Social Psychology, 70,* 1327–1343.

Downey, G., Lebolt, A., Rincon, C., & Freitas, A. L. (1998). Rejection sensitivity and children's interpersonal difficulties. *Child Development, 69,* 1074–1091.

Dunphy, D. C. (1963). The social structure of urban adolescent peer groups. *Sociometry, 26,* 230–246.

Durbin, D. L., Darling, N., Steinberg, L., & Brown, B. B. (1993). Parenting style and peer group membership among European-American adolescents. *Journal of Research on Adolescence, 3*(1), 87–100.

Easterbrooks, M. A., & Emde, R. N. (1988). Marital and parent–child relationships: The role of affect in the family system. In R. A. Hinde & J. Stevenson-Hinde (Eds.), *Relationships within families: Mutual influences* (pp. 83–103). New York: Oxford University Press.

Elder, G. H, Jr., Caspi, A., & Downey, G. (1986). Problem behavior and family relationships: Life course and intergenerational themes. In A. M. Sorenson, F. E. Weinert, & L. R. Sherrod (Eds.), *Human development and the life course: Multidisciplinary perspectives* (pp. 293–340). Hillsdale, NJ: Erlbaum.

Elicker, J., Englund, M., & Sroufe, L. A. (1992). Predicting peer competence and peer relationships in childhood from early parent–child relationships. In R. D. Parke & G. W. Ladd (Eds.), *Family–peer relationships: Modes of linkage* (pp. 77–108). Hillsdale, NJ: Erlbaum.

Erikson, E. H. (1959). *Identity and the life cycle.* New York: Norton.

Feeney, J. A., & Noller, P. (1990). Attachment style as a predictor of adult romantic relationships. *Journal of Personality and Social Psychology, 58*(2), 281–291.

Feiring, C. (1996). Concepts of romance in 15-year-old adolescents. *Journal of Research on Adolescence, 6*(2), 181–200.

Feiring, C., & Lewis, M. (1993). Do mothers know their teenagers' friends? Implications for individuation in early adolescence. *Journal of Youth and Adolescence, 22*(4), 337–354.

Feldman, S., & Downey, G. (1994). Rejection sensitivity as a mediator of the impact of childhood exposure to family violence on adult attachment behavior. *Development and Psychopathology, 6,* 231–247.

Freud, A. (1958). Adolescence. *Psychoanalytic Study of the Child, 13,* 255–278.

Furman, W., & Wehner, E. A. (1994). Romantic views: Toward a theory of adolescent romantic relationships. In R. Montemayor (Ed.), *Advances in adolescent development: Volume 3, Relationships in adolescence* (pp. 168–195). Newbury Park, CA: Sage.

Gilligan, C. (1982). *In a different voice.* Cambridge, MA: Harvard University Press.

Gold, M., & Yanof, D. (1985). Mothers, daughters, and girlfriends. *Journal of Personality and Social Psychology, 49*(3), 654–659.

Gottman, J. M., & Katz, L. F. (1989). Effects of marital discord on young children's peer interactions and health. *Developmental Psychology, 25,* 373–381.

Grych, J. H., & Fincham, F. D. (1990). Marital conflict and children's adjustment: A cognitive-contextual framework. *Psychological Bulletin, 108,* 267–290.

Hazan, C., & Shaver, P. (1987). Romantic love conceptualized as an attachment process. *Journal of Personality and Social Psychology, 52*(3), 511–524.

Hetherington, E. M., Cox, M., & Cox, R. (1978). The development of children in mother-headed families. In H. Hoffman & D. Reiss (Eds.), *The American family: Dying or developing?* (pp. 117–156). New York: Plenum Press.

Hetherington, E. M., Cox, M., & Cox, R. (1979). Play and social interaction in children following divorce. *Journal of Social Issues, 35,* 26–49.

Hetherington, E. M., Cox, M., & Cox, R. (1976). Divorced fathers. *Family Coordinator, 25,* 417–428.

Hetherington, E. M., Cox, M., & Cox, R. (1982). Effects of divorce on parents and children. In M. E. Lamb (Ed.), *Nontraditional families: Parenting and child development* (pp. 233–288). Hillsdale, NJ: Erlbaum.

Kalmuss, D. (1984). The intergenerational transmission of marital aggression. *Journal of Marriage and the Family, 46,* 11–19.

Kobak, R. R., Cole, H. E., Ferenz-Gillies, R., & Fleming, W. S. (1993). Attachment and emotion regulation during mother–teen problem solving: A control theory analysis. *Child Development, 64,* 231–245.

Kobak, R. R., & Sceery, A. (1988). Attachment in late adolescence: Working models, affect regulation, and representations of self and others. *Child Development, 59,* 135–146.

Laursen, B., & Williams, V. A. (1997). Perceptions of interdependence and closeness in family and peer relationships among adolescents with and without romantic partners. In S. Shulman & W. A. Collins (Eds.), *Romantic relationships in adolescence: Developmental perspectives. New directions for child development,* No. 78 (pp. 3–20). San Francisco: Jossey-Bass.

Lewis, M., & Feiring, C. (1989). Early predictors of children's friendships. In T. J. Berndt & G. W. Ladd (Eds.), *Peer relationships in child development* (pp. 246–274). Hillsdale, NJ: Erlbaum.

Lewis, M., Feiring, C., McGuffog, C., & Jaskir, J. (1984). Predicting psychopathology in six-year-olds from early social relations. *Child Development, 55,* 123–136.

Long, N., Forehand, R., Fauber, R., & Brody, G. (1987). Self-perceived and independently observed competence of young adolescents as a function of parental marital conflict and recent divorce. *Journal of Abnormal Child Psychology, 15,* 15–27.

Martin, B. (1990). The transmission of relationship difficulties from one generation to the next. *Journal of Youth and Adolescence, 19*(3), 181–199.

Mounts, N., & Steinberg, L. (1995). An ecological analysis of peer influence on adolescent grade point average and drug use. *Developmental Psychology, 31,* 915–922.

Mueller, C., & Pope, H. (1977). Marital instability: A study of its transmission between generations. *Journal of Marriage and the Family, 39,* 83–93.

Park, K., & Waters, E. (1989). Security of attachment and preschool friendships. *Child Development, 60,* 1076–1081.

Parke, R. D., MacDonald, K. B., Burks, V. M., Carson, J., Bhavnagri, N., Barth, J. M., & Beitel, A. (1989). Family and peer system: In search of linkages. In K. Kreppner & R. M. Lerner (Eds.), *Family systems and life span development* (pp. 65–92). Hillsdale, NJ: Erlbaum.

Patterson, G. R. (1977). Accelerating stimuli for two classes of coercive behaviors. *Journal of Abnormal Child Psychology, 5,* 335–350.

Peterson, J. L., & Zill, N. (1986). Marital disruption, parent–child relationships, and behavior problems in children. *Journal of Marriage and the Family, 48,* 295–307.

Pettit, G. S., Harrist, A. W., Bates, J. E., & Dodge, K. A. (1991). Family interaction, social cognition and children's subsequent relations with peers at kindergarten. *Journal of Social and Personal Relationships, 8,* 383–402.

Pistole, M. C. (1989). Attachment in adult romantic relationships: Style of conflict resolution and relationship satisfaction. *Journal of Social and Personal Relationships, 6,* 505–510.

Porter, B., & O'Leary, K. D. (1980). Marital discord and childhood behavior problems. *Journal of Abnormal Child Psychology, 80,* 287–295.

Putallaz, M. (1983). Predicting children's sociometric status from their behavior. *Child Development, 54,* 1417–1426.

Putallaz, M. (1987). Maternal behavior and children's sociometric status. *Child Development, 58,* 324–340.

Putallaz, M., & Heflin, A. H. (1990). Parent–child interaction. In S. R. Asher & J. C. Coie (Eds.), *Children's status in the peer group* (pp. 189–216). New York: Cambridge University Press.

Quinton, D., Rutter, M., & Liddle, C. (1984). Institutional rearing, parenting difficulties, and marital support. *Psychological Medicine, 14,* 107–124.

Reese, M., Creasey, G., Bergner, R. Criss, M., & Ottlinger, K. (1995, March). *Late adolescent conflict resolution as a function of previous exposure to interparent conflict.* Paper presented at the biennial meetings of the Society for Research in Child Development, Indianapolis.

Rice, K. G. (1990). Attachment in adolescence: A narrative and meta-analytic review. *Journal of Youth and Adolescence, 19*(5), 511–538.

Rutter, M. (1988). Functions and consequences of relationships: Some psychopathological considerations. In R. A. Hinde & J. Stevenson-Hinde (Eds.), *Relationships within families: Mutual influences* (pp. 332–353). New York: Oxford University Press.

Rutter, M., & Quinton, D. (1984). Long-term follow-up of women institutionalized in childhood: Factors promoting good functioning in adult life. *British Journal of Developmental Psychology, 2,* 191–204.

Savin-Williams, R. C., & Berndt, T. J. (1990). Friendship and peer relations. In S. S. Feldman & G. R. Elliott (Eds.), *At the threshold: The developing adolescent* (pp. 207–307). Cambridge, MA: Harvard University Press.

Sharabany, R., Gershoni, R., & Hofman, J. E. (1981). Girlfriend, boyfriend: Age and sex differences in intimate friendship. *Developmental Psychology, 17*(6), 800–808.

Shaver, P. R., & Hazan, C. (1988). A biased overview of the study of love. *Journal of Social and Personal Relationships, 5,* 473–501.

Simpson, J. A. (1990). Influence of attachment styles on romantic relationships. *Journal of Personality and Social Psychology, 59*(5), 971–980.

Sroufe, L. A., & Waters, E. (1977). Attachment as an organizational perspective. *Child Development, 48,* 1184–1199.

Steinberg, L. (1989). Pubertal maturation and parent–adolescent distance: An evolutionary perspective. In G. Adams, R. Montemayor, & T. Gullotta (Eds.), *Advances in adolescent development* (Vol. 1, pp. 71–97). Beverly Hills, CA: Sage.

Steinberg, L. (1996). *Adolescence* (4th ed.). Boston: McGraw-Hill.

Steinberg, L., & Steinberg, W. (1994). *Crossing paths: How your child's adolescence triggers your own crisis.* New York: Simon & Schuster.

Steinmetz, S. (1977). The use of force for resolving family conflict: The training ground for abuse. *Family Coordinator, 26,* 19–26.

Sullivan, H. S. (1953). *The interpersonal theory of psychiatry.* New York: Norton.

Tardif, S. (1984). Social influences on sexual maturation of female *Saquinas oedipus oedipus. American Journal of Primatology, 6,* 199–209.

Vaillant, G. E. (1974). Natural history of male psychological health: II. *Archives of General Psychiatry, 31,* 15–22.

Vaillant, G. E., & Milofsky, E. (1980). Natural history of male psychological health: XI. Empirical evidence for Erikson's model of the life cycle. *American Journal of Psychiatry, 137,* 1348–1359.

Vaillant, G. E., & Vaillant, C. D. (1981). Natural history of male psychological health: X. Work as a predictor of positive mental health. *American Journal of Psychiatry, 138,* 1433–1440.

Waters, E., & Sroufe, L. A. (1983). Social competence as a developmental construct. *Developmental Review, 3,* 79–97.

Youniss, J. (1980). *Parents and peers in social development: A Piaget–Sullivan perspective.* Chicago: University of Chicago Press.

Youniss, J., & Haynie, D. L. (1992). Friendship in adolescence. *Developmental and Behavioral Pediatrics, 13*(1), 59–66.

11 Romantic Relationships in Adolescence
The Role of Friends and Peers in Their Emergence and Development

Jennifer Connolly and Adele Goldberg

The romantic preoccupations of adolescent youth – meeting potential partners, negotiating new situations, and learning the norms and nuances of love relationships – are central to the social activities of North American youth. In this new venture, adolescents find that it is their peers who are most willing to share in their desire to sort through the subtleties that characterize dating, love, and romance. Not only do friends act as a major conduit for romantic relationships, they typically *are* the romantic partners! In view of this overlap, the goal of this chapter is to explore the linkages between adolescents' romantic relationships and those with their peers. We focus particularly on development in early adolescence since the emergence of romantic relationships is characteristic of this time.

In adolescence, peer relationships undergo substantial differentiation, as the distinction between dyads and groups becomes increasingly important. Adolescents' peer relationships include small cliques of close friends and larger peer networks, as well as one-on-one friendships (Blyth, Hill, & Thiel, 1982). Whether peer relationships are dyadic or group-based likely shapes their links with romantic relationships, and we will attend to these differences in this chapter. We also recognize that children can be more or less successful in their peer relationships (Parker & Asher, 1987). In discussing the links between peer and romantic relationships, we will give some consideration to the kinds of difficulties that might arise in romantic relationships when adolescents' peer relationships are atypical and conversely whether, in turn, difficulties in romantic relationships might have consequences for peer relationships.

As a framework for exploring peer–romantic linkages, we will make use of two organizing themes. First, we will consider the links between peer and romantic relationships from the perspective of relatedness and autonomy. These two interpersonal processes are integral to relationships across

266

the life span (Baxter, 1988), and they undergo important developmental changes in adolescence. We explore their development in the interplay between peer and romantic relationships. Second, the complexity of romantic relationships will be considered. Current theories of adult love emphasize that romantic relationships entail a range of features and components (Sternberg, 1987). Extending this perspective, we examine the linkages between adolescents' peer and romantic relationships in terms of behaviors, feelings, concepts, and motives.

Relatedness and Autonomy in Adolescence

Relatedness and autonomy are interpersonal processes that are central to psychological development in adolescence (Allen, Hauser, Bell, & O'Connor, 1994; Blatt & Blass, 1996; Erikson, 1968; Sullivan, 1953). Developmental theorists refer to *relatedness* as those processes that underlie interactions with another person which are conducted in a warm, close, and mutually fulfilling manner (Camarena, Sarigiani, & Petersen, 1990; Sharabany, Gershoni, & Hofman, 1981; Sullivan, 1953). Similar to such constructs as *bonding* and *attachment,* relatedness is generally construed as the "self-in-relation-with-others," the processes by which individuals come to experience closeness and intimacy with others. Adolescence is generally viewed as a central period for the developmental maturation of interpersonal relatedness, and adolescents' friendships are a critical venue within which this development takes place (Collins & Repinski, 1994; Furman & Buhrmester, 1992; Sullivan, 1953).

Autonomy, on the other hand, is typically viewed as the capacity for independent thought, feeling, and action (Allen et al., 1994; Hodgins, Koestner, & Duncan, 1996). Initially, autonomy was defined with reference to adolescents' desire to achieve independence from parental influences (Blos, 1979; Steinberg & Silverberg, 1986). More recently, however, researchers have focused on the capacity for self-determination and the expression of developmentally appropriate self-reliance (Hill & Holmbeck, 1986; Ryan & Lynch, 1989). Arising out of the processes of exploration and individuation, autonomy can be construed as the "self-as-separate-from-others," or the capacity of the self to act in accordance with personally defined choices and values. As with interpersonal relatedness, adolescence has been viewed as a critical period for the autonomous differentiation of the self (Hill & Holmbeck, 1986). Although the family is crucial to the process of self-differentiation, the capacity to make decisions and act independently of the influence of peers is also a critical developmental achievement of adolescence (Berndt, 1979; Brown, Clasen, & Eicher, 1986; Fuligni & Eccles, 1993; Selman & Schultz, 1990; Steinberg, 1986).

Traditionally, relatedness and autonomy have been treated as distinct lines of development. Currently, though, there has emerged a new interest in the dialectic between these two processes in diverse interpersonal interactions (Baxter, 1988; Guisinger & Blatt, 1994). Arising chiefly from research on the family context, there is now a new understanding of the manner in which development in one process facilitates development in the other (Allen et al., 1994; Barber, 1997). More recently, both peer and romantic relationships have been probed as contexts in which relatedness and autonomy are critical. Peer relationships have attracted attention because issues such as intimacy and conformity have long been of interest to developmental psychologists (Barber & Olsen, 1997; Selman & Schultz, 1990; Williams & Connolly, 1997). Likewise, adult attachment theorists stress that complementary levels of relatedness and autonomy are integral to secure romantic attachments (Hazan & Shaver, 1987, 1990; Shaver, Papalia, Clark, Koski, Tidwell, & Nalbone, 1996). In this chapter, we explore relatedness and autonomy in romantic relationships and their reciprocal links with peer relationships.

Multidimensional Views of Adult Romantic Love

Given the paucity of information on adolescent romantic relationships, we suggest that a useful starting point is to consider what is known about romantic love in adulthood. This topic has been of interest to social psychologists for many years. Pioneering theories were largely focused on typologies of romantic love styles (e.g., Lee, 1973). More recently, theorists have approached this topic by delineating the underlying components of romantic love and drawing connections to other relationships and other emotional experiences (Bierhoff, 1992; Hatfield & Rapson, 1993; Hazan & Shaver, 1987; Sternberg, 1987). In this chapter we emphasize two theoretical discussions that we view as particularly helpful in exploring the links between adolescents' peer and romantic relationships. Elaine Hatfield and her colleagues (Hatfield & Rapson, 1987, 1993) distinguish the passionate form of love associated with romance from the companionate form of love associated with friendship. They suggest that passionate love entails a motivational state of physiological arousal, the individual's cognitive view of romantic love, as well as the emotional and behavioral expressions of love. Exploring the motivational bases of love relationships, Robert Sternberg (1987) suggests that romantic love can be motivated by needs for intimacy and commitment, as well as by passion. In his view, these motivational needs emerge sequentially over the course of an individual relationship, with passion emerging as the initial motivating force, followed by intimacy, and then commitment. When intimacy, passion, and commitment are conjointly present in a relationship, consummate romantic love may be assumed to exist.

Drawing on these theoretical perspectives, our discussion of peer–romantic linkages distinguishes the emotional and behavioral dimensions of romantic relationships from the conceptual and motivational components. Emotions and behaviors give overt and visible expression to romantic relationships. Cognitive concepts define the expectations adolescents have of romance and the appraisals they make about themselves in romantic relationships. Motives identify the interpersonal needs that are met within romantic relationships. Adopting a developmental perspective, we suggest that romantic emotions, behaviors, motives, and concepts respond to distinct psychosocial pressures and progress at different rates across adolescence. Because of this, we believe that it is valuable to consider each of these components separately. Nonetheless, we recognize that this distinction is somewhat artificial and that romantic motives, concepts, emotions, and behaviors are, in reality, entwined, with reciprocal influences between them.

Romantic Emotions

Positive Emotions

Romantic relationships entail a wide spectrum of positive feelings (Davis & Todd, 1982). In their analysis of the construct of love, Hatfield and Rapson (1987) distinguish between the experience of "being in love" associated with passionate love and the experience of closeness associated with companionate love. Passionate love includes attraction, preoccupied fascination, and an intense longing to be with another person. Companionate love includes intimacy, closeness, support, and mutual understanding. Both kinds of love, that of being passionately in love and that of companionate intimacy, characterize romantic relationships (Hatfield & Rapson, 1993; Sternberg, 1986). In our discussion of these positive emotions, we focus especially on intimacy because of its clear links with peer relationships.

Intimacy. Intimacy is often viewed as an essential feature of close friendships, associated with feelings of mutual understanding, support, closeness, and warmth. According to Sullivan (1953), such intimacy is experienced first in the relationship between a parent and a child. Later in development, intimacy with a person other than a parent is experienced in the close relationships that develop between best friends, usually in the period preceding adolescence. These friendships, which are typically between children of the same sex, are the first opportunity we have to observe intimacy that arises out of reciprocity between two individuals who are of equal status. In adolescence, emergent sexual needs must be integrated with the preexisting intimacy needs, and together they give rise to romantic relationships (Sullivan, 1953). Youngsters who have experienced genuine intimacy in the context of a close friendship move into the adolescent period with an experiential basis for establishing closeness and intimacy with a romantic partner.

Sullivan wanted to document developmental lines of interpersonal growth, and in this context he emphasized the role of preadolescent friendships as precursors to romantic love. He was far less concerned with adolescents' concurrent friendships and the psychosocial functions that they might serve during adolescence. Nonetheless, ongoing transactions between romantic relationships and concurrent friendships are likely, with the lines of influence flowing both ways. Friendships may influence intimacy in romantic relationships and, at the same time, romantic relationships may influence intimacy in relationships with friends (Sharabany & Wiseman, 1993). Although there is little research on this topic, we speculate that the nature of these reciprocal influences changes across the course of adolescence. In early adolescence, friendships and romantic relationships are likely to mutually enhance the experience of intimacy in both relationships. For example, from observations of close-friend cliques, we know that sexuality and romantic relationships are common topics of discussion in these groups (Simon, Eder, & Evans, 1992). These discussions may well encourage romantic intimacy by legitimizing their occurrence within the romantic relationship, as well as providing models of how to establish such intimacy. At the same time, reciprocal self-disclosure between friends in these matters of romance likely increases the intimacy and closeness felt among the friends themselves. One consequence, then, of early romantic relationships is a heightening of emotional engagement with friends.

Later in adolescence, the nature of these reciprocal processes may well change. The romantic relationships of young adolescents are not usually characterized by high levels of intimacy or closeness (Furman & Buhrmester, 1992). As they mature, however, there is an increase in their intimacy (Connolly & Johnson, 1996). When this occurs, the potential for a decline in intimacy with friends arises. In the popular media, a well-known scenario is that of the best friend who is abandoned with the onset of a romantic relationship. Consistent with this, a withdrawal of intimate involvement with friends as commitment to a romantic relationship increases has been described among young adults (Johnson & Leslie, 1982). This negative effect on friendships may reflect a substitution of intimacy with a romantic partner for previously experienced intimacy with a friend, as well as reduced opportunities for spending time in each other's company.

Negative Emotions

There is now ample documentation that adults' romantic relationships are the source of many negative emotions as well as positive ones (Hatfield & Rapson, 1987). Envy and jealousy of a romantic partner's outside interests, despair over a broken relationship, and anger at a romantic partner are all potential risks of romantic relationships (Salovey & Rodin, 1989). Their occurrence in the romantic relationships of adolescents remains relatively unexplored. Nonetheless, studies that have considered the possibility of negative emotions report that they are part of the affective experience of adolescents' romantic relationships. For example, adolescents report that these relationships can be a source of conflict and jealousy (Gagne & Lavoie, 1993; Levesque, 1993). They also say that romantic partners can make them feel shy and self-conscious (Connolly, Ben-Knaz, Goldberg, & Craig, 1996). As well, believing that they are too tied down and overcommitted is a major component of negative feelings in these relationships (Feiring, 1996).

Might there be a role for adolescents' peer relationships in how adolescents experience and resolve these feelings? There has been little exploration of this issue. However, we propose that there are some ways in which peer relationships might be linked to experiences of negative romantic emotions. First, one might highlight the supportive role played by adolescents' friends when a romantic relationship is under stress or coming to an end. Friendships provide a context to talk out these problems and, if the relationship is terminated, to find support and validation. One might also note that envy and jealousy in romantic relationships are similar to the conflicts experienced in friendships in that they arise when there are difficulties in adolescents' ability to express their own views and work to resolve interpersonal tension in a way that is beneficial to both parties. The role of friendships in the development of conflict resolution skills has long been noted (Hartup, 1996), and it is likely that they form a basis on which adolescents can develop skills to manage conflict in romantic relationships.

Relatedness and Autonomy

Implicit in the preceding discussion is the role of interpersonal related-ness in supporting the development of romantic feelings. Central to adoles-cent maturation of relatedness is the increase in intimacy with friends relative to that with parents (Furman & Buhrmester, 1992). Intimacy with romantic partners occurs as an extension of this process, building on the foundation of relatedness with friends. Adolescents' struggle for autonomy may also play a role in the growth of romantic emotions. It is well docu-mented that susceptibility to peer pressure is high in the early years of ado-lescence, with a marked decline during midadolescence (Berndt, 1979). It is possible that this decline in responsiveness to peer pressure is linked to increased intimacy with a romantic partner relative to that with friends. Likewise, friends' capacity to maintain separate interests and conduct activ-ities apart from each other, as well as the ability to resist peer pressure, may be linked, via autonomy processes, to the growth of romantic relationships.

The successful negotiation of conflict in romantic relationships leads to a consideration of the possible role of autonomy in understanding these negative romantic emotions. Defining one's needs in relation to those of another person and negotiating mutual goals are essential features of an individual's autonomy (Selman & Schultz, 1990). Adolescents are centrally concerned with learning to negotiate conflict in their relationships with their friends, and it is likely that there is considerable overlap between skills learned in this context and those with romantic partners. Initially, handling conflict in a romantic relationship and managing feelings of jeal-ousy or envy draw on those skills that adolescents have developed in the context of their close friendships. Later in adolescence, we can anticipate that these conflict resolution skills might be elaborated in romantic rela-tionships and that this would feed back into conflict negotiation with friends. Generalizing across both of these relationships, personal autonomy is strengthened as adolescents gain confidence in their ability to resolve conflict successfully in both interpersonal contexts.

Romantic Behaviors

Dating and Romantic Activities

The activities that give behavioral expression to romantic relationships are closely tied to adolescents' involvement in their peer groups. Beginning in early adolescence, peer relationships differentiate in structure and in size. Building on the best-friend relationships of preadolescence, the early years of adolescence are characterized by the appearance of cliques of same-sex close friends (Crockett, Losoff, & Peterson, 1984; Dunphy, 1963). By the middle years of adolescence, teenagers also participate in large peer groups composed of same- and cross-sex peers, who can be acquaintances as well as close friends (Blyth et al., 1982; Connolly & Konarski, 1994; Dunphy, 1963). In late adolescence, these large groups become less salient as adolescents' romantic relationships become centered on the couple itself and associations among these couples take priority over group activities (Dunphy, 1963).

Adolescents' progression in dating activities is similar to the changes noted in peer group structure. For example, young adolescents' romantic encounters typically occur in the context of a group of peers (Connolly et al., 1996; Feiring, 1996) and only later take the form of couple dating (Hansen, 1977). The possibility that these parallel changes in peer and romantic activities are causally linked was raised by Dunphy (1963) in his ethnographic research with the peer groups of Australian youth. Dunphy proposed that there is a progression from the same-sex cliques of close friends to the mixed-sex peer crowd, both of which precede the emergence of romantic relationships. A primary function of these peer groups is to create access to potential romantic partners. Recently, we investigated this hypothesis by studying the emergence of romantic relationships among adolescents followed longitudinally from Grades 9 to 11. Supporting Dunphy's proposals of the romantic functions of adolescent peer groups, we found that same-sex cliques in Grade 9 facilitated the emergence of mixed-sex peer groups in Grade 10, which in turn increased the likelihood of participation in romantic relationships in Grade 11 (Connolly, Furman, & Konarski, 1995).

Sexual Behaviors

The expression of sexuality is an integral feature of romantic relationships among adults and plays a large role in the romantic relationships of adolescents as well (Brooks-Gunn & Furstenberg, 1989). Apart from sexual intercourse, however, and particularly the occurrence of first intercourse, little is known about adolescents' behavioral expressions of sexual desire. There are some indications, however, that adolescents' sexual activity is linked to their friendship patterns. Adolescents are more likely to associate with teenagers whose pattern of participation in sexual activities is similar to their own than with adolescents who differ in this respect (Billy & Udry,

1985). Moreover, reciprocal processes exist. As the friend associations continue, there is a tendency for friends to influence each other's sexual activities. Girls more than boys are influenced by friendships in their sexual activity. Girls who are heavily invested in their peer groups are more likely to be early initiators of sexual activity than girls are who are less involved (Miller, Christopherson, & King, 1993).

Relatedness and Autonomy

Romantic behaviors reflect aspects of adolescents' struggles with relatedness and autonomy. Previously, we noted that adolescents' separation from parents in early adolescence is facilitated by the simultaneously occurring desire for increased contact with friends (Blos, 1979). Early adolescents view the peer group as an important source of friendship and social activity (Brown, Eicher, & Petrie, 1986). Romantic relationships are embedded within this trend on the part of adolescents to decrease their reliance on their parents and to increase their contacts within their peer groups.

Although it facilitates familial autonomy, increased interaction with friends creates its own set of challenges to adolescent autonomy, with pressures for conformity to peer standards, including those regulating romantic relationships. The peer group, while providing a safe context for initial exploration of dating behaviors, can also be a source of pressure to conform to expectations about romantic activities. For example, dating in early adolescence is associated with attributes of the peer group, as well as with adolescents' sexual maturation. Even less physically mature adolescents might participate in dating if that is a feature of their peer group (Dornbusch et al., 1981). Later in adolescence, however, experience with dating likely gives older adolescents the self-confidence to relinquish dependency on the group and form romantic relationships in which the couple is the center of activity. Older adolescents are more likely to report dissatisfaction with membership in peer crowds, believing that such groups restrict their autonomy (Brown et al., 1986). The movement toward couple dating that occurs in later adolescence thus may reflect adolescents' increasing capacity to be autonomous of the peer group. Susceptibility to peer pressure, including social pressure for peer involvement, is known to decrease from middle to late adolescence, following substantial increases from early to middle adolescence (Berndt, 1979; Brown et al., 1986). We speculate that the decline in responsiveness to peer pressure is facilitated by adolescents' shift toward greater involvement in romantic relationships.

Romantic Concepts

Expected Romantic Relationships

Not only do adolescents participate emotionally and behaviorally in romantic relationships, they also form concepts and expectations about these relationships (Furman & Wehner, 1994). In this section, we distinguish between two categories of adolescents' romantic concepts, those of their expected romantic relationships and those of their actual romantic relationships. Expected romantic concepts are similar to the notion of general views of romantic relationships (Furman & Wehner, 1994) in that they are shaped by the accumulation of experiences in romantic and friend relationships. We extend this notion of general views of romance by suggesting that romantic expectations can arise prior to the initiation of actual romantic relationships and derive, at least in part, from portrayals of idealized romantic relationships. Even younger children could be expected to have notions about boyfriends and girlfriends, about dating, marriage, and romantic love. Well before the time when they might actually have a romantic relationship, then, children begin to form a conceptual framework in which these relationships are seen as unique, and this shapes their expectations about eventual romantic relationships.

How children and adolescents might think about these ideal romantic relationships, and whether peer relationships play a role as a source for their thinking, are issues that are just now being explored. Ethnographic research among adolescent girls indicates that their cliques are a primary context for discussions of romance (Simon et al., 1992), and we speculate that it is within this small-group context that adolescents explore romantic expectations and norms. Recently, we inquired about expectations of romantic relationships among children in Grades 5 to 8 (Connolly et al., 1996). We were interested in the linkages to several possible sources of influence, including media portrayals, the relationship they observed between their parents, their relationship with their best friend, and their relationships with their parents. We evaluated their perceptions of intimacy, passion, commitment, and negative emotions in all of these interpersonal contexts, allowing us to compare the strength of their linkages with expected romantic relationships. Most of the adolescents in the study were in the early stages of romantic activity, reporting that they had begun to spend time in mixed-sex groups but that they did not often date as a couple. Given the current obsession with depictions of heterosexual romance in the popular media, at least in North America and Europe (Ward, 1995), it is perhaps not surprising that we found that media romance had the strongest links with expectations of romantic passion, as well as commitment and negative emotions. Other relationships were, however, also associated with romantic expectations. Friendships were connected to notions of intimacy in romantic relationships, whereas relationships with their mothers were linked to commitment. These results lend support to the view that during childhood and early adolescence, a cognitive framework for expectations about romantic relationships is constructed prior to the initiation of actual romantic relationships. These ideal concepts may grow out of actual relationships with parents and friends. They are also influenced by media images and observations of adults' romantic relationships.

Actual Romantic Relationships

Distinct from their expectations about romantic relationships, adolescents form cognitive impressions of the nature and quality of their actual romantic relationships. Adolescents' perceptions of these relationships quite naturally reflect their actual experiences in these relationships. They are, however, also influenced by the quality of other interpersonal relationships, as well as by their expectations of romance. In two recent studies (Connolly & Johnson, 1996; Furman & Wehner, 1994), links between romantic relationships and perceptions of two critical interpersonal relationships, those with best friends and parents, have been examined. Perceptions of romantic relationships are connected to both of these relationships. Comparing the influence of these two relationships, however, suggests that friendships show stronger links than do parents, particularly as the romantic relationship increases in duration. The salience of the links with best friends likely arises because the two relationships share commonalities, particularly in domains such as intimacy and companionship, which underlie successful relationships. Further evidence that friendships provide a formative substrate for perceptions of romantic relationships comes from our longitudinal research concerning the emergence of adolescents' romantic relationships (Connolly et al., 1995). In this study, we examined the influence of antecedent friendship perceptions on later romantic perceptions and compared this to the influence of antecedent romantic perceptions on later friendship perceptions. The results favored the former set of influences, with initial friendships influencing perceptions of later romantic relationships.

In addition to the influences of these relationships, already established expectations of romantic relationships likely play a role in adolescents' perceptions of their actual relationships. In the study of adolescents in Grades 5 through 8 reported earlier (Connolly et al., 1996), we also inquired about their perceptions of their actual romantic relationships, in addition to their expected romantic relationships. There was substantial overlap between expected and actual romantic relationships, with expected romantic relationships nonetheless rated as more passionate, intimate, and committed than actual romantic relationships. As these were young adolescents who had limited romantic experience, it is probable that the influence of romantic expectations was particularly high. Among older adolescents, the relative importance of relationship expectations likely declines.

Relatedness and Autonomy

Adolescents' conceptions of their expected and actual romantic relationships are likely tied to their progress with relatedness and autonomy. Those persons with whom adolescents feel most intimate may well be those who exert the greatest influence on their conceptions of romance. Hence we might expect that the increased importance of friendships, relative to that of parents, reflects the shift in intimacy from parents to friends. Likewise, as adolescents' actual romantic relationships deepen and mature, they likely exert greater influence over their romantic views.

As adolescents gain autonomy from both parents and peers, conceptions of romance are likely to become increasingly personal and reflective of individual experiences. Media influences likely wane among older adolescents as they become increasingly reliant on their own understanding of the dimensions of romance and less dependent on stereotyped images. In a similar fashion, susceptibility to peer pressures to conform to specific expectations regarding romance decreases among older adolescents.

Romantic Motives

Developmental Sequence of Motives

Romantic relationships are motivated not only by sexual attraction but also by social and emotional needs. Focusing on the range of motivations within a relationship, Sternberg (1987) has proposed that not all of them are equally present at one time. Instead, passion emerges first in the course of a relationship, whereas intimacy and commitment take longer to develop and so emerge later. As these motivating needs emerge, a relationship can change from infatuation, characterized by passion alone, to romantic love, characterized by the joint presence of intimacy and passion, to consummate love, characterized by intimacy, passion, and commitment. In this chapter we enlarge on this theory of the sequential emergence of motives within a relationship to consider their sequential emergence over the course of adolescence, as well as the role of peers and friends in facilitating this sequence. We incorporate affiliation with peers into this sequencing of motives because of the centrality of this need in adolescence (Furman & Wehner, 1994). Our model of romantic motives thus has four stages, incorporating the need for affiliation with peers into Sternberg's trilogy of motives.

The first phase of romantic relationships in adolescence is the *initial infatuation* stage, in which physical attraction and passion are the prominent features. In this early stage, attractions or "crushes" are directed toward a particular person and are largely unaccompanied by any actual interaction or intimacy. This stage is not dissimilar to that described by Feinstein and Ardon (1973) in the progression of dating in adolescence as an initial "awakening." Not necessarily leading to actual romantic encounters, however, these initial romantic attractions of young adolescents most often exist as "possibilities," forming the substance of discussion in close-friend cliques. Researchers who have examined the content of friends' discussions have found that young adolescents more often talk about romance and sexuality with their closest friends rather than with their parents (Papini, Farmer, Clark, & Snell, 1988; Simon et al., 1992). It is likely that these discussions among same-sex close friends, accompanied by the occasional foray into actual encounters or phone calls, provide young adolescents with opportunities to articulate their romantic desires, obtain guidance about romantic norms, and gain peer approval for these interests.

Parallelling changes in the context of adolescents' peer relationships, later in adolescence there emerges a second phase of romantic relationship development, which we label *affiliative romantic relationships.* This stage coincides with the appearance of mixed-sex peer groups. At this time, casual dating within the context of a peer group is initiated and is characteristic of adolescents' initial social contacts with romantic partners. The passionate needs of adolescents' romantic relationships are now accompanied by affiliative motives, as adolescents' romantic relationships are conducted largely in the context of the peer group. These affiliative needs emphasize companionship with romantic partners as well as with friends, all of whom are experiencing similar life circumstances. Feiring (1995) conducted in-depth interviews with 15-year-old adolescents and reported that affiliative concerns figure prominently in their descriptions of their romantic involvements. We speculate that it is within this group context that adolescents can increase their comfort in their interactions with romantic partners, without, however, the more complex demands for intimacy that occur when the relationship is conducted independently of the group.

As adolescents gain confidence and experience in romantic relationships, there occurs the possibility for intimacy with a romantic partner, as expressed through emotional closeness, sharing, and support. This characterizes a third phase, *intimate romantic relationships,* in which passion and affiliation are now accompanied by emotional intimacy. The appearance of such intimate relationships coincides with the relative decline in the importance of the peer group as a social context, noted by Dunphy (1963), and marks the transition to a dyadic relationship as a romantic couple. Without the peer group to structure and regulate their interactions, adolescents have opportunities to develop and experience greater intimacy with a romantic partner. Based on her interviews with adolescents, Feiring (1996) reports a gradual increase in references to intimacy in romantic relationships among the older adolescents. Moreover, we have found that older adolescents with long-term romantic relationships report higher levels of intimacy in these relationships, compared to younger adolescents and those with short-term relationships (Connolly & Johnson, 1996). These relationships are now quintessentially romantic in the sense that they encapsulate both passion and intimacy, as well as affiliation, with a love relationship.

A final phase, that of *committed romantic relationships,* occurs at the end of adolescence and in the young adult years. At this point, commitment joins with passion, affiliation, and intimacy in motivating and defining romantic relationships. This presence of commitment leads to long-term relationships in which there is a conscious decision to maintain the relationship permanently. This type of relationship represents what many would view as the adult ideal of the committed long-term love relationship, often leading to marriage or other forms of socially acknowledged partnerships.

Evidence supportive of this sequencing of motives can be found in our study of the romantic expectations of young adolescents (Connolly et al., 1996). These adolescents were asked to identify the ways in which romantic relationships were different from other relationships. The descriptors of romantic relationships that these adolescents gave were first sorted into four categories: passions, affiliation, intimacy, and commitment. In our model of the developmental sequencing of romantic motives, we expect that in early adolescence, romantic relationships appear largely as infatuations. Consistent with this, we found that passion was the most frequently mentioned distinguishing feature attributed by young adolescents to romantic relationships (51%). A little more than half of these passionate descriptors (30%) referred to physical attraction (e.g., "hugging and kissing"), whereas 21% referred more broadly to "love" or "being in love." Descriptors highlighting affiliation and intimacy followed next in frequency, with 11% and 9% of the adolescents referring specifically to these motives. Also consistent with our model in which commitment should occur quite late in the developmental sequencing of motives, we found that references to this motive in romantic relationships was mentioned by only 5% of the adolescents. Although these conceptions are not synonymous with the actual expression of needs, they do reveal the romantic views that are salient during early adolescence.

Relatedness and Autonomy

The sequencing of romantic motives that we have outlined can be connected to the evolution of relatedness and autonomy across adolescence. Initial infatuations and affiliative romantic relationships parallel the emergence of adolescents' needs for connectedness with peers. Both of these types of romantic relationships are embedded in particular peer relationships, first cliques and then peer networks. Moreover, it is likely that these peer and romantic relationships mutually reinforce the desirability of the other. This increased peer connectedness is reflected in the sensitivity of adolescents to the norms and standards imposed by the group on both peer and romantic behavior, and this conformity likely extends to romantic relationships as well. Intimate and committed romantic relationships, on the other hand, imply some degree of distancing and autonomy from the peer group. Emphasizing the couple as the unit of interaction, intimate and committed romantic relationships are characterized by a move away from close friends as well as the peer network. This distancing from the influence of peer relationships leads to increased independence from the peer group and to enhanced autonomy in relation to peers.

Problems in Relationships

In the normal course of events, development proceeds with healthy adjustment building on preceding patterns of adaptation. In a similar fashion, when difficulties occur, the consequences can accumulate across developmental stages. In this section, we examine the consequences of problematic peer relationships for the developmental course of romantic relationships, as well as the converse condition in which difficulties in romantic relationships have negative consequences for peer relationships.

Problematic Peer Relationships

Broadly speaking, peer relationship problems arise from two distinct social styles: withdrawal from social interaction and aggressiveness in social interaction (Parker & Asher, 1987). Both patterns might well present difficulties for the emergence and development of romantic relationships. Considering first the circumstances of withdrawn youth, their social behavior patterns are typically associated with a lack of inclusion in peer groups, and with skill difficulties centered on initiation and maintenance of friendships (Rubin, Hymel, Mills, & Rose-Krasnor, 1991). It seems likely that in adolescence, these youth are more likely to encounter difficulties in finding acceptance in a same-sex clique, with subsequent difficulties in establishing connections with a mixed-sex peer group. Given these circumstances, the behavioral trajectories of their romantic relationships may be delayed and may focus directly on couple relationships, without the supportive learning environment provided by informal dating within the context of a peer group. Although a delayed onset of romantic relationships is not necessarily a negative factor for adjustment, the rapid onset of dyadic dating without the buildup of group experiences may not be advantageous for these youth. In addition to peer group difficulties, socially withdrawn youth may suffer from a lack of experience with close friendships. Since these relationships are fundamental to learning the skills of intimate interactions, socially withdrawn youth may experience difficulty in establishing appropriate degrees of intimacy with a romantic partner, leading to either avoidance of intimacy or perhaps too intense intimacy. Difficulties might also manifest in their conceptual framework for understanding romantic relationships. Socially withdrawn youth lack the friendship context in which to explore ideas related to romantic relationships. This may render them particularly prone to accept without question the images of romance portrayed in the media and other sources of information. Discrepancies between ideal and actual romantic relationships may be more striking for these youth, with a resulting lack of satisfaction with actual relationships.

A different set of romantic consequences may be encountered by youth whose peer difficulties are due to aggressive behavior patterns. These youth, although often rejected by the larger peer group, are not typically socially isolated. Instead, aggressive youth often establish friendships, although typically the cliques of friends with whom they congregate are similarly deviant in their behaviors and attitudes (Cairns, Cairns, Neckerman, Gest, & Gariepy, 1988). What might be the consequences of these patterns of aggression for youth as they enter romantic relationships?

We believe that there is an increased risk that youth who are aggressive in their peer group will extend this aggression to romantic contexts when they enter adolescence. In a recent study of over 1,000 children in Grades 5 through 8, we explored several forms of peer-related aggression, including bullying and sexual harassment (Connolly, McMaster, Craig, & Pepler, 1998; McMaster, Connolly, Pepler & Craig, 1997). Childhood bullying is a common form of peer aggression in which physical and verbal harassment is persistently directed by a more powerful child or group of children toward weaker children (Olweus, 1991). Consistent with previous research in high schools (AAUW, 1993), we used a definition of sexual harassment that included a range of behaviors from mild harassment, such as name-calling, jokes, or leering looks to more extreme behaviors such as unwanted touching or sexual contact. There is a strong similarity between bullying and sexual harassment in that both involve the repeated exertion of power through aggressive means by one individual over another. One might there-fore anticipate that youth who have shown a pattern of bullying would be those most likely to sexually harass other adolescents who, by virtue of gender or behavior, are perceived as weak. Our results show that sexual harassment occurs in elementary schools, as well as high schools, with up to 41% of students in Grade 8 reporting that they had been a victim of unwanted sexual harassment from a peer. We also found that the likelihood of sexually harassing other youth was much greater among those self-iden-tified as bullies (50%) than among those not identified as bullies (21%).

Aggressive patterns of social interaction may also influence adolescents' selection of romantic partners and the quality of their interactions in these relationships. It has been noted, for example, that the romantic partners of youth with antisocial behavior patterns are often characterized by similar antisocial behaviors (Capaldi & Crosby, 1997; Quinton, Pickles, Maughan, & Rutter, 1993). The patterns of interaction that develop between these aggressive romantic partners are likely to include both psychological and physical aggression and are often accompanied by earlier than expected sexuality (Capaldi, Crosby, & Stoolmiller, 1996). Although the aggressive behavior patterns that develop in the romantic relationships of these youth have largely been attributed to familial aggression, links to peer aggression have also been noted. Young adults who are physically violent with a romantic partner are likely to report having been physically aggressive with their peers in adolescence (O'Leary, Malone, & Tyree, 1994; Riggs, O'Leary, & Breslin, 1990). In our study of early adolescent bullying and sexual harassment (Connolly, McMaster, Craig, & Pepler, 1998), we found that those youth who bullied other children were more likely to report physical aggression in a romantic relationship than youth who had never bullied other children.

In considering the romantic consequences of peer-related aggression, those youth who are the victims of bullying, harassment, and interpersonal aggression should also be considered. Much less is known about the conditions that lead a child to be victimized or the long-term consequences of such victimization. Nonetheless, there is some evidence that being subjected to such aggression is not random. Children whose personal attributes mark them as unable to defend themselves are those most likely to become the victims of aggression (Perry, Kusel, & Perry, 1988). As these children move into adolescence, one may anticipate that they would carry forward their victim status and be at risk for involvement in violent romantic relationships.

Finally, it is worthwhile to consider the possibility that youth whose previous peer relationships were less than satisfactory might experience corrective influences from a positive romantic relationship. Sullivan (1953) believed that same-sex friendships in the preadolescent period could provide naturally occurring therapeutic experiences for children whose previous relationships had been unsatisfactory. There is reason to believe that romantic relationships may serve a similar function. Among women who have experienced emotional deprivation in childhood, a stable romantic attachment with a well-adjusted partner had a positive impact on the women's mental health (Quinton et al., 1993). The possibility thus exists for adolescents to experience beneficial changes in their peer relationships as a consequence of a positive romantic relationship. This could take the form of diverting these adolescents from deviant peer groups into the more benign friendship circle of the romantic partner. Alternatively, a supportive romantic relationship might provide a shy teenager with the self-confidence to initiate new social interactions with peers.

Problematic Romantic Relationships

In addition to the influences that problematic peer relationships can have on romantic relationships, negative romantic relationships may adversely influence peer relationships. One can imagine, for example, that a relationship with a romantic partner who is unacceptable to an adolescent's peer group may lead to a rupture with that circle of friends and a drop in available social support from these friends at this critical time. As well, the tendency for adolescents in friendship cliques to influence each other's behavior patterns in both positive and negative ways implies that the deviant romantic relationship of one member of a clique may lead other clique members toward greater deviance in their own romantic relationships. We speculate that these influences between peer and romantic relationships are most likely to occur during the early adolescent years, when susceptibility to peer pressure is high and romantic activities are closely tied to the peer group. In later adolescence, such reciprocal influences may subside as adolescents evolve toward greater separation from the peer group.

Relatedness and Autonomy

Recently, it has been argued that disturbances in romantic relationships can be attributed to difficulties in balancing the competing demands of interpersonal relatedness and autonomy (Blatt & Blass, 1995; Zuroff & Fitzpatrick, 1995). Success in romantic relationships is viewed as the result of a healthy balance between togetherness in the relationship and opportunities for personal expression. Although it is largely the family that has been identified as the context for unbalanced development of relatedness and autonomy (Allen et al., 1994), we speculate that difficulties with relatedness and autonomy in peer relationships might be equally problematic, with negative implications for romantic relationships. Adolescents who are socially withdrawn or aggressive with their peers may experience impaired development of intimate relatedness, and those who are overly sensitive to threats to their sense of autonomy may become overly conforming to peer pressures. Their difficulties with interpersonal relatedness and autonomy may then transfer to their romantic relationships, where they would be prone to similar sorts of problems.

Conclusions

Romantic relationships are an essential feature of social development in adolescence. As well, they are clearly linked to the structure and quality of adolescents' relationships with their friends and their peer groups. As with adults, there are multiple components to adolescents' romantic relationships. Romantic development in adolescence takes place in all of these components, with peers and friends contributing to this development in distinct ways. These linkages between peer and romantic relationships can be understood as part of the growth of the core psychosocial processes of adolescence. Adolescents are centrally concerned with the management of relatedness and the negotiation of autonomy in their relationships, and we have suggested that these processes encompass their romantic relationships as well. Finally, reciprocal influences between peer and romantic relationships occur. Healthy relationships promote adaptive influences, whereas problematic relationships can have adverse effects.

Future Directions

We believe that a consideration of relatedness and autonomy within the multiple components of romantic relationships can provide a useful framework for examining the linkages between adolescents' peer and romantic relationships. This framework helps to situate adolescents' romantic relationships within a general developmental perspective and provides a map for studying the transition to adult romantic relationships. However, further elaboration of several issues raised in this chapter is warranted. A careful delineation of intimacy and autonomy in romantic relationships, highlighting the distinctions from intimacy in peer relationships and autonomy in parental relationships, would enrich our understanding. As well, we should examine the synergies between relatedness and autonomy both within and across these relationships, such that development in one relationship advances development in the other. The details of the progression in romantic relationships from adolescence to adulthood also require further elucidation. We have begun to address this question in the context of problematic romantic relationships. These links need to be more fully explored in the context of healthy romantic relationships as well. In this chapter, we have focused largely on the influence of adolescents' peer networks on their romantic relationships. Less emphasis has been given to how romantic relationships might influence adolescents' peer networks. These reciprocal effects have been delineated among adults, and it would be beneficial to examine them in adolescence. Finally, the impact of the adolescent peer culture, as transmitted through peer groups as well as through the popular media, would benefit from further discussion. It is clear that the media are a critical influence on adolescents, yet there is very little information on the psychological processes by which this occurs.

Among those issues that have not yet been addressed in this chapter are questions surrounding diversity in human experience and their implications for romantic relationships. This chapter has been written from the perspective of mainstream North American culture. To what extent, for example, do cultural patterns of behavior impact on romantic relationship development in adolescence? Cultures vary widely in their encouragement or tolerance of socialization in mixed-sex groups and adolescent dating. The consequences for development of omitting the early affiliative phase of romantic relationships are unknown, although one might speculate that traditional values are more readily maintained in cultures that encourage youth to begin romantic relationships at a later age and at the dyadic couple phase. Cultures also vary in their expectations regarding the balance between interpersonal relatedness and autonomy (Markus & Kitayama, 1991). Cultures that place greater value on interdependence in human relationships than is the case in Western culture may well impose different constraints on the manner in which adolescents express relatedness and autonomy in both their peer and romantic relationships. Finally, the chapter has explored peer–romantic linkages with the underlying assumption that the individual adolescent's romantic strivings are congruent with those of the peer group. For youths whose sexual orientation is directed to same-sex relationships, this assumption cannot be made (Savin-Williams & Rodriguez, 1993). For these youths, the emergence and development of romantic relationships occur without support from friends, the peer group, or the popular culture. Whether and how these factors differentially influence the interplay between peer and romantic relationships is an issue of some importance.

Summary

It is fitting that developmental psychologists are now acknowledging the significance of adolescents' romantic relationships. These relationships are a critical context of development in adolescence, and they provide a framework for conducting intimate relationships in adulthood. Understanding adolescents' romantic relationships will shed light on the processes by which adult intimate relationships, both adaptive and nonadaptive, are formed. Peers and friends are an essential component of romantic development, and understanding the reciprocal influences between peer and romantic relationships remains an important challenge for developmental psychologists.

References

AAUW (1993). *Hostile hallways: The AAUW survey on sexual harassment in America's schools.* Washington, DC: American Association of University Women Educational Foundation.

Allen, J., Hauser, S., Bell, D., & O'Connor, T. (1994). Longitudinal assessment of autonomy and relatedness in adolescent–family interactions as predictors of adolescent ego development and self-esteem. *Child Development, 65,* 179–194.

Barber, B. K. (1997). Adolescent socialization in context – The role of connection, regulation, and autonomy in the family. *Journal of Adolescent Research, 12,* 5–11.

Barber, B. K. & Olsen, J. E. (1997). Socialization in context: Connection, regulation, and autonomy in the family, school, neighbourhood and with peers. *Journal of Adolescent Research, 12,* 287–315.

Baxter, L. A. (1988). A dialectical perspective on communication strategies in relationship development. In S. W. Duck (Ed.), *A handbook of personal relationships: Theory, research, and interventions* (pp. 257–273). New York: Wiley.

Berndt, T. (1979). Developmental changes in conformity to peers and parents. *Developmental Psychology, 15,* 608–616.

Bierhoff, H. W. (1992). Twenty years of research on love: Theory, results, and prospects for the future. *German Journal of Psychology, 15,* 95–117.

Billy, J. O. G., & Udry, J. R. (1985). Patterns of adolescent friendship and effects on sexual behavior. *Social Psychology Quarterly, 48,* 27–41.

Blatt, S. J., & Blass, R. B. (1996). Relatedness and self-definition: A dialectic model of personality development. In G. Noam & K. Fischer (Eds.), *Development and vulnerability in close relationships* (pp. 309–338). Hillsdale, NJ: Erlbaum.

Blos, P. (1979). *The adolescent passage: Developmental issues.* New York: International Universities Press.

Blyth, D. A., Hill, J. P., & Thiel, K. S. (1982). Early adolescents' significant others: Grade and gender differences in perceived relationships with familiar and non-familiar adults and young people. *Journal of Youth and Adolescence, 11,* 425–449.

Brooks-Gunn, J., & Furstenberg, F. (1989). Adolescent sexual behavior. *American Psychologist, 44,* 249–257.

Brown, B. B., Clasen, D. R., & Eicher, S. (1986). Perceptions of peer pressure, peer conformity dispositions, and self-reported behavior among adolescents. *Developmental Psychology, 4,* 521–530.

Brown, B. B., Eicher, S., & Petrie, S. (1986). The importance of peer group ("crowd") affiliation in adolescence. *Journal of Adolescence, 9,* 73–96.

Cairns, R., Cairns, B., Neckerman, H., Gest, S., & Gariepy, J, (1988). Social networks and aggressive behavior: Peer support or peer rejection? *Developmental Psychology, 24,* 815–823.

Camarena, P. M., Sarigiani, P. A., & Petersen, A. C. (1990). Gender-specific pathways to intimacy in early adolescence. *Journal of Youth and Adolescence, 19,* 19–32.

Capaldi, D. M., & Crosby, L. (1997). Observed and reported psychological and physical aggression in young and at-risk couples. *Social Development, 6,* 184–206.

Capaldi, D. M., Crosby, L., & Stoolmiller, M. (1996). Predicting the timing of first sexual intercourse for adolescent males. *Child Development, 67,* 344–359.

Collins, W. A., & Repinski, D. J. (1994). Relationships during adolescence: Continuity and change in interpersonal perspective. In R. Montemayor, G. Adams, & T. Gullotta (Eds.), *Personal relationships during adolescence. Advances in adolescent development* (vol. 6, pp. 7–36). Thousand Oaks, CA: Sage.

Connolly, J., Ben-Knaz, R., Goldberg, A., & Craig, W. (1996, March). *Conceptions of romance in early adolescence.* Paper presented at the biennial meetings of the Society for Research on Adolescence, Boston.

Connolly, J., Furman, W., & Konarski, R. (1995, March). *The role of social networks in the emergence of romantic relationships in adolescence.* Paper presented at the meeting of the Society for Research in Child Development, Indianapolis.

Connolly, J., & Johnson, A. (1996). Adolescents' romantic relationships and the structure and quality of their close interpersonal ties. *Personal Relationships, 2,* 185–195.

Connolly, J. A., & Konarski, R. (1994). Peer self-concept in adolescence: Analysis of factor structure and associations with peer experience. *Journal of Research on Adolescence, 43,* 385–403.

Connolly, J. A., McMaster, L., Craig, W., & Pepler, P. (1998, February). *Romantic relationships of bullies in early adolescence.* Paper presented at the biennial meeting of the Society for Research on Adolescense, San Diego, CA.

Crockett, L., Losoff, M., & Peterson, A. C. (1984). The perceptions of the peer group and friendship in early adolescence. *Journal of Early Adolescence, 4,* 155–181.

Davis, K. E., & Todd, M. J. (1982). Friendship and love relationships, *Advances in Descriptive Psychology, 2,* 79–122.

Dornbusch, S., Carlsmith, J., Gross, R., Martin, J., Jennings, D., Rosenberg, A., & Duke, P. (1981). Sexual development, age, and dating: A comparison of biological and social influences upon one set of behaviors. *Child Development, 52,* 179–185.

Dunphy, D. (1963). The social structure of urban adolescent peer groups. *Sociometry, 26,* 230–246.

Erikson, E. H. (1968). *Identity: Youth and crisis.* New York: Norton.

Feinstein, S. C., & Ardon, M. S. (1973). Trends in dating patterns and adolescent development. *Journal of Youth and Adolescence, 2,* 157–166.

Feiring, C. (1995). *Conscious views of romance in middle and late adolescence.* Unpublished manuscript.

Feiring, C. (1996). Concepts of romance in 15-year-old adolescents. *Journal of Research on Adolescence, 7,* 214–224.

Fuligni, A. J., & Eccles, J. S. (1993). Perceived parent–child relationships and early adolescents' orientation toward peers. *Developmental Psychology, 29,* 622–632.

Furman W., & Buhrmester, D. (1992). Age and sex differences in perceptions of networks of personal relationships. *Child Development, 63,* 103–115.

Furman, W., & Wehner, E. A. (1994). Romantic views: Toward a theory of adolescent romantic relationships. In R. Montemeyer, G. Adams, & T. Gullotta (Eds.), *Advances in adolescent development: Volume 3, Personal relationships during adolescence.* Beverly Hills, CA: Sage.

Gagne, M. H., & Lavoie, F. (1993). Young people's views on the causes of violence in adolescents' romantic relationships. *Canada's Mental Health, 20,* 11–15.

Guisinger, S., & Blatt, S. J. (1994). Individuality and relatedness: Evolution of a fundamental dialectic. *American Psychologist, 49,* 104–112.

Hansen, S. (1977). Dating choices of high school students. *The Family Coordinator, 26,* 133–138.

Hartup, W. W. (1996). The company they keep: Friendships and their developmental significance. *Child Development, 67,* 1–13.

Hatfield, E., & Rapson, R. L. (1987). Passionate love: New directions in research. *Advances in Personal Relationships, 1,* 109–139.

Hatfield, E., & Rapson, R. (1993). Love and attachment processes. In M. Lewis & J. Haviland (Eds.), *Handbook of emotions* (pp. 595–604). New York: Guilford Press.

Hazan, C., & Shaver, P. R. (1987). Romantic love conceptualized as an attachment process. *Journal of Personality and Social Psychology, 52,* 511–524.

Hazan, C., & Shaver, P. R. (1990). Love and work: An attachment-theoretical perspective. *Journal of Personality and Social Psychology, 59,* 270–280.

Hill, J. P., & Holmbeck, G. N. (1986). Attachment and autonomy during adolescence. *Annals of Child Development, 3,* 145–189.

Hodgins, H. S., Koestner, R., & Duncan, N. (1996). On the compatibility of autonomy and relatedness. *Personality and Social Psychology Bulletin, 22,* 227–237.

Johnson, M. P., & Leslie, L. (1982). Couple involvement and network structure: A test of the dyadic withdrawal process. *Social Psychology Quarterly, 45,* 34–43.

Lee, J. A. (1973). *The colors of love: An exploration of the ways of loving.* Don Mills, Ontario: New Press.

Levesque, R. (1993). The romantic experience of adolescents in satisfying love relationships. *Journal of Youth and Adolescence, 22,* 219–251.

Markus, H., & Kitayama, S. (1991). Culture and the self: Implications for cognition, emotion, and motivation. *Psychology Review, 98,* 224–253.

McMaster, L., Connolly, J., Pepler, D., & Craig, W. (1997, June). *Peer to peer sexual harassment in early adolescence: A developmental perspective.* Paper presented at the annual meeting of the Canadian Psychological Association, Toronto, CA.

Miller, B. C., Christopherson, C. R., & King, P. K. (1993). Sexual behavior in adolescence. In R. Gullotta, G. Adams, & R. Montemayor (Eds.), *Adolescent sexuality* (pp. 57–76). Newbury Park, CA: Sage.

O'Leary, K. D., Malone, J., & Tyree, A. (1994). Physical aggression in early marriage: Prerelationship and relationship effects. *Journal of Consulting and Clinical Psychology, 62,* 594–602.

Olweus, D. (1991). Bully/victim problems among schoolchildren: Basic facts and effects of a school based intervention program. In D. Pepler & K. Rubin (Eds.), *The development and treatment of childhood aggression* (pp. 411–448). Hillsdale, NJ: Erlbaum.

Papini, D., Farmer, F., Clark, S., & Snell, W. (1988). An evaluation of adolescent patterns of sexual self-disclosure to parents and friends. *Journal of Adolescent Research, 3,* 387–401.

Parker, J. G., & Asher, S. R. (1987). Peer relations and later adjustment: Are low-accepted children at risk? *Psychological Bulletin, 102,* 357–389.

Perry, D., Kusel, S., & Perry, L. (1988). Victims of peer aggression. *Developmental Psychology, 24,* 807–814.

Quinton, E., Pickles, A., Maughan, B., & Rutter, M. (1993). Partners, peers, and pathways: Assortative pairing and continuities in conduct disorder. *Development and Psychopathology, 5,* 763–783.

Riggs, D. S., O'Leary, K. D., & Breslin, F. C. (1990). Multiple correlates of physical aggression in courting couples. *Journal of Interpersonal Violence, 5,* 61–73.

Rubin, K., Hymel, S., Mills, R., & Rose-Krasnor, L. (1991). Conceptualizing different developmental pathways to and from social isolation in childhood. In D. Cicchetti & S. Toth (Eds.), *Internalizing and externalizing expressions of dysfunction* (pp. 91–122). Hillsdale, NJ: Erlbaum.

Ryan, R. M., & Lynch, J. H. (1989). Emotional autonomy versus detachment: Revisiting the vicissitudes of adolescence and young adulthood. *Child Development, 60,* 340–356.

Salovey, P. & Rodin, J. (1989). Envy and jealousy in close relationships. In C. Hendrick (Ed.), *Close relationships* (pp. 221–246) Newbury Park, CA: Sage.

Savin-Williams, R. C., & Rodriguez, R. G. (1993). A developmental clinical perspective on lesbian, gay male, and bisexual youths. In R. Gullotta, G. Adams, & R. Montemayor (Eds.), *Adolescent sexuality* (pp. 77–102). Newbury Park, CA: Sage.

Selman, R. L., & Schultz, L. H. (1990). *Making a friend in youth: Developmental theory and pair therapy.* Chicago: University of Chicago Press.

Sharabany, R., Gershoni, R., & Hofman, J. E. (1981). Girlfriend, boyfriend: Age and sex differences in intimate friendships. *Developmental Psychology, 17,* 800–808.

Sharabany, R., & Wiseman, H. (1993). Close relationships in adolescence: The case of the kibbutz. Special issue: Kibbutz adolescents. *Journal of Youth and Adolescence, 22*(6), 671–695.

Shaver, P. R., Papalia, D., Clark, C. L., Tidwell, M. C., & Nalbone, D. (1996). Androgyny and attachment security: Two related models of optimal personality. *Personality and Social Psychology Bulletin, 22,* 582–597.

Simon, R., Eder, D., & Evans, C. (1992). The development of feeling norms underlying romantic love among adolescent females. *Social Psychology Quarterly, 55,* 29–46.

Steinberg, L. (1986). Latchkey children and susceptibility to peer pressure: An ecological analysis. *Developmental Psychology, 22,* 433–439.

Steinberg, L., & Silverberg, S. (1986). The vicissitudes of autonomy in early adolescence. *Child Development, 57,* 841–851.

Sternberg, R. J. (1986). A triangular theory of love. *Psychological Review, 93,* 119–135.

Sternberg, R. J. (1987). Liking vs. loving: A comparative evaluation of theories. *Psychological Bulletin, 102,* 331–345.

Sullivan, H. S. (1953). *The interpersonal theory of psychiatry.* New York: Norton.

Ward, L. M. (1995). Talking about sex: Common themes about sexuality in the prime-time television programs children and adolescent view most. *Journal of Youth and Adolescence, 24,* 595–615.

Williams, S., & Connolly, J. (1997, April). *Rethinking intimacy and autonomy: A lifespan approach.* Paper presented at the meeting of the Society for Research in Child Development, Washington, DC.

Zuroff, D. C., & Fitzpatrick, D. (1995). Depressive personality styles: Implications for adult attachment. *Personality and Individual Differences, 18,* 253–265.

12 "You're Going Out with *Who?*"
Peer Group Influences on Adolescent Romantic Relationships

B. Bradford Brown

One of the hallmarks of American adolescence is the broadening and intensification of peer relationships (Brown, 1990; Hartup, 1993). During this life stage young people typically expand the time spent with peers, rely more on peers for advice and support, and work out their identities and aspirations within the context of peer relationships. The peer system itself expands, most notably with a new form of dyadic association: romantic relationships. To a limited extent, researchers have explored various facets of this new form of relationship: its connection to family structure and processes, its impact on the emotional and sexual lives of young people, its associations with participants' personal characteristics such as sex role orientation or attachment style, and its role in the social mandate of mate selection and marriage. Rarely, however, have researchers given concurrent attention to two other critical components of adolescent romantic relationships: the social context in which they are primarily embedded, that is, the social world of peers and the changes or metamorphosis that they manifest across adolescence. Both of these components are addressed in several other contributions to this volume, but they are the focal interests of this chapter.

My mission is to urge investigators to approach adolescent romantic relationships from a *developmental-contextual* perspective. I suggest that these relationships change dramatically in form, substance, and function over the course of this stage of life, and that they both shape and are shaped by the broader peer context in which they are rooted. More specifically, after sketching out the major features of the developmental-contextual perspective, I present a heuristic model of a prototypic, four-phase sequence through which adolescents pass in their development of romantic interests, skills, and relationship experiences. In each phase I discuss the character of romantic activity and key features of the peer context. Finally, I suggest

291

some applications of this model to future research on the role of peers in adolescent romantic relationships.

One of the most daunting tasks in studying adolescent romantic relationships is simply defining them – especially if one takes the position that they change substantively over this period of life. In this chapter I regard relationships as romantic if they are dyadic peer associations that are perceived by the participants or their close peer associates to include strong feelings of liking and caring and at least the potential for sexual activity. The strong feelings may be genuine or feigned for the sake of impression management. One individual may have romantic interests in another (feelings of liking and caring, combined with some sense of sexual attraction), but these must be shared by the couple – again, in reality or at least in appearance to peers – for the association to be considered a romantic relationship.

A Developmental-Contextual Perspective

Our "romanticized" image of a romantic couple is one of isolation: two individuals walking alone across a wind-swept shore, cuddling by themselves in front of a roaring fire, or so entranced by each other that they lose all sense of the masses of humanity surrounding them. Although such precious (and precarious) moments of isolation exist in any relationship, the truth is that romantic ties are generally negotiated in a series of social contexts – especially during the preadult years. Parents and other relatives, characters in mass media, and other adults in the community model romantic relationships and attempt to instill culturally prescribed values and orientations that will help youngsters engage successfully in this type of relationship. Religious organizations and juvenile justice authorities place restrictions on both the private and public conduct of romantically involved couples. Peers provide opportunities to meet and interact with romantic partners, to initiate and recover from such relationships, and to learn from one's romantic experiences. For all their emphasis on privacy and exclusivity, romantic relations are really a social affair.

There is also much to be learned, much to be accepted before a young person can be judged proficient at romantic relationships. The nature of one's initial forays into the romantic world are typically quite different from the romantic ties that characterize the later stages of adolescence or early adulthood. In short, one's romantic inclinations and abilities develop over time, and they do so in several social contexts.

For adolescents, peers serve as something between a guiding or inspiring and a controlling social context for romantic relationships. However, both the nature and degree of peer influence can be expected to change over the course of adolescence. As young people's romantic interests and orientations change across adolescence, the support they require from peers, and the interference they are willing to tolerate, shift substantially.

Some Initial Caveats

Before presenting an overview of the four phases, some general comments are in order. First, I am not the only scholar to propose a developmental sequence in adolescents' romantic experiences. The most widely cited phase model is that of Feinstein and Ardon (1973), who proposed a four-stage progression from sexual awakening through practicing and acceptance of the sexual role to permanent object choice. As is apparent from the stage titles, their model is based on object relations theory (Mahler, 1972) and focuses on intrapsychic issues related to adolescents' negotiation of pubertal libidinal drives. Because of its Freudian roots, this model pays little attention to context or to the social nature of ties with romantic partners. It does suggest, however, that adolescents do not simply "jump right in" to romantic relationships, but rather that they struggle with issues of identity and proficiency in coping with the demands of the romantic role. Connolly and Goldberg (this volume) also articulate four stages of romantic relationships, but with more of an emphasis on individuals' conscious orientations to the relationship rather than their unconscious libidinal drives. Their stages are labeled *infatuation, affiliative, intimate,* and *committed.*

Others have noted a progression in dating activities or features of romantic relationships without specifying a stage or developmental sequence. For example, McCabe (1984) noted that dating activity commonly begins with a period of casual, short-term relationships before individuals negotiate more serious, longer-term "steady" relationships with just one partner. Still others point to multiple functions that dating can serve without suggesting any developmental sequence to these functions. Skipper and Naas (1966), for example, specified four major functions served by dating relationships: socialization (regarding what members of the other sex are like and how to interact effectively with them), status grading or achievement, recreation, and mate selection. These functions closely reflect the dominant features of the four stages that I will articulate. There are also clear connections between my four phases and those of Feinstein and Ardon, as well as those of Connolly and Goldberg.

Thus, several authors have espoused the notion that orientations and competencies related to romantic relations evolve during adolescence.

Others emphasize the multiple functions that romantic activity can serve but stop short of putting these into a developmental framework. The developmental sequence that I present later clearly builds on these ideas.

In addition to developmental changes, adolescent romantic relationships are subject to historical changes, which can alter the nature of one or more stages or the initiation and sequencing of stages. Spreadbury (1982) noted a steady increase over the first half of the 20th century in the percentage of adolescents – particularly early adolescents – reporting casual dating activity. This implies that the age of initiation into romantic relationships declined significantly between 1910 and 1950. Bell and Chaskes (1970) reported a historical trend toward greater serial monogamy in adolescent relationships and toward going steady at earlier ages than previous generations, suggesting that age of entry into more advanced stages of romantic relationships has also dropped historically. On the other hand, Gordon and Miller (1984) found that by the early 1980s, long-term monogamous relationships were giving way to more casual dating patterns, which evolved into the group dating pattern (mixed-sex groups engaging in social activities without splitting into clearly discernible romantic pairs) that was common among middle-class youth in the 1990s. Such historical changes affect when the sequence of romantic stages begins, how quickly adolescents move among stages, and the features that characterize each stage. As a result, it is best to construe developmental models as malleable, capable of adjusting to the shifting norms or demands of a particular context or historical epoch.

Of course, these broad historical trends must be considered within the context of persistent individual variability in the age at initiation and duration of time within each developmental stage or phase. I do not wish to suggest that all adolescents move through the developmental sequence in lock-step fashion. In some cases, young people may skip a phase altogether; in other cases – such as the transition to a new school or a move to a new community or a residential college environment – young people may "recycle" through the phases. There is even cultural variability in the importance adolescents assign to romantic relationships (Griffin, 1985). Reasons for and implications of individual and subgroup variability in initiation and sequencing of romantic stages become important questions to pursue in future studies. Most American adolescents, however, can be expected to cycle through the phases sequentially at about the same time as most members of their peer group. Later, I suggest some of the dilemmas faced by adolescents who are normatively "off time" in their negotiation of the developmental stages.

I also want to emphasize that sexuality plays an important role in each phase of romantic relationships (see Miller and Benson, this volume, for a fuller exposition of this topic), although, as Feinstein and Ardon's (1973) model implies, it is manifest in very different ways across phases. Sexual feelings and interests are an important trigger for the developmental sequence, even though opportunities for sexual activities with a partner may be quite limited in the initial phase of my model. Thornton (1990) reported that the probability that teenagers would report having had hetero-sexual intercourse was significantly correlated with the age at which they began dating, and there was a noticeable spike in rates of sexual intercourse 1 year after respondents reported their first steady relationship. By the college years, males are likely to measure the level of intimacy in a romantic relationship by its degree of sexual involvement (Roscoe, Kennedy, & Pope, 1987); college students rate sexual activity with someone besides one's partner as the second strongest indicator (behind the more nebulous notion of "spending time with someone else") of infidelity in a relationship (Roscoe, Cavanaugh, & Kennedy, 1988).

Nevertheless, sexual activity is not the primary defining feature, or nec-essarily even the strongest impetus, to the developmental sequence that I will discuss. Indeed, there is some evidence that sexual maturation is not as strong a predictor of initiation of romantic activity as social factors (Dornbusch et al., 1981). Sexual activity – especially frequency of hetero-sexual intercourse – is not as common among adolescents as one might think: In Thornton's (1990) sample of white 18-year-olds, two-thirds reported no incidence of sexual intercourse in the past month, and only 20% reported having sex more than twice. Still, the connection between sexual expression and romantic relationships varies considerably across cultures, as Coates illustrates in her chapter in this volume.

Finally, I employ the term *phases* rather than *stages* intentionally to emphasize the more informal nature of this developmental sequence than standard developmental stage theories. The developmental sequence is nei-ther fixed nor inevitable nor unrepeatable. Some adolescents steadfastly remain in one phase, and others skip that phase altogether. The phases are quite distinctive for some teens but tend to overlap or blend together for others. It is possible to renegotiate the sequence. Moving into a new social context (especially the transition to a residential college setting) can prompt individuals comfortably settled in the third phase of the sequence to slip back into the earliest phase and work their way back up the sequence. These are not so much regressions as renegotiations within a new and often developmentally more sophisticated environment. However, to the extent that the social context supports the developmental sequence and prescribes a general timetable for negotiating the phases, adolescents will probably pay some social or emotional price for stepping off the normative developmental track in pursuing romantic interests and relationships. For this reason, adolescents may devote considerable energy to locating a social context in which developmental norms match their individual interests or abilities in the pursuit of romantic relationships.

The Developmental Sequence

With these caveats in mind, I now offer an overview of the four phases. Please bear in mind that they are intended to describe not the progression through a specific relationship, but rather developmental shifts in individuals' basic orientation toward romantic relationships.

1. *Initiation Phase.* A defining feature of the transition to adolescence is pubertal development, which includes a surge in sexual drives (Katchadourian, 1990). This spurs an interest in sexual expression and relationships, which, for the preponderance of youths, who are heterosexually oriented, inspires a new dimension to interactions with the other sex. Ironically, young people who have followed the normative trend in peer relationships over the course of childhood have systematically withdrawn from other-sex interaction. Scholars point out that the tendency to socialize in same-sex groups reaches its peak just prior to adolescence (Maccoby, 1988). Thus, these youths need to become reoriented toward and reacquainted with the other sex – but with a markedly different objective: as potential romantic and sexual partners rather than just as friends and playmates. Those who do not face biological urges because of delayed physical development may be swept up in the normative push toward other-sex and romantic relationships anyway by powerful forces in the peer group and the media. Gay and lesbian youths do not need to reorient toward other-sex relationships, but they are prompted by biological urges to add a new dimension to same-sex relationships (see Diamond, Savin-Williams, & Dube, this volume) – usually in the face of strong peer and broader societal pressures against homosexual expressions.

As a result, this initial phase of adolescent romantic activity tends not to focus on the quality or features of romantic relationships, but rather on characteristics within the self. The basic objectives of the initiation phase are to broaden one's self-concept to include "effective romantic partner" and to gain confidence in one's capacity to relate to potential partners in romantic ways. In other words, the focus is on the *self* (self-image and personal competencies), not on relationships. Typically, adolescents in this phase must also achieve some skill in initiating romantic relationships. Actual relationships with romantic partners, however, can be superficial or short-lived and still be quite satisfying. Indeed, a succession of short-term, superficial romantic relationships is probably more adaptive in this phase than deep, lasting affiliations.

2. *Status Phase.* As adolescents gain confidence in their ability to interact effectively with potential romantic partners and to negotiate short-term romantic relationships, the focus turns from the self to the self's *connections* to others – but not as much toward the prospective partner or relationship as to the broader peer culture in which such relationships will be enacted. Young people confront the pressures of having the "right kinds" of romantic relationships with the "right people," and of beginning and ending these relationships in socially sanctioned ways. Typically, in early and middle adolescence, individuals are preoccupied with fitting in, finding a crowd, being popular, achieving status, or at least being accepted by a group of peers (Coleman, 1961; Eder, 1985; Newman & Newman, 1976). Romantic relationships become vehicles (or possibly obstacles) to achieving these objectives. Thus, in pursuing romantic partners, adolescents must consider the consequences of a particular relationship for their image or status among peers. Romantic relationships are an important means of establishing, improving, or maintaining peer group status. Dating the "wrong" person or conducting romantic relationships in the "wrong" way can seriously damage one's standing in the group. These concerns can easily overshadow one's interest in the relationship itself. This makes it difficult to sustain relationships that are too heavily focused inward, on the quality of the interaction or needs of the couple.

3. *Affection Phase.* At some point, however, there is a shift away from the context in which the relationship exists toward the relationship itself. Through the modest array of romantic activities and relationships that occur in the first two phases, adolescents typically gain sufficient confidence in their orientations and abilities to risk a deeper, more sustained level of romantic relationship. At the same time, the power of the peer group seems to wane as young people become satisfied with (or resigned to) their status and reputation in the peer culture and sufficiently confident in their emerging self-concept to be less dependent on the judgment of others. The more intensive romantic relationships that characterize this phase are themselves more rewarding, both emotionally and sexually. Thus, the relationships often become a source of passion and preoccupation. Indeed, I would argue that it is not until this point that true and meaningful attach-

ments to romantic partners can occur (see Furman & Simon, this volume, for a description of the central features of attachment in romantic relationships). Much of the popular music and literature about adolescent romance is focused on capturing the essence of relationships in this phase – often in an idealized or stylized way.

Of course, individuals do not divorce themselves from the peer group or other social contexts in the phase of these more affectional romantic ties. Yet, I would expect that, in this phase, the relative salience of romantic relationships increases, somewhat at the expense of other social bonds. Peers serve important functions in this phase, but they cannot exercise the same level of control over romantic relationships that they did in earlier phases.

4. *Bonding Phase.* To achieve truly mature relationships, individuals must supplement the passion of the affection stage with more pragmatic and personal concerns about the possibility of long-term commitment to one's romantic partner. There is a fourth shift that should occur in late adolescence or young adulthood, which adds an important new perspective to romantic relationships. The issue is whether or not one can and should form an extended, lifelong bond to one's partner. In American society, this bond is intended to be exclusive; there is no longer any question about the feasibility of pursuing more than one romantic partner at a time. Prototypically, the objective of the bonding phase is to get married "for better or worse." However, it is possible to enter into a committed or bonded relationship outside the institution of marriage (which currently remains a limited option for gay and lesbian couples). In any case, practical as well as emotional factors enter into one's evaluation of romantic affiliations in this final phase. Because the median age at first marriage in the United States is the mid-20s, it could be argued that this phase does not occur until after individuals have moved beyond adolescence. Indeed, one's capacity to approach romantic relationships from this perspective may be a signpost of the transition from adolescence to adulthood. Nevertheless, I later explore it briefly as a phase that adolescents must come to grips with in their later romantic relationships, and one that links adolescent and adult worlds within the domain of romantic relationships.

Development in Context

As I have already indicated, my objective is not simply to point out the evolving nature of adolescent romantic relationships, but also to emphasize the ways in which that evolution is influenced by (and, in turn, influences) one's social context. The assertion that romantic affiliations are shaped by social contexts will raise few eyebrows, but many may be more skeptical about my focus on the peer group rather than other social contexts – the family, school, community, or broader American society – which could easily be regarded as more salient than peers. I maintain that the importance of peers, relative to these other social contexts, has been seriously underestimated by previous studies. To date, evidence of the preeminence of the peer context is indirect but intriguing.

Many would assume that the family plays a particularly central role in adolescents' pursuit of romantic activities. Indeed it does (see Gray and Steinberg, this volume), but probably to a lesser extent than one might expect. In a study of Arab and Jewish youth in Israel, Mikulincer, Weller, and Florian (1993) found that fewer adolescents reported family rules about dating than about any other domain. Nguyen and Williams (1989) reported that, regardless of amount of time spent in the United States, Vietnamese refugee parents strongly endorsed traditional family values, which emphasize absolute obedience to parental authority. Yet, these parents tended to approve of adolescent freedom of choice in dating and marriage partners. The extent to which parents in other ethnic groups shy away from regulating or setting boundaries on adolescent romantic interactions is simply not known, but these studies suggest that one cannot assume that all parents are heavily involved in direct management of their children's romantic ventures.

By contrast, the peer group has been portrayed as extensively involved in the romantic lives of its members. From interviews with a diverse sample of 400 American teenage girls, Thompson (1994, p. 233) ascertained that "[b]roken-hearted narrators portrayed friends as dividers, regulators, and warners. . . . They stigmatized girls who did not follow the rules. They warned each other to be careful not to give it up to just anyone, not to get hurt. Their first job was to keep each other from making a variety of mistakes – from going too far to picking the wrong guy to wearing the wrong style. Their second job was to commiserate when, after all, things went wrong: to build a friend's courage, resolve, and sense of self back up again." Dickinson (1975) provided a clever illustration of the power of influence that peers have in this domain in a comparison of dating behaviors among southern Black adolescents at two time points 10 years apart, before and after their high school was merged (because of desegregation efforts) with an all-White high school in town. Between the two time points, the average age at which dating began, the typical activities on dates, and the frequency of "parking" (typically, sexual activity) all changed dramatically for Blacks in the direction of conformity to White norms. Whereas the two racial groups had been distinctive on almost all measures in the initial survey, by 1974 their behavior was indistinguishable on all but two or three variables, even though the two groups seemed to remain socially segregated in daily interactions. Dornbusch et al. (1981) found chronological age to be stronger than pubertal development as a predictor of initiation into dating. The most sensible explanation of this finding is that age-graded, normative changes in peer group activities constitute a more compelling influence on romantic involvement than the heightened sexual urges that accompany biological changes in adolescence. Teenagers can be swept up in peer group expectations to date even if their bodies haven't yet sent out signals of interest in the sexual component of this activity, or they may delay acting on physiological impulses until the peer group provides the normative structure for romantic ventures.

Of course, the peer group does not operate in a monolithic fashion on American adolescents (Brown, 1990). Gargiulo, Attie, Brooks-Gunn, and Warren (1987) found that dating began later and was less extensive for a group of adolescent girls who were pursuing a professional career in dance than among a comparison group of nondancers. Further, menarchal status (pubertal development) was related to dating activities for the dancers but not the nondancers. Peer expectations for the age of initiation into romantic relationships also differ significantly among adolescents in different peer crowds (Brown, 1998). It is reasonable to assume marked individual variability in adolescents' attentiveness to peer group norms about dating, their reliance on friends for guidance in romantic ventures, and their willingness to allow romantic relationships to supplant other forms of peer association.

In the following sections, I flesh out this developmental-contextual model by presenting the data that support the organization of phases outlined earlier and by considering the roles that peers play in each phase of adolescent romantic relationships. Much of what is presented, particularly about peers, is conjecture and inference because of the paucity of scientific studies in this area. My interest is not in affirming and summarizing previous research but in providing a conceptual framework for subsequent work in this area. Because friends and peer groups appear to be much more active and instrumental in the early phases of dating, my comments concentrate on the first two phases of the model. These are the phases in which, relatively speaking, little research has been conducted on adolescent romantic relationships.

The Initiation Phase

According to many people, adolescents always have sex and romance on their minds. In truth, however, romantic interests emerge slowly during early adolescence and must be heavily nurtured by the social context. Connolly, Ben-Knaz, and Goldberg (1996) noted that only 30% of their middle school sample expressed an interest in romantic relationships. Mitman and Packer (1982) asked a group of middle school youths to rate their level of concern, at the beginning of their seventh-grade year, about each of 32 items covering academic, social, and personal issues; romantic relationships ranked 20th on their list. When the investigators measured their sample's concerns again several months into the (seventh-grade) school year, the "romantic relationships" item had climbed to number 10 and was the second highest social concern (behind fears that older students would bully or beat them up). Yet, romantic relationships did not load on any of the five major factors to emerge in a factor analysis that Mitman and Packer performed on their 32 items; apparently, at this age, romantic relationships were not yet well integrated into the broader context of these youngsters' lives.

In part, this may be because individuals typically enter adolescence with remarkably limited understanding of dating and romance. Jackson (1975) queried a sample of White, lower-class 11- and 12-year-olds about what the word *dating* meant. The most common answer for both sexes was "When you go out with the other sex," but among boys the second most common answer was "It's dumb!" – a generic put-down that could easily mask their difficulty in defining the term clearly. In fact, when asked what one usually does on a date, three-quarters of the boys and nearly half of the girls in this sample confessed that they simply didn't know. The proliferation of television shows about teenagers in recent years and the modest historical trend toward earlier initiation into dating may have improved young people's knowledge about dating activities, but I suspect that the majority of American youth still enter adolescence quite naive about romantic relationships.

It is difficult for adults to appreciate the awesome task that is set before youngsters (in the United States) in early adolescence: Heterosexual youths must suddenly "reverse course" in other-sex interactions, seeking intimate, affectionate relationships with peers who have been routinely ignored or derided prior to this time. Gay and lesbian youths must come to grips with their sexual orientation, then add a new dimension to their same-sex relationships, and do so in the face of pressures from their immediate peer group or the broader society against harboring romantic affections for same-sex peers. Such changes simply do not occur immediately and easily. Heightened interest at this stage in sexual expression advances the salience of romantic relationships, but they must be approached in terms of the more compelling needs of early adolescence: to fit in, to be accepted, to establish a reputation among peers, to achieve a clear and stable sense of identity (Brown, 1990; Erikson, 1963; Newman & Newman, 1976). Thus, romance first emerges in adolescence as an *identity* issue, not a relational issue. To understand the role of the peer group in facilitating adolescent romantic relationships, it is helpful to appeal to principles in theories of identity formation, as well as those of socialization theories.

Erikson (1963) portrayed early adolescence as a period of disruption, when puberty and its libidinal drives sever the sense of psychological and interpersonal continuity that individuals had achieved in middle and later childhood. The resulting effort in adolescence to construct an integrated sense of identity is meant to restore the lost sense of continuity and sameness, not only between one's past, present, and future selves, but also between one's self-image and the image others appear to have of oneself. A healthy sense of identity requires a commitment to some work or occupational role (locating an *occupational niche*), acceptance of whatever it means to be a man or woman in one's society (achieving an appropriate *sex-role identity*), and adoption of a set of values or guiding principles (*ideology*) that make sense of one's vocational and sex role orientations. To be viable, these efforts not only have to be sensible to the individual but also acceptable to the culture or society in which that person lives.

Some disciples of Erikson regarded this as an overwhelming task that was best accomplished in two phases. Adolescents, they argued, first have to work on *fitting in* before they can concentrate on *standing out*. Their initial task is to achieve a sense of *group identity* or acceptance, an affiliation with peers who can guide their subsequent efforts to derive an autonomous, individuated sense of identity (Newman & Newman, 1976). Applied to romantic relationships, this framework implies that adolescents must first prove to their peer group that they are (among other things) viable candidates for a romantic relationship, particularly in terms of their (configured) sex role identity. Only then can they focus on defining the particulars of their romantic interests, as distinctive from normative group standards and practices.

Of course, the peer group, for its part, has to be there to set standards, guide and judge potential members, and accept certain individuals into the fold. The group is expected to encourage and direct adolescents' efforts to begin the pursuit of romantic relationships, to provide a supportive environment in which group members can explore their romantic interests and sharpen their romantic self-image.

The Character of Romantic Activity

Most individuals do not immerse themselves in romantic relations at the outset of adolescence. The average age at which individuals begin dating – engaging in social activities as an identifiable romantic (or at least potentially romantic) couple – varies between 14 and 16 years of age (Douvan & Adelson, 1966; Gordon & Miller, 1984; Thornton, 1990), but relatively few early adolescents report steady dating relationships prior to age 14 (Thornton, 1990). Few 10- to 14-year-olds indicate that they date more than rarely, and the average duration of romantic relationships in this age group is less than 3 months; many relationships last for a matter of days (Connolly et al., 1996; Eder, 1993; Feiring, 1996). Furthermore, initial romantic relationships appear to be superficial in comparison to other types of peer associations – particularly friendships. There is no empirical support for the assumption that when adolescents begin to date, the intimacy of their friendships declines (Blos, 1979; Broderick & Weaver, 1968; Lempers & Clark-Lempers, 1993; Werebe, 1987). As I indicate later, however, this is not necessarily the case in later phases that feature more intense and long-term romantic alliances.

One reason for the superficial nature of early forays into romantic relationships is the awkwardness and uncertainty that adolescents feel in these ventures. In a small interview study of White, middle-class girls, Place (1975, p. 167) discovered that "all the girls agree that their very first dates were full of apprehension and often painfully awkward. The first date presents a dilemma concerning proper behavior and often the dilemma is repeated when dating a new partner. The girls are not sure how they learned dating behavior but were in agreement that the right words and right actions come with dating experience." This is confirmed in retrospections about initial dating experiences among college youths studied by Spreadbury (1982). More males than females recalled feeling happy on their first date but also awkward; females were more likely to recall feeling scared. Although statistically significant, the sex differences in emotional responses were not that dramatic. Essentially, early adolescents are too focused on how they are doing and how the date is going to invest much in the relationship itself. As Larson, Clore, and Wood note in their chapter in this volume, learning to recognize and regulate new feelings that are aroused by romantic interests is often an extraordinarily difficult task for youngsters at this age.

Because romantic *relationships* are rare, ephemeral, and not highly salient to youths in the initiation phase, it is easy to overlook the extensive romantic *activity* that characterizes this phase and the extent to which romantic interests affect peer interactions. Eder (1993) conducted an intensive ethnographic study of middle school girls, focusing particularly on their behavior in informal settings such as the lunchroom. Much of the lunchroom conversation among these girls focused on boys and employed teasing as a conversational device. Several girls teased another about liking a certain boy or being liked by a boy; or the group as a whole made jokes about a particular boy or group of boys. If a boy joined them at the table, one or more girls teased him as a means of expressing their attraction to him. It was not unusual for an entire group to fix their affections on a particular boy and to share with each other their romantic interest in him. Because the boy was likely to pay all of them equal attention – or no attention at all – it was unusual for jealousies to arise over their shared interest in this one person.

The romantic partnerships that *did* emerge from these interactions, according to Eder, were superficial and ephemeral. Moreover, they tended to be confined to interaction at school, that is, in a public arena with peers as an attentive audience. One might question whether they constituted a relationship or a performance, and whether the target of the young person's words and actions was the alleged romantic partner or the peers who were observing.

Lest one suspect that the behavior Eder (1993) observed applies only to teenage girls, I recently had occasion to witness their male equivalent while driving my sixth-grade son and his male friends to a weekend campout. To while away time in the car, the boys began a game of "truth or dare." But since a moving car (with a stern chauffeur) afforded few opportunities for dares, the game quickly evolved into demands for honest answers to pointed questions. The favorite query was "Who do you like?" One after the other, the boys were commanded to offer up the name of the object of their romantic affections, then treated to the group's evaluation of this person, then regaled with the group's fantasies about the happy couple in various romantic activities. Laughter and teasing whiled away the miles, growing most raucous with playful accusations that perhaps it was another *boy* who one of the group *really* liked.

Though many would dismiss all of this as frivolous early adolescent banter, I regard it as the very serious business of initial romantic activity.

Through these interactions within same- and mixed-gender groups, early adolescents learn how to negotiate the initial steps in a romantic relationship: how to talk about a romantic interest, how to approach that person and let her or him know of one's interest, how to acquire an evaluation of the person from one's friends, how to fend off the meddling interest of peers, how to compete with others for the attention and affection of a potential romantic partner, how to restrain new and awkward emotions when talking with an attractive peer, how to prove one's romantic inclinations to a peer group that demands this of its members. This is the essence of peer socialization into the romantic role (Skipper & Naas, 1966). It is also the emergence of peer collaboration in defining romantic interests and nurturing competencies in initiating romantic relationships.

The Peer Context

Early adolescents juggle a complex developmental agenda that includes coping with new romantic impulses; struggling to maintain self-esteem and build self-confidence in the face of major physical, cognitive, and social changes; and finding acceptance within a new and more complex peer group system (Brown, 1990). Peer relationships serve to assist in all components of this agenda. In seeking acceptance into a peer group, early adolescents often must display (or feign) interest in romantic relationships; in working out their questions and interests regarding sex and romance with friends, they forge collaborative ties that solidify their position within a peer group; through positive feedback from peers about their interactions with potential romantic partners, they gain confidence in their ability to engage in romantic relationships and they elaborate their configured sex role identity (see Feiring, this volume).

Some argue that sex role identity and romantic or sexual interests are so central to this stage of life that they prompt a major restructuring of peer group relations. In a classic observational study of Australian youth, Dunphy (1969) traced a metamorphosis in peer groups across early and middle adolescence. The changes seemed to be designed expressly to foster young people's transition into the heterosocial organization of adult society. Dunphy noted five stages of peer group structure, beginning at the outset of adolescence with *isolated, monosexual cliques.* Clique leaders tended to be youths who were most advanced in their interest in the other sex. As these leaders began to interact with each other in formative romantic relations, they drew their respective cliques into the second stage of peer group structure, in which leaders modeled appropriate modes of interaction with the other sex while other clique members watched or attempted to follow suit. The leaders' relationship brought the two sexes in close proximity, thus giving clique members a target group of other-sex members on whom to concentrate their romantic initiatives. The leaders could even urge reluctant members into action by subtle or more overt matchmaking. Ultimately, two or more opposite-sex cliques would effectively merge for socializing purposes, driving the members into the third stage of group structure.

This peer group structure is perfectly suited to the general outline of the first phase of romantic relations that others have observed. The initial emphasis is on conversations within one's same-sex clique about romantic relations – the sort of banter that both Eder (1993) and I observed among girls and boys, respectively. Then, modest forays into romantic alliances are attempted, but, as Eder observed, in the public, group context. The most heterosocially advanced boys and girls lead the way, but their relationship (with a romantic partner) is not as important as their performance (their public behavior with the partner). It is the performance that sparks discussion among the same-sex peer group, and the discussion serves as appraisal of and guidance about one's romantic self; it restores the continuity between self-image and one's image among others. The group discussion also provides articulation and reinforcement of group norms regarding romantic relationships. Norm violators are "prosecuted" in this setting through teasing, gossip, remonstrations, or ostracism if necessary to ensure that group boundaries of acceptable behavior are maintained (Simon, Eder, & Evans, 1992). Members may still challenge these boundaries and remain in the group, but only if the group is willing to tolerate their deviant self-image.

Although this peer group metamorphosis may work well for most young people in the late elementary and early middle school years, there are two groups for which it does not seem very adaptive. The first is those who are "off time" in terms of their sexual and romantic interests. Early developers, who are ready for more involved relationships, should find the teasing and public dissection of their romantic alliances menacing. In turn, their more sophisticated approach to romantic partners can be intimidating to their clique-mates. One solution is to abandon their age peers in favor of older adolescents who are more involved in romantic relationships. Typically, however, this leads them into more deviantly oriented peer groups who encourage delinquent activity and health-compromising behaviors (Caspi, Lyham, Moffitt, & Silva, 1993; Stattin & Magnusson, 1990). This helps explain the negative correlations many have observed between the age at which dating begins and several undesirable behaviors (e.g., Pawlby, Mills,

& Quinton, 1997; Simmons & Blyth, 1987). Late developers, on the other hand, may be perplexed and threatened by the efforts of their clique leaders to draw closer to an other-sex group of peers. Their reluctance to engage in the "romance games" that preoccupy their clique-mates can undermine their efforts to secure a place in a peer group and forge a positive self-concept. Peer groups can be remarkably cruel in early adolescence, particularly toward those who do not toe the line in terms of peer group standards. This situation is captured poignantly in such films as *Welcome to the Dollhouse,* in which an unattractive late maturer is nicknamed "Weiner dog" and confronted in the lunchroom by the entire cheerleading squad, who just want to know, "Is it true that you're a lesbian?"

The second group for which the peer group metamorphosis is ill suited is gay, lesbian, and bisexual youths. As depicted by Dunphy (1969), the early adolescent peer group is exclusively heterosocially oriented. Samet and Kelly (1987) found that Israeli students expected peers who had a romantic relationship to conform more closely (than those without such a relationship) to the gender-appropriate sex role. One of five cardinal norms regarding romantic relationships that Simon et al. (1992) discerned in their ethnographic study of White, middle-class, early adolescent girls was that romantic partners must be male. A group's emphasis on heterosexual orientation and its derision of same-sex attractions clearly would undermine healthy self-concept development among those who harbor such attractions. Studies are underway to examine how gay and lesbian youths cope with these forces in their social system (see Diamond et al., this volume).

Dunphy (1969) observed but chose to ignore a critical feature of early adolescent peer groups, namely, that each has a distinctive reputation based on the values and activities that typify its members. Peer crowds serve a broader purpose than simply nurturing heterosocial interests and competencies (Brown, Mory, & Kinney, 1994). They sketch out prototypic lifestyles (*provisional identities*) and establish the social hierarchy within a particular peer system. The provisional identities give early adolescents a preformatted self-image that they can adopt temporarily, with confidence that other group members will support it and accept them, while they develop the confidence to search for a more personal sense of identity (Newman & Newman, 1976). Part of this provisional identity is a configured sex role identity – a set of prescriptions for sex role–appropriate behavior, including acceptable goals and behaviors in romantic interactions. To the extent that crowds differ in their provisional identities, adolescents should find it easier to fit into a group that matches their own romantic interests, abilities, and interactional style.

Some studies have demonstrated marked differences in friendship patterns among youths in different crowds (Eckert, 1989; Kinney, 1993). Although there is scant evidence to affirm it, I suspect that this dynamic applies to the romantic sphere as well: Different crowds emphasize different patterns of romantic interactions and different attitudes toward romantic relationships. Some peer groups foster an image of romance as conquest rather than mutual care; some groups identify romantic partners by sexual as opposed to social activity; some regard romance as inherently heterosexual, whereas others consider sexual orientation irrelevant. Crowds should also differ in their timetable for moving from one phase of romantic relationships to the next, and they should vary in their willingness to retain members who are faster or slower than most group members in proceeding through the phases.

This variability among crowds is adaptive in several ways. It allows adolescents to locate a crowd that is compatible with their own emerging sex role identity and with their interest in moving quickly or slowly toward more intense and mature romantic relationships. It also should make it easier for sexual minority youths to locate a peer group that can nurture their orientations and identity issues. On the other hand, the variability increases the chance that some crowds will encourage sexist attitudes, condone behaviors such as date rape, or endorse other worrisome norms regarding romantic behaviors and self-images.

Status Phase

In the initiation phase, early adolescents quickly discover that romance is a *public* behavior that provides feedback from friends and age-mates on one's image among peers. Romantic activity, then, can become a tool in impression management, a means by which a young person can manipulate her or his reputation among peers in order to achieve or maintain membership in a particular peer group. Romantic behavior is also a *qualifier,* something that can mark an adolescent as a good or bad candidate for membership in a particular peer group. Dating itself is a source of peer status for adolescents. A sociometric study of high school youths in one small Midwestern community revealed that adolescents whose sociometric ratings placed them in the popular category reported more frequent dating than any other group except the controversial adolescents – those high in both "like most" and "like least" nominations from peers (Franzoni, Davis, & Vasquez-Suson, 1994). The most active daters were both admired (for their romantic prowess) and disliked, perhaps because they stole away dating partners from others or because their romantic activity limited the time available to interact with other peers.

Adolescents move out of the initiation phase when they begin to realize that the peer group is concerned not simply with *whether or not* one has romantic skills and interests, but also with the type of person to whom one directs romantic attention. Some may question how this is distinctive from the initiation phase. Isn't learning who to like and dating the right people a central part of learning how to be a romantic partner? A distinction that some have noted is that the initial learning is a *corporate* affair, but applying what has been learned to actual relationships is a *competitive* activity (Douvan & Adelson, 1966; Simon et al., 1992). It is acceptable for all members of a group to fix their attention on the same romantic partner in the initiation phase because no one is really going to have a relationship with that person; they are simply learning together how to play the part. But once proficiency has been achieved, several group members could begin vying for the affections of the same prospective partner. New, stronger norms emerge at this juncture (Simon et al., 1992), and relationships with friends or group members become more complex and ambivalent (Douvan & Adelson, 1966).

The most compelling and controversial evidence of the status factor in adolescent romantic relationships comes from studies of what Willard Waller (1937) referred to as the *rating/dating complex*. In his investigation of undergraduates at Pennsylvania State University over half a century ago, Waller noted that students no longer approached dating as a means of courtship and mate selection; instead, the emphasis was on thrill seeking and exploitation. Rather than long-term, monogamous relationships, undergraduates seemed to prefer to date around and to select as dating partners those who had "high marks" on a set of gender-specific criteria. These patterns served to enhance the student's own peer status. A spirited debate ensued for several decades over the accuracy of Waller's observations (see Herold, 1974, for an insightful review), but it remained focused on late adolescents and considered status and courtship as competing models of dating orientation. Few recognized the possibility of a developmental sequence in these orientations. Although we might expect most college youth to be moving on toward more serious intentions in their dating activities, early and middle adolescents have good reason to be preoccupied with issues of status and prestige.

An early component of identity development is to feel accepted by one's peers, to fit in with a crowd (Erikson, 1963; Newman & Newman, 1976). But the American social system demands more than that. Self-esteem is contingent on being highly regarded and accepted by a high-status crowd. Romantic relationships quickly become associated with this identity objective. Gordon (1981) refers to early-20th-century novels, such as Willa Cather's (1918) *My Antonia* or Fannie Kilbourne's (1918) *Betty Bell,* which sketch key features of the status phase. The heroines illustrate the prestige that comes from being asked out or, particularly, becoming the steady dating partner of a high-status boy. The novels also feature the finer points of gaining status through romantic activity, as when one heroine hopes she has been widely noticed being walked home by a member of the football team. More recent ethnographies verify that the same dynamics (but, again, not just among women) are alive and well in the contemporary American secondary school (Eckert, 1989; Eder, 1985). Romantic activity continues to be part of establishing one's reputation among peers, one's place in a particular peer group.

Franzoni et al. (1994, p. 471) confess that "the role of dating in the acquisition and maintenance of social status is an almost completely unexamined area." Nevertheless, young adolescents are aware that prestige or status plays an important part in romantic relationships. Roscoe, Diana, and Brooks (1987) cataloged the reasons for dating that were given by a sample of 6th graders, 11th graders, and college students. Status was the third most common reason among the two younger age groups, but it wasn't among the top five reasons given by college students. The percentage listing status faded across the three age groups. When asked to list desirable characteristics of a dating partner, early adolescents tended to emphasize personal and prestige factors, whereas the oldest group focused on partners who shared their interests or who had goals for the future. When asked what the advantages were of having a dating partner, Feiring's (1996) 15-year-old respondents were most likely to list companionship and intimacy – characteristics more compatible with the affection phase of romantic relationships (as one might expect at that age). Yet, status was still listed by 20% of the girls and about 10% of the boys.

In their attention to the status component of romantic activities, adolescents in this phase often craft relationships that remain superficial, short-lived, and public – though less so than in the initiation phase. In an interview study of White, middle-class suburban teens, Feiring (1996) discovered that nearly 90% claimed to have had a romantic relationship at some point in the past year, but only 20% were currently dating someone. Relationships tended to be casual, intense, and brief. Although partners might spend an hour a day on the phone with each other, most still preferred group social activities to couple-alone events. Moreover, girls in particular often expressed concern that the relationship was demanding "too much commitment."

The critical feature of the status phase is that adolescents pursue dating relationships or make decisions about romantic partners with a cautious eye on the expectations or reactions of their friends and their peer group. "Is this dating partner acceptable to my friends?" "Will this relationship help me to gain entry to the group?" "What will it do to my reputation to be seen with this person?" Hollywood captures the angst of these questions in poignant fashion. In *Lucas,* the new girl in town is swept into the popular crowd when she is courted by the football hero – and the geekish late maturer who loves her is left to concoct a scheme to raise his own social status in order to win back her affections. In *Flirting* and *Zebrahead,* couples struggle to establish a romantic alliance that violates peer group norms against cross-racial relationships. In *Can't Buy Me Love,* a boy pays a popular girl to date him for a month so that he can secure a spot in the popular crowd. In *Beethoven,* a girl is ecstatic that a popular jock actually knows her name. In *Weird Science,* two geeks manage to create (via computer) a beautiful genie of sorts who vaults them into stardom among the school's status elite and into romantic relationships they could only dream about beforehand.

The degree to which adolescents use romantic relationships to achieve, enhance, or maintain their popularity or prestige among peers probably varies among peer crowds. Groups at or near the top of the status hierarchy – populars, preppies, jocks, and so on – are likely to be much more attentive to the status consequences of romantic as well as friendship relationships than groups further down the hierarchy (Eder, 1985). Yet, even adolescents in groups that lack this status consciousness must be attentive to their standing within their own group and to the ways a particular romantic partner might affect that standing (e.g., Eckert, 1989; MacLeod, 1995).

Some individuals go so far as to feign romantic interest in someone simply to foster their own position in the peer group; they may maintain a relationship with this person if it serves their own status interests. In most cases, however, romantic feelings are governed by the heart (or, perhaps more accurately, by hormones) as well as the head. Some teenagers thus find themselves in the predicament of harboring affection for a peer who is either so far above them in status as to be unreachable or so undesirable among one's peers as to jeopardize their standing in the group. Such potential conflicts make the short-term, superficial nature of romantic relationships in this phase particularly adaptive.

These strict guidelines and limitations on romantic partners strike many as unhealthy and constraining. Both Husbands (1970) and Douvan and Adelson (1966) argued that by following a prescribed role or script in dating, American adolescents fail to take the risk of being themselves for fear that their partner will misunderstand or disapprove and break off the relationship. Dating becomes a game of impression management rather than a mode of identity revelation or self-exploration; American adolescents are too busy playing the romantic role to learn much about themselves *within* the role. These scholars' misgivings seem persuasive, but they lack developmental vision. Adolescents must first feel accepted before they can risk self-exploration, and they must then gain security in their self-concept before risking self-expansion in a relationship. Restoring that sense of continuity and sameness is a cautious, step-by-step process. Peer group prescriptions for dating partners and dating activities allow teenagers to ease into the romantic role before they need to work on fitting the role to their more autonomous sense of identity. Nevertheless, it is fair to say that adolescents are not entirely genuine in their romantic relationships at this age. Behavior in the relationship is guarded. Adolescents worry too much about being rejected by their peer group or their partner to feel free to express their true selves within a relationship. To the extent that they feel their self-image compromised in these relationships, rather than explored or expanded, they are likely to suffer emotionally (Harter, Marold, Whitesell, & Cobbs, 1996).

The Peer Context

In the status phase, peers move well beyond their earlier role of discussing romance and encouraging interactions with potential romantic partners. Indeed, the collaborative spirit of the initiation phase is more difficult to maintain amid the competitive atmosphere of the status phase. Eder (1993) commented that, whereas liking the same boy seemed to bring sixth-grade girls together, it was a source of tension and jealousy among eighth-grade girls. The difference, she emphasizes, was that the sixth graders rarely actually interacted with boys, so there was little reason for rivalry.

Nevertheless, there are a number of ways in which the peer group typically facilitates individual development during this phase. Perhaps the most obvious way is by creating a social status hierarchy among peer crowds or by articulating the criteria for status and acceptance within one's own friendship clique (see Simon et al., 1992, for a depiction of how norms regarding romantic relations emerge in the peer group). Knowledge of the group hierarchy and of membership criteria for various groups gives adolescents a clear sense of which peers are desirable romantic partners, which are prime candidates for romantic relationships (by virtue of being very similar to self in status), and which are to be scrupulously avoided – if one wishes to maintain a good reputation with friends. The travails of falling in love with someone too distant from oneself in peer prestige form one of the most hackneyed plots in films about American teenagers (e.g., *Breaking Away, Grease, Pretty in Pink, Say Anything, Stand by Me*).

Typically, in this phase, peers are also major brokers of relationships. They take on the role of matchmaking. One of the more fascinating mechanisms for assuming this function is their role as a messenger service. The most straightforward way of initiating a romantic liaison, asking someone out, is rarely done. Instead, an elaborate communications system is invoked prior to this event to ensure that when someone *is* asked out, the answer will be "yes." For example, if Rene is interested in Luis, she first asks her friends what they think of him. If Luis passes this test, Rene may ask one of her friends to ask one of his friends to ask Luis if he is interested in Rene (is everyone still with me here?). The response works its way back through the message service to Rene. If the answer is "Forget it!" Rene may deny the entire episode as rumor and innuendo; if the answer is more encouraging, she can confidently approach Luis to initiate a dating relationship. Of course, this communication system also allows an adolescent to discover a peer's interest and respond to it without the potential awkwardness of a direct confrontation. It is much easier for Luis to ask his friends to convey the message that he is not interested in Rene than to say so directly to her face.

The messenger service is particularly useful in helping adolescents avoid direct rejection, which, as Downy, Bonita, and Rincon (this volume) note, can be especially traumatic for adolescents just beginning to venture into romantic relationships. The messenger service is also especially useful for gay and lesbian teens who are interested in establishing romantic connections with a peer context that discourages or derides same-sex relationships. In this case, adolescents must develop a messenger service that is more discreet, and more adept at ascertaining not only whether a particular person is interested in their friend but also whether or not this person is receptive to same-sex relationships.

Peers can be instrumental in subsequent steps in the romantic relationships as well. They can suggest appropriate social activities, ways to respond to conflict in the relationship, interpretations of a partner's troublesome behavior, and even methods for ending the relationship without threatening one's standing in the group. Yet, there is a down side to the close scrutiny that peers give to romantic relationships in this phase. A faulty messenger system can bungle the inquiry about a potential partner and cause an adolescent considerable embarrassment. Well-meaning friends may try to "torpedo" a relationship that they believe is detrimental to the adolescent's standing in the group (see, e.g., John Hughes's film *Pretty in Pink*). Most noteworthy is that as adolescents gain confidence in their romantic skills and as they come to grips with their position in the peer group, they can come to resent peers' efforts to meddle in their romantic affairs. These attitudes are usually a sign that adolescents have matured in their appreciation of romantic relationships; they are making the transition to the third phase.

Affection Phase

From Erikson's (1963) perspective, identity development is a social process. A successful resolution of the identity crisis, however, requires individuals to adopt an identity that is personal and unique. Adolescents cannot continue to rely on group norms and provisional identities to define their self-concept and determine their behavior. They must move on to define the particulars of their own unique position within the group and the broader society. In a similar fashion, romance cannot remain a strictly public activity, directed by the peer group and motivated simply by the objectives of group acceptance or peer prestige. As adolescents become comfortable with (or resigned to) their position within the peer system, and confident that they can engage in romantic relationships successfully, they tend to be drawn more deeply into the relationship. At this point they are prepared to let the relationship itself be the focal point of their romantic activity, diminishing their attentiveness to group norms and friends' expectations. In the affection phase, romance – like identity – becomes a *personal* and relational affair.

The Character of Romantic Activity

Gordon and Miller (1984) found that over half of their sample of seniors from several Connecticut high schools rated going steady as the primary objective of high school social life. The importance of steady relationships did vary appreciably among schools and probably varies historically as well. Yet, these older students' focus on steady dating is revealing of their interest in more stable and long-term romantic relationships. So is their characterization of a good steady relationship: an exclusive relationship (mentioned more often by girls) that provides affection, friendship, and security; is preceded by dating; and fosters personal understanding. Smaller percentages noted that it involves having a good time and sexual activity. In this sample, such relationships were infrequent – on average, the students reported having had two or three steady partners – but more durable than romantic alliances in early phases. They lasted between 2 and 10 months, rather than a matter of days or weeks, as in earlier phases (Eder, 1993; Feiring, 1996).

The more serious relationships of the affection phase seem to alter the pattern of social interaction. In Gordon and Miller's (1984) study, those who were currently involved with a romantic partner reported that a typical weekend night was spent either with that partner or with a group of same-sex peers. Those without a current partner were more likely to socialize in a mixed-sex group. Time allocation is also significantly different. My own data on high school youths indicated that adolescents in romantic relationships reported spending less time (on weekends) with friends but, ironically, more time with a larger group of peers (the crowd) than those who were currently without a boyfriend or girlfriend or who had never had such a relationship. Among German youth, Silbereisen, Noack, and von Eye (1992) found a contrasting shift in preferred leisure contexts related to experience in romantic relationships. As youths expressed interest in finding their first romantic partner, they tended to change from preferring private to public contexts for leisure activities because of the greater opportunities to meet potential dating partners. Those more experienced in romantic relations, however, made the opposite shift in preferred leisure contexts, perhaps to avoid the social scrutiny so central to earlier phases, so that they could concentrate on nurturing their romantic alliance.

A key factor differentiating relationships in this phase from earlier romantic encounters is *depth*. Partners in an affection-oriented relationship probe deeper into each other's personalities, generate deeper feelings of commitment for the relationship, express deeper levels of caring for each other, and typically engage in more extensive sexual activity as well. All of these things generate strong emotional responses, so that even though emotions were substantial in earlier phases, they can become especially intense and overwhelming at this stage. Moreover, the intimacy achieved in these relationships allows participants to express to each other strong feelings about issues in their lives beyond the relationship. In many ways, then, these are emotionally charged relationships. Managing these emotions becomes a critical and challenging task for partners, both as individuals and as a relational unit (see Larson et al.'s chapter in this volume for a lengthier discussion of these challenges). Hollywood portrayals of teenage romance most commonly try to capture the essence of the emotionally charged relationships of this phase rather than the relationships typical of earlier phases (see, e.g., *Boys 'n the 'Hood, Endless Love, Say Anything*).

Because few investigators have traced the relational histories of adolescents, it is not clear whether individuals who have experienced a relationship that is characteristic of the affection phase will stick exclusively to this type of relationship, or will cycle between more serious relationships and the more casual dating or romantic alliances that were typical of earlier phases. I suspect that the latter pattern is more common, but it would be interesting to study the factors that differentiate adolescents who follow each pattern.

There is much to be learned in the affection phase. Adolescents must expand their relationship skills to be able to manage longer-term, more intimate relationships. Patience, empathy, trust, and a sense of mutuality become salient traits. Partners must diminish their efforts at impression management in favor of more honest self-disclosure. Conflict management skills are also important, as is the capacity for *relationship monitoring:* being able to sense how the relationship is going, what the partner is feeling or needing, when it is appropriate to strive for a more intimate or serious level of association, and when one should temporarily suspend efforts to deepen the relationship. At this point, the processes of exchange that Laursen and Jensen-Campbell (this volume) discuss become particularly meaningful; and, as I have already mentioned, the need for emotional regulation is heightened. The affection phase also presents the first clear opportunity for genuine attachments to form (see Furman and Simon, this volume) in the context of romantic relationships. Many of these factors are reflected in the three most important dating goals that Miller, Bettencourt, DeBro, and Hoffman (1993) discovered in their sample of college students: avoiding conflict in a relationship, maintaining emotional closeness with one's partner, and achieving narcissistic goals (sexual intimacy, making a positive impression).

All of these features are important components of identity development, especially for women. Because of their stronger orientation toward relationships compared to men (Connolly & Johnson, 1996; Gilligan, 1992), women may regard their success or failure in romantic relationships in this phase as a reflection of their *general* self-worth – not just as an indicator of their adeptness at dating or attracting romantic partners (see Feiring's chapter in this volume for a fuller discussion of this issue). For this reason, women may demand more support from friends in their romantic experiences, may have less confidence than men in negotiating these relationships, and may take more time to recover from a bad experience or an undesirable ending to a serious romantic liaison. Of course, not all males and females conform to this gender difference; boys, too, can be profoundly affected in identity development by their success or failure in romantic relationships.

It is common for changes in sexual activity to accompany shifts in the quality of romantic relationships. McCabe and Collins (1983) compared the actual and desired sexual activity among a sample of 16- to 25-year-old Australian youths at three levels of romantic activity: first date, casual relationship (several dates), and going steady. Sexual activity was more extensive at each level of relationship. Miller, McCoy, and Olson (1986), on the other hand, found higher rates of sexual intercourse and more liberal attitudes toward sexuality among adolescents who were dating several individuals concurrently than among those who focused on just one partner (although sexual activity was highest among those who were going steady or engaged to be married). Thus, there appeared to be two patterns of sexuality: one for those who dated and slept around and another for those who waited for a serious relationship. Others have depicted an even broader array of sexual styles (Buzwell & Rosenthal, 1996), whose association with styles or features of romantic relationships is not well established (see Graber, Britto, & Brooks-Gunn, this volume, for more discussion of this issue). Of course, these patterns or styles are likely to vary by both history and context: Phinney, Jensen, Olsen, and Cundick (1990) discovered that the correlation between age of initial dating and initial heterosexual intercourse was significant for White youths but not for Blacks; in fact, Blacks in her sample reported a lower median age for first sexual intercourse than for first date.

The Peer Context

As an adolescent's romantic relationships grow more serious and sustained, the rest of his or her peer social network (not to mention family, school, and other social contexts) must adjust to the new features and depth of these relationships. Most notably, the locus of primary influence is likely to tip more noticeably away from the larger peer group or crowd toward the smaller circle of close friends. This shift is reflected in the final two stages of Dunphy's (1969) model of peer group structure. In early adolescence, peer groups are transformed from isolated, monosexual cliques to loosely associated mixed-sex groups. By middle adolescence (Stage 4), cliques have become more fully integrated in terms of gender and have formed into a coalition of cliques (a *crowd,* in Dunphy's terms) for the purposes of major social activities. At this stage, which I suspect begins before but overlaps with the affection phase of romantic relationships, deciding who is in the crowd and who is not – who gets included in or excluded from crowd social events – is a major preoccupation of crowd leaders. Toward the end of adolescence, however, the alliances between cliques that form a crowd begin to break down, and cliques tend to operate more independently, as they did in Stage 1 or Stage 2 of Dunphy's model. The difference, however, is that late adolescent cliques are cross-gender rather than single-sex groups. Their smaller size is conducive to more stable membership and is quite comparable to the "small circle of friends" that characterizes social patterns among American adults. Within the clique individuals can nurture stable and intense friendships, as well as intense romantic relationships, love triangles, and so forth. The dynamics of these cliques are well captured (though perhaps overdramatized) in the film *St. Elmo's Fire.* As is illustrated in this film, when a couple who are both clique members breaks up, the entire clique can be plunged into emotional and interpersonal turmoil until all of the issues related to the dissolution of the relationship have been worked through. In other words, the intense feelings that are characteristic of romantic relationships in this phase are not confined to the couple; they spill over into the peer group and its pattern of interactions as well.

In this phase, individual friends and the friendship group take on a set of significant roles. They continue as matchmakers and cheerleaders, encouraging an adolescent's ventures into more serious romantic liaisons. But they also become *private eyes,* keeping tabs on a romantic partner's actions to ensure that she or he is faithful to the relationship. To be sure, individuals and groups vary in the degree of fraternizing, flirting, and fooling around (with persons other than the romantic partner) they will tolerate. But if a teenager oversteps the norms of the group, repercussions can be expected – beginning, of course, with a message to the group member that his or her romantic partner has been unfaithful. If for this or other reasons the couple gets into a fight, peer group members may assume a second role: *arbitrator.* A new version of the messenger service (from the status phase) may be enacted to convey partners' reactions and feelings back and forth to each other. These may replace or supplement direct communication between the couple. In some cases, the couple's conflict may be the primary focus of group discussion until the issue is resolved (or the relationship abandoned).

Peers expand their vital role as a *support system* in this phase. Especially for teenagers who cannot turn to parents, older siblings, or other relatives for advice, friends become the sympathetic ear or the wellspring of ideas on how to respond to new or confusing situations in a relationship. When the romance ends, peers offer advice on how to end the affair and consolation during the recovery period. Over the long term, the intimacy between close friends does not appear to be affected by the intense feelings adolescents develop for romantic partners (Feiring, 1996), so that friends can pick up where they left off after the romance is over.

As supportive as peers can be for group members or close friends, they can also be fiercely indignant toward individuals (especially nonfriends or nongroup members) who are perceived to have acted unethically or inappropriately in a romantic relationship. In instances of severe or persistent violation of group norms regarding romantic relationships, the peer group can serve as *judge and jury,* determining which party is guilty and how that person should be punished. It makes sense that a peer group will favor one of its own members over an outsider, but how typical this pattern is I honestly do not know. To the offended party the group extends sympathy and encouragement. To the offender it can mete out appropriate punishment: remonstrations, lectures, shunning, ostracism, or whatever. In this regard, things can be especially awkward for an adolescent who has not moved with the group from the status to the affection phase of romantic relationships. Someone who is still feigning interest in a romantic partner or pursuing superficial relationships to improve his or her standing in the group can easily run afoul of the peer group if the target of the person's romantic overtures is looking for a deeper, more personal relationship.

Although close friendships appear to be maintained across affection-oriented romantic relationships, they may be more heavily tested than in previous phases. The intensity of romantic experiences can steal both time and affect from close friendships. The advantage in intimacy, trust, and companionship that friends have maintained over romantic partners in early phases of romantic relationships disappears by the end of high school, when this phase is more common (Lempers & Clark-Lempers, 1993). Particularly if an adolescent does not also have a romantic partner, he or she may feel abandoned when a close friend becomes more intimately involved with a boyfriend or girlfriend. It is difficult to get teenagers to confess jealousy or resentment over a friend's romantic partner because such feelings violate the norms of friendship. Indeed, such feelings among male friends could easily be interpreted by peers as indicators of one boy's homosexual inclinations, so in most instances they will be carefully suppressed. Yet, I have witnessed these friendship dynamics time and again among groups of teens I work with in the community. With maturity, particularly as both members of a friendship pair gain experience with more serious romantic relationships, adolescents learn to compensate for time or affect lost when a friend pursues a romantic interest, typically by broadening their friendship network or finding a boyfriend or girlfriend of their own.

In sum, the peer group continues to be restructured in this phase, assuming an organization that is not only conducive to the more serious and sustained romantic relationships that are typical at this time, but also one that prepares adolescents for normative patterns of social interaction in adult society. The functions that friends serve again seem to change to accommodate the needs of romantic development. However, because peer groups are growing smaller, more stable, and couple oriented at this stage, they are more vulnerable to the vicissitudes of members' romantic relationships. Trauma in one member's romantic activities can reverberate throughout the group. Of course, these group dynamics are likely to differ from one crowd to the next, according to crowd norms about romantic relationships, as well as among individuals, according to their commitment to the group and their reliance on its members for support. Moreover, this portrait of the peer context remains remarkably speculative in the absence of close scrutiny by social scientists.

Bonding Phase

A healthy restoration of continuity and sameness demands the reconnection of past, present, and future selves. At some point in late adolescence, individuals should feel the need to look beyond the present and make realistic plans for the future. "How will my emerging sense of identity launch me into specific, concrete roles in adult society?" "How can I enter into sustaining relationships that will define my position in the adult community?" American society expects late adolescents to become preoccupied with these questions as they "polish off" their quest for identity and prepare for entry into adulthood. This long-term, pragmatic view should be extended to romantic relationships as well, especially because they are the crux of the next "crisis" in Erikson's (1963) lifelong sequence of developmental stages: intimacy versus isolation.

The Character of Romantic Relations

In this phase, individuals are expected to maintain the depth of relationships typical of the affection phase but to replace some of the emotionality of those romantic alliances with a more pragmatic perspective. The key issues for relational partners are whether or not they can commit to a lifelong partnership with each other, how confident they are about the prospect of building a life together, how willing they are to put up with each other's shortcomings as well as strengths, and how open they are to accommodating unforeseeable changes that are bound to occur to the partner. These are sobering concerns. They highlight the transformation in relational orientation that must take place between the affection and bonding phases. In the former, the focus in romantic relationships was on self-exploration and self-discovery (within a relational context). The objective was to probe deeply into the self in order to discover and accept one's personal, unique sense of identity. With the transition from Stage 5 to Stage 6 in Erikson's theory, individuals must take that carefully crafted sense of identity and risk losing it in an attempt at *identity fusion* with their partner. A truly mature relationship, from Erikson's perspective, requires partners to become so close that the boundaries of their identities are blurred. They remain distinctive personalities but inseparable as a couple – like two clearly discernible human forms in a sculpture who seem to emerge from and merge into each other.

These developmental mandates compel romantic partners to look at each other (and their relationship) in pragmatic and objective terms. All emotions and passions aside, do I like this person as a friend? Can I put up with his irritating habits? Do I feel comfortable with her values and lifestyle? Would we make an effective team in raising children, working out problems, or serving the community? To be sure, not all late adolescent or adult couples who make a lifelong commitment to each other have reached the level of romantic relationship featured in the bonding phase. Not all individuals, I would argue, graduate to this phase. The literature on courtship and mating stipulates other scripts for entering into lifelong relationships than the one specified by Erikson. It would be helpful in future research to identify factors that prompt some individuals to transcend the emotional fervor of affection-oriented relationships and achieve this more mature orientation. Related issues are whether or not both members of a committed couple must operate from the bonding perspective for the relationship to be successful or, indeed, whether a bonding perspective is truly more adaptive for couples over the long term than the more adolescent emphasis on status or emotional attachment.

Evidence for this final phase of romantic relations, and for the more general sequencing of phases, is admittedly thin. However, some corroboration emerges from the rationales that different age groups give for dating or their characterizations of a desirable romantic partner. Roscoe, Diana, and Brooks (1987) compared the reasons for dating given by early, middle, and late adolescents (6th graders, 11th graders, and college students). Early and middle adolescents tended to emphasize recreation and status, whereas late adolescents were more likely to list companionship, sexual activity, or mate selection. In describing features of a desirable dating partner, the younger respondents focused on personal and prestige factors, whereas the oldest group emphasized "shares my interests" and "has goals for the future." "Early adolescents tended to weight more heavily superficial features (e.g., dresses fashionably) and their approval by others (e.g., approved of by parents, well liked by many people) than did late adolescents," the investigators concluded (p. 66). "It appears that with maturity and/or experience, late adolescents become more independent in their ratings and more future oriented in their views of dating."

The Peer Context

By the time most individuals are ready to enter the bonding phase, the peer context has already been transformed, according to Dunphy (1969) into a structure compatible with normative adult forms of social interaction. Thus, no major restructuring of the peer context appears to be necessary at this point. Nevertheless, it would seem adaptive for peers to withdraw somewhat from their heavy involvement in group members' romantic lives, but at the same time remain supportive of members and brutally candid about romantic relationships. The decision to fuse one's identity with someone else is an intensely personal one with far-reaching, lifelong consequences. It is certainly not the business of peers, even close and long-standing friends, to make this decision for someone else. Yet, friends can be very effective sounding boards as individuals think through their commitment to romantic partners. Friends also may be able to judge a person's partner, or the quality of the couple's relationship, more objectively because they lack the deep emotional feelings or sexual passion that the person brings to the relationship.

In this phase, peer influences seem to lack both the collaborative and the competitive spirit that characterized their role in earlier phases. The intensity of peer influence and the compulsion to attend to peers' advice or admonitions is likely to fade as well. Still, peers can be the purveyors of cultural norms. The importance of loyalty, equality, respect, long-term commitment, and ethnic, religious, or socioeconomic homogeneity in a romantic relationship will be encoded in the group's norms, just as they are in the norms of the larger subculture, culture, or society in which individuals live. A key issue is whether or not there is convergence in these norms among the major social contexts in which late adolescents or young adults are situated. Particularly in the case of immigrant youths, the peer group continues to be a major voice in defining and interpreting cultural values. How do norms and practices within the former culture fit within the current social context? Often adolescents will look to peers rather than parents to address this issue (Brown, Hamm, & Myerson, 1996; Nguyen & Williams, 1989).

Conclusion

From giggle-ridden conversations about who the cutest person is at the next lunchroom table to schemes to win the affection of the most popular peer at school to sobering contemplation about sustaining a loving relationship with a particular person over the next five decades, romantic interests and relationships in American society undergo dramatic changes over the adolescent and young adult years. Accompanying these changes are major transformations in the structure and content of peer relations, which seem either to stem from or significantly affect adolescents' experiences in romance. In this chapter I have outlined a four-phase sequence to describe the developmental course of romantic interests and expressions. I have appealed to Erikson's theory of identity development, as well as to several research studies, to provide both the rationale for and some supportive evidence of these developmental changes. The portrait of peer group processes and influences in each phase of the model has been much more speculative for lack of solid research evidence. Yet, it is strongly suggestive of an intimate connection between development and context in this domain of adolescents' lives. It also implies a strong connection between romantic activities and peer relationships more generally, a connection that has been underrepresented and, I would argue, underrated in previous research.

From this brief exploration of the connections between the peer context and romantic activities, I would like to emphasize five concluding points. First, *romantic interests and activities constitute a complex developmental phenomenon in American adolescents.* By restricting research to romantic relationships that manifest features of long-term, committed, adult relationships, investigators have missed most of the activity that individuals engage in during adolescence; even studies of dating ignore much of the preliminary development of romantic orientations, skills, and self-concepts so central to the serious relationships individuals encounter in later adolescence. A proper understanding of adolescents' romantic relationships must proceed from the broader perspective of the full developmental range of romantic orientations and experiences. Even when investigators focus on a particular type of relationship or phase of romantic development, it is helpful for them to have the big picture in mind. For researchers to do so effectively, much more attention must be devoted to the earlier phases of the developmental sequence. The current heavy concentration of research on relationships in the affection and bonding stages must be redirected toward the experiences of younger adolescents.

Second, the developmental-contextual perspective adopted here demands that *researchers be careful not to separate romantic couples from the social context in which their relationship is situated.* I have emphasized the peer context in this chapter because I believe it is heavily influential during the adolescent years, yet seriously underrepresented or inadequately measured in many research studies. Other contexts, however, are also vitally important. Gray and Steinberg (this volume) illustrate the critical role that the family plays in adolescents' romantic experiences. Feiring (this volume) points to the influence of community or cultural expectations for sex roles and configured gender identities. Coates (this volume) explores the powerful influences of ethnic and neighborhood context, and emphasizes the reciprocal nature of influences between romantic relationships and social contexts. More careful study of each social context is sorely needed. Yet, researchers also must move to a higher level of analysis, considering how these various major social contexts interact – whether they serve to reinforce each other or, as I have pointed out in the case of some immigrant youths (Nguyen & Williams, 1989), present young people with contradictory expectations about romantic relationships.

An extension of this second point is to be mindful of broader sociohistorical forces at work on adolescent romantic relationships: historical changes and national or cultural differences. I have been careful to emphasize that this chapter focuses on the experiences and developmental trajectories of adolescents in the United States because my ideas are based on studies and observations of U.S. samples. Researchers who have studied teenage romance in other countries have presented a markedly different picture. Husbands (1970), for example, contrasted the superficiality of the American dating system with the tendency among European adolescents to date fewer individuals for longer periods of time, with stronger consideration in each relationship of the potential for lifelong commitment (mate selection). In some nations, patterns of gender segregation or an intensive focus on school and studying undermines opportunities to locate or interact with romantic partners. Such factors can affect the developmental course of romantic relationships and the roles that peers play in this process. In a similar fashion, historical changes affect romantic relations. Changes in health care and nutritional habits have lowered the age of puberty during the past century, thus increasing the possibility of teenage pregnancy, which alters a significant component of peer relations: sexual activity (see Graber et al., this volume). In the United States, the historical shift from formal dating to more informal interaction in small, mixed-sex groups allows teenagers to get to know each other on a casual, friendly basis before declaring any romantic intentions. All of these factors can affect the sequencing of phases or the character of relationships within each phase.

A third point is that *researchers must be attentive to variability in norms governing romantic relationships within a particular peer system.* Such a pattern may be influenced not only by societal norms regarding mate selection or marriage but also by the organization of adolescents' relationships with peers. Eckert (1989), for example, implies that different peer crowds will emphasize different values and orientations toward romantic activity. Crowds are likely to feature different timetables for moving from one phase to the next. Within a given population of American adolescents, one may find groups that are still making awkward approaches to potential romantic partners, under the watchful eye of a clique of same-sex companions, at the same time that other age-mates are embroiled in long-term dating relationships within the context of a larger, heterosocial peer crowd. The level of diversity and flexibility within a given peer system may be a significant predictor of adolescents' successful progression through phases of romantic activity.

Fourth, *just as there is normative variability within the larger peer system, there is also individual variability.* Adolescents do not all move in lock-step fashion through any developmental sequence. The variability apparent in pubertal and sexual maturation is also likely to be observed in maturation of romantic interests and experiences (see Silbereisen et al., 1992). At issue is whether youths who are off time in romantic development manifest the same departures from healthy developmental outcomes that have often been observed among youths who are off time in physical maturation. I have suggested some reasons why this may be the case at various points in the romantic developmental process; Douvan and Adelson (1966) also provide both empirical and theoretical arguments about the dangers of precocious dating. This issue demands much more careful research attention.

Finally, *multiple research methods must be brought to bear on the study of developmental changes in and peer influences on adolescent romantic relationships.* I have cited work that relies upon self-report data as well as participant observation, individual or focus group interviews, and even diary material. No single methodology is superlative, particularly in capturing the dynamics – such as status seeking or jealousy over a friend's success in romance – that are difficult for adolescents to acknowledge. Authors must continue to explore creative methodologies for collecting information on these intriguing subjects.

Romantic interests launch adolescents on an exciting, precarious journey of self-discovery and, hopefully, interpersonal fulfillment. It is important not to lose sight of this fact in our careful, scientific scrutiny of adolescents' romantic relationships. If our science drains this dimension of adolescent development of its wonder and rapture, we can be sure that we have missed the mark. "You're going with *who*?" Such remonstrations from one adolescent to another should never puzzle nor dismay us.

References

Bell, R. R., & Chaskes, J. B. (1970). Premarital sexual experiences among coeds, 1958 and 1968. *Journal of Marriage and the Family, 32,* 81–84.

Blos, P. (1979). *The adolescent passage.* New York: International Universities Press.

Broderick, C. B., & Weaver, J. (1968). The perceptual context of boy–girl communication. *Journal of Marriage and the Family, 30,* 618–627.

Brown, B. B. (1990). Peer groups and peer cultures. In S. S. Feldman & G. R. Elliott (Eds.), *At the threshold: The developing adolescent* (pp. 171–196). Cambridge, MA: Harvard University Press.

Brown, B. B. (1998, February). *Can peer expectations for autonomy explain crowd differences in behavior?* Paper presented at the biennial meetings of the Society for Research on Adolescence, San Diego, CA.

Brown, B. B., Hamm, J. V., & Meyerson, P. (1996, March). Encouragement, empowerment, enmeshment: Ethnic differences in approaches to parental involvement with peer relationships. In B. Brown (Chair), *Buzz off or butt in?: Parental involvement in adolescent peer relationships.* Symposium presented at the biennial meetings of the Society for Research on Adolescence, Boston.

Brown, B. B., Mory, M., & Kinney, D. A. (1994). Casting adolescent crowds in relational perspective: Caricature, channel, and context. In R. Montemayor, G. R. Adams, & T. P. Gullotta (Eds.), *Advances in adolescent development: Volume 6,*

Personal relationships during adolescence (pp. 123–167). Newbury Park, CA: Sage.

Buzwell, S., & Rosenthal, D. (1996). Constructing a sexual self: Adolescents' self-perceptions and sexual risk-taking. *Journal of Research on Adolescence, 6,* 489–513.

Caspi, A., Lynam, D., Moffitt, T. E., & Silva, P. A. (1993). Unraveling girls' delinquency: Biological, dispositional, and contextual contributions to adolescent misbehavior. *Developmental Psychology, 29,* 19–30.

Cather, W. (1918). *My Antonia.* Boston: Houghton-Mifflin.

Coleman, J. S. (1961). *The adolescent society.* New York: Free Press.

Connolly, J. A., Ben-Knaz, R., & Goldberg, A. (1996, March). *Early adolescents' conceptions of romantic relationships.* Paper presented at the biennial meeting of the Society for Research on Adolescence, Boston.

Connolly, J. A., & Johnson, A. M. (1996). Adolescents' romantic relationships and the structure and quality of their close interpersonal ties. *Personal Relationships, 3,* 185–195.

Dickinson, G. E. (1975). Dating behavior of Black and White adolescents before and after desegregation. *Journal of Marriage and the Family, 37,* 602–608.

Dornbusch, S. M., Carlsmith, J. M., Gross, R. T., Martin, J. A., Jennings, D., Rosenberg, A., & Duke, P. (1981). Sexual development, age, and dating: A comparison of biological and social influences upon one set of behaviors. *Child Development, 52,* 179–185.

Douvan, E., & Adelson, J. (1966). *The adolescent experience.* New York: Wiley.

Dunphy, D. (1969). *Cliques, crowds, and gangs.* Melbourne, Australia: Cheshire.

Eckert, P. (1989). *Jocks and burnouts.* New York: Teachers College Press.

Eder, D. (1985). The cycle of popularity: Interpersonal relations among female adolescents. *Sociology of Education, 58,* 154–165.

Eder, D. (1993). "Go get ya a French!": Romantic and sexual teasing among adolescent girls. In D. Tannen (Ed.), *Gender and conversational interaction* (pp. 17–31). New York: Oxford University Press.

Erikson, E. H. (1963). *Childhood and society* (2nd ed.). New York: Norton.

Feinstein, S. C., & Ardon, M. S. (1973). Trends in dating patterns and adolescent development. *Journal of Youth and Adolescence 2,* 157–166.

Feiring, C. (1996). Concepts of romance in 15-year-old adolescents. *Journal of Research on Adolescence, 6,* 181–200.

Franzoni, S. L., Davis, M. H., & Vasquez-Suson, K. A. (1994). Two social worlds: Social correlates and stability of adolescent status groups. *Journal of Personality and Social Psychology, 67,* 462–473.

Gargiulo, J., Attie, I., Brooks-Gunn, J., & Warren, M. P. (1987). Girls' dating behavior as a function of social context and maturation. *Developmental Psychology, 23,* 730–737.

Gilligan, C. (1992). *In a different voice.* Cambridge, MA: Harvard University Press.

Gordon, M. (1981). Was Waller ever right?: The rating and dating complex reconsidered. *Journal of Marriage and the Family, 43,* 67–76.

Gordon, M., & Miller, R. L. (1984). Going steady in the 1980s: Exclusive relationships in six Connecticut high schools. *Sociology and Social Research, 68,* 463–479.

Griffin, C. (1985). *Typical girls?: Young women from school to job market*. London: Routledge & Kegan Paul.

Harter, S., Marold, D. B., Whitesell, N. R., & Cobbs, G. (1996). A model of the effects of perceived parent and peer support on adolescent false self behavior. *Child Development, 67,* 360–374.

Hartup, W. W. (1993). Adolescents and their friends. In B. Laursen (Ed.), *Close friendships in adolescence* (pp. 3–22). San Francisco: Jossey-Bass.

Herold, E. S. (1974). Stages of date selection: A reconciliation of divergent findings on campus values in dating. *Adolescence, 9,* 113–120.

Husbands, C. T. (1970). Some social and psychological consequences of the American dating system. *Adolescence, 5,* 451–462.

Jackson, D. W. (1975). The meaning of dating from the role perspective of non-dating pre-adolescents. *Adolescence, 10,* 123–126.

Katchadourian, H. (1990). Sexuality. In S. S. Feldman & G. R. Elliott (Eds.), *At the threshold: The developing adolescent* (pp. 352–387). Cambridge, MA: Harvard University Press.

Kilbourne, F. (1918). *Betty Bell*. New York: Harper and Brothers.

Kinney, D. (1993). From "nerds" to "normals": Adolescent identity recovery within a changing social system. *Sociology of Education, 66,* 21–40.

Lempers, J. D., & Clark-Lempers, D. S. (1993). A functional comparison of same-sex and opposite-sex friendship during adolescence. *Journal of Adolescent Research, 8,* 89–108.

Maccoby, E. E. (1988). Gender as a social category. *Developmental Psychology, 24,* 755–765.

MacLeod, J. (1995). *Ain't no makin' it: Aspirations and attainment in a low-income neighborhood*. Boulder, CO: Westview Press.

Mahler, M. (1972). On the first three subphases of the separation-individuation process. *International Journal of Psychoanalysis, 53,* 333 338.

McCabe, M. P. (1984). Toward a theory of adolescent dating. *Adolescence, 19,* 159–170.

McCabe, M. P., & Collins, J. K. (1983). The sexual and affectional attitudes and experiences of Australian adolescents during dating: The effects of age, church attendance, type of school, and socioeconomic class. *Archives of Sexual Behavior, 12,* 525–539.

Mikulincer, M., Weller, A., & Florian, V. (1993). Sense of closeness to parents and family rules: A study of Arab and Jewish youth in Israel. *International Journal of Psychology, 28,* 323–335.

Miller, B. C., McCoy, J. K., & Olson, T. D. (1986). Dating age and stage as correlates of adolescent sexual attitudes and behavior. *Journal of Adolescent Research, 1,* 361–371.

Miller, L. C., Bettencourt, B. A., DeBro, S. C., & Hoffman, V. (1993). Negotiating safer sex: Interpersonal dynamics. In J. Pryor & G. Reeder (Eds.), *The social psychology of AIDS infection* (pp. 85–123). Hillsdale, NJ: Erlbaum.

Mitman, A. L., & Packer, M. J. (1982). Concerns of seventh-graders about their transition to junior high school. *Journal of Early Adolescence, 2,* 319–338.

Newman, P. R., & Newman, B. M. (1976). Early adolescence and its conflict: Group identity versus alienation. *Adolescence, 11,* 261–274.

Nguyen, N. A., & Williams, H. L. (1989). Transition from East to West: Vietnamese adolescents and their parents. *Journal of the American Academy of Child and Adolescent Psychiatry, 28,* 505–515.

Pawlby, S. J., Mills, A., & Quinton, D. (1997). Vulnerable adolescent girls: Opposite-sex relationships. *Journal of Child Psychology and Psychiatry, 38,* 909–920.

Phinney, V. G., Jensen, L. C., Olsen, J. A., & Cundick, B. (1990). The relationship between early development and psychosexual behaviors in adolescent females. *Adolescence, 25,* 321–332.

Place, D. M. (1975). The dating experience for adolescent girls. *Adolescence, 10,* 157–174.

Roscoe, B., Cavanaugh, L. E., & Kennedy, D. R. (1988). Dating infidelity: Behaviors, reasons and consequences. *Adolescence, 23,* 35–43.

Roscoe, B., Diana, M. S., & Brooks, R. H. (1987). Early, middle, and late adolescents' views on dating and factors influencing partner selection. *Adolescence, 22,* 59–68.

Roscoe, B., Kennedy, D., & Pope, T. (1987). Adolescents' views of intimacy: Distinguishing intimate from nonintimate relationships. *Adolescence, 22,* 511–516.

Samet, N., & Kelly, E. W. (1987). The relationship of steady dating to self-esteem and sex role identity among adolescents. *Adolescence, 22,* 231–245.

Silbereisen, R. K., Noack, P., & von Eye, A. (1992). Adolescents' development of romantic friendship and change in favorite leisure contexts. *Journal of Adolescent Research, 7,* 80–93.

Simmons, R. G., & Blyth, D. A. (1987). *Moving into adolescence: The impact of pubertal change and school context.* Hawthorne, NJ: Aldine.

Simon, R. W., Eder, D., & Evans, C. (1992). The development of feeling norms underlying romantic love among adolescent females. *Social Psychology Quarterly, 55,* 29–46.

Skipper, J. K., & Naas, G. (1966). Dating behavior: A framework for analysis and an illustration. *Journal of Marriage and the Family, 28,* 412–420.

Spreadbury, C. L. (1982). First date. *Journal of Early Adolescence, 2,* 83–89.

Stattin, H., & Magnusson, D. (1990). *Pubertal maturation in female development.* Hillsdale, NJ: Erlbaum.

Thompson, S. (1994). Changing lives, changing genres: Teenage girls' narratives about sex and romance, 1978–1986. In A. S. Rossi (Ed.), *Sexuality across the life course* (pp. 209–232). Chicago: University of Chicago Press.

Thornton, A. (1990). The courtship process and adolescent sexuality. Special issue: Adolescent sexuality, contraception, and childbearing. *Journal of Family Issues, 11,* 239–273.

Waller, W. (1937). The rating and dating complex. *American Sociological Review, 2,* 727–734.

Werebe, M. G. (1987). How adolescents perceive their relationships. *Adolescence, 22,* 129–142.

13   The Cultured and Culturing Aspects
of Romantic Experience in Adolescence

Deborah L. Coates

A General Overview

In this chapter the significant reciprocal influences of culture and romantic
experiences during adolescence are considered. The meaning of culture in
relation to the concepts of ethnicity and race, cross-cultural perspectives,
reciprocity between culture and romantic behavior, the influence of romantic experience on identity, and the significance of developmental timing for
romantic experience are considered. The relevance of these considerations
for research and clinical intervention applications is also discussed. In this
chapter, *culture* is defined as a group's particular adaptation to a social
environment that is characterized by a shared psychological reality or
worldview; shared customs, language, and practices; and the general protection offered by belonging to a distinct group (Coates & Vietze, 1996;
Markus, Kitayama, & Heiman, 1997). Culture and romantic experiences
are reciprocally related such that some experiences teach adolescents about
romance. These can be referred to as *cultured* experiences because they are
largely based on accepted mores and practices from the past. The cultured
experiences of adolescents acculturate them about what romance is and
what its significance should be for them. Adolescent romantic experiences

I would like to thank the editors of this volume and also Peter Vietze and
Douglas Kimmel for helpful comments on early drafts of this chapter. I
would also like to thank L. Cortes, L. Jeu, Y. Martins, M. Presinal, L.
Romero, R. Schiffino, and P. Valdez – research honors students at Hunter
College – for helpful dialogue on romantic experience in the honors
research seminar that I conducted in January 1996. I also appreciate assistance from M. Raven Rowe, another student in the seminar, in helping me
locate materials, and for her exceptionally able help in stimulating and challenging some of the ideas presented in early drafts of this chapter.

and perspectives probably also influence and modify the romantic cultural practices of a society over time. In this sense, romantic experiences of adolescents are culturing for a society. A dynamic change can occur in society regarding the meaning and significance of romantic experience, as well as in romantic practices as a result of how adolescents behave in romantic exchanges. Both perspectives contribute to understanding the developmental significance of romance, as well as of other human behaviors.

The experiences of some African-descent adolescents in the United States are used in this chapter as specific examples of some of the developmental processes to which the discussion refers. A rather lengthy introduction is provided to explore the pseudoscientific concept of *race* and its influence on how culture is viewed in the United States and among most behavioral scientists because this discussion is often ignored in work on culture. This discussion is based on the experiences of two groups in the United States, often designated as *Blacks* and *Whites* because of their historical significance and because these contrasts are often used in behavioral research (see Jones, 1997, for a further discussion)

Issues of Culture, Race, and Ethnicity

Defining Culture. At the outset, it is important to note that *everyone's* behavior is infused with cultural influences. Because culture cannot be separated from an individual's behavior and is a pervasive aspect of all human actions, it is not something that can be relegated to groups designated as *ethnic minorities.* Often the person who is studying the culture of another group must do so by contrasting this group's culture with his or her own. This sets up necessary limitations in perspective and methodology that will be addressed in this chapter in relation to romantic experience in adolescence. These limitations are important because culture, race, class, gender, and other status variables are not politically, socially, or emotionally neutral in society and cannot be so in social science research, despite the researcher's goal of scientific objectivity. Culture accounts for significant variation in all experience and is a prevailing force that is often overlooked in interpreting variation in romantic behavior. It also may account for variance in the developmental significance of romantic experience. Romantic interactions may influence the development of identity and the achievement of adult developmental goals differently across cultures.

A broad discussion of culture as a social and psychological construct, or the history and characteristics of the interdisciplinary area known as *cultural psychology,* is beyond the scope of this chapter. There are excellent discussions of this elsewhere (Akbar, 1994; Appiah, 1992; Coates & Vietze, 1996; Cole, 1996; Marimba, 1992; Markus et al., 1997; Miller & Goodnow, 1995; Myers, 1984, 1988, 1991; Ogbu, 1988; Shweder & Sullivan, 1993). Markus et al. (1997) present a view of culture that best represents the fluidity of the cultural processes and the important view that culture not be considered as an entity such as a set of values or a context that can be separated from behavior, but rather as a "variable, open and dynamic system." Diop (unpublished interview, 1976) has described culture as playing a protective role for the individual. It helps to ensure the cohesion of a group. Common practices, the feeling of belonging to the same cultural present and to a historical past, create a collective consciousness. Few studies other than broad cross-cultural comparisons try to understand how culture is dynamically integrated with behavior, how it operates as a psychological reality, and how cultural practices are engaged, accepted, rejected, and the like (see Markus et al., 1997, and Cole, 1996, for a more complete discussion).

Conceptualizing Culture and Its Influence. There are some general issues that need to be identified because they are central to how culture can be considered in understanding how it relates to adolescent experience. The first issue has to do with how to conceptualize culture and its influence on adolescent experience. Although culture is recognized as being of central importance, in many discussions of psychological theory and research it is only marginally considered. At best, culture is a secondary variable in most psychological research. Most research on adolescence examines culture by studying a particular group, sometimes comparing it with another group designated as culturally different. This is inadequate since cultural variables are not well conceptualized but merely assumed to be operational. According to Cole (1996), it has been extremely difficult for psychologists to conceptualize variable that capture *how* culture influences mental processes and behavioral experiences. For example, culture cannot be separated from individual actions, nor is it monolithic; rather, it consists of several components like artifacts, values, and attitudes. These may be culturally consistent or inconsistent, depending on the way in which an individual chooses to act. Consider a young woman's decision to get dressed in the morning. In some situations she may not realize she has choices, but in others she may choose a Western pants suit or an Eastern sari. Which represents her cultural perspective or what is inside her head as she makes this choice? Others may make assumptions about her values or attitudes based on her choice of dress or hairstyle, but they could be quite wrong without exploring what is in her head and how and why she made this choice in this particular situation. This situational and individual variation in broadly accepted cultural artifacts, practices, and values makes it difficult to manipulate experimentally a cultural variable that applies across groups. This problem makes it difficult to explore variables like romantic experience that occur as both observable behavior and internal mental processes since there is little methodological or widely accepted theoretical foundation that treats cultural influence as a central framework for understanding behavior on which to build research. Several scholars have theorized about how worldview influences behavior, yet these ideas are not broadly translated into strategies for understanding how these views influence individual behavior (Akbar, 1994; Hilliard, unpublished workshop materials, 1976; Myers, 1991; Nobles, 1985, 1989). Those studying romantic or any other adolescent experience may need to start by recognizing that nothing exists or evolves outside of culture. It may also be important to recognize that some aspects of romantic experience, such as love or passion, may not be universally experienced or valued, whereas mating may be. This requires a focus on human action as the unit of analysis and not on cultural classifications such as ethnicity, as suggested by Cole (1996). This may require different methodological approaches, discussed later in this chapter.

Differentiating Culture, Race, and Ethnicity. The second issue that requires consideration in the study of romantic experience and adolescent development is how *race, ethnicity,* and *culture* are interrelated. These terms often intersect and are sometimes treated as if they are synonymous. In some instances they may overlap. This overlap may be real, that is, ethnic groups within a culture may have a common cultural worldview. For example, many European ethnic groups have a common experience and easily accommodate the banner of European or Western culture. On the other hand, the overlap may not really exist but may be assumed, as when persons thought to be of a similar race may not share similar cultural experiences. African-descent people from the United States, the Caribbean, and the African continent have somewhat more dissimilar cultural experiences, yet they share some common racial ancestry. For the purpose of this chapter and in general, race, ethnicity, and culture should not be considered synonymous. Ethnicity often represents smaller subgroups within a larger cultural grouping such as nation-of-origin or continent-of-origin groups, religious groups, or a group that is native to a geographical area. Social scientists have attempted to understand the complexities of distinctions between ethnicity, culture, race as social referents. Some tend to see ethnicity as a complex set of cultural practices and identities that largely overlap with and sometimes encompass race (Phinney, 1989, 1996). This and other simple definitions (e.g., Betancourt & Lopez, 1993) of a common nationality, culture, or language fail to capture the meaning of ethnicity in the United States, particularly in relation to cultural practice. Phinney (1996) suggests that ethnicity is a necessary label for discourse and research, and believed that it encompasses the dynamic influence of culture, identity, and social status on behavior. However, given the dynamic nature of culture to which she refers, these characteristics of ethnicity probably do not operate in a static fashion within ethnic groups. Within a particular ethnic group, some mores and expectations about romantic experience may be similar to those of the larger cultural group, and other mores and expectations may be more closely related to those of other ethnic groups. This pattern probably varies across ethnic groups. However, a particular ethnic group may have unique ways of acting on these expectations. Thus, one could see significant variation in dating and marriage rituals across ethnic groups, as well as within ethnic groups in a particular culture.

One of the unique characteristics of the national culture in the United States is that it is thought to be a blend of many different cultures. However, it is not as much a blend of different cultural perspectives as it is a culture that expects the assimilation of cultural groups to European or Western norms. It is also a culture that assimilates or appropriates portions of other cultures on its own terms, often relegating cultural artifacts such as dress, music, foods, and ritual practices to an outsider or fringe status. This makes the issue of defining cultural values for specific ethnic groups in the United States a complex challenge.

The Overarching Culture of Race and Racism in the United States. Few social scientists explore how the social history of the concepts *race* and *color consciousness* influences their research (Stanfield, 1993; see also Appiah, 1996). Through its long history in science, and more recently in political science, sociology, and psychology, race is often thought to be a valid biological construct useful in classifying the human species. However, today it is largely thought to be an arbitrary way of classifying the human family socially that was created to distinguish between the variety among people based on presumed physical, historical, cultural, national, and/or geographical variation (Farber-Robertson & Spencer, 1996; Jones, 1997; Stanfield, 1993). Race, like sex and ethnicity, has been used to construct a social reality and, as such, has a powerful influence on identity. It often overlaps with cultural group, though the original concept has lost its scientific credibility.

The social significance of race has to be considered in the context of racism. Racism is the classification of persons based on false biological differences to support the notion that some racial groups are superior or inferior to others. *Cultural racism,* defined as denying the relevance of alternative cultural practices and perspectives, is a powerful mechanism of social control. The concept of race and the practice of cultural racism have been used to preserve a sense of privilege and entitlement for persons of European descent, usually self-labeled as White. Although this group appears to enjoy and to expect this privilege, they are often unaware of it. Although a discussion of how this occurred is beyond the scope of this chapter, given the history and ecology of Europe, it is important to note that this is a social reality. The concept of race is not often a useful biological term for understanding cultural practices and behavior. However, it is a meaningful and significant social construct that results in White social privilege being maintained. In almost every aspect of day-to-day experience, individuals attribute meaning to arbitrary classifications such as Black and White or African American and Hispanic without any clear reference to what these terms mean in other than superficial, stereotypic ways. Likewise, the terms White and Black have been used overwhelmingly in social science research as a shorthand reference for two groups coded for skin color. Skin color has been used as an obvious and sometimes subtle marker for other assumed differences (e.g., biological/genetic, cognitive, intellectual, social, economic, cultural). However these skin-color terms have little association with genetic and behavioral variability specifically as related to cultural practice. Superficial or even real differences that do exist between skin-color groups are often treated not as neutral differences but rather as the basis of hierarchical social systems that value and reward only the traits of one group, typically the White male. It is important to understand how research participants and researchers may derive meaning about the inherent superiority and inferiority of populations based on these arbitrary classifications and how these classifications, if used synonymously with culture, can distort or confuse how culture influences romantic experience in adolescence. It is also important to understand how the perceptions and behavior of an individual are affected by experiences with the hierarchical social systems that derive from these notions and how the person experiences associated individual, institutional, or cultural racism toward a group with which he or she identifies. (For a detailed discussion of constructs such as cultural racism and White privilege see Jones, 1997; and for a discussion of how whiteness and blackness have been used to maintain hidden signs of racial superiority, see Morrison, 1992.) Racism is experienced intensely during adolescence, according to an account of adolescence in girls from various ethnic groups by Taylor, Gilligan, and Sullivan (1995). They state that some adolescents have reported patterns of exclusion, scapegoating, capitulation, forced isolation, or relationships that they sense are false based on race consciousness.

Some Considerations in Understanding Culture and Adolescent Romance

Cross-Cultural Perspectives on Romantic Experience

Hatfield and Rapson (1996) and Hinde (1997) have reviewed much of the research on close relationships, love, and sex from a cross-cultural perspective. These reviews provide documentation for cultural variation in romance and emphasize cultural differences. The authors' review of the many diverse cultures seems to suggest that North Americans and Western industrialized societies value romantic love highly, although the significance of romantic love, as an intensely preoccupying experience, is becoming more universal than it used to be. During the Renaissance, love and physical pleasure became highly associated as a reaction to the repressive policies of the Church. This view of love as romantic passion has become the Western view of love and has distorted the principle of selflessness, which is an essential aspect of romantic love in other cultures. This distortion occurs because the overemphasis on love as passion that is perpetuated by well-known Western cultural myths tends to overshadow other aspects of romantic love. Romantic stories during the Middle Ages, such as the story of Sir Lancelot and Lady Guinevere, and later of Romeo and Juliet, and even later of *West Side Story,* further enhance this cultural outlook. Since the study of romantic love is limited, and since we have not explored fully the cultures of Africa, China, India, and the Middle East, the notion that passionate love is universal is not fully supported. A more interesting question involves determining how the developmental significance of romantic experience varies across cultures. In the United States the role of culture in romantic experience has been explored primarily among adults, largely in Western industrialized countries. Limited studies among teens focus on sexual experiences and their consequences, not on romantic relationships or romantic experience. This research is also limited because it often fails to conceptualize culture beyond static demographic references to racial or ethnic groups. Few studies explore the dynamic of culture and romantic experience or the role of romantic experience.

Sources of Cultural Influence in Adolescence

At least three cultural perspectives influence adolescents: (1) the cultural perspective of each adolescent in relation to national, ethnic group, community, and family values and mores; (2) the broader teen culture that exists in contrast to the culture of adulthood; and (3) the specific peer culture that most influences a particular adolescent. A concentric circle model that is sometimes used by ecology of development theorists best represents the superordinate relationship among these sources of cultural influence. Family culture represents the most direct source of broad cultural influence and may also include style of communicating, traditions, values, and expectations about moral and social order within close relationships (Sillars, 1995). Neighborhoods are another particularly salient dimension of this first level of cultural influence for adolescents, particularly in shaping identity, and include civic supports, churches, schools, and youth-based and community-based organizations (Committee on the Status of Black Americans, 1989; McLaughlin, 1993). The broader teen culture includes these same characteristics, often differently expressed, and is often portrayed by the media – music, films, television, and teen-oriented magazines. Adolescents are also immersed in the culture of large age cohorts and smaller peer groups that extend across a school or community context and operate as a system of values and expectations about styles, values, and the like (Brown, 1990; Larson & Richards, 1991).

National, community, and family cultural perspectives can be both general and specific. There are broad general values or worldviews that are characteristic of particular cultures. In the Western worldview and in Northern American society, great value is placed on individual expression of freedom and choice. This can be contrasted with the Eastern worldview, in which what is seen as best for the social group to which one belongs is more important than individual freedom and choice. More specific cultural perspectives within the broader culture may be those of an ethnic or cultural group with which one chooses or is forced to identify. Also, it is often the case that adolescents are categorized into socioeconomic and racial groups that are thought to overlap with some ethnic and/or cultural groups.

Adolescents may or may not be aware of these cultural perspectives, but they are probably influenced by them. In some cases, adolescents do not have to or may not choose to identify with a cultural group. In the

United States, adolescents who belong to the dominant ethnic group – European – which often corresponds with the group classified as White, do not have to or choose to identify with an ethnic group and most often are not classified as ethnic by others. They may think of themselves as American, treating this as an ethnic group. This privilege is not often claimed by or extended to adolescents who belong to ethnic groups that are not European, such as adolescents who are of African, Asian, Native American, or Hispanic descent. The choice of whether or not to belong to an ethnic group within the larger North American society is one that may have some influence on how much culture influences romantic experience. For example, adolescents who claim a specific ethnic identity may be more susceptible to cultural influence and more able to describe its influence.

The Reciprocal Relationship Between Culture and Romantic Behaviors

The Concept of Romantic Behavior as Cultured and Culturing Experience. Most developmental theories suggest that relationships between social interactions and developmental behavioral outcomes are bidirectional. That is, social relations influence and are influenced by behavioral outcomes. Romantic behavior as a cultured experience and a culturing behavior suggests that a reciprocal and dynamic exchange can exist between cultural practices and romantic experience, and between the romantic behavior of an individual adolescent and cultural practices. Adolescent romantic behavior is characterized by dynamic changes over *cohort time,* and these changes may influence what is acceptable cultural practice for an adolescent at any point in historical time.

Cultured Romantic Experiences. Romance is an acculturating or cultured experience because it always occurs within the context of specific cultural expectations. The cultural practices adolescents experience influence how they perceive and engage in romantic behaviors. The occasion of romantic experience can open a window of opportunity that allows parents and other socializing agents to use these adolescent experiences and interests to teach an adolescent about some aspects of cultural expectations, specifically about romantic choices and behavior, within the socializing cultural group. It can also afford the adolescent the opportunity to learn about aspects of the romantic partner's culture through shared activities. In order to understand how romance is a cultured experience, it is necessary to understand variations in cultural, ethnic group, and family practices that relate to the adolescent stage of development, as well as the adolescent's peer group culture. Often organizations are created to foster ethnic vitality and use dance, music, drama, and art to create ethnic cohesion and to divert adolescent interest from negative influences (Ball & Heath, 1993). These organizations are also sources of culturally relevant information about romantic experiences.

Adolescents exist within large cultural and smaller ethnic groups. Cultural and ethnic characteristics are both group and individual characteristics. One can characterize the group using superficial characteristics like social expectations, but an individual adolescent may not display the characteristics of the group despite claiming membership or being assigned membership by others. Adolescents assimilate a variety of lessons about romance from their particular culture and so are cultured about romance. Adolescents who do not feel strictly bound by the cultural expectations of their group might choose a romantic partner or custom from a different cultural group and, by doing so, may be criticized by members of their own cultural group. This criticism serves to teach or culture them about what is acceptable romantic behavior and romantic partners. This may include emphasizing or deemphasizing heartfelt desires for a particular type of companion. This issue is discussed further, using examples from Cole (1996), in the section on operationalizing culture in research.

Romantic relationships that cross cultural or ethnic boundaries may be particularly significant in shaping or teaching culture to adolescents. This ethnic group boundary crossing might be a type of risk behavior for some adolescents. In cases where romantic partners are from similar cultural backgrounds, romance provides cultural experiences, but these experiences may be less salient in reinforcing values, attitudes, and traditions, particularly romantic ones, since they don't draw as much attention to the romantic partners. Cross-ethnic relationships, on the other hand, draw more attention and thus may be more meaningful in acculturating the adolescent about what is acceptable. Cultural influences on romantic experience take on a particular significance if one romantic partner is from an ethnic group that often enjoys special privilege and power and the other is from a group that is disenfranchised. In these cases, the partner who is disenfranchised may use the romantic liaison as a way of being cultured into the other partner's group. This probably occurs only late in adolescence intentionally, but it may occur unintentionally earlier in adolescence. In the opposite case, an adolescent from a more powerful cultural group may use romantic liaisons to reject cultural practices they wish to escape or deny. Young or midadolescent girls described as white sometimes express romantic interest in boys who are members of ethnic minorities by U. S. Census standards or boys who could be characterized as lower income or from a different religious or cultural background. This boundary crossing can elicit a number of responses in a parent all of which, except completely ignoring the adolescent, let adolescents know that their behavior has some influence on their parents and their own destiny. Social agents responsible for providing an adolescent with cultured experiences either stress or deemphasize romantic liaisons at particular ages, and there is probably some degree of cultural variation found here.

Romantic Behavior as a Culturing Process. An adolescent who resists the assimilation of romantic lessons from his or her culture of origin may play a role in bringing about some cultural change or may be a culturing agent in that particular group. These individuals seem to be willing to cross boundaries, which may allow them to participate in culturing their particular group and render them willing to accept something new or different in unacceptable romantic practices or partners. This may also be true of youths who do not resist a cultural ideal but who also conjointly follow other cultural traditions, along with their own, elaborating on them and using them to influence their own cultural traditions. Also, when an adolescent chooses an unacceptable romantic partner, this often alerts those adults responsible for providing cultured experiences to shape the adolescent's thinking toward what is expected by the larger cultural group, as described earlier. Conflicts that arise result in the adolescent's either being cultured or, if he or she resists this strongly, in being a culturing agent. This may be especially likely to happen when adolescents from several diverse cultural or ethnic groups identified in the United States, or in another large sociopolitical context with several cultural groups, coexist.

Another example of how adolescent behavior may influence cultural practices is found in the phenomenon of group dating among young adolescents. It has gradually become more common for romantic exchanges and social interaction with romantic partners to occur in unsupervised group settings and in group dates, particularly among younger adolescents (see also Brown, this volume). This may account, in part, for the greater acceptance and expectation among parents and other social institutions of dating at younger and younger ages. Examples of this reciprocity can also be seen in how the peer group culture often influences adolescents to be romantic or to be romantic in a specific way. Individual behavior, however, also influences the peer group's acceptance of particular romantic rituals and behavior. The influence of adolescent culture on society, as seen in and created by the film, music, and television media, is also an example of how reciprocal relationships between culture and adolescent behavior operate. For some adolescents, these influences may be more unidirectional, with film, music, and print media messages teaching adolescents how to behave romantically. On the other hand, many superficial aspects of the peer culture of some African-descent adolescents often seem to be copied and "sold" to many other cultural groups, as in the case of hip-hop music and the wearing of athletic sneakers and head gear.

Cultural Perspectives on Some African-Descent Adolescents and Romantic Behavior

Characteristics of Indigenous African-Descent People Relevant to Romantic Experience

Among some African American adolescents who are descendants of U.S. slaves, there are a number of cultural characteristics that may distinguish them from adolescents from other ethnic groups, including some others of African descent, like some Puerto Ricans, Haitians, Jamaicans, and African-continent immigrants. These characteristics, although not extensively or comprehensively documented, have been described in various ethnographies about indigenous African Americans (Burton, 1990; Stack, 1974) and in other research on African American families (Cauce, Higara, Graves, Gonzales, Ryan-Finn, & Grove, 1998; McAdoo; 1993). This cultural group has been contrasted with European Americans in terms of worldviews or basic cultural values by Myers (1978) and Hilliard (1976). The worldview of this group consists of many elements, only a few of which are discussed here.

It has been suggested that a traditional African worldview would include a focus on self-knowledge; spirituality and the interdependent web of creation; an unconditional love orientation; and a focus on connectedness to the group. In contrast a European American worldview would stress external knowledge or facts based on numbers and counting; materialism and competition; conditional love, based on appearance, for example; and primacy of individual concerns over those of the group. Other cultural values/characteristics that have been emphasized, but not studied well, among indigenous African Americans are religiosity, an emphasis on mother–daughter relationships, and primacy of the extended family (Cauce et al., 1998; McAdoo, 1993; Taylor, 1988). Taylor et al. (1995) present an ethnographic description of girls' cultural stories and describe some African-descent girls as experiencing a free flow of information from their mothers about relationships, including romantic ones. They seem to learn considerably more about their mothers' frustrations and joys in romance than do girls they described as white or Hispanic. Carothers (1990) has also described this in a sample of African-descent girls. These characterizations may be getting at some fundamental differences in cultural perspective between these large cultural groups that may relate to romantic experience, but they are problematic in that they are characterized too broadly to be applicable in specific face-to-face interactions. Among indigenous African Americans, there are probably several ethnic groups that share some similar cultural characteristics and that have some characteristics that are unique. However, there are no definitive studies to help us understand this or to clarify how these orientations are expressed among adolescents as an aspect of peer culture. Orientation to religion, use of language or a particular dialect of American English, orientation to work and achievement, parenting practices, styles of intimacy and social exchange, and music preferences are examples of some characteristics that might distinguish among ethnic groups within the indigenous African-descent cultural group and between and among European-descent and other cultural groups.

The Oppositional Frame of Reference

Indigenous African Americans are an involuntary immigrant group, unlike other African-descent groups and other ethnic and cultural groups that have immigrated to the United States. Ogbu (1994) suggests that this creates another cultural difference that he describes as an *oppositional cultural frame of reference.* This frame of reference can be thought of as a cultural inversion. Using the European–Western cultural tradition as a standard, Ogbu suggests that some African American adolescents consciously or unconsciously reflect the opposite values, traditions, mores, and so on in their behavior. This serves to indicate that they are not dominated or subsumed by a European cultural perspective. Some African-descent ethnic groups, through constant struggle and conflict with a dominant cultural group, create an oppositional cultural frame of reference as a way of defending themselves against being unaccepted, socially or economically, into the cultural mainstream. The oppositional culture acts as a protection or defense that helps to maintain a sense of self-worth in a hostile environment (Ogbu, 1994). An obvious example of this is found in language use. African-descent ethnic language, and some other cultural forms such as jazz and rap music, are constantly being created as aspects of this language and culture are incorporated into the mainstream by European-descent Americans. This incorporation renders them somewhat useless in maintaining the oppositional and self-enhancing cultural framework.

The phenomenon that Ogbu terms an oppositional frame of reference could also be interpreted as striving for a unique identity in a context that affords little recognition of one's personhood (Fordham & Ogbu, 1986). Indigenous African Americans often use unique names for their children, that is, names with unusual spellings and pronunciations. This may be a way of establishing a unique identity for the child in anticipation of the racism and social isolation that the child may encounter. Cross (1995) provides a similar interpretation of the positive value of *oppositional identity* as part of the pathway to self-esteem. He characterizes oppositional identity as an appropriate early developmental defense against the reality of racism and as a precursor to the development of an ethnic identity. It is also useful as a way to encounter a culture that does not include the individual and a healthy position from which to attempt inclusion in other cultural groups.

Romantic Behavior as Cultural Adaptation in the Oppositional Framework. It is possible that indigenous African-descent young women may experience serious romantic role conflict when they attempt to integrate oppositional perspectives on what to expect in a romantic partner and what to expect from themselves as a romantic partner with other views of romantic behavior. They may idealize European romantic notions while also tending to be more pragmatic about the complexities and difficulties of a romantic relationship. This pragmatism, often learned from their mothers, as described by Carothers (1990), teaches them what not to expect from a romance and about the things that can go wrong in romantic relationships. They also are not likely to experience much validation from the broader culture for their more pragmatic view of romance and so tend to struggle more with adopting a positive image of themselves as a romantic partner. Most young women in the United States grow up with stories about heterosexual romance in which the male romantic partners appear to be wild, fantastic, and able to transform themselves at will into other personas. The focus in these stories is not on the female as the object of the romantic episode but rather on the power that the male romantic partner has over himself and ultimately over her. Hamilton (1995) has collected a set of such stories found in the oral tradition of African-descent persons in the United States.

In early adolescence, these girls may tend to adopt a more European view of romantic possibility and develop idealized scripts, reflecting what the broader European population expects, about a romantic partner, namely, passionate, idolizing love. Anderson's (1990) ethnographic account of the sex and family codes among some African inner-city poor youths suggests that this is the case. This may not be true of all adolescents from African-descent backgrounds because many have experienced different cultural influences. Some of these young women may adopt an oppositional framework to survive numerous assaults on their self-worth. In doing this, they may change their views of romance and become more pragmatic, expecting less and less and, even in late adolescence, beginning to shun romantic entanglements. This allows them to devalue romance and preserve their integrity by convincing themselves that they don't need a Western-type romantic partner. They adopt a "what's in it for me?" attitude that often focuses on material gifts as a reflection of romantic interest by a partner. They may also come to think of themselves more and more as undesirable romantic partners.

For many African-descent adolescents, an oppositional cultural frame of reference or one that strives for uniqueness coexists with cultural practices that are viewed by these adolescents as mainstream. Some African-descent adolescents have created distinct romantic rituals that are similar to, and often merge over time with, those of the dominant culture. These include ritualistic dancing know as *slow* dancing and being excessively affectionate in public. There may be other practices that fit this pattern or stem from this oppositional frame of reference that are not well documented. African-descent adolescents are aware of how their dating and romantic practices fit or don't fit with what happens among European and other cultural and ethnic groups. Therefore, as Miller and Goodnow (1995) suggest, this creates a situation that makes it necessary to accept multiple identities or to become extremely isolated within the oppositional framework.

It is possible and often desirable, in a society where several cultural perspectives coexist, to adopt various cultural points of view. This multicultural perspective may increase interpersonal and intrapersonal flexibility, thus increasing opportunities for self-development and achievement of developmental goals. Adolescents who adopt multiple cultural and ethnic group identities may be more likely to cross cultural boundaries for romantic experience and thus encounter opposition or acceptance by a variety of cultural groups. How these scenarios affect development for these adolescents has not yet been addressed.

Cultural Isolation Among Indigenous African-Descent Girls

It is fairly well documented that adolescent peer groups are described as segregated both racially and socioeconomically (e.g., Steinberg, 1996). Damico and Sparks (1986) found that girls described as Black were most likely to be socially isolated among Black boys and among White boys and girls. Because of this isolation based on skin color, some indigenous African-descent girls who belong to socially isolated peer cliques may be most likely to have limited cultural experiences and least likely to learn about the cultures of other ethnic groups through romantic exchange. This social isolation for some African American girls, in comparison with other adolescents, makes it more likely that these girls may miss opportunities to participate in the larger adolescent peer group culture, and they may develop severely oppositional dating behavior that may incorporate characteristics such as increased expectations for sexual intimacy and for material tokens of affection. They may also be more likely to accept oppositional cultural norms in dating behavior from African-descent boys. This isolation may also make it more likely that parents' values about romantic experience are challenged and disregarded, since parents may become less oppositional (i.e., conservative in values) because of their parental role and adult status. These girls may develop more oppositional perspectives on romantic expectations, with respect to ethnic and family values, since they may need to do more to protect their self-esteem given their peer-based social isolation. Among this group, girls who do cross ethnic boundaries for romantic exchange may have a unique opportunity to explore whether cross-cultural romantic exchange enhances self-esteem or whether self-esteem is a precursor to being able to have a cross-cultural romantic relationship. It is not possible, given the limitations of this chapter, to discuss all of the ways in which oppositional identity relates to other important variables such as socioeconomic status, individuation processes, or how an oppositional identity may be intensified or accelerated in romantic liaisons, but these considerations also merit attention. It is also important to consider how these processes occur for isolated boys. Anderson (1990) has conducted some preliminary work on lower-income, inner-city, African-descent boys' need to use sexual conquests to enhance their status, since other forms of competition in the larger society are often unavailable to them. However, this work, although interesting and insightful, may not be generalizable to other populations of African-descent youth.

The Majority Rule

The terms *majority group* and *minority group* are also relevant to a discussion of cultural considerations, and of African-descent and other ethnic groups. These terms reflect a current but diminishing social and statistical reality in the United States. That is, some groups are larger and more dominant, often through physical force and ideological universality, and thus can consider themselves the majority, whereas other groups are smaller and less dominant and are referred to by the dominant group as the minority. However, this majority status is alleged by persons who claim to be White through a hegemonic valuing of one shared characteristic – so-called White skin. The U. S. 1990 Census[1] classifies about 76% of the population as "white, not of Hispanic origin." The remaining population is classified as falling into distinct skin color or ethnic groups creating a majority and a minority group. The Census could have classified persons by some different ethnicity system that made many more ethnic distinctions, but instead it created a majority White group that reflects a social reality in the U.S. but not the global population (e.g., White persons make up about 6–10% of the global population, clearly not a majority). Many of the persons listed as "other" and as "non-White" may view themselves as belonging to more than one race or ethnic-origin group. In fact, most persons probably have ancestors from more than one of these classifications. European-descent persons in the United States tend to blur ethnic and race distinctions among themselves, perhaps because this gains them access to privilege, and over the years more ethnic groups have been considered White. This allows one group to maintain a majority status and gain privilege by allowing only what they term non-White persons to be ethnic and therefore minorities. Because these classifications exist and are often associated with other discriminatory social practices, members of these minority groups often have to include collective experiences of oppression and exploitation as part of their ethnic identity (see Phinney, 1996) and thus cannot often remember and value their own culture. The group labeled White also often does not enjoy the protection of belonging to a distinct and unique cultural group. This loss of culture because of these designations can make explorations of cultural influence difficult. This also raises a host of issues when members of the dominant group conduct research on minority groups based on their own experiences, since they tend to devalue cultural influence.

The tension and conflict of being bicultural, that is, part of a minority culture in a majority cultural situation, create tensions and conflicts that express themselves as some minority parents try to teach their adolescent to have an ethnic identity but also to fit into the broader majority culture (Peskin, 1991; Taylor et al., 1995). Both the cultural orientation of a group and an individual's adaptation or acculturation to that group must be considered in charting cultural influence. LaFromboise, Coleman, and Gerton (1993) outline an alternation model that posits that a person can usually gain competence in two cultures, achieving an identity in both and moving between them. Sometimes this cultural shifting may take place across more than two cultures. It is important to note that all adolescents "have culture," that is, their behavior is part of a particular set of dynamic cultural experiences. Most social science research has assigned ethnic group classifications to all but White or European-descent adolescents. This approach limits both theory and methodological approaches to understanding the impact of cultural values on romantic experience in adolescence and vice versa. As the majority finds its own individual cultures and discovers how someone from the majority shifts among them, rather than assuming that one cultural reality represents majority culture, cultural variation in all cultural groups can be better examined.

Identity and the Developmental Significance of Romance

Establishing an identity is a primary developmental process that receives heightened attention during adolescence and has been studied extensively by developmentalists (Steinberg, 1996). Identity emerges as a result of certain maturational processes, but the expression of an identity is largely dependent on the cultural or social context. The process of identity development, as well as the type of identity that emerges, depends largely on the historic, geographical, cultural, and social status characteristics of an individual. Romantic experience, also bound by these same characteristics, may play an important role in establishing an identity during adolescence. Research on how romantic experience shapes the self is especially informed by looking at cultural variables, particularly if one uses a looking-glass or symbolic interaction perspective on the origins of self (Coates, 1985). Some cultural groups may stress the value and importance of romantic relationships, and it may be that among these adolescents romantic experience plays a significant role in the development of identity. Exploring the relationship between identity and romantic experience may offer an opportunity to move beyond a cultural differences approach in understanding cultural influences on romantic experience to one that focuses on differences in the developmental significance of romantic experience for identity and for other important aspects of the mind. We understand very little about how this might occur, but several important areas of theory and research point to interesting directions for future work. Some of these will now be discussed.

The Window of Ethnic Identity

An earlier discussion of race, racism, and majority versus minority designations is useful in thinking about the development of identity and the significance of ethnic identity and romantic experiences in shaping identity. Ethnic identity may be the closest mirror of the self since, as Allport (1954/1958) suggests, we all cling to our own families, ethnic groups, or clans because our self could not be itself without them. Unfortunately, most studies of how identity is related to ethnicity and culture have been focused only on so-called ethnic minorities and have used a cultural differences approach (see the reviews by Frable, 1997, and by Porter & Washington, 1993). They also have tended to use small and somewhat unique samples and therefore are limited in generalizability. Research and theory on the development of ethnic identity among the most common ethnic groups in the United States by Phinney (1989, 1992), Cross (1995), Cross and Fhaegan-Smith (1996), Spencer and Markstrom-Adams (1990), and Pyant and Yanico (1991), for example, largely describe differences across broad ethnic groups.

The questions of how ethnic identity may influence the pursuit of romantic relationships and how romantic experiences may shape ethnic identity is also important. These questions may lead to a better understanding of how ethnic identity shapes the overall identity of adolescents. Adolescents who must accept an ethnic identity sometimes represent themselves as having two identities. They either refer to themselves as Filipino, Italian, Mexican, *and* American or as being Black and able to "act White." In an ethnographic study of ethnicity and achievement in a multiethnic high school, Peskin (1991) found that this duality in self-representation existed among many students. These adolescents are usually aware of the need for more than one identity and of the importance of situational fluidity in identity. Acting White, for example, is an option accepted for some students who do so in the classroom, where they want to achieve so as to fulfill personal goals. Because of this awareness, they may be better able to articulate how romantic experiences are related to identity processes. On the other hand, the process may not be so accessible since adolescents in multiethnic schools tend not to discuss ethnicity (Peskin, 1991). More detailed accounts of how adolescents experience ethnicity choices and reactions to these choices are needed before we can clearly understand how this process operates.

Peskin (1991) also reports that adolescents in the multiethnic school that he observed operated in a climate where no one ethnic group was considered more acceptable than the others. This situation may create opportunities to cross ethnic boundaries for friendship and for romantic partners. Adolescents who cross ethnic boundaries, whether in multiethnic situations or situations where they are socially isolated, offer interesting opportunities to study how identity influences romantic choices and how romantic experiences shape identity. It may be that students who see themselves as Mexican and American, or as from an African heritage but able to adopt some European behaviors, will be more willing to cross boundaries. Romantic experiences may have a unifying effect on identity in adolescents in whom the distinction between the dual traditions is weak, but it may tend to sharpen distinctions among adolescents who have more clearly articulated views of themselves as coming from one or the other ethnic tradition. Ethnic identity may have more salience for African-descent adolescents with a long history of social isolation and experiences with communities that devalue their cultural orientation. In this case, these adolescents might tend to view the characteristics and existence of a romantic partner as an important component of ethnic identity.

The Relevance of Social Identity Theory. Social identity may play a more significant role in the lives of adolescents who are forced, often by skin color, to accept a particular ethnicity. Psychologists who study group processes have pointed out how groups strive to maintain individual identity and a place within a particular social context and political system. Group processes have been critical for creating social change. This has been demonstrated by the group process among persons of African descent that provided critical impetus to the civil rights movement in the United States and among other groups seeking change in Eastern Europe and in South Africa more recently (see Abrams & Hogg, 1990, for a further discussion). Cultural perspectives are often at the heart of ethnic group striving to maintain a social identity. Often these identities are linked to maintaining social traditions in addition to creating social change that seems necessary to the group's well-being. These group cultural perspectives often may lead to individual identity as persons who are identified, either voluntarily or involuntarily, as members of the group try to determine their relationship to the group's cultural perspectives. In understanding the cultural influences on adolescent romance, it may be important to begin with an assessment of whether or not individuals know that they are part of an ethnic group, how they value that ethnic group membership, and more specifically how they interpret group messages and rules regarding romantic relationships. Social identity theory suggests that group membership plays a central role in identity formation and self-enhancement through motivational processes (Abrams & Hogg, 1990). Understanding how these group identity processes and motivational processes operate in choosing a romantic partner may be critical to creating an accurate picture of how cultural practice influences romantic behavior in adolescents. An especially interesting situation may involve adolescents who choose particular romantic partners as a way of denying or enhancing their identity (see Deaux & Ethier, 1998, for a fuller discussion of social identity processes). In these considerations, it is also important to note the distinctions necessary between social and personal identities and the complex relationships between multiple identities that most persons negotiate, as discussed by Deaux (1993).

The Special Case of Marginal-Status Adolescents. Some indigenous African American adolescents, especially those who develop an oppositional identity, may provide an especially distinctive window on how the development of identity is related to romantic experience. Because the social conditions of minority status require these adolescents to develop an intensely ethnic identity that is often attacked and devalued, it may be that romantic experiences have more salience for them. These adolescents generally have undervalued status in the larger society and may look to romantic partner characteristics or to the number of romantic partners as a way to enhance their self-esteem. Adolescents whose current and future social status is perceived to be marginal understand that they are embedded in a society that does not value their potential contribution. This may increase their identity achievement need and the need for validation of identity through romantic experience. Although this may occur for all adolescents, the particular sociocultural conditions of minority status adolescents may make this validation of identity through romantic experience more intense, and it may occur earlier in their development. It may occur earlier because the need for self-validation and enhanced self-esteem is greater in these adolescents than it is in other adolescents who may not be aware of these needs until much later, when the process of individuation begins. Marginal adolescents may seek to increase their status through romantic relationships. Therefore, romance may have greater salience for them. The ending of relationships may seem more threatening, devastating, and debilitating to these adolescents. They may also seek out multiple romantic relationships simultaneously and engage in more intense romances in an attempt to compensate for identity and status needs that are not met through other sources of social validation. This hypothesis needs further development and elaboration, but it holds some promise for understanding the romantic behavior of some adolescents. Gay and lesbian adolescents of African descent may also represent an especially marginalized group. These adolescents may find that their ethnic identity is less salient than a gay identity, but this depends on a number of factors and needs to be explored further (Greene, 1996; see also Diamond, Savin-Williams, & Dubé, this volume).

Self-efficacy and Romantic Experience. Romantic experience may also play an important role in activating aspects of identity such as self-efficacy. Bandura (1995) suggests that individuals rely on emotional and physiological mood states to judge their performance. Thus, these mood states are a source of efficacy beliefs, and they influence the nature and function of self-efficacy. Some romantic experiences during adolescence may function to enhance a positive mood and thus increase perceived self-efficacy. In other cases, romantic experiences that stimulate a despondent mood may reduce self-efficacy. Because romantic experiences are a source of mood elevation or depression, they may influence how self-efficacy develops. Self-efficacy beliefs are strongly linked to cognitive, motivational, affective, and selection processes (Bandura, 1995). They are therefore essential to the overall well-being of an adolescent, and romantic experiences may be a key factor in explaining these self-efficacy beliefs. For a further discussion of this topic, see the chapter by Larson, Clore, and Wood in this volume.

How does the experience of romantic relationships affect self-efficacy for African American adolescents? This process may also be more intense for these adolescents because experiences that contribute to self-efficacy and competence are less available to some of them due to racism and racist stereotypes about their abilities or family and social circumstances. Since some of their first strong feelings of self-efficacy may come from successful romantic experiences, rather than from experiences in other areas, such as academic achievement, these experiences may buffer them from the inability to obtain the benefits of self-efficacy beliefs that arise from other sources of these beliefs. These relationships merit further exploration.

The Significance of Developmental Timing in Romantic Experience

The timing of events and experiences is a key conceptual framework in the study of development and is well documented in the study of biological and psychological events (Turkewitz & Devenny, 1993). Lerner, Perkins, and Jacobson (1993) discuss the central role of interactional timing for biological and contextual variables that is central to a developmental-contextual view of development. This point of view stresses that individual diversity occurs because of the vast array of differences in the timing of interactions between organismic and cultural variables that exist and create developmental change. It may also be true that the planned or cultured timing of romantic experiences with biological development may vary across cultures. In other words, particular patterns of the timing of romantic experiences with biological events may exist within cultures and vary across cultures. For example, in some cultures initiation of romantic experiences may be timed to occur with the appearance of secondary sex characteristics, whereas in other cultures this initiation could be encouraged earlier or much later than the biological events because of a particular cultural group's desire to delay or accelerate reproduction. This need to accelerate or delay reproduction could also be viewed as an individual's attempt, within the developmental-contextual framework, to try to shape his or her own developmental change. Individuals could be helped to time events so that passionate romantic experience occurs only when they are ready to form long-lasting relationships that may lead to reproductive outcomes. Some of the variation in the rates of teenage sexuality and pregnancy, and failures of pregnancy interventions among some cultural groups, might be better explained from this point of view.

Another issue of timing has to do with which type of cultural influence is most salient at a particular point in the developmental trajectory of romantic experience. Different types of cultural influences, such as family, peers, and the media, on romantic behavior may be more salient at different points along the trajectory of romantic experiences that are possible in adolescence and beyond. These influences may vary across cultural groups. For example, expectations of parents and messages from the media may be more salient in influencing romantic behavior in preadolescence and early adolescence, whereas the peer group culture is probably the most important influence in middle adolescence. Family, national and ethnic influences become more salient in late adolescence and young adulthood. This timing by influence interaction may vary by cultural group and may be observed by examining patterns across ethnic groups. Ethnic groups may only represent generalized, stereotypic monoliths of culture and may not approximate the dynamic of cultural influences one needs to explore in studying cultural influence on development. For example, although African-descent adolescents exist in a larger culture that often makes them very conscious of the low status of their ethnic identity and of various cultural practices associated with being of African descent in the United States, not all of them internalize this influence in the same way. Some African-descent adolescents may be intensely focused on their ethnic identity early in adolescence and consequently on how particular romantic partners may increase their social status. Thus, they may experience peer group influences on romantic experiences much earlier than African-descent adolescents who do not focus on this aspect of their experiences. The significance of cultural influence on romantic relationships may also be a function of the type of romantic relationship being considered. Romantic relationships that are casual, for example, may be more influenced by the peer group and the media, whereas more serious, long-term relationships may be more influenced by family and neighborhood cultural values and customs. Although the initiation of these different types of romantic relationships may correspond with a developmental period, this may not always be the case.

Questions and Issues in Developing a Research Agenda on Culture and Romantic Experience

Several research directions have been implied in this discussion of culture and romantic experience. In addition, there are a number of strategies and issues that need to be considered in charting a research agenda that explores the relationships between culture and romantic experience. In summary, based on the preceding discussion, there are four categories of concern that are highly relevant for understanding cultural influences on romantic experience and the developmental significance of romantic experience as a function of culture: (1) operationalizing culture and cultural influences on behavior; (2) avoiding misleading normative interpretations of adolescent experiences; (3) using research designs that are sensitive to developmental timing; and (4) seeing the big picture: identifying important issues and questions for future research.

New Ways to Operationalize Culture

A number of social scientists have suggested that previous approaches to the study of culture in general, and in the case of African Americans and other ethnic minorities, are seriously flawed (Betancourt & Lopez, 1993; Cole, 1995, 1996; Stanfield, 1993). These criticisms focus largely on how poorly cultural characteristics have been conceptualized and measured. Using ethnic categories and terms like *racial* and *ethnic/racial groups* perpetuate a misunderstanding of culture and racist attitudes about the inherent superiority of persons designated as White or as having no ethnicity or race/genetic designation, as is the case in many studies. These ethnic/race categories are assigned to individuals without understanding what specific cultural practices, interactions, and activities they are meant to represent. Indeed, they are assigned, analyzed, and interpreted without exploring the degree of overlap and uniqueness associated with prevailing cultural practices observed the United States that exist across static assignments to ethnic groups. There is some appreciation of the limitations of ethnic group categorizations like White and Black and the assumptions of particular ethnic groups (e.g., African Americans, Hispanic or Latino Americans, European Americans). However, this idea is not well integrated into research designs. Rather than trying to develop a system of smaller and more precise groupings of ethnic membership, it might be more instructive to develop better descriptions of cultural practices from the perspective of key individuals that may represent segments of an ethnic group.

Miller and Goodnow's (1995) *cultural practices* approach to understanding how culture influences development defines *cultural practices* as what people can be observed to do that are open to the observation of a researcher and/or a social group. Usually this is thought of as recurrent, repeated sequences of activities (Miller & Goodnow, 1995; Scribner & Cole, 1981). Although this approach would be adequate for understanding some aspects of romantic experience, such as ritualized dating practices and the public display of romantic feelings, it cannot address internalized experiences like "falling in love" and "falling out of love" or the more spiritual aspects of love's selflessness.

Cole (1996) also suggests several other ways in which we could redefine how culture is considered in research. He suggests that cultural psychology must be transformed from a cross-cultural psychology to a psychology that represents Wilhem Wundt's *second psychology.* This view of cultural psychology would shift the emphasis from culture as an independent variable to culture as the dependent variable. The assumption that culture cannot be separated from experience and behavior is paramount here. There are several important assumptions or characteristics of an approach that does not separate culture as an independent variable from mind, thought, or behavior, as suggested by Cole (1996), for studying adolescent romantic experiences: (1) mediated action in a context must be emphasized; (2) the analysis must be grounded in everyday life events; (3) mental development occurs as a joint, mediated activity of many people; (4) individuals are the active agents in their development but often do not act in settings of their own choosing; and (5) methodologies and sources from the humanities, and from the social and biological sciences, are useful. It is important to note here that this paradigm shift, changing the study of culture from an independent to a dependent variable, would require a major reconsideration of psychology's traditional logical-positivist research designs and assessment strategies. Principally this would require a shift, as Cole (1996) suggests, from the use of concepts like *context* and *situation* to the use of terms like *activity* and *practice,* particularly at the level of the individual mind. Ethnic group analyses are useful only in determining the supraindividual unit of analysis. This overarching level, sometimes viewed as the cultural situation, does not easily show how culture is experienced by the individual and is a source of influence. It merely provides a starting point for understanding cultural influence. We cannot get a complete view of how culture is expressed as romantic behavior by studying romantic behavior across different cultural groups. Understanding variations in individual actions and choices, and in how artifacts and practices are mediated by individuals, requires a different kind of design focus as the unit of cultural analysis described by Cole (1996) is interpreted here.

This research paradigm may be guided best by in-depth ethnographic studies of individuals, who may be targeted as having experience within particular cultural niches, rather than conducting cross-cultural studies to begin to understand the supraindividual level of culture. This will afford us the opportunity to gain the necessary details that allow understanding of cultural practices. The study of life narratives is a qualitative methodology that might well suit this research objective (for examples, see Josselson & Lieblich, 1995). Approaches might include exploring stories about first romantic encounters and the array of subsequent romantic experiences for an individual, from romantic liaisons to passionate romantic love. Several ethnographies about a particular segment and set of experiences of African-descent people in the United States offer some useful perspectives on how to address the inherent biases and distortions that exist when researchers from outside of a cultural perspective, and with certain powers and privileges, do research on that culture (Anderson, 1990; Burton, 1990; Gilyard, 1991). Journalists sometimes can also provide useful ethnographies of the cultural experiences of a particular group. David Zucchino's sympathetic portrait of the daily struggles and stresses of one family living on public assistance is an example (Zucchino, 1997). Self-examination of status considerations, privilege, and power in relation to how data gathering is prescribed and data are interpreted may also help researchers who enter other cultural groups to avoid some pitfalls in interpreting these cultural stories. Crossing over into another cultural group to interpret that group's experiences, usually known as *cross-cultural research,* should not be done casually. Cross-cultural research is defined here as research that is conducted when someone with one set of cultural practices enters another culture to interpret it. It may be important to use adolescents and members of particular cultural groups to collect these cultural descriptions. Obviously, what adolescents may be willing to tell another adolescent who is involved, for example, in cross-cultural dating may be very different from what they might tell a graduate student or senior researcher with whom they do not share any cultural similarities.

Avoiding Misleading Normative Interpretations of Adolescent Romantic Experience

Often a Western scientific approach to reality assumes that if this tradition hasn't heard of, discovered, or found a phenomenon, then it does not exist. In studying romantic love and romantic experiences among adolescents, it is assumed that these constructs are meaningful within the same material reality that exists for European-descent adults. It may be that we have misconceptualized the romantic experiences of some cultural groups using the notion of passionate, emotionally based love. Is it beyond the capacity of the academic or scientific communities to acknowledge that perhaps this is not the basis of romantic experiences among some adolescents? This question needs to be explored in research questions that challenge traditional notions of romantic experience.

Using Traditional Research Designs That Are Sensitive to Developmental Timing and Reciprocal Relationships Among Cultural and Psychological Variables

For some research questions, longitudinal and cross-sequential designs that examine differences in romantic experiences may be particularly instructive given the nature of romantic experiences and cultural influences. In studying the intersection of romance and culture using traditional psychometric and ethnographic approaches, it may be instructive to consider whether the developmental influence of culture on romantic experience is sensitive to developmental period. Several questions emerge from this consideration that help to shape a research agenda. For example, are the broad cultural practices that an early adolescent is exposed to more important in shaping orientations toward romance in early adolescence or is the culture of the peer group more significant later in adolescence?

It may be that generalized teen culture and broad cultural practices are more salient early in adolescence, peer culture in middle adolescence, and family and community practices in late adulthood. Such a timetable may vary by ethnicity. Research on culture and romantic experience should explore the impact of critical periods for cultural influence. It is also important to include in our research agenda studies of how romantic experiences and interactions shape or change cultural perspectives of groups and of individuals as a corollary to understanding how culture affects romantic experiences. Hughes, Seidman, and Williams (1993) offer some helpful considerations when using these traditional approaches that may allow researchers to examine how the cultural perspectives of the researcher and the research participants influence major phases of the study.

Seeing the Big Picture: Other Important Issues and Questions

It is not possible to present an exhaustive taxonomy of how culture and romantic experience could be studied, yet such a taxonomy needs to be developed. Explorations of how romantic experience is influenced by culture and how culture influences romantic experience can help us to appreciate how some watershed developmental goals are achieved during adolescence. We understand a good deal about such phenomena as increased intimacy in relationships with peers and decreased intimacy in relationships with parents during adolescence (Rice & Mulkeen, 1995; Steinberg, 1996; Youniss & Smollar, 1985) and about representation of self and others in interpersonal relationships during adolescence and adulthood (Banaji & Prentice, 1994; Berscheid, 1994; Harter & Monsour, 1992; Steinberg, 1996). An exhaustive taxonomy of the features of indirect and direct cultural influence that are potentially or actually related to romantic experience might include several factors. Some obvious candidates are (1) personality traits that are valued in a particular culture (e.g., introversion, extroversion, compliance, individualism); (2) value placed on the expression of intimacy within a relationship both privately and publicly; (3) gender role orientations; (4) age norms for social behaviors; and (5) representations of romantic behavior in the media. Peer group and family characteristics might include (1) meanings, linguistic and otherwise, ascribed to intimacy; (2) communication patterns about intimacy and romantic exchange; (3) patterns of attachment; (4) orientation toward self-efficacy; and (5) exposure to intimate violence.

Implications for Practice from Perspectives on Culture and Romance

It is difficult to draw conclusions about practical settings in which we find adolescents and the potential for romantic experience when research findings are so limited. However, one strategy that may have some merit is developing clinical and intervention strategies that stem from considerations of how oppositional identity functions to affect the romantic and sexual behavior of young, indigenous African American girls. A better appreciation of the impact of social isolation on African American girls' identity and the mediating role of this on perceptions of romance and romantic behavior may offer more effective strategies for addressing problems like teenage pregnancy than have been explored in the past. Social network analysis interventions, which build social networks to improve support resources and enhance self-esteem, previously described by Coates (1990), may be useful here. A second strategy involves integrating an understanding of masculinity among indigenous African American boys into clinical and school-based applications. Some of the perspectives articulated here, particularly those related to oppositional identity and to racism in U.S. society, may be helpful in articulating interventions that emphasize the unique forms of masculinity that have developed among African American males. Frustrations they have experienced in other roles (e.g., provider, protector, community leader) may have been channeled into more intense male bonding than might be seen in other groups (Franklin, 1994). This intrasex bonding may be more developed than in other cultural niches and therefore more important in developing intervention strategies with this group. Majors (1994) offers helpful suggestions in this regard.

Future research data that are generated using some of the strategies just outlined may be quite useful for professionals in clinical practice and in schools that are trying to help teenagers handle sometimes painful and difficult romantic situations. These strategies hold more promise than traditional cross-cultural psychometric approaches for providing details that lend themselves to useful and meaningful applications.

A Concluding Comment

This chapter has outlined and briefly discussed a subset of the many complex issues related to the study of culture and romantic experiences. The chapter stressed the importance of considering the reciprocal nature of culture and romantic experience. It also outlined how romance must be considered as both an experience that teaches culture and as behavior that can shape the cultural practices of a group or an individual. Therefore, romance is both a cultured and a culturing experience. Examples drawn primarily from the cultural experiences of African American youth, using a national, ethnic group, worldview, community, and family values perspective, were offered to illustrate the concepts discussed. The chapter also recognized the contributions to romantic experience of other cultural perspectives, such as that of adolescent culture. Identity may be a central construct from which to understand culture and romantic experience, and aspects of ethnic identity may be very sensitive to romantic experiences.

Note

1. The U.S. Census population classification terms are political categories and do not reflect self-selected terms that many ethnic groups prefer, such as *Latino/Latina* instead of *Hispanic,* and so on.

References

Abrams, D., & Hogg, M. A. (1990). *Social identity theory: Constructive and critical advances.* New York: Springer-Verlag.

Akbar, N. (1994). *Light from ancient Africa.* Tallahasee, FL: Mind Productions and Associates.

Allport, G. (1954/1958). *The nature of prejudice.* Garden City, NY: Doubleday Anchor Books.

Anderson, E. (1990). *Streetwise: Race, class and change in an urban community.* Chicago: University of Chicago Press.

Appiah, K. A. (1992). *In my father's house: Africa in the philosophy of culture.* New York: Oxford University Press.

Appiah, K. A. (1996). *Color conscious: The political morality of race.* Princeton, NJ: Princeton University Press.

Ball, A., & Heath, S. B. (1993). Dances of identity: Finding an ethnic self in the arts. In. S. B. Heath & M. W. McLaughlin (Eds.), *Identity and inner-city youth: Beyond ethnicity and gender* (pp. 69–93). New York: Teachers College Press.

Banaji, M., & Prentice, D. A. (1994). The self in social contexts. *Annual Review of Psychology, 45,* 297–332.

Bandura, A. (1995). Exercise of personal control and collective efficacy in changing societies. In A. Bandura (Ed.), *Self efficacy in changing societies* (pp. 1–45). New York: Cambridge University Press.

Berscheid, E. (1994). Interpersonal relationships. *Annual Review of Psychology, 45,* 79–129.

Betancourt, H., & Lopez, S. R. (1993) The study of culture, ethnicity and race in American psychology. *American Psychologist, 48,* 629–637.

Brown, B. (1990). Peer groups. In S. Feldman & G. Elliott (Eds.), *At the threshold: The developing adolescent* (pp. 171–196). Cambridge, MA: Harvard University Press.

Burton, L. (1990). Teenage childbearing as an alternative life-course strategy in multi-generational black families. *Human Nature, 1,* 123–143.

Carothers, S. (1990). Catching sense: Learning from our mothers to be black and female. In F. Ginsburg & A. L. Tsing (Eds.), *Uncertain terms: Negotiating gender in American culture* (pp. 233–247). Boston: Beacon Press.

Cauce, A. M., Higara, Y., Graves, D., Gonzales, N., Ryan-Finn, K., & Grove, K. (1998). African American mothers and their adolescent daughters: Closeness, conflict and control. In B. J. Leadbeater & N. Way (Eds.), *Urban adolescent girls: Current research and future trends* (pp. 100–117). New York: New York University Press.

Coates, D. L. (1985). Relationships between self-concept measures and social network characteristics for black adolescents. *Journal of Early Adolescence, 5,* 319–338.

Coates, D. L. (1990). Social network analysis as a mental health intervention with African American adolescents. In F. C. Serafica, A. I. Schwebel, R. K. Russell, D. D. Isaac, & L. B. Myers (Eds.), *Mental health of ethnic minorities* (pp. 5–37). New York: Praeger Press.

Coates, D. L., & Vietze, P. M. (1996). Cultural considerations in assessment, diagnosis and intervention. In P. J. W. Jacobson & J. A. Mulick (Eds.), *Manual of diagnosis and professional practice in mental retardation* (pp. 243–256). Washington, D.C: American Psychological Association Press.

Cole, M. (1995). The supra-individual envelope of development: Activity and practice, situation and context. *New Directions for Child Development, 67,* 105–118.

Cole, M. (1996). *Cultural psychology: A once and future discipline.* Cambridge, MA: Belknap Press of Harvard University Press.

Committee on the Status of Black Americans (1989). Identity and institutions in the black community. In G. D. Jaynes & R. M. Williams, Jr. (Eds.), *A common destiny: Blacks and American society* (pp. 161–204). Washington, DC: National Academy Press.

Cross, W. E., Jr. (1995). Oppositional identity and African American youth: Issues and prospects. In W. D. Hawley & A. W. Jackson (Eds.), *Toward a common destiny: Improving race and ethnic relations in America* (pp. 185–204). San Francisco: Jossey-Bass.

Cross, W., & Fhagen-Smith, P. (1996). Nigrescence and ego identity development: Accounting for differential black identity patterns. In P. Pedersen, J. Draguns, W. Lonner & J. Trimble (Eds.), *Counseling across cultures (4th edition).* Newbury, CA: Sage Publications.

Damico, S., & Sparks, C. (1986). Cross-group contact opportunities: Impact on interpersonal relationships in desegregated middle schools. *Sociology of Education, 59,* 113–123.

Deaux, K. (1993). Reconstructing social identity. *Personality and Social Psychology Bulletin, 19,* 4–12.

Deaux, K., & Ethier, K. A. (1998). Negotiating social identity. In J. K. Swim & C. Strangor (Ed.), *Prejudice: The target's perspective* (pp. 301–323). New York: Academic Press.

Farber-Robertson, A., & Spencer, L. (1996). *Journey toward wholeness: The next step from racial and cultural diversity to anti-oppression and anti-racist multiculturalism.* Boston: Universalist Association Press.

Fordham, S., & Ogbu, J. (1986). Black students' school success: Coping with the burden of acting white. *The Urban Review, 18,* 176–206.

Frable, D. E. S. (1997). Gender, racial, ethnic, sexual, and class identities. *Annual Review of Psychology, 48,* 139–142.

Franklin, C. W., II. (1994). Men's studies, the men's movement, and the study of black masculinities: Further demystification of masculinities in America. In R. G. Majors & J. U. Gordon (Eds.), *The American black male: His present status and his future* (pp. 3–19). Chicago: Nelson-Hall.

Gilyard, K. (1991). *Voices of the self: A study of language competence.* Detroit: Wayne State University Press.

Goodnow, J., Miller, P., & Kessel. F. (Eds.). (1995). *Cultural practices as contexts for development,* Special Issue, *New Directions in Child Development, 67.* San Francisco: Jossey-Bass.

Greene, B. (1996). Lesbians and gay men of color: The legacy of ethnosexual mythologies in heterosexism. In E. D. Rothblum & L. A. Bond (Eds.), *Preventing heterosexism and homophobia* (pp. 59–70). Thousand Oaks, CA: Sage.

Hamilton, V. (1995). *Her stories: African American folktales, fairy tales and true tales.* New York: Blue Sky Press.

Harter, S., & Monsour, A. (1992). Developmental analysis of conflict caused by opposing attributes in the adolescent self-portrait. *Developmental Psychology, 28,* 251–260.

Hatfield, E., & Rapson, R. L. (1996). *Love and sex: Cross-cultural perspectives.* Boston: Allyn & Bacon.

Hinde, R. (1997). *Relationships: A dialectical perspective.* Hove, East Sussex, U.K.: Psychology Press.

Hughes, D., Seidman, E., & Williams, N. (1993). Cultural phenomena and the research enterprise: Toward a culturally anchored methodology. *American Journal of Community Psychology, 21,* 687–701.

Jones, J. M. (1997). *Prejudice and racism* (2nd ed.). New York: McGraw-Hill.

Josselson, R., & Lieblich, A. (Eds.). (1995). *Interpreting experience: The narrative study of lives* (Vol. 3). Thousand Oaks. CA: Sage.

LaFromboise, T., Coleman, H. L. K., & Gerton, J. (1993). Psychological impact of biculturalism: Evidence and theory. *Psychological Bulletin, 114,* 395–412.

Larson, R., & Richards, M. (1991). Daily companionship in late childhood and early adolescence: Changing developmental contexts. *Child Development, 62,* 284–300.

Lerner, R. M., Perkins, D. F., & Jacobson, L. P. (1993). Timing, process and the diversity of developmental trajectories in human life: A developmental contextual perspective. In G. Turkewitz & D. A. Devenny (Eds.), *Developmental time and timing* (pp. 41–59). Hillsdale, NJ: Erlbaum.

Majors, R. G. (1994). Conclusion and recommendations. In R. G. Majors & J. U. Gordon (Eds.), *The American black male: His present status and his future* (pp. 299–315). Chicago: Nelson-Hall.

Markus, H. R., Kitayama, S., & Heiman, R. J. (1997). Culture and "basic" psychological principles. In E. T. Higgins & A. W. Kruglanski (Eds.), *Social psychology: Handbook of basic principles* (pp. 857–913). New York: Guilford Press.

Marimba, A. (1992). *Yrungu: An African-centered critique of European cultural thought and behavior.* Trenton, NJ: World African Press.

McAdoo, H. (Ed.). (1993). *Black families.* Newbury Park, CA: Sage.

McLaughlin, M. W. (1993). Embedded identities: Enabling balance in urban contexts. In S. B. Heath & M. W. McLauglin (Eds.), *Identity and inner-city youth: Beyond ethnicity and gender* (pp. 36–68). New York: Teachers College Press.

Miller, P. J., & Goodnow, J. J. (1995). Cultural practices: Toward an integration of culture and development. *New Directions for Child Development, 67,* 5–16.

Morrison, T. (1992). *Playing in the dark: Whiteness and the literary imagination.* Cambridge, MA: Harvard University Press.

Myers, L. (1984). The psychology of knowledge: The importance of world view. *New England Journal of Black Studies, 4,* 1–12.

Myers, L. (1988). *Understanding an Afrocentric world view: Introduction to an optimal psychology.* Dubuque, IO: Kendall/Hunt.

Myers, L. (1991). Expanding the psychology of knowledge optimally: The importance of world view revisited. In R. L. Jones (Ed.), *Black psychology* (3rd. ed., pp. 15–28). Berkeley, CA: Cobb & Henry.

Nobles, W. (1985). *Africanity and the black family: The development of a theoretical model.* Oakland, CA: Black Family Institute Publication.

Nobles, W. (1989). Psychological nigrescence: An Afrocentric review. *The Counseling Psychologist, 17,* 253–257.

Ogbu, J. U. (1988). Cultural diversity and human development. *New Directions for Child Development, 42,* 11–29.

Ogbu, J. U. (1994). From cultural differences to differences in cultural frame of reference. In P. M. Greenfield & R. R. Cocking (Eds.), *Cross-cultural roots of minority child development* (pp. 365–392). Hillsdale, NJ: Erlbaum.

Peskin, A. (1991). *The color of strangers, the color of friends: The play of ethnicity in school and community.* Chicago: University of Chicago Press.

Phinney, J. S. (1989). Stages of ethnic identity in minority group adolescents. *Journal of Early Adolescence, 9,* 34–49.

Phinney, J. S. (1992). When we talk about American ethnic groups, what do we mean? *American Psychologist, 51,* 918–927.

Porter, J. R., & Washington, R. E. (1993). Minority identity and self-esteem. *Annual Review of Sociology, 19,* 139–161.

Pyant, C. T., & Yanico, B. J. (1991). Relationship of racial identity and gender-role attitudes to black women's psychological well-being. *Journal of Counseling Psychology, 38,* 315–322.

Rice, K. G., & Mulkeen, P. (1995). Relationships with parents and peers: A longitudinal study of adolescent intimacy. *Journal of Adolescent Research, 10,* 338–357.

Scribner, S., & Cole, M. (1981). *The psychology of literacy.* Cambridge, MA: Harvard University Press.

Shweder, R. A., & Sullivan, M. A. (1993). Cultural psychology: Who needs it? *Annual Review of Psychology, 44,* 497–523.

Sillars, A. L. (1995). Communication and family culture. In M. A. Fitzpatrick & A. L. Vangelist (Eds.), *Explaining family interactions* (pp. 375–399). New York: Sage.

Spencer, M. B., & Markstrom-Adams, C. (1990). Identity processes among racial and ethnic minority children in America. *Child Development, 61,* 290–310.

Stack, C. B. (1974). *All our kin: Strategies for survival in a black community.* New York: Harper & Row.

Stanfield, J. H., II. (1993). Epistemological considerations. In J. H. Stanfield II & M. D. Rutledge (Eds.), *Race and ethnicity in research methods* (pp. 16–36). Newbury Park, CA: Sage.

Steinberg, L. (1996). *Adolescence,* (4th ed.). New York: McGraw-Hill.

Taylor, J. M., Gilligan, C., & Sullivan, A. M. (1995). *Between voice and silence: Women and girls, race and relationship.* Cambridge, MA: Harvard University Press.

Turkewitz, G., & Devenny, D. A. (1993). Timing and the shape of development. In G. Turkewitz & D. A. Devenny (Eds.), *Developmental time and timing.* Hillsdale, NJ: Erlbaum.

Youniss, J., & Smollar, J. (1985). *Adolescent relations with mothers, fathers and friends.* Chicago: University of Chicago Press.

Zucchino, D. (1997). *Myth of the welfare queen: Portrait of women on the line.* New York: Scribner.

14   What's Love Got to Do with It?

Adolescents' and Young Adults' Beliefs About Sexual and Romantic Relationships

Julia A. Graber, Pia R. Britto, and Jeanne Brooks-Gunn

Over the past 30 to 40 years, dramatic changes have taken place in our society in adolescents' and young adults' entry into sexuality, marriage, and parenting. The links between sexual activity and marriage began to erode with increased options for contraception, changes in societal norms, and opening up of economic opportunities for women (Alan Guttmacher Institute [AGI], 1994; Furstenberg, 1995, in press; Smith, 1994). Subsequent eroding of the link between the establishment of a stable marriage as a necessary condition of parenting has occurred due to myriad social policies and societal norms on divorce and the support of children (Cherlin, 1988; Furstenberg, 1995). Adolescent and young adult transitions to sexuality, marriage, and childbearing occur in parallel with, although not necessarily as a result of, the development of romantic relationships.

In our culture, a prevailing belief is that sexual intimacy is inappropriate if it does not occur in the context of love, and often a legally or religiously sanctioned arrangement (i.e., marriage). However, the strength of this belief varies across historical periods; the dimension of the relationship; and the gender, age, and context of the individuals involved. The timing and co-occurrence or patterning of sex, love, and stable, long-term relationships occur in societal and historical contexts (Elder, 1974, 1985; Hagestad, 1986; Hardy, Astone, Brooks-Gunn, Shapiro, & Miller, 1998; Hareven, 1977). Thus, the beliefs and behavior of youth are shaped by historical, economic, familial, and social forces that define appropriate behavior and, ultimately, expectations for relationships. Such factors have also shaped the

The authors were supported by grants from the National Institute of Child Health and Human Development (NICHD; HD24770, HD32376) during the writing of this chapter. We would also like to acknowledge the support of the NICHD Research Network on Child Well-Being and the National Institute of Mental Health Family Research Consortium.

formation of social policies over time, resulting in an interconnected set of forces that influence adolescents' beliefs and expectations about the role that stable, romantic relationships will play in their adult lives.

Drawing upon examinations of sexual behavior, marriage, and child-bearing from multiple disciplines, we provide support for the hypothesis that youth growing up in low-income environments experience a loss of confidence in long-term relationships and their stability. These altered expectations influence subsequent decisions for the timing of childbearing. To delineate this thesis, we provide an overview of the connections among sexual behavior, relationships, and childbearing. Expectations and behaviors are examined in adolescent and young adult relationships in the areas of commitment and length of relationships, fidelity, and the timing of marriage and childbearing, as well as how public policy influences expectations and childbearing. Again, some experiences may apply to the lives of many youth, whereas other experiences are most influential or unique to a sub-group of youth. Both types of processes or experiences are considered in connection with how and for whom contextual forces influence adolescent expectations and behaviors.

Whereas other chapters in this volume consider the developmental processes involved in different aspects of romantic relationships, such as the meaning of relationships in the lives of adolescents, how individuals develop these relationships, and types and progressions of such relationships, our focus is on the factors that shape expectations for relationships. In particular, we are considering the effect of different contexts of adolescent experiences on the expectations and behaviors of youth as they begin to take on adult roles and behaviors. Our discussion is limited to romantic relationships with other-gender partners and to those romantic relationships that include sexual exploration and ultimately intercourse. We are not considering romantic relationships that do not have a sexual component; that is, we are not focusing on the types of romantic relationships or experiences in relationships that may be precursors to sexually intimate relationships. For example, dating, falling in love, "crushes," and the like may or may not lead to or include a sexual component; hence, these experiences are not our focus.

Adolescence has generally been considered a period of transition from childhood to adulthood, with commensurate changes in nearly every aspect of the adolescent's life as the individual progressively acquires the various roles of an adult (Graber, Brooks-Gunn, & Petersen, 1996; Lewin, 1939). With a more adultlike appearance and expectations on the part of peers, family, and the self for more adultlike behaviors, adolescents begin to construct expectations for romantic relationships and begin to engage in them. Constructions of expectations for relationships are based not only on an individual's present interests and desires, but also on his or her perceptions of what adult relationships and behavior are like. This is not to say that children enter adolescence as a tabula rasa in terms of their ideas about relationships; certainly children have been exposed to familial and cultural beliefs about relationships, perhaps since they were first cognitively aware of a connection to another caring human being (Edwards, 1995; Maccoby & Martin, 1983; Stein & Trabasso, 1989). However, during adolescence, personal exposure to romantic relationships begins more fully, as has been noted by many, if not all, of the contributors to this volume. In addition, individuals advance in their ability to conceptualize their future and make longer-term plans (Keating, 1990; Nurmi, 1991). Thus, beliefs about romantic relationships and their eventual outcomes become more salient in the adolescent years.

Connections among Sexual Behavior, Relationships, and Childbearing

One question is whether there is an endpoint or "mature" outcome that results from the development of the romantic lives of adolescents. Because there is presently so much variation in how adults define and engage in romantic relationships, it is difficult to identify what the mature state is. One approach is to consider what role such relationships serve in the lives of adults. From this approach, stable, long-term romantic relationships have served historically and culturally as the basis for childrearing, with most couples marrying prior to having children (Furstenberg, Levine, & Brooks-Gunn, 1990; Johnston, Bachman, & O'Malley, 1995; Smith, 1994). Thus, a primary outcome of the development of romantic relationships in adolescence and young adulthood has been marriage and childrearing. In fact, national surveys indicate that most adolescents expect to marry and rate having a stable, happy marriage as very important to them (Johnston et al., 1995). However, although the desire for marriage is still prevalent, this goal is not universal since some individuals do not want to marry.[1] Also, the ideal age at which one expects to marry has increased over the past few decades, with clear variations by social class, to be discussed in more detail later (Bingham, Stemmler, Crockett, & Petersen, 1995; Graber & Brooks-Gunn, 1996a). Not all youth who value or desire the goal of marriage perceive it as attainable in their adult lives (Cherlin, 1988; Furstenberg, in press).

We contend that increased instability in romantic relationships (or at least the perception that stability is an unlikely aspiration) has an effect on the expectations and choices that adolescents and young adults make about their future relationships. That is, perceived instability of romantic relationships has probably not eroded the *desire* for romantic relationships, but instead may have altered the *structure* of the romantic relationships in which adolescents and young adults engage or hope to attain. Historic or social changes may influence the expectations and behaviors of many or all youth, whereas economic or familial factors may be altering the expectations and behaviors of a subset of the population of youth who live in unique economic or family situations. Young adults and teens, who have fewer financial and educational resources, are those most likely to enter into nonmarital relationships when starting a family (National Center for Health Statistics, 1993).[2]

It might be asked why we examine trends in sexual behavior or its connection to marriage in a discussion of forces that shape beliefs about romantic relationships. There are several answers to this question. The first and perhaps most obvious one is that although sexual behavior and romantic relationships are not synonymous for adolescents or adults, the two overlap. At least for earlier cohorts of youth (i.e., high school students in North Carolina and Florida seen in the early 1980s), about one-quarter of the adolescents seen in a large survey study indicated that they had their first intercourse experience in the context of a stable dating or romantic relationship, as indexed by "going steady," and another 30% of adolescents indicated that their first partner was someone they knew well and liked a lot even if they were not actually going steady (Rodgers, 1996). In addition, fewer than 15% of adolescents surveyed in the North Carolina survey study reported that this was their only sexual experience with that partner (Rodgers, 1996). Although these data are less than adequate proxies for describing adolescent relationships, it has certainly been accepted that one aspect of negotiating romantic relationships in adolescence, and undoubtedly in adulthood, is learning how to manage sexual desires and behaviors (Brooks-Gunn & Furstenberg, 1989; Brooks-Gunn & Paikoff, 1997).

The second reason for considering the role of sexuality as a potential component in adolescents' relationships is that parents and adults in general, and society overall, have a vested interest in regulating the sexual behavior of youth. In fact, nearly every society has mechanisms for doing this (Brooks-Gunn & Paikoff, 1993, 1997). The desire for limits and regulations on sexual behavior among unmarried youth stem from moral beliefs about the acceptability of premarital sex, as well as the need to regulate out-of-wedlock childbearing (Brooks-Gunn & Paikoff, 1993, 1997; Zabin & Hayward, 1993). Increasing rates of pregnancy and out-of-wedlock childbearing among adolescents and young adults over the past 25 years (AGI, 1994) would suggest that regulation of sexual behavior, either by others or by adolescents themselves, has deteriorated, at least for some youth. Thus, figuring out how to manage sexual behavior while at the same time developing healthy relationship skills has been an ongoing challenge for youth faced with their own desires for physical and emotional intimacy and with parental and societal pressures for limiting these behaviors.

Finally, trends in out-of-wedlock births indicate that both the belief in the link between marriage and childbearing and beliefs about the attainability of marriage are changing in connection with or at least parallel to one another. In particular, the United States has the highest rate of teen pregnancy in the industrialized world. In 1995, the rate was 57 births per 1,000 adolescent girls between the ages of 15 and 19 (Child Trends, 1997). About half as many boys as girls become parents prior to age 20; boys are also more likely to be older rather than younger teens when they become parents (AGI, 1994). Even though the birth rate is no longer increasing, the number of teens is increasing, so the number of births to adolescents has begun to increase. Thus, adolescent mothers, in particular, are a significant subgroup within the population of adolescent girls.[3] Of note is that out-of-wedlock childbearing is more common in certain contexts than others; specifically, it is more common in poor neighborhoods, among lower-income families, and among youth with less education (Brooks-Gunn, Duncan, Klebanov, & Sealand, 1993; Furstenberg, Brooks-Gunn, & Chase-Lansdale, 1989; Hofferth & Hayes, 1987).

Adolescent mothers have less education than their peers, are less likely to be employed, if they are employed have lower-wage jobs, overall have lower incomes, are more likely to be single parents, and, if they marry, are more likely to divorce (Brooks-Gunn & Chase-Lansdale, 1995; Furstenberg et al., 1989; Hofferth & Hayes, 1987). Thus, several of the correlates of adolescent motherhood make it much less likely that these adolescents will move out of poverty. In addition, poverty increases the risks faced by young mothers and their children due to exposure to high crime and overcrowding, lowered residential stability, difficulty in coping with the demands of daily living, reduced social support, and reduced access to services (Brooks-Gunn & Chase-Lansdale, 1995; Halpern, 1993; Osofsky, Hann, & Peebles, 1993). Beliefs and expectations for relationships among low-income youth are likely to be associated with who chooses to have children in the adolescent or young adult years and who chooses to have children out of wedlock. It should also be noted that we most often discuss out-of-wedlock childbearing and related issues in connection to income rather than race. Race and income are often confounded in examination of these issues; however, in the few studies that have examined processes by both race and income, similarities are often found across racial groups for youth in similar income groups (e.g., Hardy et al., 1998).

For the reasons reviewed, it is of interest to consider adolescent beliefs about relationships and their behaviors in them. It is also clear that the behaviors and expectations of youth growing up in low-income environments, including families and neighborhoods, or of youth who choose to become parents as teens may be different from those of other youth. These differences are no doubt predicated on environments in which these youth grow up and the unique constraints that these contexts may place on adolescent and young adult relationships. In the following sections, we consider aspects of the association of sex and romantic relationships and the potential effect that different adolescent relationship patterns may have on subsequent choices pertaining to marriage and childbearing. We focus on how some experiences may be more common to most adolescents and how some experiences may apply to only some adolescents.

Sex Within and Outside of Committed Romantic Relationships

We have argued previously that sexual intercourse among adolescents has become a normative behavior, at least when considering the actual behavior of adolescents (Graber, Brooks-Gunn, & Galen, 1998). Adolescents and children are bombarded with sexual messages in their everyday immediate environment. Advertisements, MTV and other television programs, their friends, and adult society all paint an enticing and permissive picture of sexual behavior. Thus, sex has come to be viewed by adolescents as integral to teen life (Sugland, Wilder, & Chandra, 1996). However, it is important to note that even though adolescents may view sexual intercourse as normative for themselves or their peers and even though premarital intercourse has become more accepted for adults, most adults still believe that it is not acceptable for adolescents to have intercourse (Smith, 1994).

The extent to which intercourse is linked to committed or romantic relationships varies among adolescents. The past century has seen dramatic changes in patterns of marriage and sexual behavior, with the most rapid behavioral changes occurring in the past 30 years. Currently, even though expressions of sexual behavior are seen as the foundation of committed relationships, they are not limited to them (Thompson, 1994). In examining age at first intercourse and the contexts in which it occurs, as well as patterns of intercourse, there are three significant shifts in sexual behavior and marriage that are of note for the present discussion. First, it became more acceptable, at least for adults, to engage in intercourse in nonmarital relationships (provided that neither party was married); thus, the rates of first intercourse prior to marriage rose. Historically, societal norms were that sexual behavior was confined to the establishment of a permanent relationship as sanctified by marriage (Smith, 1994). Due to economic changes and the entry of women into the labor force, postponement of marriage for women to older ages has contributed to the growing acceptance of premarital sexual activity (Furstenberg, 1995). For example, 23% of women born in the years 1951–1955 had their first sexual intercourse with their husband (i.e., after marriage) compared to 2% of women born in the years 1971–1975 who had had intercourse (National Center for Health Statistics, 1997). This trend represents a distinct generational shift in beliefs as to whether intercourse should be confined to marital relationships.

Second, the number of unmarried adolescents who have had intercourse increased dramatically over the past 30 years. Since the 1960s, there has been an increase in sexual behavior, in particular intercourse, among adolescents. (See AGI, 1994, and Miller & Benson, this volume, for reviews of rates and historical trends in age at first intercourse.) There is some evidence that factors that differentiated the sexual behavior of youth are disappearing. Specifically, prior differences among girls based on family income are disappearing such that girls from higher-income families are about as likely to have intercourse during middle to late adolescence (ages 15–19) as girls from low-income families (AGI, 1994; Forrest & Singh, 1990).

Finally, among adolescents, there has been an increase in the number of adolescents having sex at earlier ages. Again drawing upon information compiled in the late 1980s (AGI, 1994), approximately 23% of 14-year-olds, 30% of 15-year-olds, 42% of 16-year-olds, 59% of 17-year-olds, and 71% of 18-year-olds reported having had intercourse. Each of these factors has contributed to the variability in patterns of sexual behavior within and outside of relationships that is exhibited among adolescents.

In general, nonmarital sexual behavior has become the most common context for intercourse for adolescents and young adults; notwithstanding this fact, romantic relationships are seen as a prerequisite for sex. As indicated, in surveys conducted in the early 1980s, about 25% of both boys and girls had intercourse for the first time with someone with whom they were going steady, and another 30% indicated that their first partner was someone they knew well. In the National Center for Health Statistics survey of 1995, approximately 75% of adolescent girls (ages 15–19) who had had intercourse indicated that they were going steady with their first partner.

Only a small minority of adolescent girls have their first intercourse experience with someone they have just met. In addition, about 50% of sexually active adolescent girls take about 18 months before they have sex with a subsequent partner. Although this is not a definitive indication that they have taken the time to develop a relationship with this person, the delay does seem indicative of a continuing sexual and romantic relationship with the first partner followed by establishment of a new relationship once the first relationship ends. Thus it appears that for the most part, even though adolescents are indulging in sexual behavior, it is in the context of a committed relationship.

Several factors account for variation in the context of first intercourse and subsequent movement to another partner. The timing of initiation of intercourse (i.e., at younger or older ages in adolescence) is considered an important factor in making this transition in terms of the subsequent developmental outcomes of adolescents (Graber et al., 1998). In particular, age at first intercourse is associated with differences in type of relationship at first intercourse and with rapidity of movement from one partner to the next (AGI, 1994). For example, adolescent girls who have intercourse for the first time at younger ages move more quickly to a second partner than girls who make this transition later in adolescence. In part, this may be due to younger girls being less mature in their relationship skills overall. Consequently, the first sexual relationship of young girls may be less enduring or stable. It is also likely that such differences are associated with the propensity for younger girls to be in more casual relationships when they first have intercourse. Whereas the majority of adolescent girls report going steady with their first partner, girls who have their first intercourse experience prior to age 16 are somewhat more likely to report that this person was just a friend (15.1%) in comparison to girls who have intercourse for the first time at later ages, for whom only 7–9% were just friends (National Center for Health Statistics, 1997). Similar to other domains of adolescent functioning that are influenced by developmental transitions (Graber et al., 1998), the timing or onset of adolescent sexuality appears to have an impact on sexual behavior within committed relationships of adolescent girls.

An adolescent's sexual style is another influence on both adolescent beliefs and behavior vis-à-vis sex in committed relationships. Buzwell and Rosenthal (1996) have developed a categorization scheme of sexual style that is based on the development of a sexual identity or *sexual self*. Sexual self goes beyond selecting a sexual preference to include an individual's perceptions of her or his qualities, such as sexual efficacy, sexual self-esteem, and sexual attitudes. In a study of 470 high school students in Melbourne, Australia, five sexual styles emerged in adolescents' responses across these domains (Buzwell & Rosenthal, 1996): sexually naive, sexually unassured, sexually competent, sexually adventurous, and sexually driven. (1) The naive and unassured were more often virgins (males and females) but also included adolescents who had had intercourse. Naive youth were more often girls (76%) who reported low rates of exploration and low confidence in sexual arenas. In assessing attitudes toward intercourse within and outside of committed relationships, naive youth reported the most committed beliefs or endorsements of the need for commitment prior to intercourse. (2) The unassured were also more often virgins (74%) and more often boys (84%) who also lacked confidence in their sexual abilities and exhibited high levels of anxiety but moderate interest in sexual activity. (3) The competent group was characterized by an overall sense of comfort with their sexual attitudes and behaviors and confidence in their ability to regulate behaviors. This group had a more equal distribution of boys and girls. Interestingly, both competent and unassured youth reported that commitment was of relatively moderate to high importance for sexual behavior. (4) The adventurous group was similar to the competent group in that they were also high in confidence and comfort. In addition, these youth (85% boys) indicated high levels of exploration but lower endorsements of commitment as a prerequisite to sex. (5) Finally, the sexually driven group had very positive reports of their self-esteem and attractiveness but rated commitment in relationships prior to sex as of very little importance, at least in comparison to other groups. This group was almost exclusively composed of boys (97%) but included some virgins (29%), although fewer than in other groups.

As might be expected, these groups differed not only in their attitudes about sex and relationships (i.e., in terms of commitment) but also in their behaviors. In particular, the naive and unassured had had the fewest number of sexual partners in the past 6 months, as would be expected given that these groups were composed of more virgins than in other groups. The sexually competent group had an intermediate number of partners, and the adventurous and driven reported having more partners in the past 6 months than other groups (about 1 to 1.4 partners, respectively). Of note is that the competent group, which was the largest of the groups, was somewhat closer in behavior to the adventurous and driven than to the other groups. The sexually competent had about as many one-night stands (ever) as the sexually driven (.91 and 1.11, respectively). Interestingly, the competent youth were fairly conscientious about avoiding risky behavior in sexual situations with casual partners but were less conscientious in situations with a regular partner, that is, someone with whom they had a reasonably permanent relationship. The competent adolescents may be most representative of the general population of high school adolescents, although the Buzwell and Rosenthal study was not a national, representative study but was confined to Australian adolescents in public schools. This study is unique in that the construction of the sexual self is inclusive of a range of attitudes and behaviors. In addition, this approach was predictive of beliefs and behavior regarding sex and relationships.

The research to date, albeit limited, suggests that for most adolescents, sex and romance are connected. Certainly, sexual behavior has become fairly normative for youth, especially by the middle to late adolescent years. Moreover, sexual behavior frequently occurs within committed relationships. However, these relationships are not permanent for the most part, with very few adolescents eventually marrying their first sexual partner. As indicated, historical and societal shifts in normative behavior are associated with the romantic and sexual relationships of most youth. Examinations of sexual styles are particularly informative, as this approach identifies individual differences in attitudes and behaviors. The generalizability of these styles to more diverse groups of adolescents has not yet been tested.

Buzwell and Rosenthal have, however, recently found preliminary support for a developmental course from naive and unassured to competent styles (Buzwell, 1996). Precursors to sexual styles, such as familial and contextual factors that shape and differentiate the sexual styles of adolescents, are still not known. Certainly early childhood experiences in relationships, as described by Downey, Rincon, and Bonica (this volume), likely set youth on a course for subsequent sexual and romantic behaviors and perhaps sexual styles. For some youth, early familial experiences may strengthen the connection between sexual behavior and relationships such that those youth with a high need for emotional intimacy may use sex in relationships to solidify the bond. These youth may be particularly vulnerable to disappointment and perhaps to the rejection experiences described by Downey and her colleagues when these relationships end. How contextual and familial factors may influence views about stability and the expectation for longer-term relationships will be discussed in subsequent sections. Indications that intercourse is a common component of heterosexual romantic relationships for most youth do not speak to how youth manage sexuality and balance their emotional and physical desires.

Serial versus Overlapping Relationships

Along with variability in adolescents' sexual behavior in terms of the connection to a committed or stable relationship is variation in their pattern of relationships over time. That is, like adults, most youth follow a pattern of serial monogamy, maintaining fidelity to a single partner until the relationship ends (AGI, 1994). At this point, individuals move into the next relationship, again maintaining a monogamous connection, hence the term *serial monogamy*. Although this pattern is seen as the normative one for relationships, in some cases youth engage in overlapping relationships. Youth may openly choose not to commit to one relationship over another or may engage in sexual activity with another partner more secretively. The latter situations have been examined in terms of sexual betrayal or infidelity. Among married adults, it has been estimated that 50% of men and 35% of women have at some point engaged in extramarital sexual activities (see Parkinson, 1991, for a historical review). However, such reports of a lifetime history of infidelity vary substantially from large population studies of current sexual activity of married adults (Michael, Gagnon, Laumann, & Kolata, 1994). Specifically, in any one year, the vast majority of married adults (e.g., 67% in the United States, 79% in Finland) have only one sexual partner (i.e., their spouse). Very little information is available on adolescent infidelity in committed relationships, with estimates ranging from 20% to 64%, depending on how infidelity is defined (Feldman & Araujo, 1996).

Even though infidelity may be fairly common, the acceptability of infidelity is low. Feldman and Araujo (1996), in one of the few studies to examine this aspect of sexual behavior and relationships in older adolescents and young adults, investigated the attitudes and behaviors of 300 youth between 18 and 25 years of age, conducting in-depth interviews with 60 of them. They found that the majority of these youth disapproved of betrayal; infidelity was seen as a serious violation of the implicit agreement of the relationship. The only circumstances under which betrayal (defined as petting or intercourse with someone other than the partner) was considered somewhat more acceptable was when there was a magnetic attraction for the new partner or if the couple had a bad relationship. Young men were more accepting of cheating than young women, although again, such distinctions were usually between finding it totally unacceptable versus somewhat unacceptable. These findings are comparable to those of the Monitoring the Future survey, in which 60% of boys and 76% of girls indicated that limiting oneself to one partner was not too restrictive (Johnston et al., 1995).

An examination of the association between attitudes toward betrayal and actual behavior suggests that far more youth indulge in extradyadic relationships than accept such infidelities. Thirty-five percent of youth reported that they had betrayed a partner at some point in time, and 45% had been betrayed. Overall, 57% were involved in betrayal as either the betrayer or the betrayed, suggesting that those who betray are often in relationships with partners who are also engaging in this behavior (Feldman & Araujo, 1996). Clearly, there is a discrepancy between adolescent attitudes toward betrayal and the actual practice of faithfulness in a relationship. Further investigation of this discrepancy reveals that those who have betrayed are more accepting of cheating in a relationship. In addition, unfaithful youth tend to be older, come from single-parent families, have more sexual experience, and have more sexually permissive attitudes. Even though there are gender differences in the acceptability of betrayal, there are no gender differences in the practice of betrayal. One explanation for the discrepancy between attitudes toward betrayal and unfaithful behavior could be that a double standard exists; that is, there is low tolerance for the behavior of others and a higher acceptance of one's own behavior.

Strong psychological reactions have been noted in response to being betrayed in a romantic relationship. Thompson (1994) observed a range of responses in an examination of the personal narratives about sex and romance obtained from 350 adolescent girls of diverse ethnic and racial backgrounds. One set of narratives seemed to fit the romance novel approach to sex, with stories of "broken hearts." These girls responded to betrayal with emotional distress, despondency, and depression. Other narratives were more realistic and, as such, had a more optimistic attitude; the girls treated betrayal as a mistake or "getting involved with the wrong guy" and were ready to move on. In a sample of older adolescents and youth, the primary reactions to betrayal were anger, sadness, frustration, disappointment, and mistrust of the partner (Feldman & Araujo, 1996). No gender differences were observed in the emotional reactions to betrayal or infidelity. If the partner became aware of the betrayal, about two-fifths of the relationships ended because of it.

Based on the studies available, though not drawn from nationally representative samples, it appears that there is low acceptance of betrayal and infidelity. However, the practice is more common. Interestingly, there appear to be no gender differences in the practice of betrayal. Thus, most adolescents do not expect their relationships to endure, and many will have to cope with infidelity. How these experiences translate into longer-term expectations is unclear. It may be that many adolescents view these relationships as temporary and assume that their subsequent relationships in adulthood will have more stability and commitment. Alternatively, infidelity itself may not be the experience that subsequently causes an adolescent to give up the expectation for a permanent relationship. Again, Feldman and Araujo (1996) found that discovered infidelities resulted in termination of the relationship for fewer than half of youth, suggesting that these emotionally charged experiences are not the determinant of behavioral responses in relationships among youth.

Information on the expectation of maintaining a continuous monogamous relationship suggests that some girls and young women have low expectations for such a relationship. In Thompson's work (1994) with girls' personal narratives, many girls indicated that they feared being "dumped" after having intercourse with someone. Again, these feelings were most common for girls who believed the romance novel stereotype. Being seduced and abandoned was a common theme of their stories. For girls who were relating their actual experiences, these were stories of despair; for girls who were still virgins, these expectations were rationales for not having intercourse. The girls with more positive or less despairing attitudes were actually less idealizing of their male partners. These girls often acknowledged a partner's shortcomings, and hence viewed him as unreliable and likely to stray. A study with focus groups of low-income teenage mothers suggests that these mothers believe that men cannot be trusted to be faithful and eventually would let them down (Furstenberg, 1995). Teenage mothers on welfare state that they find men unreliable, and therefore often enter into relationships expecting them to fail (Maynard, 1995). Thus, some adolescent girls, especially those who have already become mothers, expect infidelity from the men with whom they are romantically or sexually involved. However, given that infidelity is so common and that youthful relationships are not usually long-lasting, it is not just teen mothers who expect their partners to be unreliable. Similar expectations may also exist for other groups of young women and men. For some youth, the expectation of betrayal and experiences of it may ultimately lead to the postponement or avoidance of marriage.

Many adolescents are entering into sexual relationships, and are faced with the task of regulating this behavior and identifying its meaning in the context of the relationship, whether it is romantic or not. Because youth engage in intercourse at earlier ages in recent cohorts than in previous cohorts of youth, they are meeting these relationship challenges at younger ages and are exploring sexual relationships when they are less prepared to consider long-term goals and consequences of these relationships. Those who enter into sexual relationships at younger ages are perhaps the most likely to experience disappointment in these relationships due to their lack of maturity. Again, the processes that lead to rejection sensitivity, delineated by Downey and her colleagues (this volume), support the notion that prior relationship experiences have dramatic effects on the subsequent coping abilities of adolescents as they engage in sexual, romantic relationships. Some youth may be particularly disheartened by infidelities or may cling to unhealthy relationships despite such infidelities because of difficulty dealing with romantic relationships.

How adolescents interpret and cope with the challenges of their relationships is certainly influenced by several environmental conditions. It may also be that youth in certain contexts are more likely to have certain relationship experiences than youth in other contexts. Less is known about individual differences in this area. As indicated, Feldman and Araujo (1996) did find that youth from single-parent homes and those who had had more sexual experiences were the ones more likely to betray partners. Such findings suggest that contextual factors are important in shaping behaviors in relationships. How expectations may be shaped can be explored more fully by examining the factors that shape expectations for marriage and childbearing.

Timing of Marriage and Childbearing

Across historical periods, the timing of marriage in particular and childbearing via connection to marriage has been influenced by economic factors. For example, at the beginning of the 20th century, individuals moved directly from the home of their parents to a home with a spouse without living independently. Hence, men, in particular, waited to marry until their middle to late 20s in order to establish themselves financially so that they could support a family of their own. By the middle of the century, the age of first marriage had declined (U.S. Bureau of the Census, 1991). Better economic conditions in the decades that followed World War II likely account for part of this trend (Modell & Goodman, 1990). That is, part of the reason that the age of marriage was able to move down in the first place was the increased or earlier prosperity of young men entering the labor force. These men were able to establish themselves sufficiently to support families. The more recent trends from 1970 to 1990 for older ages at marriage (returning to the mean age of marriage observed in 1900) may reflect, in part, changing expectations for marriage and a dramatic weakening of the link between relationships involving sexual intercourse and marriage.

In addition, trends in the timing of marriage have been associated with the entry of women into the labor force and the economic and social changes that prompted this change in labor force participation (Cherlin, 1988). Acceptability for women to enter the labor market as young adults has led to greater financial independence for many young women. At the same time, economic conditions of the middle to late 1970s required more women of all ages to enter the labor market in order to maintain standards of living for families that were previously maintained through the wages of a sole provider.

The changing social and economic milieu has clearly altered not only the national average age at marriage but also expectations on the part of adolescents for getting married. More important, given that economic conditions are not uniform across adolescents, it appears that expectations for the timing or eventuality of marriage differ by youths' economic circumstances. The majority of adolescents, when asked if they are likely to get married, answer in the affirmative. In the Monitoring the Future survey of approximately 3,000 high school youth conducted in 1993, 76% of the males and 82% of the females expected to get married (Johnston et al., 1995). Only a small percentage of youth had no plans for marriage. Of note is that among the general population of youth who participated in the Monitoring the Future survey, even though the expectation of marriage was high, youth were somewhat less confident that their marriages would last, with 59% indicating that it was likely that they would stay married (Johnston et al., 1995).

In smaller studies of adolescent development, more affluent youth reported an expected age of marriage in the late 20s (Bingham et al., 1995; Graber & Brooks-Gunn, 1996a), whereas youth in rural working-class communities expected to marry in their early 20s (Bingham et al., 1995). This discrepancy has been attributed to the fact that fewer adolescents in the rural community expected to attend college. They entered the work force immediately after high school and therefore expected to be able to support a family at an earlier age. In contrast, adolescents in poor urban environments reported very different expectations regarding the timing and eventuality of marriage. In a Baltimore study of teenage mothers and their children, many more mothers of daughters believed it was better to delay marriage until after age 25; this was true even if the daughter herself had become a teen parent (Furstenberg et al., 1990). In a sample of over 100 low-income African American teen mothers and their male partners, most of the participants felt that they would never get married (Burton, 1994).

When the timing of childbearing is examined, a different pattern emerges. In this case, for most youth, expected ages of childbearing follow expected ages for marriage. In many reports, the expected age for having one's first child followed the expected age of marriage by about 1–2 years (Bingham et al., 1995; Graber & Brooks-Gunn, 1996a). However, low-income youth have lower expectations for getting married or assume that it will be delayed substantially. Thus, these youth often decide to have children out of wedlock rather than wait for a marriage that may never happen.

The disconnection over time between childbearing and marriage is seen in the case of unwed parenthood. In the early 1960s, 41% of adolescent girls who had babies were already married when they conceived; an additional 26% of girls who conceived married prior to the birth of the child (Bachu, 1991). Thus, about 33% of girls who gave birth did not marry. In contrast, by the late 1980s, only 19% of girls who gave birth were married at the conception or birth of the child; thus, 81% of births to adolescents occurred out of wedlock (Bachu, 1991). For teen girls who become mothers, childbearing outside of marriage has become normative (Brooks-Gunn & Chase-Lansdale, 1995), with 92% of births to African American teenage mothers and 54% of births to Caucasian teenage mothers being out of wedlock. For a large number of young mothers, the father of their child is a friend or boyfriend (Furstenberg, Brooks-Gunn, & Morgan, 1987). Economically disadvantaged women with out-of-wedlock births have lower marriage rates and so are highly likely to remain single. Additionally, adolescent mothers have higher divorce rates than other adolescents (Astone, 1993).

For example, in a 30-year study of the lives of teen mothers who gave birth in the late 1960s, their children, and their children's children, about two-thirds of the first generation of young mothers in this study married soon before or after the birth of their child (Furstenberg et al., 1987). By age 20, about 38% of these young women had never married and only 16% were currently married to the father of their child. The instability of the marriages of teen mothers may be one reason that subsequent generations of teen parents have elected not to marry and why parents of these teens have not encouraged it to the same extent as prior generations.

It should also be noted that at the same time that some youth are postponing marriage and experiencing out-of-wedlock childbearing, many of these same youth are likely to form cohabiting households (Bumpass, Sweet, & Cherlin, 1991; Loomis & Landale, 1994). Bumpass and colleagues (1991) report that in the National Survey of Families and Households conducted in 1987–1988, cohabitation may in fact account for declining marriage rates among young adults with lower educational attainment. Although a popular notion was that cohabitation was occurring among college-educated young adults, resulting in these individuals living together in the college or postcollege years prior to marrying, in fact cohabitation has become most common among young adults who have not completed high school. Although many cohabitating couples indicate that they plan to marry, uncertainty about the stability of the relationship seems to be a factor in their decision to delay marriage. In addition, 40% of cohabitating couples have children living with them; these children may be offspring of the couple or of one partner from a prior relationship (Bumpass et al., 1991). Subsequent examinations of this dataset indicate that relatively disadvantaged young adults who are cohabitating are also more likely to give birth while cohabitating than are more economically advantaged cohabitators, with childbearing and cohabitation patterns varying most by economic level for White women (Loomis & Landale, 1994). Thus, those at an educational disadvantage (and therefore a likely economic disadvantage) are those most likely to choose cohabitation over marriage and most likely to have children while cohabitating.

Explanations for Out-of-Wedlock Childbearing

Several theories have been put forth to explain the rise in out-of-wedlock births. These include economic, historical, sociological, and, more recently, contextual models (Furstenberg,1995, in press; Haveman, Wolfe, Wilson, & Peterson, 1997; Uhlenberg, & Eggebeen, 1986; Willis, 1996; Wilson & Neckerman, 1986). Adolescents' loss of confidence in marriage and marital relationships, especially among low-income youth, is affected by myriad interrelated factors. In the next sections, we focus on five hypotheses that have been presented. These can be summarized as (1) the effect of changing patterns of labor force participation for men and women and gender imbalances, (2) perceptions of health and reproductive capability, (3) families over partners as a source of support, (4) advantages to men of free riding, and (5) technological change and the decline in shotgun weddings. Other explanations exist, but these seem particularly relevant in their connection to adolescents' relationships, in particular marriage. In addition, these hypotheses are often not distinct in that several factors may be at work for adolescents, which likely have a cumulative effect in predicting their behaviors.

Changing Patterns of Labor Force Participation. We have previously noted that relative prosperity in the post–World War II decades allowed individuals to marry at younger ages because they were able to obtain jobs that would sustain a family. In the 1960s and 1970s, these trends began to change, with greater numbers of women entering the labor force for social and economic reasons. It has been suggested that economic changes have had a disproportionate impact on the lives of young men, especially young African American men and non-college-educated youth from working-class and low-income families (Cherlin, 1988; Furstenberg, 1995; Wilson & Neckerman, 1986). The rapidly increasing unemployment rate among these groups of young men over the past two to three decades not only affected men's own belief in the desirability of marriage and their ability to support a family, but also influenced the expectations of their potential partners. Concomitantly among urban African American families, women became financially more stable and economically more viable than men. Thus, from an economic perspective, young African American women have a lowered expectation for getting married due to lack of available, viable partners. Wilson (1987) has argued that for African Americans the influence of economic trends, specifically unemployment rates, is not separate from marital instability. Unemployment may be more strongly predictive of marital dissolution for African American than White families, especially for those of lower income.

Unemployment in itself does not fully describe the economic disadvantage that is experienced by young African American men as they or their partners consider the desirability of marrying. Wilson (1987), in calculating a "male marriageable pool index," observed that by the early 1980s, the pool of young African American men who would be able to support a family was depleted by unemployment, along with high mortality and incarceration rates (Blake & Darling, 1994; National Center for Health Statistics, 1991). Overall, these economic patterns lead young women to assume that a traditional breadwinner, the father, will not be available to help them raise children. The conclusion for them is to have children without marrying. And in fact, only a small percentage of low-income mothers actually marry the father of their child (Testa & Krogh, 1995).

It is certainly likely that as adolescents begin to think about relationships and their expectations for romantic relationships, they also become increasingly aware of the economic world around them. Youth who grow up in the neighborhoods that Wilson describes observe the work and family formation patterns of those around them and receive direct messages from others (i.e., school counselors, parents, other adults) about the availability of jobs. Indications that adolescents actively use their observations of the world around them in developing their expectations for relationships are presented in related work by Geronimus (1996), discussed in the next section.

Perceptions of Health and Reproductive Capability. In addition to the potentially limited expectations for romantic relationships based on the availability of marriageable African American men, it has also been hypothesized that African American women have based their decisions about childbearing (e.g., earlier versus later, married versus unmarried) in part on their potential health outcomes (Geronimus, 1994, 1996). In compiling statistics on mortality and morbidity among women in both rural and urban environments, Geronimus (1994) reported that African American women experienced more serious health difficulties and experienced them at earlier ages than their White counterparts. The poorest health and the earliest onset of poor health were observed in African American women living in low-income urban environments. Geronimus (1994) observed that there is a greater prevalence of health risks in these environments, as well as a greater chance of prolonged exposure to these risks for girls growing up in these environments. One potential outcome of these differential health trajectories is that African American women living in low-income urban environments may have fewer reproductive years, so that they are more likely to have healthier offspring and fewer complications with childbearing if they give birth at younger ages (Geronimus, 1994).

When making decisions about the context of childbearing and the feasibility of entering into a stable romantic relationship prior to having children, adolescent African American girls are faced with both of these realities: (1) the decreased pool of young men who will be available to assume the roles of husband and father in the future and (2) the prospect of their own health declining at earlier ages. However, although these economic and social-contextual conditions have been documented, it may be questioned whether adolescent girls are actually aware of these issues and utilize broader contextual information when making relationship and role transition decisions. Geronimus (1996) has recently examined adolescent girls' awareness of these processes. Drawing upon interviews with pregnant African American girls from low-income urban families, she reports that at least some of these girls are using both sets of information in their decision-making processes. In particular, when asked about the oldest age at which a woman should have a child, many of these girls (67%) listed ages in the 26- to 35-year range. By comparison, only 25% of a sample of White girls reported ages in this range, and most of them listed older ages in response to the question (see also Furstenberg et al., 1990). Reasons given for curtailing childbearing by a particular age were in line with health statistics; the pregnant African American interviewees indicated concerns that a woman would die prior to raising her child if she waited past ages 26–35 to conceive. African American girls also reported firsthand experience with the death of female relatives that had made them think about these issues. Furthermore, at least some girls also considered the longevity of their partners when making decisions regarding carrying the baby to term versus abortion. In reflecting on the exposure to violence experienced by their partners, these girls may be more prone to have a child within an adolescent relationship because they know that there is a risk that their partner may not have a subsequent chance to raise a child. Such decisions appear to be made with the understanding that the adolescent relationship may be unstable or impermanent due to the threat of premature death for those youth growing up in violent neighborhoods.

Families Over Partners as a Source of Support. Young mothers' expectations for support from the father of the child, even if they anticipate that he will avoid early death or prison, influence their choice to have children out of wedlock. Some young women perceive men to be immature, spoiled, controlling, and undependable, and thus not ready to enter into serious relationships (Furstenberg, 1995). The ability of a young man to meet the economic needs rather than the emotional needs of his partner has emerged as an important factor in the expectations of marriage of low-income adolescents (Burton, 1994). In Burton's ethnographic study of teen mothers, their families, and their partners, it was clear that the girls believed that the father of their child would be unable to provide financial resources for the child. It seemed that these girls had shifted reliance for both financial and emotional needs to themselves or their families rather than to the father of the child. Many teenage mothers are able and willing to support their children using their own resources (Brooks-Gunn & Chase-Lansdale, 1995; Willis, 1996).

In one of the few studies on the role of young fathers in out-of-wedlock childbearing, Sullivan (1993b) found that many of these youth initially sought to provide support for the child and the mother. Unfortunately, given their own economic situations (e.g., joblessness or job instability), these teens were often unable to provide even basic resources such as diapers or money. The lack of support frequently resulted in tension between the young mother and father and, in some cases, between her female relatives and the young man. Ultimately, some of these young men stopped seeing the mother and the baby because it was easier than facing the failure of visiting the child empty-handed (Sullivan, 1993).

It might be argued that adolescent girls who become parents receive more support from their own families in part because their mothers were likely to be teen parents themselves; hence, patterns across generations have been established for dealing with the needs of the young mother and her child. Certainly, when compared to children of older mothers, daughters of teenage mothers are more likely to be teenage mothers themselves (Hardy et al., 1998). However, contrary to popular belief, many daughters of adolescent mothers do delay childbearing to beyond the teen years. In the follow-up study of the Baltimore sample of teenage mothers, nearly two-thirds of the daughters of the original teen mothers delayed their first birth until age 19 or later (Furstenberg et al., 1990; see also Hardy et al., 1998).

Based on the rates of teen parenthood reviewed, families in some communities (whether having a history of teen parenting or not) are more exposed to the demands placed on all generations of the family. In addition, given that the family as a whole has experienced the economic changes and social shifts that have resulted in higher rates of out-of-wedlock childbearing for poor youth, it is not surprising that the mothers of adolescent mothers may discourage reliance on the father of the child (Merriwether-de Vries, Burton, & Eggeletion, 1996).

Several studies have found that, at least for African American families, grandparents may serve as coparents or surrogate parents of their grandchildren. Many adolescent mothers continue to reside with their own parents (Chase-Lansdale, Gordon, Coley, Wakschlag, & Brooks-Gunn, 1999; Merriwether-de Vries et al., 1996). Coresidence may provide supports via pooling of resources and responsibilities. However, residing with parents is not always an advantage for adolescent mothers but varies, depending on the age of the adolescent (Chase-Lansdale, Brooks-Gunn, & Zamsky, 1994). Younger mothers appear to benefit the most, whereas older adolescents seek more autonomy in the decisions that they make as parents. Even some nonresiding single parents rely on their families for a small percentage of their financial resources (Edin, 1995).

It should be noted that these patterns have been observed most often in African American families. However, they are probably due not to undefined correlates of race but rather to the economic disparities between African American and European American families. In the few studies to have examined out-of-wedlock childbearing across generations in both African American and European American families, patterns were similar for both races (Hardy et al., 1998). More extensive research is needed in order to describe patterns of intergenerational support.

The Low Cost of Out-of-Wedlock Childbearing for Men or Free Riding. The studies just reviewed have focused on economic and social contexts that may discourage girls and young adult women from viewing marriage as an option and lead to out-of-wedlock childbearing. Of course, changing labor force participation would also influence boys' beliefs that they would be able to support a family (Willis, 1996; Wilson & Neckerman, 1986). It has been suggested that given the economic conditions for poor youth, out-of-wedlock childbearing may offer young men the alternative of "costless fatherhood" (Willis, 1996). Given the present labor force patterns, women would be more likely than men to be able to support a child. In addition, given the surplus of women in comparison to men (i.e., the male marriageability pool index), women are more likely to choose to have children out of wedlock. For jobless men who would not be able to help support a family, there are still women who wish to have children and are more likely to support them by other means.

It is important to note that more affluent women have more options in choosing a partner who would also be able to contribute to the family (Willis, 1996). For poor women, fewer men are available, as a disproportionate number are dead or incarcerated. And those who are available are likely to be unemployed, sporadically employed, or in low-wage jobs. Hence, for these men, fatherhood does not incur the costs experienced by wealthier men who expect to help support a family. Willis (1996) further asserts that these men may find it in their best interest not to marry but rather to move from partner to partner (although little evidence exists to support this premise).

The costs of not marrying are kept low for men on the margins of the employment market because young mothers who are poor may receive support through Aid to Families with Dependent Children (AFDC), their families, and/or their own work efforts. Federal laws (i.e., the Family Support Act of 1988) stipulate that unmarried women must establish the paternity of the father of the child in order to receive AFDC benefits for the child. Once paternity is established, child support is collected from fathers, often via the judicial system (Edin, 1995; Garfinkel, McLanahan, & Robins, 1994). However, Edin (1995) has found that there is often covert noncompliance on the part of single mothers in establishing paternity or assisting in tracking the fathers of their children. Often the women indicated that they knew the fathers of their children were poor and unable to make regular payments. In some cases, these women still had romantic relationships with the men, but even if they did not, they often wanted the fathers to maintain a relationship with their child. These women believed that they were more likely to receive sporadic support from the fathers of their children and to maintain the relationship, at least when the children were younger, if they did not involve the legal system in this support (Edin, 1995). Given these desires, over half of the women Edin interviewed indicated that they gave misleading or incorrect information (e.g., old addresses, wrong social security numbers) to case workers trying to locate the fathers. These women emphasized relationship issues and possible support over the demands of a system that they felt often did not work effectively in balancing diverse concerns[4] (Edin, 1995).

Technological Changes and the Decline of Shotgun Weddings. Apart from employment patterns and similar economically based reasons for out-of-wedlock childbearing, the impact of technological change on expectations and behaviors has also been put forth as an explanation for the dramatic increase in out-of-wedlock childbearing that occurred in the past 30 years (Akerlof, Yellen, & Katz, 1996). In this model, increased availability of contraception and the legalization of abortion (i.e., technological change) altered the rate of legitimization of pregnancy. Via application of game theory, Akerlof and colleagues (1996) demonstrated how marriage rates would decrease dramatically with the introduction of these technological changes. Previously, when men and women decided whether or not to have sex, there was an implicit understanding that the couple would marry if there was a pregnancy. Once changes occurred making other options available, the equilibrium of the decision-making model also changed, so that a man and woman no longer had to commit to marriage in the case of pregnancy as long as the woman chose to have an abortion. Through game theory, connections among marriage and childbearing are based on a series of choices. Women choose whether or not to have sex, given the lowered probability of marriage, and whether or not to have an abortion in the case of pregnancy. Men, in contrast, make *social choices* about whether or not to become responsible for the child after the mother chooses to have the child. This model posits that technological change resulted in women being more likely to have premarital sex and men feeling less obligated to marry a pregnant partner.

Akerlof and his colleagues (1996) found support for the technological change model in the responses of college students to vignettes that varied the availability of abortion. Interestingly, college students in the 1990s focused less on availability of technology and more on responsibility. Overall, students felt that the man was responsible to the child but not the child's mother, and many felt that a forced marriage was a bad idea. The couple in the vignettes had been dating for a year, and students often reported that this was not long enough prior to marrying. Reports on perceptions of dating and marriage examined in the 1960s provide a marked contrast. Akerlof and colleagues (1996) note that in the 1960s, a couple who had dated for a year and had an unexpected pregnancy were generally considered to have demonstrated sufficient compatibility for marriage.

In this model, technological shifts affect the willingness to marry due to changed norms for responsibility and lowered costs to both men and women for out-of-wedlock sexual behavior. In addition, there are clear influences on the expectations for all youth. Adolescents growing up after these technological changes occurred would as a group feel less connection among sexual behavior, childbearing, and marriage. Shifts in the perception of responsibility from the relationship between the couple to the relationship with offspring would also be more likely in the general population rather than for subsets of youth. In fact, there is a less clear rationale under this explanation for greater disconnections among disadvantaged youth. In such a model, adolescent girls in disadvantaged environments would need to desire children more than adolescent girls in more advantaged environments, this being the reason to risk pregnancy without the assurance of marriage. It is perhaps more likely that lower-income girls alter the timing of their desire to have children. In our own work examining the transition to adulthood among middle- and upper-middle-class young women, we have found that 16% of young women reported having been pregnant in high school or college; nearly all had had abortions (Graber & Brooks-Gunn, 1996b). The majority of these young women expected to have children, but in their late 20s or early 30s. Although game theory applications are interesting in that they consider the influence of different costs and payoffs for each choice in the model, variability is likely to exist in the costs assigned to choices for youth from different familial and economic contexts (Graber et al., 1998). Girls who perceive futures that would be curtailed by an unexpected pregnancy are probably more likely to have an abortion than are those who do not expect the pregnancy to have much influence on other life outcomes, such as continued education, or who do not expect to marry.

Policy Considerations

For poor adolescents and young adults who have children out of wedlock, there is government assistance for the support of the child if their own resources are too low. Thus, concerns over the increase in out-of-wedlock childbearing have shifted from the well-being of children to the costs incurred by taxpayers in supporting poor children. Recent reforms at national and state levels in support for poor children and families seek to influence adolescents and young adults indirectly and secondarily to reach other goals. The purposes of these reforms are to decrease government assistance to poor families and increase the responsibility of parents for the support of their children and themselves. Within the wide range of enacted changes and proposed changes in public policy that have been labeled *welfare reform* are regulations that specifically target out-of-wedlock and teen childbearing. New regulations, such as limiting the number of years that an individual may receive benefits, would apply to all potential recipients and do not necessarily target adolescent behaviors. Again, these regulations influence the lives of all single parents rather than just adolescents. Of course, lifetime limits on eligibility will have the greatest effect on those who are youngest when they first spend their allotment and must live the rest of their lives without a safety net should a crisis occur.

At the same time, the Welfare Reform Bill of 1996 has specific requirements for teenage mothers paralleling changes in some state policies over the past few years. For example, many states require adolescent girls who have children to attend school, with the intent of encouraging them to develop self-sufficiency skills (Bloom, Kopp, Long, & Polit, 1991) and to deter them from using early childbearing as an excuse for leaving school (Ianni & Orr, 1996). The Welfare Reform Bill requires all teenage mothers to stay in school in order to receive welfare benefits and Medicaid.

Another policy requires adolescent mothers to live with their families rather than independently with their child in order to increase familial responsibility for the child. As indicated, such living arrangements may not be in the best interest of the adolescent mother or her child (Chase-Lansdale et al., 1994). It is not clear whether such legislation will be sensitive to the developmental needs of older and younger adolescents.

Policies designed to establish paternity and enforce child support payments by the noncustodial parent have been addressed via national policy that has developed over the past 25 years (Garfinkel et al., 1994). Such approaches fit with the game theory models developed by Akerlof and colleagues (1996) and the Willis free-riding model in that one method for shifting the equilibrium in childbearing and marriage is to raise the costs incurred by men in out-of-wedlock childbearing. However, methods for implementing regulations in these areas and innovative programs to guarantee support payments to all children vary state by state and, in many cases, county by county (Garfinkel et al., 1994). Some of the past policies, especially those affecting the support of children by unmarried parents, may have influenced the nature of the romantic relationships of these young adults who are parents (Edin, 1995; Furstenberg, in press; Sullivan, 1993). Will new policies begun in 1996 affect romantic relationships as well?

Conclusions

In this chapter, we have considered several levels of influence on adolescent romantic relationships, with a focus on how the negotiations or expectations of sexual involvement interact with romantic relationships. At the most simple level, our argument might be summarized as encouraging attention to individual differences and the factors associated with these differences. Moving beyond this abbreviated statement, we sought to highlight the range of factors that are presently influencing the lives of youth. Numerous policies have been devised to alter the behavior of youth, especially sexual behavior. Without a careful consideration of processes and multiple levels of influence, it is unlikely that any single approach will have the desired influence.

In addition, the focus on historical, economic, social, and familial influences on sexual behavior in and out of relationships does not fully address the psychological experiences or responses to these influences on youth. Individuals seem to begin life with different affiliative needs and/or different styles for meeting those needs. Subsequent interactions with adults and early experiences with peers foster the development of skills and strategies for meeting those needs that build the foundation for the next phase of relationships – romantic and sexual interactions.

At a 1997 conference on young adult transitions, a doctoral student in sociology commented on the changing social norms concerning the acceptability of sexual relations outside of marriage, increased access to and options for contraception, and the increased ability of women to support themselves as adults. This person asked whether the final result of these historical, economic, and social changes would be the elimination of marriage. Setting aside the obvious prevalence of religious influences on the institution of marriage, the heart of the question is perhaps what role a committed, stable, long-term relationship plays in the lives of human beings. For some individuals, this type of relationship may not be necessary to meet their affiliative needs. However, the continued prevalence of such an affiliation, as institutionalized in the form of marriage, despite increased divorce rates and increasingly prevalent cohabitation, would suggest that this relationship does have a personal or psychological value to at least some individuals. Our argument does not fully address how individuals develop different affiliative needs and desires that are subsequently acted out in different childbearing and relationship patterns. For some youth, the contextual influences we have identified may be counter to affiliative desires, leading to frustration in young adult relationships when it is difficult to attain one's desired relationship. Furthermore, it may be that certain social and economic environments are altering the desire for certain types of relationships as youth find other ways to meet affiliative needs and utilize short-term strategies to meet sexual and reproductive goals.

The title of this chapter should not imply that love has nothing to do with it. Rather, this is perhaps the one question that adolescents, young adults, and perhaps humans of all ages answer in each relationship in which they try to fulfill sexual and romantic desires. Although the answer to the question is perhaps inherently personal, the range of alternative answers is determined in part by contextual forces.

Notes

1. As Diamond, Dube, and Savin-Williams (this volume) note, gay, lesbian, and bisexual youth may have different expectations for relationships than heterosexual youth. Increases in same-sex marriages (regardless of legality) would indicate that for some lesbian, gay, and bisexual individuals, their relationship goals may have commonalities with the relationships of heterosexuals. For example, regardless of sexual orientation, youth often seek committed romantic relationships in which they can express physical intimacy.

2. In the National Longitudinal Survey of Youth (NLSY), 50% of teenage fathers live with their first-born child during the initial months of the child's life (Marsiglio, 1987). In general, about 25% of children born out of wedlock live with both biological parents at the time of birth (Bumpass & Sweet, 1989). Among young adults (less than 25 years of age), cohabitators frequently have less than a high school education (Bumpass et al., 1991).

3. Most of the descriptive reports focus on the reproductive histories of girls and women. In subsequent sections, we include information on both boys and girls in relationships whenever possible.

4. Under the Family Support Act of 1988, if fathers provided child support through payments to the state (a common stipulation), the mother on AFDC did not receive more than $50 of the support collected each month, as the rest went to offset the AFDC award. This arrangement may have discouraged poor mothers and fathers from entering into formal child support arrangements. Indeed, in Edin's interviews, some mothers indicated that when the father of their child was employed, they received more support from the father if they did not use the system than if they did.

References

Akerlof, G. A., Yellen, J. L., & Katz, M. L. (1996). An analysis of out-of-wedlock childbearing in the United States. *The Quarterly Journal of Economics, 111,* 277–317.

Alan Guttmacher Institute. (1994). *Sex and America's teenagers.* New York: Author.

Astone, N. M. (1993). Are adolescent mothers just single mothers? *Journal of Research on Adolescence, 3*(4), 353–371.

Bachu, A. (1991). Fertility of American women: June 1990. *Current Population Reports* (Series P-20, No. 454). Washington, DC: U.S. Government Printing Office.

Bingham, C. R., Stemmler, M., Crockett, L. J., & Petersen, A. C. (1995). *Community–contextual differences in adolescents' expectations for the timing of adulthood transitions.* Unpublished manuscript.

Blake, W. M., & Darling, C. A. (1994). The dilemmas of the African American male. *Journal of Black Studies, 24,* 402–415.

Bloom, D., Kopp, H., Long, D., & Polit, D. (1991). *LEAP: Implementing a welfare initiative to improve school attendance among teenage parents.* New York: Manpower Demonstration Research Corp.

Brooks-Gunn, J., & Chase-Lansdale, P. L. (1995). Adolescent parenthood. In M. H. Bornstein (Ed.), *Handbook of parenting: Volume 3, Status and social conditions of parenting* (pp. 113–149). Mahwah, NJ: Erlbaum.

Brooks-Gunn, J., Duncan, G. J., Klebanov, P. K., & Sealand, N. (1993). Do neighborhoods influence child and adolescent development? *American Journal of Sociology, 99*(2), 353–395.

Brooks-Gunn, J., & Furstenberg, F. F., Jr. (1989). Adolescent sexual behavior. *American Psychologist, 44*(2), 249–257.

Brooks-Gunn, J., & Paikoff, R. L. (1993). "Sex is a gamble, kissing is a game": Adolescent sexuality, contraception, and pregnancy. In S. G. Millstein, A. C. Petersen, & E. O. Nightingale (Eds.), *Promoting the health of adolescents: New directions for the twenty-first century* (pp. 180–208). New York: Oxford University Press.

Brooks-Gunn, J., & Paikoff, R. L. (1997). Sexuality and developmental transitions during adolescence. In J. Schulenberg, J. Maggs, & K. Hurrelmann (Eds.), *Health risks and developmental transitions during adolescence* (pp. 190–219). New York: Cambridge University Press.

Bumpass, L. L., & Sweet, J. A. (1989). *Children's experience in single-parent families: Implications of cohabitation and marital transitions* (NSFH Working Paper No. 3). Madison: Center for Demography and Ecology, University of Wisconsin.

Bumpass, L. L., Sweet, J. A., & Cherlin, A. (1991). The role of cohabitation in declining rates of marriage. *Journal of Marriage and the Family, 53,* 913–927.

Burton, L. M. (1994). Intergenerational legacies and intimate relationships: Perspectives on adolescent mothers and fathers. *ISSPR Bulletin, 10*(2), 1–3.

Buzwell, S. (1996, August). *Change and stability in adolescents' sexual selves.* Paper presented at the 14th biennial meeting of the International Society for the Study of Behavioral Development, Quebec City, Canada.

Buzwell, S., & Rosenthal, D. (1996). Constructing a sexual self: Adolescents' sexual self-perceptions and sexual risk-taking. *Journal of Research on Adolescence, 6,* 489–513.

Chase-Lansdale, P. L., Brooks-Gunn, J., & Zamsky, E. S. (1994). Young African-American multigenerational families in poverty: Quality of mothering and grand-mothering. *Child Development, 65*(2), 373–393.

Chase-Lansdale, P. L., Gordon, R. A., Coley, R. L., Wakschlag, L. S., & Brooks-Gunn, J. (1999). Young African-American multigenerational families in poverty: The contexts, exchanges, and processes of their lives. In E. M. Hetherington (Ed.), *Coping with divorce, single parenting and remarriage: A risk and resilience perspective* (pp. 165–191). Mahwah, NJ: Erlbaum.

Cherlin, A. (1988). The weakening link between marriage and the care of children. *Family Planning Perspectives, 20*(6), 302–306.

Child Trends, Inc. (1997, October). *Facts at a glance.* Washington, DC: Author.

Edin, K. (1995). Single mothers and child support: The possibilities and limits of child support policy. *Children and Youth Services Review, 17*(1–3), 203–230.

Edwards, C. P. (1995). Parenting toddlers. In M. H. Bornstein (Ed.), *Handbook of parenting: Volume 1. Children and parenting* (pp. 41–63). Mahwah, NJ: Erlbaum.

Elder, G. H., Jr. (1974). *Children of the great depression: Social change in life experience.* Chicago: University of Chicago Press.

Elder, G. H., Jr. (1985). Perspectives on the life course. In G. H. Elder, Jr. (Ed.), *Life course dynamics: Trajectories and transitions, 1968–1980* (pp. 23–49). Ithaca, NY: Cornell University Press.

Feldman, S. S., & Araujo, K. (1996, August). *Sexual betrayal in the relationships of youth.* Paper presented at the 14th biennial meeting of the International Society for the Study of Behavioral Development, Quebec City, Canada.

Forrest, J. D., & Singh, S. (1990). The sexual and reproductive behavior of American women, 1982–1988. *Family Planning Perspectives, 22,* 206–214.

Furstenberg, F. F., Jr. (1995). Dealing with dads: The changing role of fathers. In P. L. Chase-Lansdale & J. Brooks-Gunn (Eds.), *Escape from poverty: What makes a difference for children?* (pp. 189–210). New York: Cambridge University Press.

Furstenberg, F. F., Jr. (in press). The fading dream: Prospects for marriage in the inner-city. In A. M. Cauce & S. Hauser (Eds.), *Adolescence and beyond: Family processes and development.* Mahwah, NJ: Erlbaum.

Furstenberg, F. F., Jr., Brooks-Gunn, J., & Chase-Lansdale, L. (1989). Adolescent fertility and public policy. *American Psychologist, 44*(2), 313–320.

Furstenberg, F. F., Jr., Brooks-Gunn, J., & Morgan, S. P. (1987). *Adolescent mothers in later life.* New York: Cambridge University Press.

Furstenberg, F. F., Jr., Levine, J. A., & Brooks-Gunn, J. (1990). The children of teenage mothers: Patterns of early childbearing in two generations. *Family Planning Perspectives, 22,* 54–61.

Garfinkel, I., McLanahan, S. S., & Robins, P. K. (Eds.). (1994). *Child support and child well-being.* Washington, DC: Urban Institute Press.

Geronimus, A. T. (1994). The weathering hypothesis and the health of African-American women and infants: Implications for reproductive strategies and policy analysis. In G. Sen & R. Snow (Eds.), *Power and decision: The social control of reproduction* (pp. 77–100). Cambridge, MA: Harvard University Press.

Geronimus, A. T. (1996). What teen mothers know. *Human Nature, 7,* 323–352.

Graber, J. A., & Brooks-Gunn, J. (1996a). Expectations for and precursors of leaving home in young women. In W. Damon (Series Ed.), J. A. Graber, & J. S. Dubas (Vol.

Eds.), *New directions for child development: Volume 71, Leaving home: Understanding the transition to adulthood* (pp. 21–38). San Francisco: Jossey-Bass.

Graber, J. A., & Brooks-Gunn, J. (1996b). Reproductive transitions: The experience of mothers and daughters. In C. D. Ryff & M. M. Seltzer (Eds.), *The parental experience in midlife.* (pp. 255–299). Chicago: University of Chicago Press.

Graber, J. A., Brooks-Gunn, J., & Galen, B. R. (1988). Betwixt and between: Sexuality in the context of adolescent transitions. In R. Jessor (Ed.), *New perspectives on adolescent risk behavior* (pp. 270–316). New York: Cambridge University Press.

Graber, J. A., Brooks-Gunn, J., & Petersen, A. C. (1996). Adolescent transitions in context. In J. A. Graber, J. Brooks-Gunn, & A. C. Petersen (Eds.), *Transitions through adolescence: Interpersonal domains and context* (pp. 369–383). Mahwah, NJ: Erlbaum.

Hagestad, G. O. (1986). Dimensions of time and the family. *American Behavioral Scientist, 29*(6), 679–694.

Halpern, R. (1993). Poverty and infant development. In C. H. Zeanah, Jr. (Ed.), *Handbook of infant mental health* (pp. 73–86). New York: Guilford Press.

Hardy, J. B., Astone, N. M., Brooks-Gunn, J., Shapiro, S., & Miller, T. L. (1998). Like mother, like child: Intergenerational patterns of age at first birth and associations with childhood and adolescent characteristics and adult outcomes in the second generation. *Developmental Psychology, 34,* 1220–1232.

Hareven, T. K. (1977). Family time and historical time. *Daedalus, 106,* 57–70.

Haveman, R., Wolfe, B., Wilson, K., & Peterson, E. (1997). *Do teens make rational choices? The case of teen nonmarital childbearing* (DP #1137-97). Madison: Institute for Research on Poverty, University of Wisconsin.

Hofferth, S. L., & Hayes, C. D. (Eds.). (1987). *Risking the future: Adolescent sexuality, pregnancy and childbearing* (Vol. 2). Washington, DC: National Academy Press.

Ianni, F. A. J., & Orr, M. T. (1996). Dropping out. In J. A. Graber, J. Brooks-Gunn, & A. C. Petersen (Eds.), *Transitions through adolescence: Interpersonal domains and context* (pp. 285–321). Mahwah, NJ: Erlbaum.

Johnston, L. D., Bachman, J. G., & O'Malley, P. M. (1995). *Monitoring the future.* Ann Arbor, MI: Institute for Social Research.

Keating, D. P. (1990). Adolescent thinking. In S. S. Feldman & G. Elliott (Eds.), *At the threshold: The developing adolescent* (pp. 54–90). Cambridge, MA: Harvard University Press.

Lewin, K. (1939). The field theory approach to adolescence. *American Journal of Sociology, 44,* 868–897.

Loomis, L. S., & Landale, N. S. (1994). Nonmarital cohabitation and childbearing among black and white American women. *Journal of Marriage and the Family, 56,* 949–962.

Maccoby, E. E., & Martin, J. A. (1983). Socialization in the context of the family: Parent–child interaction. In P. H. Mussen (Ed.) & E. M. Hetherington (Vol. Ed.), *The handbook of child psychology: Volume 4, Socialization, personality, and social development* (pp. 1–101). New York: Wiley.

Marsiglio, W. (1987). Adolescent fathers in the United States: Their initial living arrangements, marital status and educational outcomes. *Family Planning Perspectives, 19,* 245–251.

Maynard, R. (1995). Teenage childbearing and welfare reform: Lessons from a decade of demonstration and evaluation research. *Children and Youth Services Review, 17,* 309–332.

Merriwether-de Vries, C., Burton, L. M., & Eggeletion, L. (1996). Early parenting and intergenerational family relationships within African-American families. In J. A. Graber, J. Brooks-Gunn, & A. C. Petersen (Eds.), *Transitions through adolescence: Interpersonal domains and context* (pp. 233–248). Mahwah, NJ: Erlbaum.

Michael, R. T, Gagnon, J. H., Laumann, E. O., & Kolata, G. (1994). *Sex in America: A definitive survey.* Boston: Warner Books.

Modell, J., & Goodman, M. (1990). Historical perspectives. In S. S. Feldman & G. Elliott (Eds.), *At the threshold: The developing adolescent* (pp. 93–122). Cambridge, MA: Harvard University Press.

National Center for Health Statistics. (1991). *Vital statistics of the United States, 1988. Volume II. Mortality, Part A.* Washington, DC: U.S. Government Printing Office.

National Center for Health Statistics. (1997). *Fertility, family planning and women's health: New data from the 1995 National Survey of Family Growth.* DHHS Publication No. (PHS) 97-1995. Hyattsville, MD: U.S. Department of Health and Human Services.

Nurmi, J. E. (1991). How do adolescents see their future? *Developmental Review, 11,* 1–59.

Osofsky, J. D., Hann, D. M., & Peebles, C. (1993). Adolescent parenthood: Risks and opportunities for parents and infants. In C. H. Zeanah, Jr. (Ed.), *Handbook of infant mental health* (pp. 106–119). New York: Guilford Press.

Parkinson, A. B. (1991). Marital and extramarital sexuality. In S. J. Bahr (Ed.), *Family research: A sixty-year review, 1930–1990* (Vol 1, pp. 65–96). New York: Lexington Books.

Rodgers, J. L. (1996). Sexual transitions in adolescence. In J. A. Graber, J. Brooks-Gunn, & A. C. Petersen (Eds.), *Transitions through adolescence: Interpersonal domains and context* (pp. 85–110). Mahwah, NJ: Erlbaum.

Smith, T. W. (1994). Attitudes toward sexual permissiveness: Trends, correlates, and behavioral connections. In A. S. Rossi (Ed.), *Sexuality across the life course. The John D. and Catherine T. MacArthur Foundation series on mental health and development: Studies on successful midlife development* (pp. 63–97). Chicago: University of Chicago Press.

Stein, N. L., & Trabasso, T. (1989). Children's understanding of changing emotion states. In C. Saarni & P. L. Harris (Eds.), *Children's understanding of emotion* (pp. 50–77). New York: Cambridge University Press.

Sugland, B. W., Wilder, K. J., & Chandra, A. (1996). *Sex, pregnancy, and contraception: A report of focus group discussions with adolescents.* Washington, DC: Child Trends, Inc.

Sullivan, M. L. (1993). Young fathers and parenting in two inner-city neighborhoods. In R. I. Lerman & T. J. Ooms (Eds.), *Young unwed fathers: Changing roles and emerging policies* (pp. 52–73). Philadelphia: Temple University Press.

Testa, M., & Krogh, M. (1995). The effect of employment on marriage among Black males in inner-city Chicago. In M. B. Tucker & C. Mitchell-Kernan (Eds.), *The decline of marriage among African Americans: Causes, consequences, and policy implications* (pp. 59–95). New York: Russell Sage Foundation.

Thompson, S. (1994). Changing lives, changing genres: Teenage girls' narratives about sex and romance, 1978–1986. In A. S. Rossi (Ed.), *Sexuality across the life course. The John D. and Catherine T. MacArthur Foundation series on mental health and development: Studies on successful midlife development* (pp. 209–232). Chicago: University of Chicago Press.

Uhlenberg, P., & Eggebeen, D. (1986). The declining well-being of American adolescents. *Public Interest, 82,* 25–38.

U.S. Bureau of the Census. (1991). Marital status and living arrangements: March, 1990. *Current Population Reports* (Series P-20, No. 450). Washington, DC: U.S. Government Printing Office.

Willis, R. J. (1996, October). *Father involvement: Theoretical perspectives from economics.* Paper presented at the Conferences on Father's Involvement, NICHD Family and Child Well-Being Network, Bethesda, MD.

Wilson, W. J. (1987). *The truly disadvantaged: The inner city, the underclass, and public policy.* Chicago: University of Chicago Press.

Wilson, W. J., & Neckerman, K. M. (1986). Poverty and family structure: The widening gap between evidence and public policy issues. In S. H. Danziger & D. H. Weinberg (Eds.), *Fighting poverty: What works and what doesn't* (pp. 232–259). Cambridge, MA: Harvard University Press.

Zabin, L. S., & Hayward, S. C. (1993). *Adolescent sexual behavior and childbearing.* Newbury Park, CA: Sage.

PART IV

Conclusion

15 Love Is a Many-Splendored Thing

Next Steps for Theory and Research

Wyndol Furman, Candice Feiring,
and B. Bradford Brown

Adolescent romantic relationships have received little attention from social scientists, as they have been considered to be ephemeral experiences of little significance. In contrast to this view, the authors in this volume provide a rich and varied set of theoretical ideas concerning the nature of adolescent romantic relationships. What is most striking from reading these chapters is the complexity of these relationships.

This complexity is evidenced in many ways. Witness the diversity of theoretical perspectives taken in this volume, not only across the different chapters but even within a particular one. For example, Gray and Steinberg draw on sociobiological and contextual views of family functioning. Laursen and Jensen-Campbell integrate social exchange and evolutionary theory. Larson, Clore, and Wood incorporate three theories of emotions. Miller and Benson describe the contribution of both biological and cultural processes.

The descriptions of the relationships are equally complex. Connolly and Goldberg discuss emotions, behaviors, motives, and concepts. Downey, Bonica, and Rincon delineate how rejection sensitivity may be played out in terms of relationship processes, partner selection, and the impact of being rejected by a partner. Gray and Steinberg describe multiple mechanisms that may link romantic relationships and the family of origin, and Collins and Sroufe present a series of processes that would lead securely attached individuals to be more able to navigate the new tasks entailed in dating. Brown describes the multiple and changing forms of peer influence on the development of romantic identity and romantic relationships, and Graber, Britto, and Brooks-Gunn describe the historical, economic, social,

Preparation of this chapter was supported by Grant 50106 from the National Institute of Mental Health (W. Furman, P.I).

and familial influences that affect romantic expectations. Similarly, Coates points out the need to study the multiple processes reflected in cultural contexts rather than simply treating culture as a static, unitary entity.

Numerous authors in this volume propose a number of complicated, often subtle distinctions in their accounts – for example, general gender identity versus configured gender identity (Feiring), emotional versus sexual commitment (Diamond, Savin-Williams, and Dubé), and working models versus styles (Furman and Simon). The complexity of the phenomena dictate that we approach these relationships with a range of perspectives, each quite complex in its own right.

These chapters should provide plenty of stimulation for social scientists interested in studying adolescent romantic relationships. At the same time, the complexity of the phenomenon – love's many-splendored nature – makes it evident that further work will be required, theoretically as well as empirically. In this concluding chapter, we discuss some of the directions such work may take. In part, we highlight some of the common themes echoed in these chapters, but we also focus on some of the issues *not* highlighted. Rather than just summarizing the themes that emerge in this book, we also point out some of the next steps that need to be taken – the kinds of topics that should be addressed in a sequel to this volume.

Romantic Experiences and Romantic Relationships

To begin, it is important to note that these chapters have focused on two distinct phenomena – the individual in a romantic relationship and the romantic relationship as a dyad. That is, sometimes the focus is on the romantic experiences an individual has, whereas elsewhere the focus is on the relationship itself. For example, in some sections of their chapter, Downey et al. describe the thoughts and feelings of a rejection-sensitive individual, whereas in other sections they describe the impact of rejection sensitivity on relationship processes. Similarly, Brown describes the development of an adolescent's sense of identity regarding romantic relationships, as well as developmental changes in the nature of these relationships.

An examination of the individual in a relationship and an examination of the relationship as a dyad require two different levels of analysis. After all, there is more than one person in a relationship! The difference is greater than that, however; relationships are influenced not only by the person's general characteristics and the partner's characteristics, but also by the interaction or meshing of the two individuals' characteristics, relationship-specific variables (e.g., their specific feelings and attitudes toward each other, their history together, and their expectations for the future), contextual factors, and the interaction among these variables (see Furman, 1984, for further discussion).

Consider, for example, the amount of conflict that occurs in a relationship. It may be affected by the general predisposition of both partners to engage in conflicts; in other words, it is affected by how much each of them tends to get into conflicts in their various relationships. It also may be affected by how the general predispositions of both partners interact or mesh. For example, it may be necessary for only one person to be conflict-prone for frequent conflict to occur in the relationship; alternatively, it may require two conflict-prone individuals for conflict to occur readily. Additionally, the degree of conflict may be affected by the prior history of conflict in the relationship, the feelings of the partners for each other, and their expectations about the course of the relationship in the future. Similarly, conflicts may occur in some contexts or in regard to particular issues more readily than in other contexts or issues. Finally, interactions among these different variables may occur. For example, a jealous person's tendency to engage in conflicts may be exacerbated in a relationship with a history of infidelity or in situations where competition for the partner's attention is high.

This distinction between the individual and the relationship has multiple implications for further theory development. First, most of the theoretical and empirical work to date has focused on the individual, and relatively little exists concerning relationships. In part, the lack of work on relationships may stem from the evanescent nature of many adolescent romances, as was discussed in Chapter 1. In part, it may be because we have more theories of individuals than theories of dyads in the general field of psychology that can serve as a foundation for our conceptualizations of adolescent romantic relationships. The literature on marriages may, however, be a good source for such ideas, even though obvious differences exist between marriages and most adolescent relationships.

To some extent, our conceptualizations of relationships have been constrained by our methodological approaches to studying dyads. Typically, we gather data on particular types of interaction, such as conflict, and make comparisons across dyads. Relationships, however, are composed of different types of interactions and cannot be fully captured by examining particular interactions in isolation (Hinde, 1992; Sroufe & Waters, 1977). Rather, it is essential to examine different interactions within particular relationships and how they affect each other in order to understand fully how the relationships function. In other words, our theories and methods need to reflect the idea that relationships are self-organizing systems. Accordingly, a relationship-centered approach is needed to complement the variable-centered approach that we usually take.

Second, we need to appreciate that dyadic phenomena exist that cannot be readily captured in terms of individual characteristics. For example, Laursen and Jensen-Campbell use the theoretical constructs of equity and interdependence – both of which are inherently relational. Similarly, the communication of emotions entails more than just the individuals' experience of emotions (Larson et al., this volume). Here again, the marital literature may prove useful, as Gottman (1993) and others have identified sequences of interaction, such as a mutually hostile exchange or contempt followed by withdrawal, that are predictive of dissatisfaction and divorce.

Third, we need to be more aware of the limitations in the inferences that can be drawn from individual-level data and dyadic data. Often we assess social competence by observing patterns of social interaction. Social interactions, however, are affected by all of the factors discussed in the preceding paragraphs, not just by an individual's social competence or characteristics. In other words, social competencies are usually conceptualized as characteristics of the individual, and yet what are usually measured – patterns of social interaction – are characteristics of the relationship. Thus, we need to be wary about inferring that a particular individual is unskilled in managing conflict from the observation that his or her romantic relationship is rather conflictual. Conversely, we should be wary about inferring that a conflict-prone person will necessarily have a conflictual romantic relationship. Some assessment strategies for addressing this issue are discussed more extensively elsewhere (Furman, 1984).

Fourth, not only is more theoretical work needed at the dyadic level, but we also need more elaborated theories of how the individual and dyadic levels interface. Most of the theoretical conceptualizations presented in this volume and elsewhere simply propose direct links between an individual's characteristics and his or her behavior in the dyad. That is, this type of person behaves this way in a romantic relationship. We have given little consideration to how the partner's characteristics may moderate the effect of an individual's characteristics on the pattern of interaction. Feiring proposes a few ways in which a partner's characteristics may influence a person's gender-related behavior, but the topic warrants further consideration. In the friendship literature, who the particular friend is has been shown to affect the relationship and its impact on the individual (see Hartup, 1996). One would certainly expect the same to be true for romantic relationships.

Additionally, few theories consider how the course of a relationship may be influenced by particular experiences with a partner – that is, the relationship history or relationship-specific factors. Finally, we have theorized more on how an individual's characteristics affect a relationship than on how relationship experiences may affect individuals, though in this volume the discussion of Larson et al. on the emotional impact of romantic relationships, and Feiring's discussion of the role of romantic relationships in configured gender identity are noteworthy exceptions to this pattern.

In a related vein, a number of chapters in this volume consider how other close relationships may influence romantic relationships, but we should also consider the influence that romantic relationships have on them. For example, Connolly and Goldberg point out the potential impact of romantic relationships on peer relationships, and Gray and Steinberg discuss the impact they may have on relationships with parents. Similarly, Downey et al. point out that the particular partner or kind of partner selected could lead to parental or peer rejection – a problem commonly faced by sexual minority youth. Finally, Coates points out how individuals can even influence the culture's perspectives.

Common Features and Differences

The chapters in this volume point both to features common to most adolescents' romantic experiences and to the vast differences in them. Several authors suggest that these relationships commonly serve certain developmental functions. For example, Connolly and Goldberg, as well as Gray and Steinberg, propose that romantic interest is linked to autonomy processes or individuation. Miller and Benson suggest that romantic relationships may meet the critical developmental needs of security, fulfillment, and validation. Brown and Feiring discuss the role of romantic relationships in identity development.

Evolutionary theory serves as a basis for a number of hypothesized functions. For example, in this volume Gray and Steinberg suggest that romantic interest serves to enhance status in adolescence and could protect against inbreeding in a context that entails prolonged contact between parents and reproductively mature offspring. Laursen and Jensen-Campbell suggest that passion or the intense affective arousal that characterizes some romantic relationships may facilitate pair bonding, and as such may be a product of natural selection. The idea that these relationships may eventually serve as attachments is either explicit or implicit in many other chapters (by Collins and Sroufe, Diamond et al., and Furman and Simon).

Of course, what features and functions are universal remains controversial. For example, Coates (this volume) questions whether passionate, emotionally based love is universal. Regardless of what proves to be the case in this particular instance, the point is that our conceptualizations of the roles romantic relationships play depend upon which features or functions are universal or near-universal.

Although most romantic relationships may share some common features, the diversity of the relationships is equally evident. In this volume, Diamond et al., in fact, propose four different types of relationships – passionate friendships and sexual, dating, and romantic relationships. Similarly, Miller and Benson argue that romantic ideation and sexual interaction commonly co-occur, but neither is a necessary precondition for the other. Drawing on the adult relationship literature, Laursen and Jensen-Campbell propose two other distinctions – communal versus exchange and open- and closed-field relationships.

Moreover, marked variation occurs within any of these types. Various authors in this volume, such as Larson, et al., Brown, Coates, Downey et al., and Graber et al., wisely avoid the temptation to idealize these relationships, as once happened in the early study of friendships. They recognize that these relationships can have deleterious consequences and will help short-circuit any Polyanna-like tendencies.

The variability in these relationships and relational experiences is evident from the long list of variables hypothesized to play a role. Various authors in this volume have focused on a range of personal characteristics, including sexual orientation (Diamond et al.), capacity for intimacy (Collins and Sroufe), rejection sensitivity (Downey et al.), a history of coercive sexual experiences (Miller and Benson), ability to regulate emotions (Larson et al.), aggressiveness and social isolation (Connolly and Goldberg), and configured gender identity as well as gender (Feiring). Physical attractiveness, pubertal timing, personal interests, and religion were also alluded to and are likely to play major roles as well.

Socioeconomic status, ethnicity, and culture were discussed by many authors, particularly Coates and Graber et al. These authors make a compelling argument for the importance of incorporating diversity at the center of our conceptualizations. Diamond et al. rightly argue that a normative model not only fails to capture the experiences of those who deviate from its parameters, but also does not do justice to those who follow the more common paths. In a related vein, they note that an exclusive emphasis on heterosexual relationships would lead us to focus too much on certain phenomena such as dating and to not notice other important phenomena such as passionate friendships.

These authors also point out the importance of not assuming that phenotypically similar phenomena are actually similar in function in different groups. For example, Diamond et al. argue that heterosexual dating leads to relationships, whereas same-sex dating fosters the transition to an identity as a lesbian, bisexual, or gay person. Coates argues that the validation of identity through romantic experience may occur more intensely and earlier for minority status adolescents. In effect, these relationships may serve identity and status functions that are not being satisfied in ways that are made available to majority status adolescents. Once again, an acknowledgment of the diversity of these relationships strengthens the study of all kinds.

Romantic Relationships and Other Close Relationships

Just as romantic relationships have similarities and differences, so do romantic relationships and other close relationships. In this volume, Laursen and Jensen-Campbell, Collins and Sroufe, Diamond et al., and Furman and Simon all discuss some of the unique features of adolescent romantic relationships and some of the features shared with other close relationships. The identification of such similarities and differences is essential for understanding what processes are specific to a relationship and what processes are common to close relationships or perhaps different types of peer relationships (Furman, 1993; Furman & Simon, 1998). For example, Collins and Sroufe suggest that some parallels may exist in what makes a friend and a romantic partner appealing, which would indicate that some facets of romantic attraction may really be elements of interpersonal attraction in general.

Moreover, this work may lead to a reconceptualization of phenomena. For example, based on such comparisons across relationships, Furman and Simon (this volume) have suggested that representations should be conceptualized as representations of relationships, and not as representations of attachment per se.

An examination of these relationships in their social as well as their cultural context also makes one appreciate the links among the different relationships. Not only are the links with friendships and parent–child relationships mentioned by many authors in this volume, but the ties to peer status (Brown; Connolly and Goldberg) and parents' marriage (Furman and Simon; Gray and Steinberg) are also discussed. In the literature on adult romantic relationships, the emphasis has been almost exclusively on the parallels to and influence of early parent–child relationships, with little said about the role of peers. In adolescent romantic relationships, the influence of peer relationships is unmistakable (Brown, this volume; Furman, in press), and we suspect that the same will prove to be the case for adult romantic relationships (Furman & Wehner, 1994). Thus, these chapters may serve as a healthy corrective for the neglect of peer relations by adult romantic researchers.

Finally, the importance of taking a network perspective can be seen by considering the implications of the fact that most adolescents are involved in a romantic relationship only part of the time. When adolescents are not in a relationship, the functions fulfilled by romantic relationships either are unfulfilled or are fulfilled by another relationship. For example, adolescents who do not have a romantic partner to talk to about problems may turn to their best friend. By examining when another relationship substitutes for a romantic relationship and when it does not, we can identify some of the processes that are common to different relationships and those particular to romantic relationships. We can also obtain information about the potential impact of romantic relationships by comparing the characteristics of social networks when a romantic relationship exists and when it does not. For example, some research indicates that adolescents with romantic partners interact less with friends and receive less support from friends than those without romantic partners (Laursen & Williams, 1997; Shaffer & Ognibene, 1998).

Development

The developmental background of the authors is evident, as all of them described developmental changes in these relationships and in the experiences of these relationships. In Chapter 1, we argued for the importance of studying adolescent romantic relationships and how they are distinct from adult romantic relationships. That may be too simple. The relationships in early, middle, and late adolescence also are quite distinct.

In fact, these relationships change not only in terms of the frequency of various characteristics, but also in the centrality of the various processes influencing them. For example, in this volume Laursen and Jensen-Campbell propose that distal influences wane over the course of adolescence, whereas proximal ones increase. Brown and Connolly and Goldberg propose that the links between peer relations and romantic relationships change with development, and Coates argues that cultural influences change as well. Feiring suggests that the links between romantic relationships and configured gender identity increase with age. Finally, Gray and Steinberg suggest that the partner or the quality of the relationship is not terribly important in early adolescence; it is having a relationship that matters.

The task of conceptualizing and studying developmental changes in romantic experiences is complicated by two further considerations. First, the diversity of romantic experiences implies that adolescents may take different developmental trajectories. For example, Dubé (1997, cited in Diamond et al., this volume) identified two trajectories among sexual minority men. Those who engaged in same-sex sexual contact prior to identifying themselves as gay or lesbian eventually participated in a higher proportion of sexual than romantic relationships than those who had identified themselves as sexual minorities before engaging in same-sex contact. Thus, we will have to conceptualize development in terms of individual paths rather than a single normative path.

Second, the timing, as well as the trajectory, of romantic development differs widely. For example, several authors describe the importance of pubertal timing for the emergence of romantic interest. For this and other reasons, some individuals began to date at an earlier age than others do. Early- and late-starting daters may both develop relatively stable relationships, but at different ages. Thus, observed differences among individuals of a particular age could reflect differences in the timing of their romantic development, as well as differences in the trajectories they may be pursuing (Furman & Simon, 1998). Accordingly, when we observe that an adolescent has not begun dating, we should be wary of inferring that this is necessarily indicative of some enduring characteristic of that adolescent, as it may simply be indicative of a later start or a slower timeline.

Most of our theories of development tend to account for observed differences in terms of differences in stable, traitlike features of the developing organism. We need to remind ourselves that observed differences may reflect differences in social timelines or social context, especially in a domain such as romantic relationships. After all, in early to middle adolescence, we should expect to see a great deal of fluctuation in who has a romantic partner at any given time point or in how long the relationship exists. Such fluctuations should make us appreciate that the differences we observe at any particular moment are influenced by factors other than stable individual characteristics. Perhaps the right partner just hasn't come along – a particularly salient problem for sexual minority youth.

Another way of expressing this point is to note that one should not equate chronological age with developmental status, especially in this arena, where the timelines seem to differ substantially. It may be valuable to consider ways of assessing developmental status other than age. The number of years postpuberty may be helpful for some purposes. Alternatively, it may be valuable to identify a number of common milestones in the romantic arena and use these as a way of identifying individuals at similar phases of development. For example, rather than simply making comparisons among students of the same age with different levels of romantic experience, sometimes it may be useful to make comparisons of students who have dated for the same length of time, even if they differ somewhat in age. Such milestones could include sexual ones (time since first intercourse; see Graber et al., this volume) and relational ones (time since dating alone as a couple vs. in a group), but it is important that any such milestone be sensitive to the diversity of these relationships.

Up to this point, we have focused on the development of individuals, but the development of the relationship presents equally complex issues. After all, romantic relationships can go through a series of phases, including the selection of a partner, initiation of the relationship, development of the relationship, maintenance or deepening of it, its decline, termination, and, in some instances, its reestablishment. And of course, these phases are not fully distinct, nor does one move from phase to phase in a simple, linear manner that is irreversible or even includes all phases. Some relationships may be deliberately short-term in nature; for example, Diamond et al. distinguish between dating and romantic relationships. Relationships may even vacillate in type over time between romances and friendships.

Our theories of adolescent romantic relationships have said little about these developmental phases. As a starter, we need to describe the role various processes or characteristics of individuals play in different phases of a relationship. For instance, Downey et al. (this volume) describe how a rejection-sensitive individual approaches or reacts to the different phases of a relationship. We suspect that the task of spelling out the role our hypothesized variables play is complicated by the fact that different variables may be more or less important at different phases. For example, we have suggested that attachment processes play important roles in how particular relationships develop and are maintained, but we think that they play a less important role in the initial attraction to a specific partner (Furman & Flanagan, 1997). Similarity, availability, physical attractiveness, and infatuation seem more likely to be important in the initial phase.

In many respects, the issues concerning the timing of an individual's romantic development apply to the development of relationships as well. That is, some relationships may proceed at a slower pace than others, perhaps because of fewer opportunities for the adolescents to interact. As a consequence, the adolescents in a slower-moving relationship may not be as close after a month as those in a fast-moving relationship. One could argue that this reflects a genuine difference between the two relationships, but we would caution against drawing inferences from this about the level of closeness the relationship may ultimately develop or about the characteristics of the individuals.

Finally, just as the characteristics of individuals and the characteristics of their relationships are related, so too is the development of individuals and the development of their relationships. In this volume, Larson et al. discuss the role cognitive developmental factors may play in the experience of emotions and their control, and Furman and Simon describe the role such variables may play in the development of romantic representations. Similarly, Laursen and Jensen-Campbell propose that developmental factors inhibit early adolescent romantic relationships. We believe, however, that we have just scratched the surface of this topic.

Methodological Issues

The theories proposed here have some important implications for our methodological approaches. Conversely, the resolution of a number of thorny methodological issues will depend upon our theoretical approaches.

For example, these chapters sensitize us to the idea that a wide range of perspectives exist concerning any particular relationship. An adolescent, the partner, their friends, their parents, and we scientists are all likely to have somewhat different views about what a relationship is like. In addition, Furman and Simon (this volume) distinguish between conscious and underlying, partially unconscious perceptions. In effect, we are not trying to conceptualize and measure a single phenomenon; we're interested in multiple interrelated perspectives about the relationship. Moreover, these perspectives usually do not converge very highly, nor should they be expected to, as they reflect meaningful differences in perceptions (Furman, Jones, Buhrmester, & Adler, 1988; Larson & Richards, 1994; Olson, 1977). This idea has several important implications. First, our theoretical conceptualization of the processes influencing relationships should influence our selection of measures. For example, if one thinks that the processes involved are the adolescents' perceptions of something, then one might want to assess them through a questionnaire, or perhaps an interview if unconscious processes are thought to be implicated. On the other hand, if it is actual behavior, then observations may be most appropriate. Of course, we are often uncertain about what the processes are or we may think that several processes may be implicated. In such cases, multiple approaches are required. The theoretical chapters in this volume reflect this multimethod approach, drawing upon a wide range of measures, including experience-sampling methods (Larson et al.), diaries (Downey et al.), interviews (Collins and Sroufe; Furman and Simon), and idiographic (Feiring) and ethnographic approaches (Coates), as well as more traditional questionnaires and observations. We need to continue to develop new methodological approaches, especially given the highly personal and complex nature of romantic relationships. We suspect that much of what is critical in these relationships is not evident either to us or to the adolescents themselves. After all, for centuries, writers have alluded to the mysteries of love.

In fact, it is not even clear what constitutes a romantic relationship. In part, such definitional problems seem inherent in studying social constructs with fuzzy borders, but the issues seem particularly troublesome in the present case. For example, in our own work, some adolescents report that their first relationship occurred in the very early school years. Although these relationships may have been important and may have lasted for a long time in some cases, we suspect that they are qualitatively different from later relationships. Similarly, we've had an adolescent report that one of his most important relationships was a single evening with a girl, even though he was with his parents as well and had had a number of other relationships. In effect, his fantasy of what it could be made it one of the most important relationships for him. And these same definitional dilemmas arise in terms of the boundaries between friendships and romantic relationships, especially since these relationships may change over time and since sometimes the adolescents themselves may not agree or do not know how to define the relationship.

This last example illustrates the fact that part of the definitional problems arise from the fact that romantic relationships are constantly in development. Thus, a friendship may become a romantic relationship; one evening may lead to another and another. Moreover, the nature of romantic relationships changes over the course of adolescence and adulthood. As the chapters of Connolly and Goldberg and Brown illustrate, early contacts are often short-lived (but important). In many ways, one could say that early adolescents are having romantic experiences, not relationships. Eventually, however, adolescents begin to pair off, dyadic interchanges occur more frequently, and interactions develop into relationships. One of the important challenges in the field today is developing theoretical and methodological approaches that address the changing nature of these relationships and provide a way of mapping romantic development. More generally, we will need to devote considerable attention to the definitional problems in the field. Focus groups of adolescents or perhaps questionnaires about definitional questions may prove useful.

Putting It All Together

The present volume contains 13 different theoretical chapters. Although it is unclear whether an attempt to provide a single, unified theory would prove fruitful, an important step is to begin to integrate some of these frameworks to provide broader, more comprehensive theories. Several pairings seem particularly promising.

For example, Feiring (this volume) alludes to gender role issues in lesbian, gay, and bisexual couples. A more extensive consideration of her theoretical work could enrich Diamond et al.'s (this volume) work, as Feiring's (this volume) idea of configured gender identity may offer a framework for understanding how sexual minority youth define or integrate their biological sex with their preferences or behaviors in romantic relationships. It permits a possible dialogue about the individuals' identity that is not constrained by the presumptions of heterosexism or stereotypes.

Attachment theorists have suggested that the strategies for regulating the attachment system govern the expression of emotions as well (Kobak, Cole, Ferenz-Gilles, & Fleming, 1993). Larson et al. (this volume) focused principally on the general experience of emotions in romantic relationships, but the attachment framework may prove to be a useful way of conceptualizing individual differences in the experience and expression of such emotions.

One would also want to emphasize the importance of integrating biological and social perspectives. In Chapter 1, we observed that the research on adolescent sexuality has given little attention to relational factors, and we do not want to make the reverse error of ignoring the role of biological processes in romantic relationships. Several chapters in this volume make such integrative efforts. Miller and Benson discuss not only the importance of biosocial models of sexuality, but also some biochemical underpinnings to attraction and attachment. Similarly, Larson et al. report that they have found romantic feelings to be partly instigated by puberty. Graber et al. extensively discuss the links among romance, sexuality, childrearing, and marriage while simultaneously making the point that these four are distinct and do not always co-occur. Thus, the relational perspective in this volume may help avoid the reductionistic approach to sexuality critiqued by Diamond et al. (this volume) and provide us with a richer understanding of the roles played by sexual behavior and romance.

It will be equally important to integrate these theoretical models of adolescent romantic relationships with those concerning adult romantic relationships. Such an integration can prevent us from developing a separate and isolated field of work with its own theoretical and methodological frameworks. In fact, a number of authors have made efforts to foster such integration by drawing on the adult relationship literature in their conceptualizations. Conversely, we have argued that the chapters in this volume on adolescent romantic relationships have important implications for the conceptualization of adult romantic relationships. For example, Furman and Simon provide an alternative conceptualization of working models, and many authors underscore the importance of peer as well as parental relationships. We can also benefit from the methodological approaches developed by adult researchers. In fact, the conflict resolution tasks used by marital researchers are currently being used in studies of adolescent relationships. Of course, adolescents are not likely to argue about money, as do spouses; instead, communication or the amount of time spent together are likely sources of conflict. And that observation illustrates the idea that we also need to ensure that our theories accurately capture the essential features of adolescent relationships.

Although a range of perspectives are commonly used by the authors of these chapters, the approaches taken in this volume are almost exclusively psychological. Sociological, historical, and anthropological approaches need to be incorporated. Coates provides a general psychological framework about thinking about culture, and Graber et al. discuss economic and other contextual influences, but more is to be said about the striking variation in cultural norms concerning adolescent romantic relationships. Similarly, influences of the mass media and even the Internet seem important to adolescents' ideas of romantic relationships but are alluded to only periodically (e.g., Connolly and Goldberg; Feiring). Graber et al. provide an extensive discussion of the influence of historical trends in childrearing, marriage, and sexuality. Other authors allude to specific secular trends, such as the seeming increase in group dating (Coates) and the increased frequency of intercourse in Western countries, but many other changes are also likely to be significant – for example, AIDS, the increased divorce rate, and the apparent increase in cross-gender friendships in some cultures. Such secular trends are not only important in their own right but may also alter the relations among different variables. For example, in this volume, Miller and Benson and Graber et al. suggest that sex and romance may now be less closely related than before.

Of course, what may be most needed are empirical studies. At the beginning of this volume, we observed that relatively little work has been done on adolescent romantic relationships. Moreover, much of that work has focused on factors related to romantic relationships, such as gender roles or sexual activity, rather than on relationships in their own right. Much of this work is simply descriptive or atheoretical.

Many questions remain. Certainly, the chapters emphasize different elements of romantic relationships or different factors. In fact, a careful reading of the chapters will reveal some differences in the predictions made by different authors. We have deliberately left such differences in the text, as they may provide particularly promising issues to examine empirically. That is, evidence on these issues would not only provide support for one theory, but also would be counterevidence for another.

Even when there are no contrasting predictions, these chapters make many controversial (and not so controversial) assertions that require confirmation. We suspect that some of the assertions will be proven incorrect, and we hope that some will be correct. But right or wrong, we believe that these theoretical frameworks will prove helpful in providing systematic approaches for the needed research.

References

Furman, W. (1984). Issues in the assessment of social skills of normal and handicapped children. In T. Field, M. Siegal, & J. Roopnarine (Eds.), *Friendships of normal and handicapped children* (pp. 3–30). New York: Ablex.

Furman, W. (1993). Theory is not a four letter word: Needed directions in the study of adolescent friendships. In B. Laursen (Ed.), *New directions for child development: Close friendships in adolescence* (pp. 89–103). San Francisco: Jossey-Bass.

Furman, W. (in press). Friends and lovers: The role of peer relationships in adolescent romantic relationships. In W. A. Collins & B. Laursen (Eds.), *Relationships as developmental contexts: The 29th Minnesota symposium on child development.* Hillsdale, NJ: Erlbaum.

Furman, W., & Flanagan, A. (1997). The influence of earlier relationships on marriage: An attachment perspective. In W. K. & H. J. Markman (Eds.), *Clinical handbook of marriage and couples interventions* (pp. 179–202). Chichester, U.K.: Wiley.

Furman, W., Jones, L., Buhrmester, D., & Adler, T. (1988). Children's, parents' and observers' perspective on sibling relationships. In P. G. Zukow (Ed.), *Sibling interaction across culture* (pp. 165–183). New York: Springer-Verlag.

Furman, W., & Simon, V. A. (1998). Advice from youth: Some lessons from the study of adolescent relationships. *Journal of Social and Personal Relationships, 15,* 723–739.

Furman, W., & Wehner, E. A. (1994). Romantic views: Toward a theory of adolescent romantic relationships. In R. Montemayor, G. R. Adams, & G. P. Gullota (Eds.), *Advances in adolescent development: Volume 6, Relationships during adolescence* (pp. 168–195). Thousand Oaks, CA: Sage.

Gottman, J. (1993). *What predicts divorce?* Hillsdale, NJ: Erlbaum.

Hartup, W. W. (1996). The company they keep: Friendships and their developmental significance. *Child Development, 67,* 1–13.

Hinde, R. A. (1992). Developmental psychology in the context of other behavioral sciences. *Developmental Psychology, 28,* 1018–1029.

Kobak, R. R., Cole, H. E., Ferenz-Gillies, R., & Fleming, W. S. (1993). Attachment and emotion regulation during mother–teen problem solving: A control theory analysis. *Child Development, 64,* 231–245.

Larson, R., & Richards, M. H. (1994). *Divergent realities: The emotional lives of mothers, fathers, and adolescents.* New York: Basic Books.

Laursen, B., & Williams, V. A. (1997). Perceptions of interdependence and closeness in family and peer relationships among adolescents with and without romantic partners. In S. Shulman & W. A. Collins (Eds.), *Romantic relationships in adolescence: Developmental perspectives* (pp. 3–20). San Francisco: Jossey-Bass.

Olson, P. H. (1977). Insiders' and outsiders' views of relationships: Research studies. In G. Levinger & H. L. Rausch (Eds.), *Close relationships: Perspectives on the meaning of intimacy* (pp. 1–49). Amherst: University of Massachusetts Press.

Shaffer, L., & Ognibene, T. (1998). *Links between adolescent friendships and romantic relationships.* Paper presented at the meeting of the Society for Research in Adolescence, San Diego, CA.

Sroufe, L. A., & Waters, E. (1977). Attachment as an organizational construct. *Child Development, 48,* 1184–1199.

Author Index

Note: Italic page numbers denote reference citations.

AAUW (American Association of University Women), 282, *286*
Aboud, F.E., 134, *145*
Abrams, D., 349, 350, *359*
Adams, C., 88, *97*
Adams, H.E., 136, *145*
Adams, J.S., 7, *14*
Adelson, J., 9, *15*, 26, 28, 29, 35, 40, 43, *44*, 136, *143*, 185, *208*, 220, *229*, 303, 309, 312, 326, *327*
Adler, N.E., 105, *117*
Adler, T., 409, *413*
Ainsworth, M.D.S., 125, 127, 128, *142*, 152, *170*, 195, 199, *207*
Aires, E., 222, *228*
Akbar, N., 332, *259*
Akerlof, G.A., 386, 387, 388, *391*
Alan Guttmacher Institute, 108, 109, 111, 113, *117*, 364, 368, 370, 371, 374, *391*
Alapack, R.J., 20, 29, *45*
Albrecht, R., 220, *231*
Allen, J.P., 93, *95,* 267, 268, 284, *286*
Allport, G., 348, *359*
Almeida, D., 212, *229*
Alvarez, M.M., 217, *230*
American Psychiatric Association, 152, *170*
Amsel, E., 88, *97*
Anastas, J.W., 114, *117*

Anderson, D.A., 35, *43*
Anderson, E., 344, 345, 355, *359*
Anderson, S., 152, *170*
Angleitner, A., 23, *44*
Appiah, K.A., 332, 334, *359*
Appleman, D., 111, *118*
Aral, S.O., 114, *120*
Araujo, K., 374, 375, 376, 377, *392*
Archer, J., 220, *228*
Ardon, M.S., 1, *15*, 278, *288*, 293, 295, *327*
Argyle, M., 64, *70*
Arias, I., 148, *173*
Arnett, J., 26, *43*
Aron, A., 27, *44, 74*
Asher, S.R., 154, *170*, 266, 281, *289*
Ashmore, R., 217, 226, *228*
Asmussen, L., 20, 25, 30, 35, *46*
Astone, N.M., 364, 379, *391, 393*
Attie, I., 300, *327*
Audrain, P.C., 27, *46*
Aune, K.S., 100, *117*
Aune, R.K., 100, *117*
Averill, J.R., 32, *43*
Ayduk, O., 151, 164, 166, *170, 171, 172*
Ayers-Lopez, S., 134, *143*

Bachman, J.G., 366, *393*
Bachu, A., 379, *391*
Bagby, G.J., 251, *260*

415

Subject Index

adolescent mothers, *see* teenage mothers

affect
and attachment style, 251
parent transmission processes,
254–256
affect-as-information hypothesis, 38

affiliation; *see also* companionship
and attachment style, 79–81
centrality in adolescent relationships,
84–85
cognitive representations, 79–81,
84–87
evolutionary function, 77–78
measurement, 92–93
in peer relationships, 78
in romance developmental sequence,
278–280

African Americans
cultural perspectives, 341–347
identity development, 343–349
male unemployment effects, 381
marriage expectations, 381–382
oppositional cultural frame of reference, 342–345, 358
oppositional identity, 343, 345, 350,
358
out-of-wedlock childbearing, 381–389
pragmatic romantic approach,
343–344
research approaches to, 352–356
self-efficacy, 351
sexual behavior norms, 108

sexual intercourse experience, 109
social isolation, girls, 345, 358
traditional cultural values, 341–342

age at first intercourse
sexual abuse link, 114
timing of, 371
trends, 368–370

age at first marriage
expectations, 378
trends, 109, 377–378

age factors
dating, 107, 300
developmental status, 407–408
versus puberty, dating initiation, 300
romantic emotional competence, 43
and social exchanges, 56

aggression
bullying, 282
peer relationship problems, 281–284
rejection sensitivity strategy, 156, 166
romantic relationship problems,
281–284

anger
evolutionary function, 22
and rejection expectations, 152,
155–156

antisocial behavior, 282–283
and mate selection, 282
and parental aggression, 249
romantic relationships effect of,
282–283

anxiety